Varieties of Civic Innovation

VARIETIES OF CIVIC INNOVATION

Deliberative,

Collaborative,

Network,

and Narrative

Approaches

JENNIFER GIROUARD
and
CARMEN SIRIANNI
editors

VANDERBILT UNIVERSITY PRESS
Nashville, Tennessee

This book is printed on acid-free paper.

Library of Congress Cataloging-in-Publication Data on file
LC control number 2014008052
LC classification number JF1525.P6V36 2014
Dewey class number 320.6—dc23

ISBN 978-0-8265-1999-3 (cloth)
ISBN 978-0-8265-2000-5 (paperback)
ISBN 978-0-8265-2001-2 (ebook)

Contents

Introduction   1
Jennifer Girouard and Carmen Sirianni

1. Embedding Public Deliberation in Community Governance   7
Elena Fagotto and Archon Fung

2. Ways of Knowing the Los Angeles River Watershed: Getting from
Engaged Participation to Inclusive Deliberation   23
Anne Taufen Wessells

3. Civic Innovation, Deliberation, and Health Impact Assessment:
Democratic Planning and Civic Engagement in San Francisco   45
Jason Corburn

4. Intramovement Agenda Setting: Nationalizing North Carolina's Fight
to Defeat an Anti–Gay Marriage Constitutional Amendment   75
Daniel Kreiss and Laura Meadows

5. Civic Communication in a Networked Society:
Seattle's Emergent Ecology   92
by Lewis A. Friedland

6. Accounting for Diversity in Collaborative Governance:
An Institutional Approach to Empowerment Reforms   127
by Caroline W. Lee

7. Networks and Narratives in the Making of Civic Practice:
Lessons from Iberia   159
Robert M. Fishman

8. Turning Participation into Representation: Innovative
Policy Making for Minority Groups in Brazil   181
Thamy Pogrebinschi

9. Bringing the State Back in through Collaborative Governance:
    Emergent Mission and Practice at the US Environmental
    Protection Agency   203
    Carmen Sirianni

10. A Systemic Approach to Civic Action   239
    Jane Mansbridge

    Contributors   247

    Index   251

Acknowledgments

The Ash Center for Democratic Governance and Innovation, John F. Kennedy School of Government, Harvard University, provided a welcome home while this volume was being prepared. It also sponsored several talks (followed by probing dinner conversations) that became chapters in the book. Special thanks to Archon Fung, Jenny Mansbridge, and Bruce Jackan, as well as to the regular participants in the Ash Center's Democracy Seminar. We would also like to thank the Thomas and Jane Norman Fund for Faculty Research at Brandeis University for financial support in preparing this volume. Matt Leighninger provided detailed and astute comments on the manuscript as a whole. Mike Ames, director of the press, proved yet again to be a most valued partner and critical thinker. Others at the press helped bring this to fruition, especially Joell Smith-Borne and Drew Bryan. Our biggest debt is to the contributors for sharing their research and extending the conversation on civic innovation.

JENNIFER GIROUARD
CARMEN SIRIANNI
Waltham, Massachusetts, February 4, 2014

Introduction

JENNIFER GIROUARD AND CARMEN SIRIANNI

■ Over the past decade, residents in Seattle have generated a rich civic ecology of new communications media aligned with some of the traditional newspaper and broadcast media to enhance the public sphere for democratic deliberation and civic action. They have done this through irrepressible grassroots technological innovation, institutional collaboration with universities and libraries, and support from the community technology program, an office of city government modeled partly on Seattle's famed neighborhood matching fund and participatory planning system that emerged in the prior two decades. In Brazil, not only do several hundred cities now engage in participatory budgeting, where, beginning in Porto Allegre in 1989, citizens themselves deliberate and decide upon local development priorities, but over the past decade a broad array of national policy conferences also helps inform the parameters of debate and action by legislative and administrative bodies on questions of economic development, health, and minority rights. These policy conferences operate through sequenced forums designed for deliberation and learning at all three levels of the federal system—municipal, state, and national—opening up a broad horizon for grassroots and stakeholder participation alongside core institutions of representative democracy and administrative accountability.

Such innovations, and many more in this collection and other studies, signal an era of democratic innovation and social learning (Sirianni and Friedland 2001), even as many components are not yet strongly embedded in communities or translocal networks, not yet inclusive or accountable enough to secure democratic equality, not yet linked enough to transform entire institutional fields, such as the bureaucracy, the law, the market, the educational system, and other actors (Sirianni 2009; Fligstein and McAdam 2012; Ansell and Gash 2007). Democratic innovation—as was typical in Jeffersonian, Populist, Progressive, and 1960s eras in the United States—remains uneven and uncertain, open to unexpected pathways and unintended consequences, entangled in various local and state political cultures and diverse institutional fields. "Not yet" holds out the promise of further refinement and institutionalization, while transforming civic identities and professional and organizational cultures (Dzur 2008; Boyte 2005). But the phrase should never betray a sense of inevitability. Our democracies are battered by gale force winds of various types, not least those literal storms that that will tax our civic and democratic institutional capacities to adapt to climate change, even as we seek to mitigate it. Even if we begin to mitigate in reasonably hopeful long-term ways, we will be terribly challenged to adapt to the highly disruptive community, regional, cultural, ecological, economic, and distributive costs already under way, and to do so in a manner that enhances democratic legitimacy and restrains conflict within appropriate limits. Indeed, successful climate adaptation is likely impossible without further civic and institutional innovation of the kinds that we examine in this collection.

More generally, the challenge of innovating well and aligning new models with other democratic institutions is momentous. Nothing has been easy or inevitable. As our contributors to this volume recognize, despite some of their different approaches, civic innovation can widen our opportunities for genuine democratic reform. But only a hardheaded analysis of limits, obstacles, and tradeoffs can yield sustainable and systemic change.

Our contributors come at these questions from various though often complementary angles. Elena Fagotto and Archon Fung, for instance, utilize the concept of "embeddedness" to capture the ways that innovations take root in local environments. They argue that successful interactions are repeated across time, are anchored in community institutions, and encompass multiple issues. Fagotto and Fung examine nine long-term cases of deliberation with substantial impacts on their communities, including Issue Forums in West Virginia, Hawaii, and South Dakota, and study circles in Delaware and Maryland. In doing so, they locate a number of shared characteristics—having a key catalyst (political authority) and institutional support (capacity)—and reveal the importance of institutional investment. Several intermediaries—such as AmericaSpeaks, Everyday Democracy, and the National Issues Forums—work across the field of deliberative innovation to ensure transfer of best practices and critical reflection from community to community, issue to issue, even model to model (see also Leighninger 2006; Nabatchi et al. 2012).

Carmen Sirianni examines a series of related capacity-building challenges by focusing on two programs (watersheds, environmental justice) within the US Environmental Protection Agency that seek to coproduce tools and training for local groups and fund leadership and organizational development, but also across a larger field through national and regional intermediaries (River Network, Southeast Watershed Forum), as well as through state-based agencies and civic intermediaries (Colorado Watershed Assembly). Sirianni's analysis complements local embeddedness in Fagotto and Fung with agency-wide and field-wide questions of institutional capacity, mix, and configuration. His analysis challenges stale understandings of bureaucratic organization by examining agency-wide networked team design and collaborative governance. In the process, he expands the normative basis for theorizing robust civic democracy to include national public agencies.

Anne Taufen Wessells, in turn, further enriches our understanding of the kinds of tools that community actors and agency officials can coproduce, ranging from an artistic field guide for everyday citizens to explore and claim civic ownership of the Los Angeles River to a multistakeholder matrix for ranking and selecting viable local projects to fund with state grants. Jason Corburn examines the process of generating a highly sophisticated community-based health assessment tool among twenty-five local groups in San Francisco, with a city planning agency catalyzing collaboration in a larger field that included an initially reluctant city health agency. In these and other cases, it is the mix of lay and professional knowledge, which Corburn (2005) refers to elsewhere as "street science," that is critical, not some ideal tool or organizational form.

While many of our contributors examine institutional dimensions of innovation, many also focus on narrative, frame, and informal conversation. As Caroline Lee shows in a comparative study of three conservation-planning partnerships in the United States, different tolerances for shame and disagreement might lead some to utilize backstage and informal conversation as a way to generate trust and small wins that later can be leveraged for larger purpose. Robert Fishman demonstrates the importance of a broad narrative, a "participatory storyline," of the Carnation Revolution in Portugal in the 1970s for ongoing capacities to empower poor and working-class communities in policy change and innovation. His comparison with two cases in Spain reveals the importance of narratives that are either broadly globalizing or narrowly local. On the other hand, while Brazil had its own revolution of richly intertwined and historically layered networks and narratives (Mische 2008), as well as local participatory budgeting innovations (Baiocchi, Heller, and Silva 2011), Thamy Pogrebinschi provides an analysis of contemporary national policy conferences, both in terms of substance and number of bills introduced to Congress. She demonstrates that such ambitious deliberative designs can be relatively inclusive, engaging indigenous women, people with disabilities, and gay, lesbian, bisexual, and transgender communities. Deliberative, collaborative, and networked approaches, when designed well and embedded appropriately in institutional fields, can serve ideals of democratic equality, even though there are many factors in every field that tend to reproduce participatory inequalities of income, education, class, or race. In short, there are ways to systematically and strategically "invest in democracy" (Sirianni 2009) that do not simply displace issues of justice, but locate them centrally.

Information technology must now be at the center of any robust theory and practice of democracy, though there is not general agreement on such questions as whether publics become more polarized and unequal as a result (Karpf 2012; Sunstein 2007). Several of our essays address information tools, such as participatory geographical information systems (PGIS) and planning scenarios that one might use in community health or watershed planning, but two essays in particular focus in depth on possibilities at different ends of a spectrum. Daniel Kreiss and Laura Meadows examine the campaign to defeat the anti-gay constitutional amendment in North Carolina in 2012, which, while unsuccessful, was highly consequential and instructive. Equality NC, a statewide LGBT advocacy nonprofit, formed a broad Coalition to Protect All NC Families. This coalition was a hybrid assortment of more than 125 national, regional, and North Carolina–based social, political, religious, and civil society organizations and groups. It then reached out to a wide array of bloggers and media producers around the country, leveraging the hybrid repertoires that have become characteristic of many netroots groups, such as MoveOn.org and DailyKos. Lewis Friedland, on the other hand, examines a broad range of shifting types of online civic communication at the level of a city and in the midst of critical shifts in the old media business models. But his focus is less about strategic communication and more about civic problem solving, community development, and environmental sustainability among many kinds of independent grassroots groups, sometimes mobilized against the city and other authoritative and powerful actors, but also drawn into various forms of collaboration. Grassroots groups may train their own "information stewards," but city agencies also provide capacity-building grants and offer complementary training to neighborhood staff to enable fruitful problem solving that adds public value to communities, including to communities of color and immigrants who often tend to be left behind by the communications revolution. While Friedland does not focus on strategic political action in the way Kreiss and Meadows do, his analysis reveals a significant amount of multisided strategic field building (Fligstein and McAdam 2012) among diverse types of civic organizations, public agencies, technology entrepreneurs, and old and new media.

In her concluding reflections on the essays in this collection, Jane Mansbridge calls attention to the larger deliberative systems in which these and other cases are invariably embedded, sometimes with complementary effects that enhance democracy, sometimes with displacement effects that might devalue some needed forms of democratic speech and action, including effective and fair representation. Her systems approach to deliberation is not mechanistic, but allows for dynamic emergence, reflexivity, paradox, and suboptimal configurations, thus requiring practical judgment by scholars and citizens alike. Mansbridge's analytic tools continually lead us to the big normative questions of what might constitute robust democracy amidst such complexity and institutional differentiation. These are exactly the kinds of questions we trusted our contributors to pose, even when focusing on specific types of tools, networks, places, discourses, relationships, and institutions.

References

Ansell, Chris, and Alison Gash. 2007. "Collaborative Governance in Theory and Practice." *Journal of Public Administration Research and Theory* 18: 543–71.

Baiocchi, Gianpaolo, Patrick Heller, and Marcello K. Silva. 2011. *Bootstrapping Democracy: Transforming Local Governance and Civil Society in Brazil.* Stanford, CA: Stanford University Press.

Boyte, Harry C. 2005. "Reframing Democracy: Governance, Civic Agency, and Politics." *Public Administration Review* 65 (5): 536–46.

Corburn, Jason. 2005. *Street Science: Community Knowledge and Environmental Health Justice.* Cambridge, MA: MIT Press.

Dzur, Albert W. 2008. *Democratic Professionalism: Citizen Participation and the Reconstruction of Professional Ethics, Identity, and Practice.* University Park: Pennsylvania State University Press.

Fligstein, Neil, and Doug McAdam. 2012. *A Theory of Fields.* Oxford: Oxford University Press.

Karpf, David. 2012. *The MoveOn Effect: The Unexpected Transformation of American Political Advocacy.* New York: Oxford University Press.

Leighninger, Matthew. 2006. *The Next Form of Democracy: How Expert Rule Is Giving Way to Shared Governance and Why Politics Will Never Be the Same.* Nashville, TN: Vanderbilt University Press.

Mische, Ann. 2008. *Partisan Publics: Communication and Contention across Brazilian Youth Activist Networks.* Princeton, NJ: Princeton University Press.

Nabatchi, Tina, John Gastil, G. Michael Welksner, and Matt Leighninger, eds. 2012. *Democracy in Motion: Evaluating the Practice and Impact of Deliberative Civic Engagement.* New York: Oxford University Press.

Sirianni, Carmen. 2009. *Investing in Democracy: Engaging Citizens in Collaborative Governance.* Washington, DC: Brookings Press.

Sirianni, Carmen, and Lewis Friedland. 2001. *Civic Innovation in America: Community Empowerment, Public Policy, and the Movement for Civic Renewal.* Berkeley: University of California Press.

Sunstein, Cass. 2007. *Republic.com 2.0.* Princeton, NJ: Princeton University Press.

1

Embedding Public Deliberation in Community Governance

ELENA FAGOTTO AND ARCHON FUNG

■ Public deliberations, meetings where citizens collectively discuss local problems and possible solutions, are a distinctive characteristic of American political life. While America famously has a long tradition of civic participation and self-government (de Tocqueville 2004), some citizens in some communities appear to have developed habits of regularly engaging one another in public deliberations on a breadth of topics. We call this civic and democratic achievement *embedded deliberation*. We believe that communities with embedded public deliberation are relatively rare; in most places, public decisions and the deliberations surrounding them are left primarily, often exclusively, to elected representatives and those who staff public agencies. By contrast, when the habit of deliberation is embedded in a community's political institutions and social practices, public decisions and collective actions commonly result from processes that involve discussion and reasoning that engages ordinary citizens rather than through the exercise of authority, expertise, status, political weight, or other such forms of power.

But how does embeddedness happen? What are its dimensions? Are there characteristics that make for a more fertile environment for deliberation to flourish? In order to answer these questions, we searched for communities where regular and organized deliberation had taken root and grown. We aimed to understand how what almost always begins as a limited effort to mobilize citizens and convene them to consider a public issue or political problem can sometimes grow into a regular practice that involves many different segments of a community and spans multiple issues that bear scant relation to one another. In this chapter, we use evidence from nine case studies to identify the main characteristics of embedded deliberation and understand the role that individual initiators and institutional sponsors play in promoting public deliberation. We also examine the political and social characteristics that seem to favor embeddedness.

The notion of embedded deliberation lies at a frontier of both understanding and practice of public deliberation. Empirical scholars of deliberation have focused on whether citizens' views change following discussion, whether they become polarized, whether they learn, whether their engagement in politics and civic life increases (Fishkin 1997; Barabas 2004; Sunstein 2002; Mendelberg 2002), whether deliberation and negotiation contribute to the reduction of conflict and ease of policy implementation (Coglianese 1997; Coglianese, Beierle, and Cayford 2002). Both scholars and practitioners have examined the wide variety of designs for procedures of public deliberation and have examined choices such as whether deliberations should be open to all or only to those who are chosen by lot or through some other mechanism, whether deliberation should be "empowered" with actual decision-making authority (Arnstein 1969; Fung 2004), and so on. These remarkable accomplishments in practice and understanding mark real progress in the state of deliberative practice. Embedded deliberation, however, adds to these two threads of literature by focusing on the long-term effects of public deliberation.[1] By examining how deliberation takes root and evolves, we are able to observe the way public and private institutions employ deliberation and respond to it, and how a more deliberative approach affects communities' and institutions' ability to address local problems.

Methodology

In order to understand the dynamics of embedded deliberation, we researched nine case studies of communities that had developed habits of deliberation. Because we wanted to learn about the conditions under which deliberation becomes socially and politically embedded, our selection of case studies was highly opportunistic. The advice of national experts on community-level deliberations guided us in our process of identifying communities where public deliberation was well-established. We singled out cases where deliberative practices had become fairly widespread and repeated over time and had led to some action around the issues. Hence, we selected mature or relatively mature cases, which enabled us to observe how deliberative practices evolved through time and to understand their embeddedness and impact over a period of several years. Within this category, we also selected for variety of topics, trying to obtain as broad a spectrum as possible of deliberative issues. Although we tried to include different deliberative models in our cases, our selection is by no means representative of the myriad of deliberative practices used in the United States. Since we were interested in cases where deliberation had become well-rooted, inevitably our choice of cases favored models that mobilize communities and institutions over time (such as study circles) or rely on local organizations to regularly promote deliberative methods (such as the National Issues Forums). Therefore, important deliberative formats that are used for specific one-time events (including, but not limited to, AmericaSpeaks-type events or Deliberative Polls) are not represented in our sample.

For each case, we conducted at least one field visit of several days and observed one or more deliberative events. In three cases, we attended trainings on the specific deliberative model used: the National Issues Forums model in West Virginia and Hawaii and the Indigenous Issues Forums model in South Dakota. We also conducted extensive semistructured interviews by phone or in person. In general, we interviewed the main promoters of public deliberation, participants, to register their reactions, as well as activists, policy makers, experts, and organizations that supported deliberation. We also examined all available documents from these sites to understand how deliberation was adopted and matured. Such documents ranged from simple lists of objectives taken down at the conclusion of some deliberation to internal memos, newsletters, web materials and videos, press coverage, formal reports, program evaluations, and scholarly articles, when available.

What Is Embedded Deliberation?

Understanding Public Deliberation

By public deliberation we mean a discussion where a group of citizens collectively reflects on an issue and confronts the views of other participants. Simone Chambers offers a good definition of deliberation as "debate and discussion aimed at producing reasonable, well-informed opinions in which participants are willing to revise preferences in light of discussions, new information, and claims made by fellow participants" (Chambers 2003, 309). The notion of "public" deliberation implies that the discussion happens in the public sphere, with citizens as participants, often with the purpose of gaining a better understanding of a problem and contributing to an agreed solution with ideas and resource mobilization. According to Delli Carpini, Cook, and Jacobs, we can say that public deliberation "is the process through which deliberative democracy occurs" (Delli Carpini, Cook, and Jacobs 2004, 317). Public deliberation is a critical part of deliberative democracy, "a form of government in which free and equal citizens (and their representatives), justify decisions in a process in which they give one another reasons that are mutually acceptable and generally accessible, with the aim of reaching conclusions that are binding in the present on all citizens but open to challenge in the future" (Gutmann and Thompson 2004, 7).

Deliberation is frequently contrasted with aggregative social choice procedures in which conflicting views and disagreements are managed through the voting process rather than through reason giving (ibid., 13–21). Under deliberative democratic accounts, on the other hand, citizens can confront and change their views through public deliberations, and their political discussions originate policies that are more acceptable to all and more legitimate. Far from being an alternative to representative democracy, deliberative democracy can complement it by improving the depth and quality of political discussion, and ultimately the quality of public decisions. But why is a more deliberative approach to policy making and government preferable? First, decisions that are corroborated by public deliberation are more legitimate because they are made not only by elected representatives, the voters' agents, but also by the voters themselves, the principals and the very source of legitimacy of democratic governments. Second, public deliberation may produce more reasoned policies due to the exchange of information and discussion among diverse citizens. Third, public deliberation can defuse polarization and encourage social cohesion because, even if not all citizens reach a consensus, deliberative discussions promote the appreciation of different, even opposing, opinions. Fourth, there are systemic deficits in the democratic policy making process (from unclear public preferences to lack of accountability) that can be corrected through an injection of public deliberation (Fung 2006). Finally, public deliberations can deepen civic engagement and encourage voting, volunteering, and participating in public life, thus strengthening the very fabric of democracy.

Embedded vs. Occasional Deliberation

Now that we have clarified the concept of public deliberation, consider the difference between embedded and occasional deliberation. Court juries and town meetings are perhaps the most familiar forms of public deliberation, but there are many other forms that include neighborhood planning committees, study circles on race, National Issues Forums on poverty, public hearings, and even discussions that occur on the Internet. What distinguishes deliberative meetings from other kinds of meetings are a focus on including a plurality of views by recruiting diverse participants, often the presence of a moderator, and specific rules to ensure mutual respect, listening, and the weighing of all opinions.

Our case studies drew upon different deliberative approaches. Many were informed by the study circles model, which combines public deliberation (and dialogue) with community organizing. Most of the deliberations take place in smaller groups of eight to twelve that meet in a series of sessions to explore an issue with the guidance of peer facilitators. Participants start by discussing an issue, then move on to explore concrete ways they could address the problem, and then come up with specific action ideas. At a National Issues Forum, a diverse group of participants (the number can vary greatly) gathers for a two-hour deliberation about a public policy problem, such as reforming health care or US international relations. A moderator invites participants to weigh different approaches, considering their pros and cons so the participants can deepen their understanding and appreciate the complexity of issues. The community conversations we observed in Connecticut mobilize a large and diverse group for an evening, when participants discuss public education issues in small groups and formulate concrete action plans. The Indigenous Issues Forums use small-group dialogues where participants explore tribal issues and reflect about the characteristics of a healthy dialogue. Finally, the Keiki Caucus (Children Caucus) convenes stakeholders, including legislators, advocacy groups, and public agencies, in monthly meetings to discuss pressing children's issues, prioritize needs, and assemble a legislative package.

Most of these deliberative approaches were developed by national organizations. In every case, however, those in local communities adapted the different models to their specific circumstances and needs.

More often than not, public deliberations occur in a community as sporadic events. Participants learn about deliberative methods of dialogue and there may be some follow-up activities, but there is no substantive change in the way local problems are addressed and decisions made. In that case, we have *occasional* public deliberation. When a community develops a habit of using public deliberation with some regularity, we say it has *embedded* deliberation in the way it discusses issues or faces local challenges.

No deliberative process is a guarantee for embeddedness; the same deliberative methods can be well-embedded in a community and used repeatedly as a problem-solving tool, and they can be employed only occasionally in others. The community conversations on public education we observed in Connecticut provide a good example of a deliberative format that was used only once in many communities across the state, but became well-embedded in some communities and extremely embedded in one area (Bridgeport, CT). No model ensures embeddedness, but some formats are more likely than others to favor it. Most of the deliberative formats in our sample, for example, are more inclined to take root because they are designed precisely to build capacity and mobilize communities over time, hence present a higher probability of becoming embedded. Study circles, with their series of trust-building dialogues and their focus on action and change, can be effective community-organizing tools to encourage coalition building and mobilize participants. But the National Issues Forums, with their reliance on local institutions to convene forums regularly and provide annual training, also aim to instill regular deliberative practices in communities.

Other deliberative models, on the other hand, are best for occasional deliberations aimed at providing public input and measuring the impact of public deliberation on participants' opinions. AmericaSpeaks, for example, facilitates large town meetings where citizens (often in the hundreds) deliberate for a day or more on public policy issues and provide input to policy makers. In Deliberative Polls, a random sample of participants discuss a policy issue in depth for a weekend, with the aid of materials, experts, and facilitators. Participants are polled before and after the deliberations to measure opinion shifts and show what the public would think if it had a chance to deliberate on issues and be better informed. They are designed to provide informed input from representative samples of the population, in a fashion that is clearly more oriented to influencing policy making than mobilizing communities for public action.

How Embeddedness Happens: Deliberative Entrepreneurs, Organizations, and Theories of Change

We have shed light on the distinction between occasional and embedded deliberation and how different models may be more appropriate for each purpose. But how are deliberative interventions introduced into previously nondeliberative environments? In two of the cases we examined, *deliberative entrepreneurs* played a key role in introducing deliberative reforms. As we explained elsewhere (Fagotto and Fung 2006), these entrepreneurs identified "markets," or opportunities where injecting public deliberation could improve community relations or policy making. They are often individual activists who have deep personal commitments to citizen engagement and public deliberation. They begin by planting the seed of deliberative practices informally by convening forums in their church or library, and they move on to more structured ways by building deliberative "catalysts," small centers that promote deliberation and assist organizations that seek public input or want to increase civic engagement. In South Dakota and West Virginia, individual deliberative entrepreneurs brought practices of public deliberation to their communities and later created more permanent homes for dialogue.

Other times, deliberative interventions are launched by the leaders of organizations, public or private, who after being exposed to dialogues decide to employ the same deliberative methods to further their organizations' substantive missions. In Hawaii, for example, state legislators sought to improve child welfare policies by involving stakeholders through public deliberation. In Delaware, the YWCA launched dialogues on race to remove social and economic barriers. In most of the cases in our sample, deliberation was the initiative of nongovernmental organizations, local government, or coalitions that brought the two together. This is because we selected cases where deliberation appeared more embedded, and sponsorship from organizations, rather than individual deliberative entrepreneurs, seems to deepen embeddedness. But we shall explain this in more detail in the section that describes the dimensions of embeddedness.

Second, deliberative interventions, be they the initiative of deliberative entrepreneurs or of organizations, operate with different "theories of change." There are at least two relevant schools of thought: some focus mainly upon changing the beliefs and behaviors of the citizens who participate directly in public deliberations, while others simultaneously address citizens *and* public institutions. The first believe that instilling the principles of deliberation in citizens will increase their tolerance of diversity, make them more reflective and informed, and make them more active and collaborative citizens. According to this line of thinking, in the long run social change is driven by citizens who propagate the principles of deliberation in public life.

The second school sees deliberation as an instrument to mobilize citizens, but also to directly affect the policies and capabilities of public institutions. Those in this category believe that institutions and citizens should be partners in deliberation and public action. Clearly, this theory of change requires public institutions that are willing to collaborate with citizens or even delegate some of their prerogatives in collaborative governance arrangements.

South Dakota and Delaware are good examples of the first theory of change, as the sponsors of deliberations there believed that change would start by improving the way individuals interact and respect differences. Restoring community relations could lay the foundation for more participation in public life and activism. In places like Kuna, Kansas City, and Montgomery County, on the other hand, public deliberations were used to improve the decisions of public institutions with the provision of public input, or to mobilize communities to collaborate with government to better their neighborhoods and schools.

Three Dimensions of Embeddedness

We described how embedded deliberation is a habit of using deliberative practices involving participation, discussion, and reasoning to make public decisions and take collective action. We also know about the crucial role played by deliberative entrepreneurs and organizational sponsors. But what are the dimensions that characterize embeddedness? Evidence from our cases suggests that in order to be embedded, public deliberation must be (1) iterative, (2) anchored, and (3) encompassing.

First, deliberation is embedded when its use is *iterative; almost definitionally, embeddedness requires formal practices of deliberation to be repeated with regularity over time.* This principle guided our choice of cases, as we singled out communities that had developed a habit of regularly employing deliberative practices. The extent of the iteration varies greatly across cases and fluctuates overtime within a single case, depending on, among other things, organizational capacity and resources available. Clearly, deliberation is less frequent when it is first introduced, and it occurs more often once more individuals, organizations, and government officials gain familiarity with the process and promote it in their circles. Deliberations in Montgomery County, for example, went from seven in school year 2003–2004, when the program officially started, to twenty-two in 2006–2007. Some cases present a dozen or more deliberations in a single year, like the Connecticut community conversations and the Hawaii Keiki Caucus, while others had less frequent deliberations, like the Kuna and Portsmouth study circles, with one or two deliberations per year. In most of our case studies, deliberation was introduced in the late 1990s, with West Virginia (mid-1990s) and Hawaii (early 1990s) being more mature cases, and Montgomery County the most recent (early 2000s). Given these disparities in frequency per year and in years of deliberative practice, we opted not to assign a specific value to the iterative dimension of embedded deliberation, but at a minimum, the cases we studied presented at least one or two deliberations a year for at least five years.

Second, to be embedded, deliberation must be *anchored* in the sense that deliberative practices are linked to a range of community-based or governmental organizations from which they receive support and resources. Deliberation does not happen in a *vacuum*. It requires staff and resources to train moderators, produce discussion materials, convene events, build capacity, conduct outreach, and follow up on the deliberations. This is why deliberations are often sponsored by community organizations, universities, or government offices. These institutions secure not only material resources, such as office space, funding, or staff, but also access to other organizations in their political and social networks.

Finally, one effect of anchored deliberation is that organizations may respond by altering their culture and adopting more deliberative mechanisms to operate and make decisions. If the planning commission in a city decides to engage residents to design a new development project, the planning department may later change its policies by institutionalizing a citizen body to participate in all project designs.

Third, to be embedded, deliberation must be *encompassing*, that is, a variety of topics or local problems must be treated in a deliberative fashion. While it is unrealistic and undesirable to think that all public decisions should be subject to organized public deliberation, almost every community has many areas that could benefit from greater public deliberation. The delivery of numerous public services, from health care to education and infrastructure, can be improved with participation from the beneficiaries, but also areas that are usually considered the experts' domain, such as electoral law, can benefit from public input.[2] If deliberation is initially adopted in a specific policy area but it fails to address other urgent issues, it will be only partially embedded.

In Figure 1.1 we plot our cases along the dimensions "encompassing" and "anchored." We omitted the "iterative" dimension because, since repetition over time was our selection criterion, all our cases are iterative, so this dimension has less explanatory power than the other two. Analyzing our cases along the two other dimensions offers a deeper understanding of embeddedness.

In the *vertical axis* we have the encompassing dimension, where cases are measured according to the number of issues that were submitted to deliberative treatment. The *horizontal axis* presents the anchored dimension, where cases can be less anchored when they are supported only by a deliberative entrepreneur, moderately anchored when non-government organizations back them, and very anchored when support comes from government. At a minimum, deliberation needs to be promoted by a deliberative entrepreneur, an individual who promotes the use of deliberative practices in a community. The deliberative entrepreneur often trains facilitators, networks with organizations, and identifies issues that could benefit from a deliberative treatment. Deliberative entrepreneurs also seek funding to build some infrastructure for public deliberation. Although the deliberative entrepreneur plays a key role in introducing a community to deliberative practices, unless she secures support from an established organization, deliberation will be only minimally anchored and may disappear when the entrepreneur ceases to promote it. Deliberation is more anchored when an established NGO backs it with funding, staff, or other organizational resources, including reputation and access to the organization's network. If supported by an organization, deliberation will establish itself more deeply in the community and will not depend solely on the efforts of an individual. Deliberation will be most anchored when supported by government. Very often, deliberative entrepreneurs or NGOs try to persuade government officials to adopt deliberative practices and open decision making to citizens, but success in influencing

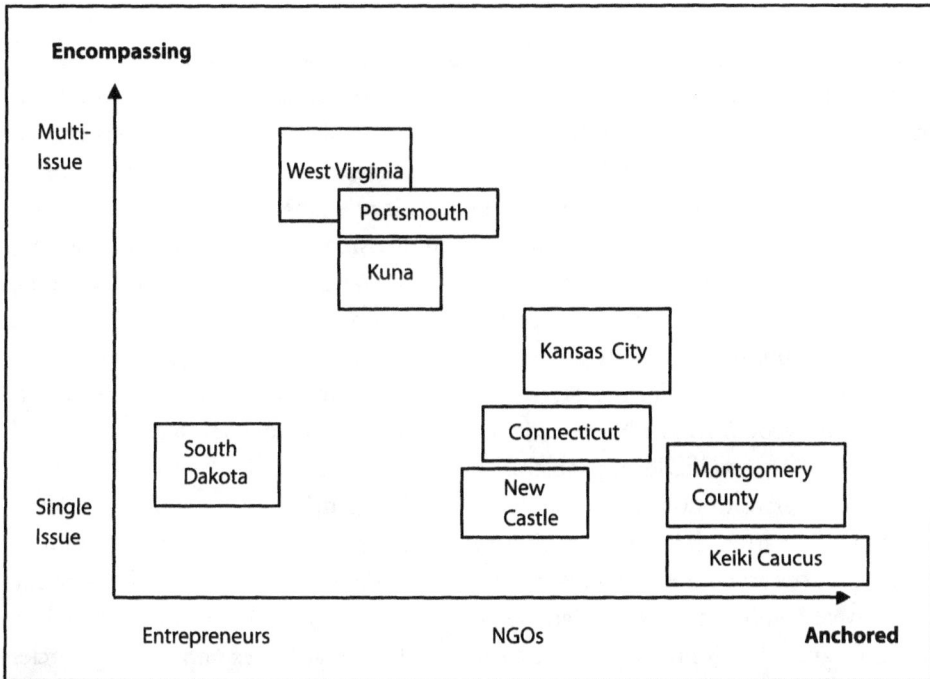

Figure 1.1 Embeddedness of Cases

government varies. When government sponsors deliberation, on the other hand, deliberation is most likely to have a durable impact, as government has the authority and resources to use public input and change its practices in response to deliberations. Let us now discuss how the cases are ordered in the figure along these dimensions.

Encompassing Dimension

In five of our cases deliberations dealt with a single issue, and consequently they rank low in the encompassing dimension. In South Dakota, deliberation was used principally to deal with tribal problems. Race relations were the focus of study circles in New Castle County, DE, and in Montgomery County, MD; more specifically, the latter encouraged dialogue on race to close the achievement gap in public schools. In Connecticut, community dialogues sought to mobilize residents and civil society to improve public education in local schools. Finally, the Keiki Caucus in Hawaii gathered legislators, stakeholders, and the public to prioritize issues related to child welfare. Obviously, in most of these cases, deliberations have occasionally expanded to include other topics. In South Dakota, for example, besides deliberations on tribal issues, there were also forums on national policy problems, and New Castle County employed study circles to address issues of disability and gender. Although some of the single-issue cases sporadically applied deliberation to more than one topic, by and large their principal focus was on one issue. That they are not encompassing, however, should not be interpreted as failure, especially considering that in these cases deliberation was adopted to focus on a specific policy area, ranging from race relations to public education and child welfare legislation. Therefore it is obvious that deliberative interventions created to promote deliberation on indigenous issues, or engage communities in discussions on public education, stuck to the areas defined in their missions.

The remaining case studies are more encompassing as deliberations discussed a broader range of issues. A cluster of three cases, West Virginia, Portsmouth, and Kuna, rank particularly high in the encompassing dimension, while in Kansas City public deliberation appears to be moderately encompassing. In the West Virginia case, we encounter National Issues Forums on national policy issues, such as health care, education, and the economy. The National Issues Forums model, however, was also adapted to deliberate on specific local problems, ranging from the lack of opportunities for youth in the state to domestic violence and underage drinking. In Kuna and Portsmouth, deliberation did not start with a focus on specific policy issues, but instead was introduced to address important community problems. In these localities, study circles were helpful in providing an arena to discuss pressing local problems, defuse tensions, and offer input to local government. In Kuna, for example, study circles improved public planning and helped clarify opinions on some contentious issues that were polarizing the community, such as the adoption of a drug testing policy in schools and the approval of a bond to finance the expansion of school facilities. The public was given a chance to weigh in using public deliberation, and its feedback was incorporated in the decisions of the local government. Also, Portsmouth held study circles on a variety of local topics, from school violence to the preparation of the city's master plan. There too, deliberation defused tensions on the decision to redistrict some public schools, which faced intense opposition from some parents who feared for the quality of their schools. After participating in study circles, parents and school officials revised their initial positions and came to an agreement on the redistricting plan. In the Kansas City case, on the other hand, deliberations were less encompassing as they revolved around two areas: supporting schools by strengthening relations with families and the community, and helping depressed neighborhoods take action on issues of crime and poverty. The program was launched to improve relations between schools, families, and the community, but it later expanded to helping neighborhoods because it became clear that unless neighborhoods became healthier, they could offer only limited support to schools.

If in single-issue cases deliberation was an instrument applied to solve problems in a specific policy area, in multi-issue ones deliberation was intended as a decision-making tool that could be applied to *any* issue. In multi-issue cases the deliberations were encompassing because they were promoted by neutral organizations whose scope was to advance the use of *deliberative methods* to engage citizens. These nonpartisan organizations convened deliberations on very different issues and acted as neutral venues where complex local problems could be discussed, irrespective of the positions of those who brought the issues before them.

Anchored Dimension

Along the horizontal axis, cases are organized according to the extent of their anchoring. As explained above, deliberation requires institutional and organizational support in order to be embedded. Without such backing, deliberation will hardly have the capacity and resources it needs to penetrate in a community and impact policies, and will more likely remain a sporadic practice.

In nearly all our cases deliberation was backed by NGOs, government, or a mixture of both. The only exceptions are the South Dakota Indigenous Issues Forum, where deliberations were supported by a small coalition of deliberative entrepreneurs. Although these entrepreneurs have established a solid web of relations with local organizations, from libraries to churches and correction facilities, to preserve their autonomy they decided not to be housed in any organization. Since so much of their approach depends on a slow process of trust building within indigenous communities, they probably prefer to rely mostly on the reputation of the deliberative entrepreneurs and their ability to cultivate trust rather than risk being confused with the programs of existing organizations.

In six of our case studies, public deliberations were supported by NGOs or by coalitions of NGOs and local government. We will examine them in order.

The West Virginia Center for Civic Life is an independent organization housed at the University of Charleston, where it held forums with students, faculty, and staff, gradually embedding deliberative practices in the university curriculum. The university provided logistical support, but all outreach activities to spread deliberation across the state and to secure funding were independently conducted by the Center for Civic Life. The center also partnered with other organizations to help them use deliberative methods.[3] In Kuna and Portsmouth, deliberation was initially promoted by coalitions of local leaders who later understood there was a need to formalize their efforts and established two nonprofit organizations, called Kuna ACT and Portsmouth Listens respectively, which served as institutional homes for engaging citizens on local policy issues. These organizations received some funding from local partners and government and served as neutral venues to convene deliberations on any topic brought before them. In West Virginia, Kuna, and Portsmouth, public dialogues were launched by a deliberative entrepreneur or by local leaders and later received some logistical support and funding from existing organizations or local government, but they remained independent from their funders in order to serve as neutral deliberative venues.

In New Castle County, Connecticut, and Kansas City, on the other hand, deliberations on specific topics were introduced by nongovernmental organizations (in Kansas City by a coalition that included the public schools). In these cases, NGOs saw deliberative interventions as an instrument to advance public dialogue and action in areas they were active in. In New Castle County, the YWCA launched study circles to promote dialogue on race relations. The YWCA's reputation and resources were instrumental in reaching out to government and businesses, which convened dialogues among their employees.[4] The Community Conversations on Public Education were launched by a foundation whose mission is to improve education for Connecticut's children by, among other things, involving communities and families. The foundation saw deliberations as a key tool to engage parents, local organizations, and schools in conversations where they could discuss problems but also become actively engaged in finding solutions to improve education. The program was managed by the League of Women Voters, whose organizational capacity, together with the foundation's resources, contributed to the success of the initiative. The Kansas City study circles program shares some similarities with the Connecticut conversations because it was supported by the local chapter of the United Way, with funding from the Kauffman Foundation, to restore trust between families and schools and improve public education. In addition, however, this initiative was supported also by a school district that viewed community involvement as essential to improving local schools. If in other cases discussed so far in the anchored dimension, government offered *some* support to deliberations and used deliberations to receive public input, in Kansas City it went one step further because the school department was a cofounder of the study circles initiative and viewed deliberation as an enabler of community engagement and change. This is why the Kansas City case occupies a position between NGOs and government on the horizontal axis.

In the two remaining cases deliberations were launched and funded by local government branches. The Montgomery County Public School District introduced a study circles program as a component of a broader initiative to close the achievement gap. The school district wanted to get parents, educators, and students to talk openly about race and build trust and the capacity to remove barriers to educational achievement. Study circles are reaching more schools in the district every year, defusing tensions and enabling collaborations. Additionally, staff members from some departments within the school district held study circles on race, a sign that public deliberation is slowly changing the organization's understanding of the achievement gap. The Keiki Caucus was launched more than fifteen years ago by two Hawaiian state legislators to draft better laws to protect children. They decided to involve stakeholders active in the area of child welfare in monthly meetings to exchange information and prioritize issues that need new legislation. This approach enabled collaboration among agencies and other stakeholders, informed legislation, and promoted a more targeted use of resources.

Three Conditions for Embeddedness

With this concept of embeddedness and the dimensions that characterize it, consider now what conditions are necessary for deliberation to become embedded. What kind of environments offer more fertile terrains to embed public dialogue and citizen engagement? Three factors seem to be important:[5]

Political Authority

As we have seen, instances of public deliberation are frequently born from the initiative and energies of civic organizations and entrepreneurs. To endure through time, however, they must also be supported by local politicians and decision makers. At minimum, they must find an environment where political leadership is not hostile. Public officials can provide resources to support deliberation over time. More importantly, however, public deliberation frequently addresses social problems and so calls for various public actions and policy changes. Without official leadership that is willing to engage citizens and at times delegate some of its authority, deliberation lacks authority and force. Though officials can often be expected to resist deliberative initiatives, endorsement from a handful of leaders can lay the groundwork for more anchored deliberations. In Hawaii, for example, the Keiki Caucus is chaired by two legislators. The Kansas City study circles were launched by a coalition led by the school superintendent and the United Way. It may well be that in certain cases, leaders have a particular predisposition for collegiality and power sharing, but in others they seem to endorse public deliberation out of more pragmatic motivations. Local government in Kuna and Portsmouth used study circles because they were dealing with thorny issues where public input became an attractive way to overcome an impasse.

Self-interest can also sometimes support deliberation. Officials sometimes make a political calculation that they need to feel the public's pulse before embarking upon a course of policy. Public deliberation can help them gauge public sentiment and reduce polarization among their constituents.

Deliberative Capacity

Sustained, embedded public deliberation also requires the maintenance of local capacities to organize and convene such discussions. At the very minimum, those capacities include the presence of trained moderators and facilitators in a community, the administrative wherewithal to organize deliberative events, and the ability to mobilize and recruit participants. Another "deliberative capacity" is the ability to gain attention of local decision makers to participate in deliberative events and to utilize their recommendations. Finally, connections between those who deliberate and local institutions—such as community newspapers and radio, churches, schools, businesses, and social service providers—extend the reach of deliberation beyond direct participants to the many others in any community who do not engage directly.[6] In our case studies, independent civic organizations such as Kuna ACT, Portsmouth Listens, and the United Way housed local deliberative capacity. In other communities, less commonly it seems, deliberative capacity is housed within governmental agencies. Provided that they can secure funding, such groups create a professional home for deliberative entrepreneurs to practice their craft, organize it, and reproduce it through time.

Demand for Democracy

Finally, we reason that lasting and durable embeddedness requires that constituencies be willing to mobilize to defend their organizations, institutions, and practices. Even in communities where local politicians or policy makers are disposed toward public deliberation, they may be replaced by others who are less favorably inclined or they themselves may cool if public engagement turns out to hamper their other priorities or agendas.

Given these very real possibilities—even tendencies—local practices of deliberation are more likely to be sustained when "countervailing" forces—such as community organizations or mobilized citizens—act politically to defend or advance practices of public deliberation. Although in our cases we were not able to identify instances where citizens mobilized to demand or defend deliberation, continued exposure to deliberative practices may generate this demand in the future, and this aspect surely constitutes an important topic for future research. More broadly, our cases obscure the importance of this political factor *because* we selected communities in which local officials were supportive of deliberation. Our cases, therefore, are likely to be unrepresentative in this regard.

These three conditions are particularly relevant for deliberative interventions that intend to mobilize communities to become actively engaged and impact the decisions and behaviors of local government, along the lines of the second theory of change discussed earlier. Political authority and demand for democracy may not be so essential when it comes to deliberations to transform individuals or to reflect on policy issues (first theory of change) because the sphere of impact of the deliberations is confined to the personal level.

Laying out these three dimensions may aid deliberative entrepreneurs and institutional sponsors in selecting promising areas in which to invest resources in deliberative reform. Given a choice, it is better to work in communities where political leaders are friendly to deliberation, where there are organizations that can be long-term allies in sponsoring forums and associated activities, and where the possibilities for forming organized constituencies seem positive. Clearly, often the promoters of deliberations lack the luxury of selecting places that are ripe for embedding it. Although they may have to choose other options to drive social change, being mindful of the conditions for embeddedness should nevertheless help them understand how to cultivate these three factors to prepare the ground for deliberative interventions in the future. These dimensions may also guide reform efforts in particular communities. It is important to gain the ear, sympathy, and commitment of policy makers, to foster linkages with appropriate civic organizations or to found new ones to support capacity for deliberation, and to organize supporters—most likely those who have participated in deliberative engagements—to back local democratic reforms as a political matter.

Looking Forward

Our aim in the pages above has been modest. We aim to open an additional line of inquiry for those examining the institutions of public deliberation and for those who seek to spread and deepen the practice of democracy in communities everywhere. Theorists of deliberative democracy have always imagined that practices of public deliberation would be embedded in this sense—that in a deliberative democracy, citizens would participate regularly in the exchange of reasons and arguments that would in turn help to determine laws and policies. Scholars and self-identified practitioners of deliberation, by contrast, have focused their energies upon understanding and creating more episodic experiments or prototypes of public deliberation. For this they can be forgiven because the political and social world in which we live is so far removed from the ideals of deliberative democrats. No one can create ongoing deliberation wholesale, with a wave of the hand.

Nevertheless, intentional interventions to create public deliberation—experimentally and episodically—in communities across the nation over the past two decades have cumulated to more sustained deliberative habits in some communities. By examining those efforts and characterizing them in a systematic way, we hope to illuminate some of the strategies that produce not just good deliberation, but public deliberation that is sustained across time and spread across issues. This exploration is of course only a beginning. We hope that by highlighting the importance of *embedded* deliberation, practitioners will be better able to instill practices that are sustained in communities and so bring them one meaningful step closer to the ideal of a democracy that is deliberative.

Notes

1. In this effort, we join perspectives such as those in Grisham (1999), Sirianni (2009), Sirianni and Friedland (2001).
2. The British Columbia Citizen Assembly, for example, was composed of citizens who met for a year to draft a proposal to reform the province's electoral law, and it inspired other Canadian provinces to follow the same model.
3. The center was established by Betty Knighton, a deliberative entrepreneur, but it later obtained the institutional backing of a university, which is why we position this case between deliberative entrepreneur and NGO in our figure.
4. The Delaware Office of Personnel and the Department of labor played a key role to involve state employees in study circles.
5. Joe Goldman suggested this framework at a research meeting at the Kettering Foundation in Dayton, Ohio, on May 24–25, 2007.

6. Successful partnership with local newspapers was instrumental to the success of public forums in West Virginia. Newspapers not only advertised public events in advance, but also published the discussion materials so that citizens could read them in advance and be more stimulated to attend.

References

Arnstein, Sherry R. 1969. "A Ladder of Citizen Participation." *Journal of the American Planning Association* 35 (4): 216–24.

Barabas, Jason. 2004. "How Deliberation Affects Policy Opinions." *American Political Science Review* 98 (4): 687–701.

Coglianese, Cary. 1997. "Assessing Consensus: The Promise and Performance of Negotiated Rulemaking." *Duke Law Journal* 86: 1255–1349.

Coglianese, Cary, Thomas C. Beierle, and Jerry Cayford. 2002. *Democracy in Practice: Public Participation in Environmental Decisions.* Washington, DC: Resources for the Future.

Chambers, Simone. 2003. "Deliberative Democratic Theory." *Annual Review of Political Science* 6: 307–26.

Delli Carpini, Michael X., Fay Lomax Cook, and Lawrence R. Jacobs. 2004. "Public Deliberation, Discursive Participation, and Citizen Engagement: A Review of the Empirical Literature." *Annual Review of Political Science* 7: 315–44.

Fagotto, Elena, and Archon Fung. 2006. *Embedded Deliberation: Entrepreneurs, Organizations, and Public Action.* Final Report for the William and Flora Hewlett Foundation, April 14.

Fishkin, James S. 1997. *The Voice of the People: Public Opinion and Democracy.* New Haven, CT: Yale University Press.

Fung, Archon. 2004. *Empowered Participation: Reinventing Urban Democracy.* Princeton, NJ: Princeton University Press.

———. 2006. "Democratizing the Policy Process." In *The Oxford Handbook of Public Policy,* ed. M. Moran, M. Rein, and R. Goodin. 669–85. Oxford: Oxford University Press.

Grisham, Vaughn L. 1999. *Tupelo: The Evolution of a Community.* Kettering Foundation Press.

Gutmann, Amy, and Dennis Thompson. 2004. *Why Deliberative Democracy?* Princeton, NJ: Princeton University Press.

Mendelberg, Tali. 2002. "The Deliberative Citizen: Theory and Evidence." In *Research in Micropolitics.* Vol. 6. *Political Decision-Making, Deliberation and Participation,* ed. M. X. D. Carpini, L. Huddy, and R. Shapiro, 151–93. Greenwich, CT: JAI Press.

Sirianni, Carmen. 2009. *Investing in Democracy: Engaging Citizens in Collaborative Governance.* Washington, DC: Brookings Press.

Sirianni, Carmen, and Lewis Friedland. 2001. *Civic Innovation in America: Community Empowerment, Public Policy, and the Movement for Civic Renewal.* Berkeley: University of California Press.

Sunstein, Cass. 2002. "The Law of Group Polarization." *Journal of Political Philosophy* 10 (2): 175–95.

Tocqueville, Alexis de. 2004. *Democracy in America.* Translated by Arthur Goldhammer. New York: Library of America.

2

Ways of Knowing the Los Angeles River Watershed

Getting from Engaged Participation to Inclusive Deliberation

ANNE TAUFEN WESSELLS

■ This chapter considers collaborative policy design in Los Angeles–area watershed management and riverfront redevelopment. Two distinct modes of collaborative engagement are examined in detail, where government actors and policy activists developed initiatives to build common regional understandings about watershed planning priorities, and to grow the constituency of citizens who are actively engaged in issues of watershed management and riverfront redevelopment, respectively. I trace a crucial relationship between formal collaborative governance initiatives, where various agencies and nonprofits are tasked with devising shared programs and plans, and the informal constituency-building work of grassroots activists and nonprofit leaders, where average citizens are invited into acts of consciousness raising, exploration, and contemplation. I suggest that the latter should be understood as an essential component of collaborative governance, populating, enabling, and supporting the more technical work of multiparty, government-led initiatives.

As overarching policy goals for the greater Los Angeles region, watershed management and riverfront redevelopment entail numerous and interrelated objectives: from the ongoing provision of adequate fresh water for millions of urban residents to the management of seasonal floods and the capacity to deal with polluted stormwater; from the protection of native species, the restoration of indigenous riparian habitat, the provision of neighborhood park space, and the creation of wetland biofunctionality to the economic redevelopment and residential densification of a postindustrial urban core.

These various policy purposes have presented an extraordinary opportunity for collaborative governance in Los Angeles, both at the level of regional agencies, organizations, and traditional policy sectors, as well as between formal governance initiatives and nonprofit groups and the citizens they are meant to represent, partner with, and serve.

The analysis offered here addresses what I understand to be two faces of the collaborative policy design challenge: first, the need to craft strategies at the highly professionalized and frequently specialized level of regional governance institutions, that is, to build shared understandings, coalitions, and policy priorities between historically disparate government sectors and public agencies; and second, the concurrent need to design ways of engaging citizens on regional issues in more prosaic and arguably far more powerful participatory, capacity-building efforts—enlisting a more sociological understanding of institutions as patterns of neighborhood, cultural, community, and recreational practice. This broadened conception of institution is crucial to collaborative governance, for it is through local sites, affiliation networks, and experiential settings that informed, capable, motivated constituencies will be built around public issues that cannot ultimately be "solved" by professionalized public interventions, however broadly construed and well-intentioned. Thus, I expand to the most liberal possible use of the term *institution*, to encompass not just the nested and various structures, rules, and norms that are designed and formally activated to "govern the commons" (Ostrom 1990), but also the social patterns and practices that enable less formal and intentionally unbounded citizen engagement with a governance issue.

Before continuing, it is also important to distinguish between the interrelated democratic ideals of *participation, inclusion*, and *deliberation* in order to support the realistic goal of accomplishing them. Deliberation signals careful consideration of various forms of knowledge, collective learning, and multiparty decision making. It "requires thoughtful examination of issues, listening to others' perspectives, and coming to a public judgment on what represents the common good" (Roberts 2004, 332). Deliberation is not the same thing as participation, and indeed the ability to listen, think, and reason collectively as to what constitutes the common good can be hindered by the wide, porous net indicated by participation (Innes and Booher 2004). For instance, public participation processes often unwittingly reinforce existing power dynamics to the detriment of less-resourced populations (Cooke and Kothari 2001), or are merely an opportunity for the public to comment on already developed programs, plans, and policies, rather than a chance to help to create them (Quick and Feldman 2011). Put simply, deliberation demands more and promises more than does participation.

Deliberation without inclusion, however, lacks engagement with the ideals of justice, democracy, and diversity that collaborative governance demands. Thus, deliberation only begins to meet the normative expectations we have for participation when it is characterized by inclusion practices, that is, "continuously creating a community involved in coproducing processes, policies, and programs for defining and addressing public issues" (Quick and Feldman 2011). Not only are more diverse stakeholders invited into the inclusive deliberative space, where they co-create the decision-making process and product(s), inclusive deliberation also engages multiple ways of knowing and is characterized by a temporal openness that enables the range of stakeholders and participants to change and evolve over time (Quick and Feldman 2011).

In the pages that follow, I elevate the significance of engaging different citizen constituencies' and institutional networks' ways of knowing issues such as watershed management and riverfront development as a key dimension of successful collaborative governance. Further, there is both agency and structure in these ways of knowing that can be strategically activated through inclusive policy design and management (Feldman et al. 2006). In order to collaborate effectively in governance networks—that is, in order ultimately to engage in inclusive deliberation and to develop collectively reasoned approaches to complex policy issues—these ways of knowing must be accessed, enrolled, and brought into productive interaction with each other. I propose that inclusive deliberation is the end game for which broad-based engagement and participation are aiming, and that it is only through the street-level enrolling of citizens as democratic agents that grassroots, neighborhood, advocacy, and nonprofit organizations grow their mission and membership and are then included in the decision-making bodies that we identify as formal collaborative governance institutions (such as working groups, task forces, stakeholder councils, and so on). Thus, effective collaborative governance must consider a full ecology of mechanisms and policy designs, such that *institutions as informal patterns* are transformed into *institutions as formal governance spaces* through this process:

1. Activating and maximizing **participation** by citizens, leading to . . .
2. Enriched **inclusion** in collaborative governance initiatives, which results in . . .
3. **Deliberation** that is vigorous and deeply democratic.

In order to examine how this is done, I present two different kinds of institutions that together help to form a robust and variegated ecology of collaborative governance: first, the formal deliberative space of a diverse group convened to prioritize watershed management projects in the basins of the Los Angeles and San Gabriel Rivers; and second, the informal endeavors of a river guide and an art gallery installation, designed to engage the leisure, cultural, and recreational practices of average Los Angeles citizens, enrolling them to participate in a growing constituency of grassroots watershed activists.

Because inclusive deliberation demands first that various people understand and care about a public issue and are motivated to work on it, and second that this work is a shared project among numerous people with varying perspectives, this chapter addresses both of these aspects of deliberation by examining the participatory mechanisms through which different, invested constituencies are activated and developed.

I start with an initiative where regional institutional actors worked together to develop a draft watershed plan. I describe this as a deliberative accomplishment of both structure and agency, where the policy design and the management approach worked to successfully enroll multiple ways of knowing into a single regional plan proposal. Over a period of months, ways of knowing watershed management at the organizational scale were effectively engaged and enrolled into a collective process and structured into a draft policy document prioritizing watershed projects throughout the region. This initiative, however, did little to engage citizens or to build relational capacity at the grass roots, which is the democratic substance from which its success was generated and on which its implementation and longevity will depend.

Second, then, as a complement to the Integrated Regional Watershed Management (IRWM) policy design and as examples of the kind of citizen engagement missing therein, I also consider two forms of public engagement designed to get more people interested in issues of watershed management and riverfront redevelopment. These are initiatives of individual policy activists within the watershed management/ river redevelopment governance network in Los Angeles: the creation of a field guide to the Los Angeles River as an art project and published book available to citizens through various nonprofit organizations and watershed events; and the creation of a public river redesign charrette, crafted as an interactive art gallery installation aimed at children. These initiatives are not public policy designs per se—they are not government-funded or government-led—but I suggest that perhaps they could be and should be, however unlikely that may seem.

I make a case here for collaborative policy designs that function as interrelated, reinforcing elements within a local ecology of governance. Different aspects of a far-reaching policy issue may present specific challenges and opportunities, and collaborating around a particularly complex set of issues—as in watershed management and urban riverfront redevelopment—can necessitate multiple, concurrent policy designs and civic engagement initiatives. The key question for civic democracy becomes whether such elements are arrayed in the field in such a way that the "core principles of collaborative governance" (Sirianni 2009, 42) are being met *in toto* by feeding into and reinforcing each other, if not in each and every initiative and policy design.[1] It is thus crucial to understand how individual policy designs function, so that when several are deployed simultaneously around a multifaceted issue, they can complement each other effectively.

In evaluating the Los Angeles examples, I explain *how* each design functions, engaging participants' ways of knowing the policy issue. The focus is on the *practice* activated and engendered by the specific collaborative design, and in particular on the *things* that structure this practice.[2] This analytic approach relies on what is known as Actor-Network Theory, a way of understanding social reality that acknowledges the role of nonhuman, material entities in shaping the form and pattern of our social interactions.[3] Most policy designs are enacted through actual things and literal mechanisms, or *actants*[4]: for instance in the institutional-level, watershed working group example that follows, the key organizing actants are a set of grant-funding guidelines, a matrix evaluation tool, project submittal sheets, and a CD version of the

draft Integrated Regional Watershed Management Plan. In the public engagement examples, the actants are the river field guide and the arrangeable pieces of the charrette
installation.

The actant that derives from and supports the enactment of a policy design will
drive who engages and how.[5] Who engages and how are the key underlying dimensions
of public deliberation. When designing policy for collaborative governance, thinking through the actants—the nonhuman, material, mundane links between people,
through which they are able to engage with each other in an ongoing, meaningful,
iterative way—is the basis for understanding and trying to predict how the policy will
perform, who will be able to participate in the performance, and whether various ways
of knowing can be held and expanded in time and space, ideally not just coexisting
but also learning from each other.

The initiatives that I examine below are not the only collaborative governance designs operating in Los Angeles watershed management and riverfront redevelopment.
Quite the opposite: these examples bump into and draw upon a myriad of other,
related designs. I focus on these three because they allow me to illustrate, in some
depth, how the actants of a particular design mediate various ways of knowing a policy
issue or issues. Because this mediating role is so crucial to productive deliberation, we
should consciously link the choice of actants within a collaborative policy design to
the citizen constituencies and institutional actors whose ways of knowing we hope to
engage in public deliberation.

IRWM Planning: Public Deliberation on Regional Priorities

Some brief background is required to understand the context of Integrated Regional
Watershed Management (IRWM) planning. The provision of adequate water quantity
for a fast growing, semiarid region has brought organizations like the Metropolitan
Water District of Southern California and the Los Angeles Department of Water and
Power under increasing pressure to conserve water resources.[6] Water quality is also
an area of growing concern and policy activity in the greater metropolitan area. The
need not only to provide fresh water clean enough for human consumption, but also
to monitor and control the discharge of polluted water into the environment, has
required a complex web of policy initiatives, programs, and regulatory enforcement.
The Los Angeles water resources community—whose government agencies include
the city and county departments of sanitation, engineering, and flood control in addition to the water providers mentioned above—faces increasing pressure to meet state
and federal mandates for total maximum daily loads (TMDLs) of nonpoint source
pollutants that accrue in the watershed.

The state has thus been actively involved in trying to build the collaborative capacity to address these dilemmas and to develop new policy approaches to help structure and adjudicate growing regional water conflicts. The most high-profile of these is

the CalFED Bay Delta program, a comprehensive initiative among twenty-five state and federal agencies to improve water supplies in the state and protect the San Francisco Bay Delta. The agencies involved recognize that such a partnership develops needed interorganizational resources and brings a legitimizing federal umbrella to a policy domain riddled with interagency conflict, regional disputes, and competing interests (Innes et al. 2006; Jacobs, Luoma, and Taylor 2003).

Over the past decade, California has also begun to play an organizing umbrella role with respect to the variegated water policy landscapes of its various regions. By creating new granting programs that require an Integrated Regional Water Management (IRWM) plan, the state of California, largely under the aegis of CalFED, is requiring that individual, local advocacy groups and water resource agencies, such as those sprinkled across the Los Angeles basin, coordinate with one another and come up with a unified presentation of prioritized projects and programs for watershed management grant funding.

The first pass at this approach to state water policy grant making—requiring regions to present a prioritized IRWM plan in order to qualify for funds—took place with the first round of grants under Chapter 8 (Integrated Regional Water Management) of Proposition 50 (The Water Security, Clean Drinking Water, Coastal and Beach Protection Act), in spring 2005. Proposition 50 was passed by California voters in 2002 and provided more than $3 billion in bond revenue for water projects, including those to fund coastal protection, CalFED, IRWM, safe drinking water, and water quality.

The first meetings of the greater Los Angeles Regional Water Management group were sponsored and convened by the City of Los Angeles Bureau of Sanitation and took place between January and May 2005 at the Los Angeles Department of Water and Power (DWP). The members of this group included not only state and federal water resource agencies, but also many of the organizations who had been working for more than two decades to grow an environmentally responsible river sensibility in Los Angeles (for instance, the River Project, Tree People, the Santa Monica Mountains Conservancy, Northeast Trees, the Los Angeles and San Gabriel Rivers Watershed Council, and Friends of the Los Angeles River).

The structure and progress of these meetings, as well as the creation of a first round of IRWM grant applications from the region, represent a collaborative governance approach to regional watershed management. Initiated by the City of Los Angeles Bureau of Sanitation, the IRWM process was structured to enlist the active participation of approximately one dozen key institutional stakeholders, and it required them to articulate and contribute their ways of knowing the project priorities within the watershed.

There are three policy documents—actants—that organized and enabled this process of collaboration and deliberation (see Figure 2.1). The first is the text of the state policy itself—Chapter 8 of Proposition 50 and the grant guidelines established therein

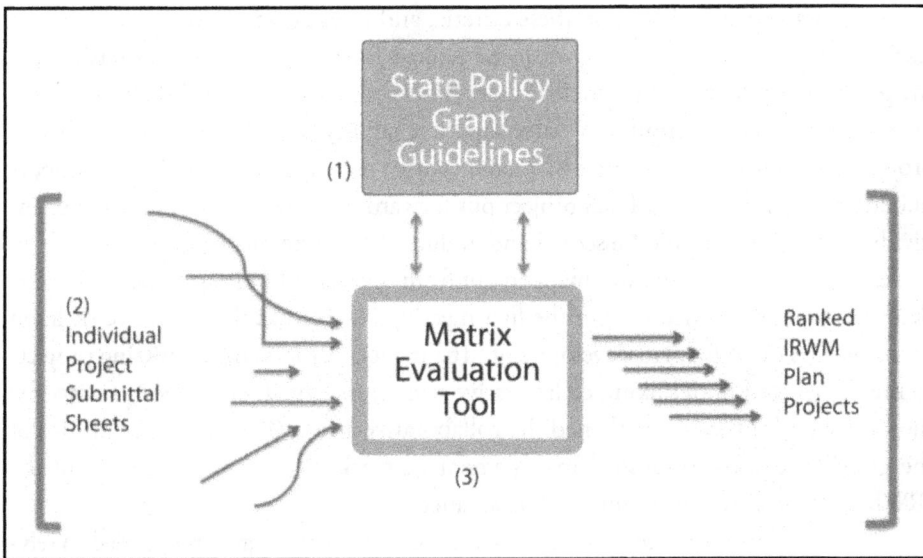

Figure 2.1 Actants of the IRWM Collaborative Policy Design: (1) state grant guidelines, (2) project summary submittal sheets for institutional stakeholders, (3) the project screening and evaluation matrix, developed from the state guidelines (1).

for the allocation of funding resources to regional IRWM plan projects.[7] Second is the project summaries generated by individual group members, describing the scope and components of various watershed projects that they knew and valued and about which they felt strongly. And third is the tool developed by the consultant team hired to manage the process: a project-screening matrix, to characterize, rank, and prioritize all the projects brought before the group by its constituent members. The matrix served as a process document throughout the life of the group's meetings, where individual watershed park projects and agency imperatives could be represented and continually evaluated, as part of a comprehensive list of watershed-wide priorities.

Participants referred to the ongoing workshop as "Prop 50 meetings," referring to the state ballot measure that would fund the first round of watershed projects, but the workshop itself formed the basis of Los Angeles' nascent Regional Water Management group.[8] The first round of meetings took place over a period of five months, between January and May 2005, at the City of Los Angeles' Department of Water and Power headquarters in downtown Los Angeles. The ongoing workshop involved more than eighty individual actors representing more than fifty organizational stakeholders.

After review of the grant guidelines, at the group's first meeting the consultants hired by the city introduced the project-screening matrix tool to the group. Developed from the criteria established by the guidelines, which emphasize the importance of "multiple benefits" for regional watershed management projects, the matrix develops a score for each project based on these criteria, and then ranks the projects relative to each other. These criteria were each to be ranked for compliance by the state: Does the project provide multiple benefits? Does it help to meet regional TMDL standards for runoff? Does it contribute to water supply reliability? Are there provisions for the project's long-term maintenance? Does the project reduce pollution? Does it support underserved communities? Each project put forward by a member organization or individual participant would be scored and evaluated on these measures.

Because the matrix tool was mapped out from the state's funding criteria for watershed management projects, from the first meeting it served as the figurative skeleton of the group's ongoing plan development. The iterative process of submitting projects to the matrix and undertaking collaborative review, managed and actively framed by the workshop leaders, strengthened the collaborative and deliberative relationships of the growing regional watershed management network, fleshing out the body of the IRWM plan and its new administrative alliances.

The matrix tool evaluated projects based on the state's measures, as opposed to relying exclusively or centrally on any one local stakeholder's way of knowing the watershed. Instead, "multiple benefits," "local and regional water supply reliability," "the attainment and maintenance of water quality standards," "the elimination or reduction of pollution," and "service to disadvantaged communities" served as dimensions through which watershed projects and knowledge would be evaluated and assessed. The matrix assigned scores to projects based on the status of their environmental review, the availability and percentage of matching funds, the agreement of multiple stakeholders, and provisions for ongoing adaptive management. The matrix depersonalized the potentially contentious first collaborative step in the workshop initiative.

The leader of the workshop meetings was a consultant with a large international environmental engineering firm, contracted to manage the process through the city's Bureau of Sanitation. She was responsible for introducing and managing the development of the matrix tool and leading the workshop meetings. Importantly, the consultant was well-known to many of the governance actors involved in Los Angeles water-resource planning, having worked in leadership positions for several of the organizations taking part in the collaborative workshop. Her management style as the workshop leader was inclusive and patient. The consultant acknowledged and answered every question that was raised, and did not appear to favor any stakeholder(s) during the meetings, even though many were clearly more informed and eager about the process than others.

Another key participant and important unofficial workshop leader was a parks advocate and project manager from a local nonprofit known for its cost-benefit modeling of ecosystem-management projects. This NGO leader has personally guided the successful creation of several major system site retrofits that involved multiple partners, both private and public, and took years to implement. She is well-known and well-respected in both the local environmental community and among city officials involved with resource management. During the first meeting the NGO leader asked two questions indicating that she was wary of the process and its purposes, but by the last meeting it was clear that she was supportive of the consultant and the organizational merit of the project-screening matrix tool, signaling to the rest of the group her investment in the collaborative effort.

Over the five-month planning process, draft matrices were compiled and scored by the workshop consultant team. Between meetings they were e-mailed to all participants, and at each meeting the current draft matrix was distributed to all attendees. At the third meeting a reasonably complete draft matrix on a CD was provided to all the participants. As a complex and highly specialized document, the screening matrix "rewards people who have done some leg work," as the NGO leader noted. The matrix tool illustrated many of the classic elements of scientific and professional policy designs: it was highly structured, favored "objective" criteria, placed discretion with the planning consultants, limited participation to qualified stakeholders, constrained the types of information involved in order to produce numerical standards, and constructed a credible logic for its use (Schneider and Ingram 1997, 196).

It follows, then, that workshop participants were not blind to the tool's inability to capture the nuances of projects. They pressed the consultant especially about their concerns: How were the project matrix criteria weighted? What about the measurement of impacts and benefits? How does the tool define organizational commitment? How does the tool define a disadvantaged community? What about the differences between stakeholder organizations, and how they might have filled out their project submittal sheets? The NGO leader noted more than once that a successful ranking from the project-screening tool was "all about the organizational ability to do leg work." And yet, over and over, participants' concerns about the matrix's instrumentality were moderated and diminished, primarily by the consultant, with the assertion that the tool and its rankings were a "document in process."

When the first draft matrix was distributed, the consultant talked about it as the first pass of the "initial screening." She seemed to be telling everyone not to worry. They were using the tool as a first-cut device. This was still just version one. The workshop group was at the start of an ongoing, long-term process; in the words of the consultant, they were throwing a wide net, getting all the projects in the pipeline, getting a handle on what's out there, getting a handle on what's fundable. The point, the consultant said at every meeting, was getting projects together, creating a database of all the projects, and beginning to rank them through the use of this "guideline document."

"The door is still open," the consultant told the group as late as the last meeting, allaying anxieties over the eventual uses of the rankings. Projects were resubmitted over the course of the workshop meetings, and various participants continually emphasized that the ranking might change. The way forms were filled out and "how things were presented" directly affected a project's score and ranking; the consultant acknowledged that sometimes there were "things that weren't included, things that didn't make it into the analysis." Workshop participants encouraged each other to go back and look again at the matrix criteria and at the state's guidelines. The matrix tool was "intended as a feedback process."

The key point here was when participants began to adopt these phrases in responding to one another's concerns. In the early meetings, it was always the consultant's voice assuring stakeholders that the plan was an ongoing process. During the second and third meetings, the NGO leader and the consultant responded to questions as a sort of tag team, and by the last meeting there were at least half a dozen participants active vocally about the progressive, collective nature of the plan they were constructing. There was joking about the ongoing project submittals, about pet parks and pet projects getting worked over and massaged until they achieved a high score and ranking. And yet, with dozens of workshop participants in attendance and the availability of individual project score sheets online, this appeared to be accepted as a reasonably transparent learning process as opposed to the deliberate manipulation of an esoteric, inaccessible policy standard.

For instance, when the second draft of matrix rankings was distributed, numerous participants noted that the popular L.A. River Plan parks—Taylor Yard, the Cornfields, Confluence—had surprisingly low scores.[9] These are favorite parks among both agency officials and nonprofit activists, many of whom were involved in the early mobilization to get them designed and promoted within their communities. There was a palpable sense within the group that the L.A. River parks deserved to be ranked higher, and there was an extended conversation about why they had not been and how this could be addressed. A city official explained that the L.A. parks had been "dumped into the tool" at the last minute, based on project descriptions developed for a different granting program. The city had not been able to allocate the staff time to conduct a careful submittal for these criteria. They would go back over the project submittal sheets and see if they could better articulate the projects' merits. This explanation and solution satisfied the stakeholders who had raised the concern. On the other hand, said one participant, there were projects at the top of the rankings that "don't belong." Others nodded and spoke out loudly in agreement. In these interchanges, the group came to collective understandings of their project priorities that depended upon their intersubjective, nontechnical assessment of the projects themselves.

The consultant noted that things are being, have been, and will continue to be updated, enabling the group to prioritize and strategize, and eventually to be "choosing what we want to get done." The most important thing, noted the NGO leader, was "getting people to work together." In particular, these conversations illustrate the working out and articulation of collective decisions as to what watershed projects will go forward. Focusing on the iterative nature of the draft plan permitted the leaders to emphasize the group's ability to determine the character of the final document. It was a successful strategy to keep participants engaged, and to dialogue, literally and figuratively, with the apparent rigidity of the state's standards. The policy tool of the published granting criteria enabled the workshop leaders to help shore up weak project submittals, without undermining the legitimacy and supposed objectivity of the project-screening tool.

The deployment of the matrix tool as an evaluation mechanism that was "not set in stone" was necessary in soliciting an authentic, representative local response to the state's standard, especially in a situation where some stakeholders started off in overly powerful positions simply by virtue of their organizational experience and institutional familiarity with the criteria. The group's leaders acknowledged that the matrix was not, in this sense, "objective": it could reward bureaucratic experience over project merit, where watershed projects have not had their benefits well-articulated on the most important state criteria.

As a result, the project submittal sheets became the most crucial and powerful policy documents, or actants. The grant guidelines and the matrix-ranking tool carried the embedded imperatives of the new state policy; they were not going to change. The project submittal sheets, on the other hand, could be revised and resubmitted until they spoke the language of the matrix tool fluently enough to have their merits translated, acknowledged, and valued.

The promise of continued revision to the matrix rankings, and the ongoing draft status of the plan, hardly guaranteed that a consensus would ultimately be reached. Moreover, the seeming flexibility and potential for spin doctoring of the project submittal sheets threatened to undo the group's acquiescence to the requirements of the state granting guidelines; why should the stakeholders accept and slavishly adhere to the matrix criteria if they are ultimately malleable and therefore prone to power plays within the group? Ultimately, the interplay between the three policy documents—the state criteria, the project submittal sheets, and the matrix-ranking tool—created associative pathways that enabled the group's connective tissue to grow and strengthen.

Ultimately, the project screening matrix tool both depended upon and *created* cooperation and collaborative commitment within the new regional water management group. Sustaining the dialectical interaction between the granting criteria and the project submittal sheets became the central vehicle in creating a forum for deliberation. The incentive from the state was substantial and its stated purpose legitimate enough for the group to accept its basic guideline parameters and strive to meet them. But as the key second step, enough stakeholders remained engaged in the process to facilitate an ongoing conversation that eventually included dozens of voices. A real turning point in the workshop came when stakeholders were addressing each other's concerns with shared understanding of how the process was working, rather than by deferring to the consultant or even the NGO leader. By the last meeting there seemed to be shared understandings that had been reached about what projects were the "best," why they should be constructed on an expedited schedule, and what kind of planning preparation needed to continue into the future. These assessments were ultimately agreed to as the first regional IRWM grant application for Proposition 50 funds, and they were submitted to the state in June 2005.[10]

L.A. River Constituency Building: Creating Personal River Experiences

In the above case of IRWM planning, the primary collaborative challenge was in bringing varied institutional stakeholders and their ways of knowing watershed management into productive, deliberative dialogue. But before an agency or a nonprofit becomes a stakeholder whose leadership is even aware of something called watershed management, there is a profound educative process that unfolds, reaching and sometimes emanating from the level of local citizens. Citizens become interested in river issues through initiatives of deliberate engagement, two of which I focus on below.

First, there is the book of river walks compiled and published by Joe Linton in 2005, *Down by the Los Angeles River: Friends of the Los Angeles River's Official Guide* (Linton 2005). Second, there is the gallery installation led by Metropolitan Transportation Authority senior planner and Latino Urban Forum founder James Rojas, in 2007, *Five Models Afloat: Art Inspired by the LA River and Participatory Model-Building*.

Neither of these initiatives represents stand-alone phenomena nor are they completely unique in their visionary, experiential approach to interpreting and promoting the Los Angeles River and the watershed spaces that surround it. There have been numerous recent publications about the river (see, for instance Gumprecht 1999; Hargreaves 2002; Morrison 2001; Orsi 2004; Price 2001), and it has been the focus of an increasing number of art installations, documentaries, websites and blogs, news pieces, and photo essays (for an early overview, see UEPI 2001). The experiences crafted by Linton and Rojas are not necessarily the most important of their kind, and they are not connected to a discrete workshop or stakeholder group. What is crucially important about each of them, though, is the degree to which they represent the efforts of individual activists to solicit and engender highly personal, immediate, aesthetic relationships with the river corridor, and by doing so to grow a viscerally motivated, increasingly powerful river constituency. In this sense, their actants bring citizens into contact with the river as art and experience, through direct personal associations that cannot be underestimated in their importance to the development of a citizen constituency for the river.

The guide created by Joe Linton draws on more than a dozen years of river restoration and bicycle path activism, including outreach, organization, and management roles with Friends of the Los Angeles River (FoLAR), the Los Angeles City Council, and the Los Angeles County Bicycle Coalition. Linton is both passionate and prolific; his field guide, gathered from extensive experience as the leader of walking and biking tours along the river, provides detailed trip descriptions for twenty-seven walking trips and twelve bike routes along, across, and near the streambed. Linton also illustrated the book himself, with maps, inspired signage, and elegant pen-and-ink drawings. The introduction lays out Linton's basic philosophy:

> I think that we all come from cultures, all over the world, where rivers are important. In Los Angeles and in many places across the country and around the world, we've literally turned our back on the rivers that have given birth to great cities. . . . I hope that this book will inspire you to go down to the river. Listen to the river. Begin to fall in love with it. Protect it. Restore it.
> —Joe Linton, *Down by the Los Angeles River*, p. 4

With a foreword by *Los Angeles Times* columnist and *Rio L.A.* author Patt Morrison, an introductory letter from FoLAR founder Lewis MacAdams, and an afterword by city councilman Ed Reyes, it is clear to any reader that Linton is well-known and well-respected within Los Angeles' river restoration and watershed movement. This contextualization emphasizes the years of activism behind the book. But the bulk of the text is truly aimed at the person rolling out of bed on a weekend morning thinking they might like to get out and about. It is filled with practical advice, directions, and very specific information about where to access the river, what kind of pathways to expect, how long an outing takes, and what kind of flora, fauna, and built landmarks one might find.

Linton has created an actant that is meant to feed and transform citizens' ways of knowing the river in practical, mundane ways: tucked into a backpack with walking shoes and a water bottle; reached for when the walking path seems to disappear, or the parking area seems not to be materializing, or one needs to double check where to make a turn, cross a bridge, or spot a historic site; left on a bedside table, with pages turned down for walks planned, bike rides enjoyed, or outings reviewed after the fact. In short, the guide is intended to bring the reader into a close personal relationship with the river—not in a single virtual episode involving interpretive images, text, and talk, but over time, at the reader's own pace, in repeated experiential episodes involving physical, tactile, self-directed exploration.

The river walks are organized geographically, clustered in the San Fernando Valley, Glendale Narrows, downtown Los Angeles, downstream (South L.A. and Long Beach), and four different tributaries. The bike rides, by virtue of the greater propulsion involved, cover more ground throughout the watershed. Linton also includes a twenty-page section on the historic bridges spanning the river. The structure of the guide enables different kinds of usage. The reader can figure out what river pathways are close to where he or she lives or works and explore based on proximity; she or he can prioritize the ones cited as "favorites" by Linton (2005, 21–22) in a "Best of" section broken into different categories; or one can simply make his or her way sequentially through the book, one site at a time.

What Linton does with this guide is create an access point to the river for those without the impetus or desire to simply go find it and start walking. The actant facilitates agency on the part of the average citizen, to expand the citizen's way of knowing the river. Also, because the river itself "is by no means a paradise" (3), the guide helps to ensure that if someone is curious about it but not able or willing to join an official FoLAR river walk, that person will be reasonably well-prepared for where to look for a good physical introduction, and what she or he will find. The guide empowers citizens and residents to forge their own relationship with the river, and it smooths the exploratory legwork of doing so.

Performing this translation—helping people to become not just vaguely curious about the watershed or familiar with river scenes from a media article or a documentary, but increasingly knowledgeable about it and capable of exploring and enjoying it on their own—is a deep-seated constituency-building accomplishment. It is an accomplishment that becomes more established every time an individual opens the guide and goes out to explore a new stretch of the river and every time a new, different citizen opens the book. Bringing citizens and residents into an association with the river in this way, enlisting them in its strange and unique beauty, is arguably the most crucial—and unpredictable—enrollment that is performed in the watershed movement. The guide is not deployed to achieve explicit, foreseeable alterations to the organizational power and existing patterns of the movement. Linton makes it clear that he has an environmentalist's vision for the river and hopes to see it restored to a "swimmable, fishable, boatable, river" (FoLAR mission statement, State of the River Report, 2005). An actant such as the field guide, however, simply performs the associative work of bringing citizens into direct relationship with the river, and as a result into the social construction of the watershed movement. Ultimately, there is no way to know what is possible and what is hopelessly idealistic with respect to the river, except by persisting in trying to bring it back to life:

> It tells a story of nature's persistence. As much as we have bulldozed, concreted, and generally trashed the Los Angeles River, it's still around, and it's still full of life. . . . It has willow trees growing three stories tall, graceful herons and egrets hunting, mother ducks with a dozen ducklings in tow, fish, turtles, and much more. Yes, it's degraded. Yes, there's a lot of trash hanging in those trees (and we need to do more about that). But it is a real river. It was a real river a thousand years ago, and it will still be one a thousand years from now.—Joe Linton, *Down by the Los Angeles River*, p. 3

Linton is clear that no one plan is going to do the work of transforming the Los Angeles River; he even pointed out that the 1996 Los Angeles River Master Plan did not include Taylor Yard, which has become the river's showcase park project (Linton 2003). The point, and the essence of his approach, is that what will ultimately transform the river is a critical mass of people who care about the river, and people will only really care about the river if they have a direct, personal relationship with it. La Gran Limpieza, the annual Great Los Angeles River Clean Up, is not primarily about the literal cleanup of the river (Linton 2005). Certainly, tons and tons of trash are picked out of the riverbed and disposed of, and the river is better for it. But the volume of waste that is collected remains a drop in the bucket compared with the trash that is left in the riverbed and what will quickly reaccumulate. The larger purpose of the event, as with the field guide, is its associative, enrollment function. By bringing people down to the river and exposing them both to its beauty—existing and potential—and to its abuse, the watershed movement gains new participants and builds the organizational capacity and political constituency to eventually accomplish transformational change.

This kind of fine-grained enrollment is similar to the performance created by the site-building charrette designed by James Rojas as a gallery installation in the early spring of 2007. Timed to coincide with the city's release of the draft River Revitalization Master Plan, the installation created a three-dimensional, interactive opportunity to explore different ideas for the five nodes identified by the official planning study. *Five Models Afloat* built on two previous—and ongoing—efforts: the one by the master planning team to elicit participatory feedback from different neighborhoods across the city between October 2005 and March 2007, and the one by Rojas himself to explore tactile, personal representations of the riverscape, first mounted and presented about a year earlier in a 2006 installation titled *River Dreams*.

The *Five Models Afloat* installation was open to the public for about a month, between mid-February and late March of 2007. It was located at Gallery 727, a space that Rojas co-owns, on Spring Street in downtown Los Angeles. The river site–building charrette was designed with children in mind, to let them explore possibilities for the river that they discover and choose for themselves, rather than having options presented to them by a team of experts. Rojas deliberately planned the installation for a young audience, saying the river restoration "will come in their lifetime, not ours" (Pool 2007). Rather than relying solely on uniform, neatly assembled model-building materials—foamcore, balsa wood, and so on—Rojas presented participants with a random assortment of found objects with which to imagine and embellish the basic topography of the river sites. Rubber tubing, toothpaste tops, bottle caps, and miniature figurines were among some of the objects assembled by gallery visitors; Rojas documented many of the model creations on film to serve as a record of some of the more inventive site interpretations and river visions (Pool 2007).

A crucial and organizing characteristic of the charrette installation designed by Rojas is that it breaks down the pervasive planning and development assumption—among residents and citizens of all ages—that someone else makes decisions about and is responsible for constructing the urban landscape and built environment. Like the *Down by the River* field guide, *Five Models Afloat* invites individual citizens into a personal and immediate way of knowing the river and hence a relationship with the watershed's future. It may not bring people directly to the river's edge, but it casts them in the role of active participants in imagining its possibilities.

The challenge of how to interest and engage individuals who are not conversant with—or interested in—the operative language of a master plan public participation meeting, and perhaps offer them a different, more immediate and personal experience, is met by the charrette installation designed by Rojas. Two things are striking about the design of the charrette, and both are related to the participatory role of the site-building components as direct, tactile experience.

First, they were not wholly predetermined. Participants were presented with a model of the river corridor, and the five nodes of opportunity identified by the planning team, as a set of existing conditions that were embedded as constraints within the model. But the selection of representative, material site conditions and land uses was left entirely to the participant-builder. These elements were chosen from what might be termed a junk box, found objects and tiny household elements that are at once totally familiar and utterly new when superimposed on the untouchable, unimaginable river corridor. In this way, the categories of known and unknown are broken down and recast through the lens of these objects, chosen and enlisted by each participant to translate and represent each person's individual, creative ideas. The actants are enrolled in crafting a personal, creative way of knowing the river.

Second, the materiality of the site-building charrette, and in particular its movable components, are marked by tactile three-dimensionality. Rather than interpreting images on a screen, text on a presentation board, or site plans that have been otherwise flattened out, the materiality of the site elements allow the participants to see, feel, and arrange the various components, and experience the many relationships involved—of themselves to each site's characteristics, and between components being superimposed at each site. This is facilitated despite being a "virtual" watershed experience; the participant is not at the river but is imagining and experiencing her or himself as an invested, thinking, experimenting, choosing member of the river's visioning team, which may be just as important.

By enabling immediate, experiential modes of engaging with the river and the watershed, such "designs" elicit the most crucial element of citizen engagement, which is the sense of being aware of and invested in a policy issue in a personal, direct, and meaningful way (see Figure 2.2). Citizens' ways of knowing the policy issue are seeded, activated, and strengthened.

Public investment in such experiential modes of policy design for citizen engagement that fed into a programmatic structure would enable key collaborative outcomes that are hard to engender in private, one-off efforts through deeper public institutionalization. The individual experience of taking a river walk or playing with an interactive public art installation could be translated into an intentionally relational setting. *Who can I share this experience with? Where are the others who care about this? Where can I find out more about how to get involved? Is there a place where I*

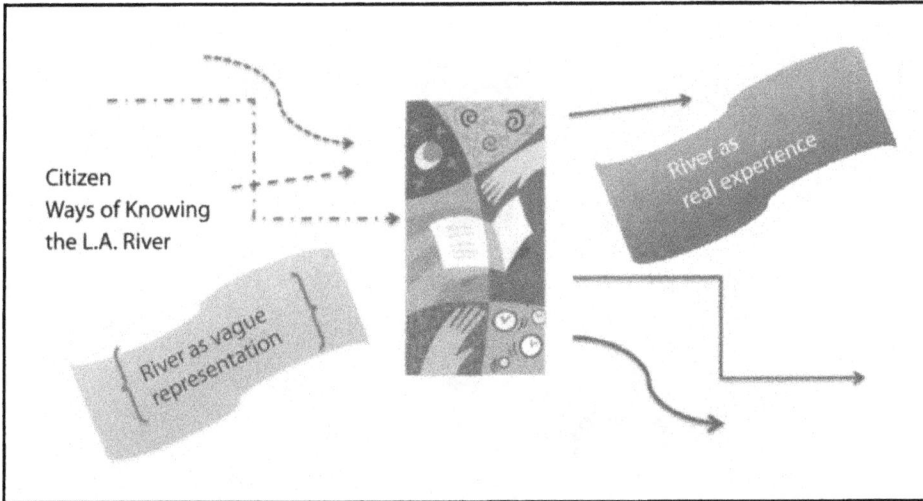

Figure 2.2 Actants such as the river field guide book and the charrette installation pieces enrolled citizens' vague ways of knowing the river, translating them into real experiences.

can come back again and again, bring my friends, learn more, find out about what I can do to make a difference? These are the questions that collaborative governance designs should be seeking to elicit from citizens, in whatever ways possible, and without a lapse in time and space in providing answers, a lapse in which such motivations and good intentions are quickly squandered. They are also questions that collaborative policy designs must be poised to actually answer, with discrete projects, trainings, and opportunities for ongoing, collective engagement. In short, government should both interest citizens in public issues as well as make it easier for them to involve themselves in addressing them.

Discussion and Conclusion

In order for a policy design to bring about collaboration and deliberation, it must consciously activate ways of knowing a policy issue that are salient to particular stakeholders and publics. Collaborative governance is accomplished through an ecology of interrelated policy designs, where ways of knowing are being strengthened and brought into sustained interaction in ways that are highly intentional, depending on the desired collaborative outcomes in particular settings. In the individual examples examined above, none of the initiatives would function successfully as aspects of collaborative governance without the existence of the other designs, and other kinds of designs, in a sustained field of interaction.

In the case of IRWM planning, the participants in the workshop had different ways of knowing and valuing watershed projects, whether as sites to slow storm water and help to prevent flooding, or as parks for underresourced neighborhoods, or as

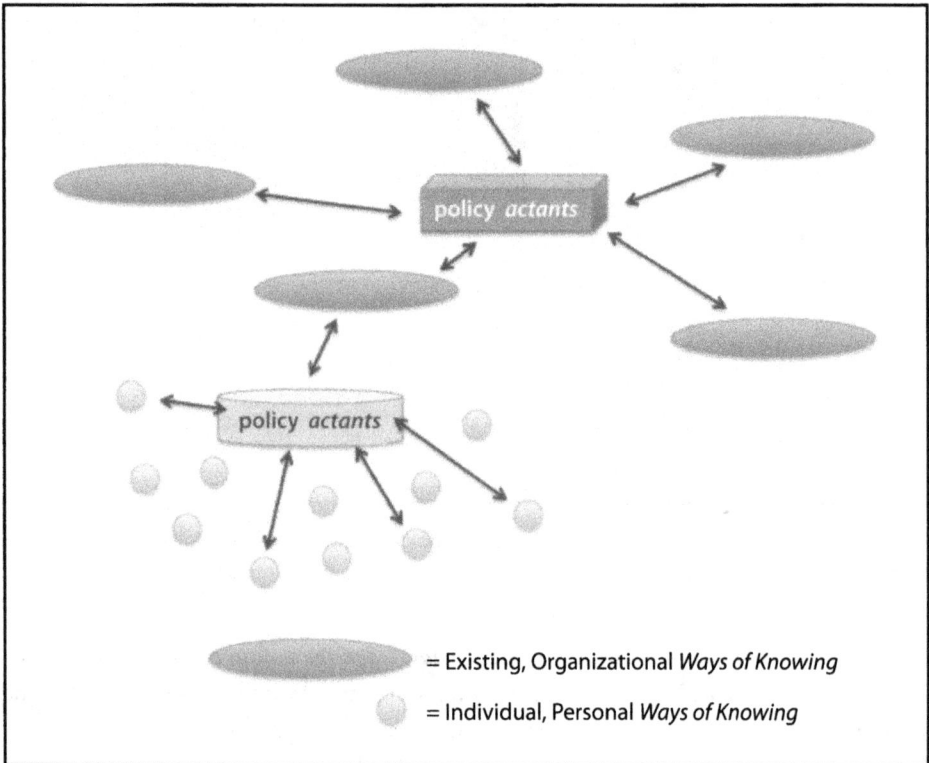

Figure 2.3 The actants designed into a policy must fit their collaborative governance purpose. For instance, facilitating deliberation between organizational ways of knowing, or enrolling citizens into more active ways of knowing, and thus growing participation in, and enriching the organizational way of knowing.

initiatives to aid in groundwater recharge and pollution mitigation. The actants of the IRWM planning process enrolled all these ways of knowing and created a space where a conversation could emerge about the relative priority of these policy objectives, at individual sites and between sites within the watershed. The policy design and the inclusive managers who led the initiative facilitated this public deliberation at an intersectoral, institutional level. The groups represented in the workshop have citizen members—indeed, many of them are defined and driven by their citizen membership—but the workshop itself was highly professionalized. The collaborative purpose was to structure and enact institutional collaboration at the regional level.

The constituency-building, public engagement examples, however, illustrate some of the ways that the membership groups in the IRWM workshop develop the citizen activism that underpins their existence and institutionalization. If you stop a person on the street in Los Angeles and give him or her a copy of the IRWM planning matrix, in all likelihood that person's way of knowing the river and the watershed will not match up with the dense spreadsheet you have placed in her or his hands. The actant of the

IRWM collaborative design does not suit all purposes of public deliberation; it is overly technical and specialized for purposes of citizen engagement. If we seek to engage the person on the street in Los Angeles in the issues of watershed management and river-front redevelopment, we need a collaborative policy design with different actants at its center. The field guide and charrette installation illustrate what these different actants might look like and how they enable different and more readily accessible opportunities to make meaning and strengthen ways of knowing the policy issue.

A possible problem for collaborative governance is that the participatory actants do not necessarily connect to a forum or clear opportunity pathway for public delib-eration. For instance, the field guide may enroll citizens into new and stronger ways of knowing the river and the watershed, and those citizens may become members of orga-nizations such as Friends of the Los Angeles River (FoLAR). FoLAR, in turn, partici-pates in deliberative governance structures such as the IRWM planning workshop. The issue, however, of whether citizens are being well-represented in such public delibera-tion is an open question, one not addressed by the immediate and open-ended purpose of visceral engagement strategies. In a best-case scenario, citizens become so interested and invested in the river that they begin to seek out public and private opportunities for sharing their ways of knowing, dialoguing, and becoming involved in planning for the watershed's future. Certainly, the more people that identify as watershed citizens, the more likely they are to press their claims as democratic agents in this regard.

This chapter has explored the relationship between different modes of collabo-rative governance, focusing in particular on the actants that grow different ways of knowing a public issue and that enable their sustained interaction in formal delibera-tive spaces. I suggest that these actants are important elements of policy design, not just for practices of inclusive governance, but also, potentially, for building widespread citizen engagement and public participation on issues such as watershed management, so that formal governance institutions are able to accomplish inclusive, robust forms of deliberation.

Notes

1. Carmen Sirianni identifies eight core principles of collaborative governance and policy design (2009), emphasizing the need for government action to engage and develop self-governing citizens: (1) coproduce public goods, (2) mobilize community assets, (3) share professional expertise, (4) enable public deliberation, (5) promote sustainable part-nerships, (6) build fields and governance networks strategically, (7) transform institution-al cultures, (8) ensure reciprocal accountability.
2. This approach is central in exposing the structure/agency duality in collaborative gover-nance, as pioneered by Feldman et al. (2006).
3. For a brief, informal discussion of Actor-Network Theory, as set forth by Bruno Latour, and its relationship to both Los Angeles watershed management as well as public man-agement practice, see Wessells (2007).

4. An actant is a thing, a material mechanism, or entity that provides an associational link between individual people and thus structures the performance of a social practice. As such, the actant has agency, and potentially the imprint of intentionality, on the part of the person who has created or deployed it (hence its significance for policy design). As general examples, consider actants such as personal computers, digital networks, and .pdf files, and the social practice of sharing professional reports and papers. The actants have had a transformative effect on the social practice over the past several decades, and participation in the performance of the social practice is sharply defined and delimited by the characteristics of the actants; having a computer, access to a server, the right software become prerequisites for participation in the network performance which constitutes the social practice.

5. This concern with how particular policy content works, and what kinds of responses it structures and elicits, is descended from the theoretical work of Anne Schneider and Helen Ingram (1993, 1997). For an earlier, related analysis see "Behavioral Assumptions of Policy Tools," *The Journal of Politics* 52 (2): 510–29.

6. The overall volume of local water use—water quantity—faces growing constraints as other western states claim their legal shares of Colorado River water, and transfers within the state of California come under increasing pressure and scrutiny. A deal long expected to guarantee future water transfers for urbanized Southern California, from former agricultural lands in the Imperial Valley in inland San Diego County, now looks less certain; historic appropriations of water by greater Los Angeles from Mono Lake and the Sierra Valley were reversed by court order in 2005, and large transfers from Northern California's Bay-Delta region, via canals stretching to metropolitan Los Angeles through the state's Central Valley, are increasingly scrutinized by governance actors concerned about the resultant environmental degradation throughout the watersheds of the Bay Area. Despite tremendous advances in technological processes for water purification and desalinization, the Southern California water resources community recognizes that the ability to import water adequate to meet the profligate thirst of its growing regional population poses a serious water supply issue for the twenty-first century, and it has invested heavily in addressing this problem (Ingram 1990; Ingram and Fraser 2005; Lach, Rayner, and Ingram 2005).

7. The Proposition 50 grant guidelines were published by the state of California in December 2004 and presented and reviewed at the group's first meeting in January 2005. According to the grant guidelines, a region must have a water management group, as well as evidence of progress toward an Integrated Regional Water Management plan standard, in order to qualify for these funds. The City of Los Angeles Bureau of Sanitation, as a local agency with statutory control over water resources planning, was eligible to coordinate such a regional water management group. The Bureau of Sanitation sponsored the effort to do so, and to organize grant applications to the state for this funding.

8. The creation of this group and its first draft plan have implications well beyond the allocation of Proposition 50 funds. According to one participant, in spring 2005 "there [were] five park and water bonds at play in the state legislature." The implication was that the current grant-funding guidelines were likely to be replicated for the distribution of additional bond monies, such as Proposition 50, Chapter 5 (River Parkway Funds), Proposition 40 (The California Clean Water, Clean Air, Safe Neighborhood Parks, and

Coastal Protection Act), and Proposition O (a storm water management bond passed by the City of Los Angeles in 2004).

9. Because of the difficulty of controlling nonpoint source pollution and the resultant necessity of better managing the flows of polluted storm water through the watershed in order to achieve TMDL standards, urban parks and open spaces are important sites of nonstructural watershed management and ecological remediation. In adequate numbers and appropriately designed, urban parks have the capacity to absorb runoff and slow flood events, becoming sites of storm water management, slowing sediment transport, catching and filtering suspended pollutants, and aiding in groundwater recharge.

10. The grant application for project implementation funding was not successful, but the group's application for a planning grant was. In fall 2005 a far more ambitious IRWM process was launched, with a new consultant team and a longer timeline. The group's core membership remained the same, and the first meetings were marked by excitement, cooperative energy, and strong attendance, as opposed to the smaller, more wary initial meetings at DWP nine months earlier.

References

Cooke, B., and U. Kothari, eds. 2001. *Participation: The New Tyranny?* London: Zed Books.

Feldman, M. S., A. M. Khademian, H. Ingram, and A. S. Schneider. 2006. "Ways of Knowing and Inclusive Management Practices." *Public Administration Review* 66 (6s): 89–99.

Gumprecht, B. 1999. *The Los Angeles River: Its Life, Death, and Possible Rebirth.* Baltimore, MD: Johns Hopkins University Press.

Hargreaves, G., ed. 2002. *LA River Studio Book.* Cambridge, MA: President and Fellows of Harvard College.

Ingram, H. 1990. *Water Politics: Continuity and Change.* Albuquerque: University of New Mexico Press.

Ingram, H., and L. Fraser. 2005. "Path Dependency and Adroit Innovation: The Case of California Water." In *By Fits and Starts: The Dynamics of U.S. Environmental Policy Change*, ed. F. R. Baumgartner. New Haven, CT: Yale University Press.

Innes, J. E., and D. E. Booher. 2004. "Reframing Public Participation: Strategies for the 21st Century." *Planning Theory and Practice* 5 (4): 419–36.

Innes, J. E., S. Connick, L. Kaplan, and D. E. Booher. 2006. *Water Management in California: CALFED as an Emergent Form of Governance.* Irvine, CA: UC Irvine Center for Organizational Research.

Jacobs, K. L., S. Luoma, and K. Taylor. 2003. "CALFED: An Experiment in Science and Decision-making." *Environment* 45 (1): 30–41.

Lach, D., S. Rayner, and H. Ingram. 2005. "Taming the Waters: Strategies to Domesticate the Wicked Problems of Water Resource Management." *International Journal of Water* 3 (1): 1–17.

Linton, J. 2003. Research interview. A. T. Wessells. Los Angeles.

———. 2005. *Down by the Los Angeles River: Friends of the Los Angeles River's Official Guide.* Berkeley, CA: Wilderness Press.

Morrison, P. 2001. *Rio L.A.: Tales from the Los Angeles River.* Los Angeles: Angel City Press.

Orsi, J. 2004. *Hazardous Metropolis: Flooding and Urban Ecology in Los Angeles.* Berkeley: University of California Press.

Ostrom, E. 1990. *Governing the Commons: The Evolution of Institutions for Collective Action.* Cambridge, UK: Cambridge University Press.

Pool, B. 2007. "River Project is Child's Play—and More." *Los Angeles Times*, March 18.

Price, J. 2001. "Paradise Reclaimed: A Field Guide to the Los Angeles River." *L.A. Weekly*, August 10–16, 23–39.

Quick, K. S., and M. S. Feldman. 2011. "Distinguishing Participation and Inclusion." *Journal of Education Planning and Research* 31 (3): 272–90.

Roberts, Nancy. 2004. "Public Deliberation in an Age of Direct Citizen Participation." *American Review of Public Administration* 34 (4): 315–53.

Schneider, Anne, and Helen Ingram. 1993. "Social Constructions and Target Populations: Implications for Politics and Policy." *American Political Science Review* 87 (2): 334–47.

———. 1997. *Policy Design for Democracy.* Lawrence: University of Kansas Press.

Sirianni, Carmen. 2009. *Investing in Democracy: Engaging Citizens in Collaborative Governance.* Washington, DC: Brookings Press.

UEPI. 2001. *Re-envisioning the L.A. River: A Program of Community and Ecological Revitalization; Report on 40 Forums, Events, Activities, and Projects Held During 1999-2000.* Los Angeles: Urban and Environmental Policy Institute, Occidental College.

Wessells, Anne Taufen. 2007. "Reassembling the Social: An Introduction to Actor-Network Theory by Bruno Latour." Book review. *International Public Management Journal* 10 (3): 351–56.

3

Civic Innovation, Deliberation, and Health Impact Assessment
Democratic Planning and Civic Engagement in San Francisco

JASON CORBURN

■ In November 2002 community members and city officials met in San Francisco's Mission District to discuss how the health and planning departments might support the Mission Anti-displacement Coalition's (MAC) "People's Plan." The People's Plan was a land use, zoning, and community development plan drafted by the MAC and endorsed by thousands of local residents. The document proposed, among other things, zoning and land use changes that would promote the development of more affordable housing, preserve industrial-sector jobs, and stop the demolition of existing buildings. At the same time, the city's planning department announced that they were set to launch a planning process aimed at developing new zoning controls for the Mission District and the surrounding Eastern Neighborhoods of San Francisco. At the meeting with the city agencies, representatives from the MAC—already aware that the health department had analyzed the human health impacts of specific development projects—asked the agency to help them review the likely health impacts of the goals and objectives of their People's Plan. Having spent years organizing the community to draft the People's Plan, the MAC was reluctant to lead a health assessment—which they had never done before—without the assistance and experience of the San Francisco Department of Public Health (SFDPH or DPH).[1]

The health department agreed to work with the community coalition to explore the process and content of a community-based health impact assessment. By March 2003 the SFDPH helped facilitate a community meeting that was considered the first meeting of the Mission Neighborhood Community Impact Assessment process.[2] During the meeting the DPH asked residents to envision the elements that make their community "healthy," and much of the discussion focused on affordable housing. Regular meetings between the MAC and the DPH continued, and discussions shifted from envisioning the healthy neighborhood to building an evidence base. Community residents also requested that the assessment consider how neighborhood changes were influenced by regional dynamics like the high-tech economy. As the MAC and the DPH discussed the agenda for a broader health impact assessment, the city's planning department released a new rezoning plan for the city's Eastern Neighborhoods, which include the Mission District, Showplace Square–Potrero Hill, and South of Market areas. The planning department also announced that they were preparing both an environmental and social impact assessment of the rezoning plans and that these assessments would be done independently using experienced consultants. The MAC and DPH agreed that they should meet with the planning department to explore adding health analyses into the environmental or social impact assessments.

Merging Participatory Planning with Health Impact Assessment

This chapter highlights the planning process and outcomes of the Eastern Neighborhoods Community Health Impact Assessment (ENCHIA), the process that emerged in response to the planning department's rezoning plan. During the ENCHIA, community groups and city agencies collaborated in a participatory planning process that built new working relationships, gathered new evidence to assess health impacts of planning proposals, and generated a new analytic process, called the Healthy Development Measurement Tool (HDMT), that could be applied to future urban planning and policy decisions. More than twenty-five different interest groups participated in the ENCHIA and met monthly for close to two years. Through a consensus-based collaborative process, the ENCHIA produced a vision of the healthy city, established goals and indicators necessary to implement this vision, and gathered and mapped data to populate these indicators. The group also analyzed more than thirty non-health-specific policies that might promote the healthy city vision. Ultimately the ENCHIA would have a significant influence on planning decisions not just in San Francisco but also on healthy planning and health equity coalition building across the entire Bay Area. This chapter examines the political factors that contributed to the local and regional success of the ENCHIA and the implications for designing planning processes that promote healthy and equitable urban governance.

Framing Healthy City Planning

The MAC and the DPH met again with the planning department in January 2004 to discuss how the assessments of the Eastern Neighborhoods rezoning plan might include human health. Miriam Chion, a senior planner with the San Francisco's planning department at the time, suggested that the health assessment process the MAC and DPH had already started ought to be expanded to include the rezoning plan. Rajiv Bhatia, director of environmental health at the San Francisco Department of Public Health, recalled that in the meeting Paul Maltzer, director of environmental review for the planning department, acknowledged that public health was already part of the environmental assessment process but rejected the idea of including such social determinants of health as housing affordability, displacement, and social cohesion in the Environmental Impact Report (EIR). Maltzer was also candid about the political obstacles to broadening the scope of the California Environmental Quality Act (CEQA), including the likelihood of litigation. He emphatically stated that the environmental review process was not the right venue for addressing community needs and he refused to initiate any changes unless directed to do so by city leaders.[3] With the planning department refusing to include the social determinants of health in the pending environmental review process, the MAC looked to the DPH to take the lead. MAC leaders requested that the health assessment of the People's Plan be expanded to include the Eastern Neighborhoods rezoning plan, and the DPH agreed to work with the group. The planning department agreed to participate in the health assessment process, but made no commitments to incorporate its findings into either the environmental or social impact assessment.

Deliberative Democracy and Health Impact Assessment

As the MAC and SFDPH began organizing the new health assessment, both groups recognized that they needed a strategy to identify and recruit new participants from beyond the Mission District. An added challenge was that this new HIA would likely need to propose healthy land use and policy changes, since the final rezoning plan had not been released. According to Rajiv Bhatia, the political controversies that already surrounded the HIA meant that its legitimacy was likely to rest as much in the process and representativeness of participants as in its proposals and recommended outcomes.[4]

Aiming to ensure that the process was inclusive and democratic, the SFDPH researched models of participatory HIA, such as the Merseyside Model for Health Impact Assessment, and public processes used to address controversial science policy issues, such as the Danish Consensus Conferences and Science Shops used in Europe (Fischer, Leydesdorff, and Schophaus 2004; Scott-Samuel, Birley, and Arden 2001; Wachelder 2003). The DPH also aimed to design a process that embodied the values of the World Health Organization's consensus statement on HIA, commonly called the Gothenburg Statement, which emphasized democratic participation, equity, and transparency in the analytic process (Quigley et al. 2006, 3).

Building on international models of participation and HIA, the SFDPH and the MAC drafted a set of guiding principles for designing their health assessment that included:

- evaluating social and economic effects not considered in environmental impact assessment,
- using a broad definition of health to consider the comprehensive effects of planning,

- creating meaningful participation opportunities for socially marginalized stakeholders,
- allowing participating stakeholders to have power in determining the scope of the assessment,
- valuing community experience as evidence,
- providing scientific methods and data as a response to questions emerging from the process, and
- using deliberative and consensus-building methods in decision making (SF-DPH 2007a).

The SFDPH also recognized that they needed to build support within their own agency for a participatory HIA.[5] Staff from the environmental health unit began meeting with other units across the health agency, explaining their objectives for the HIA and seeking expert input. The SFDPH also aimed to build support for the process outside of city government. The agency met with more than forty interest groups and private organizations from across the Bay Area that might participant in the assessment. These meetings helped the DPH learn about concerns different interest groups had with the proposed rezoning plan and other issues the agency wasn't aware of but which could impact the quality of life in the Eastern Neighborhoods.[6] Combining aspects of participatory science–policy processes, consensus building, and knowledge gleaned from the informational meetings, the DPH and MAC designed a process called the Eastern Neighborhoods Community Health Impact Assessment (ENCHIA) and collaboratively drafted a new set of goals and objectives (Table 3.1) and a process map outlining the stages of a proposed eighteen-month public process (Figure 3.1).

The Eastern Neighborhoods Community Health Impact Assessment

On November 17, 2004, more than thirty different nonprofit and private sector organizations and four public agencies, in addition to the Departments of City Planning

Table 3.1 ENCHIA Goals and Objectives

Identify and analyze the likely impacts of land use plans and zoning controls on health determinants, including housing, jobs, and public infrastructure

Provide recommendations for land use policies and zoning controls that promote community priorities

Demonstrate the feasibility of health impact assessment methods

Promote meaningful public involvement in land use policy by making explicit competing interests and facilitating consensus

Develop capacity for interagency working relationships

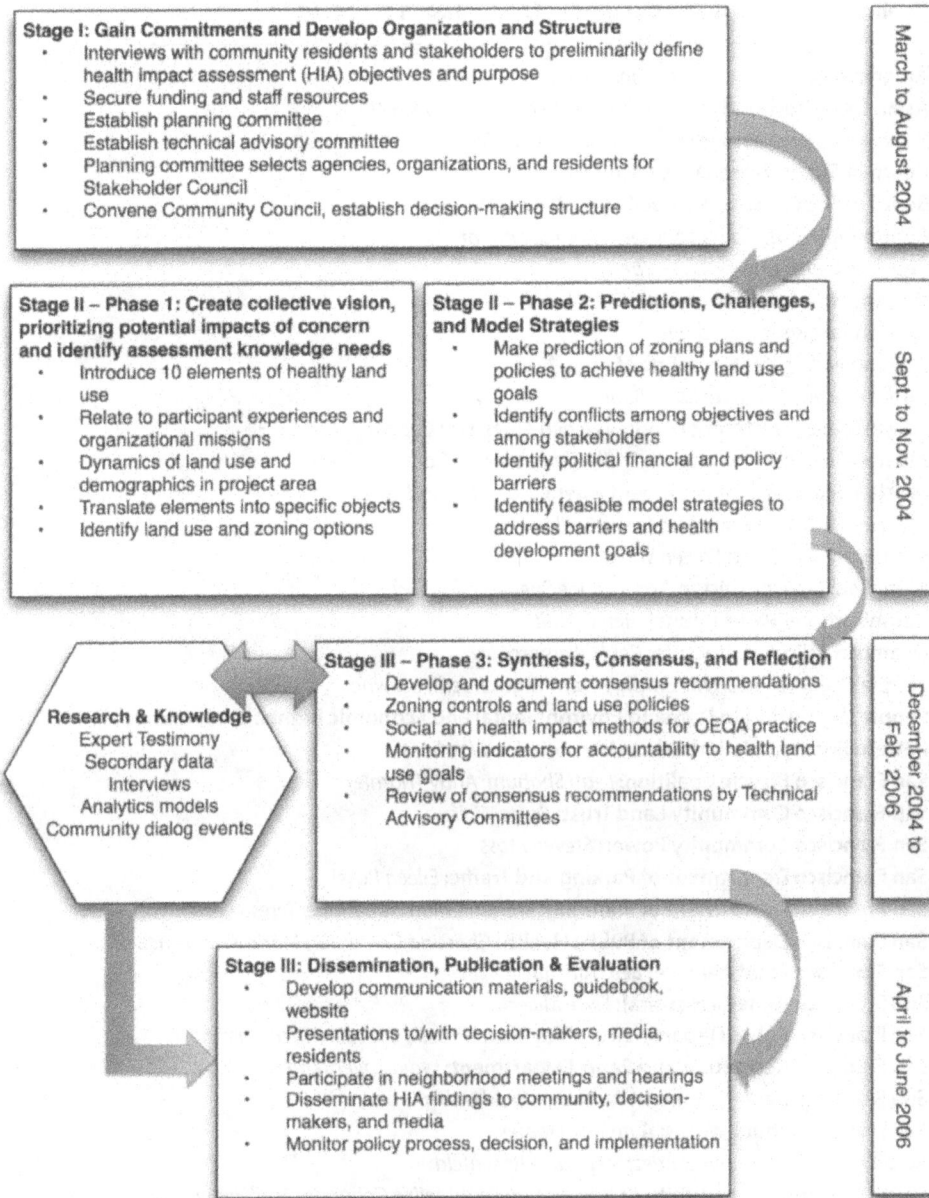

Stage I: Gain Commitments and Develop Organization and Structure
- Interviews with community residents and stakeholders to preliminarily define health impact assessment (HIA) objectives and purpose
- Secure funding and staff resources
- Establish planning committee
- Establish technical advisory committee
- Planning committee selects agencies, organizations, and residents for Stakeholder Council
- Convene Community Council, establish decision-making structure

March to August 2004

Stage II – Phase 1: Create collective vision, prioritizing potential impacts of concern and identify assessment knowledge needs
- Introduce 10 elements of healthy land use
- Relate to participant experiences and organizational missions
- Dynamics of land use and demographics in project area
- Translate elements into specific objects
- Identify land use and zoning options

Stage II – Phase 2: Predictions, Challenges, and Model Strategies
- Make prediction of zoning plans and policies to achieve healthy land use goals
- Identify conflicts among objectives and among stakeholders
- Identify political financial and policy barriers
- Identify feasible model strategies to address barriers and health development goals

Sept. to Nov. 2004

Research & Knowledge
Expert Testimony
Secondary data
Interviews
Analytics models
Community dialog events

Stage III – Phase 3: Synthesis, Consensus, and Reflection
- Develop and document consensus recommendations
- Zoning controls and land use policies
- Social and health impact methods for OEQA practice
- Monitoring indicators for accountability to health land use goals
- Review of consensus recommendations by Technical Advisory Committees

December 2004 to Feb. 2006

Stage III: Dissemination, Publication & Evaluation
- Develop communication materials, guidebook, website
- Presentations to/with decision-makers, media, residents
- Participate in neighborhood meetings and hearings
- Disseminate HIA findings to community, decision-makers, and media
- Monitor policy process, decision, and implementation

April to June 2006

Figure 3.1

and Public Health, joined the Community Council of the ENCHIA and attended the first meeting (Table 3.2). The meeting focused on stakeholders getting to know one another, a review of how a consensus-building process works, and a group visioning exercise where participants brainstormed about the elements of a healthy neighborhood. The early objectives for the HIA process were to have group discussions about

Table 3.2 ENCHIA Participants, November 17, 2004

American Lung Association: *Linda Weiner*
Asian Neighborhood Design: *Peter Cohen; Fernando Marti*
Board of Supervisors, Ammiano: *Angela Calvillo*
Board of Supervisors, Daly: *Rachel Redondiez*
Board of Supervisors, Maxwell: *Greg Asay*
Center for Human Development: *Andrea Spagat*
Charlie's Place: *Charlie O'Hanlon*
Citizens Housing Corporation: *Scott Falcone*
GCA Strategies: *Debra Stein*
Jackson Pacific Ventures: *Ezra Mersey*
Jardiniere/Nextcourse: *Larry Bain*
Low Income Investment Fund: *Gretchen Ames; Erin Coppin*
Mission Community Council: *Emily Claassen; Kyle Fiore*
Mission Economic Development Agency: *Luis Granados*
Mission SRO Collaborative: *Jazzie Collins*
Morrison & Foerster: *Steven Vettel*
Municipal Transportation Agency: *Joe Speaks*
Neighborhood Parks Council: *Jeff Condit*
Okamoto Saijo Architecture: *Paul Okamoto*
People Organized to Win Employment Rights: *Jerin Browne*
People Organizing to Demand Environmental and Economic Rights: *Oscar Grande*
Potrero Boosters Neighborhood Association: *Joe Boss*
San Francisco Bicycle Coalition: *Leah Shahum; Andy Thornley*
San Francisco Community Land Trust: *Bruce Wolfe*
San Francisco Community Power: *Steven Moss*
San Francisco Department of Parking and Traffic: *Eileen Ross*
San Francisco Department of Planning: *Miriam Chion; Sue Exline; Teresa Ojeda*
San Francisco Department of Public Health: *Christina Carpenter; Maria X. Martinez*
San Francisco Food Alliance: *Beth Altshuler*
San Francisco General Hospital: *Elyse Miller*
San Francisco Police Department: *Officer Glen Ghiselli; Captain Albert Pardini*
San Francisco Recreation and Parks Department: *Lydia Zaverukha*
San Francisco Redevelopment Agency: *David Habert*
San Francisco Youth Works: *Aumijo S. Gomes*
SEIU Local 790: *Bob Hernandez; Stephanie Rosenfeld*
South of Market Community Action Network: *Angelica Cabande; April Veneracion*
South of Market Employment Center: *Cindy Mendoza*
South of Market Family Resource Center: *Judith Baker*
Tenants and Owners Development Corporation: *Tim Dunn*
Transportation for a Livable City: *Tom Radulovich*
Urban Habitat: *Lila Hussein*
Walk San Francisco: *Emily Drennen; Wesley Kirkman*

---

the elements of a healthy place, how land use does or does not influence these elements, and how the rezoning proposals might influence these elements in a positive or negative way. Meeting agendas, summaries, presentations, and a range of supporting documentation were regularly posted and available to the public on the project website (*www.sfdph.org/phes/enchia.htm*).

Another early objective was distinguishing for participants how the HIA process was going to be *different* from other assessment processes of the Eastern Neighborhoods rezoning plans. Many participants asked at early meetings, "How is this process different from the environmental and social impact assessments?" A matrix was developed by the DPH comparing the ENCHIA process with the proposed environmental and social impact assessment processes (Table 3.3). The categories the DPH selected reflect, in part, their view of what makes HIA important and different as a public-knowledge-generating process. For example, the DPH emphasized each process's institutional setting, analytic scope, orientation toward evidence gathering and research methods, roles for the public and nonexperts, use of evidence, and public accountability of both procedures and outcomes.

The first meetings of the ENCHIA were spent in small and large groups building a vision of the "healthy city." Substantive work of participants during early ENCHIA meetings focused on deliberating over and working toward consensus on the elements of a "healthy place." Discussions ranged from the physical characteristics of places to social relationships to measurable health outcomes. One ENCHIA participant described the healthy city as a place "where you feel good about living, raising your family, spending leisure time . . . you know, where you, your kids, and your mother-in-law would like to live." Others suggested a healthy place was more tangible: "A healthy place is one that helps people recover when they are down, and not just those living there, but visitors too." Still other participants emphasized change: "The measure of healthy place is if people and institutions can learn about what is not working and are committed to fixing it." As part of the discussions the group drafted pictures to help map some of the more tangible characteristics of a healthy place. A set of common elements for the healthy city began to emerge, and facilitators from the SFDPH organized these to include basic living conditions, a secure livelihood (e.g., a "healthy paycheck"), social interaction in public places, diverse political representation, and living near extended families. Six specific elements were selected and became the Healthy City Vision (Table 3.4), and the group decided to use these to frame their future. The Healthy City Vision included the following categories: environmental stewardship, safety and security, public infrastructure, access to goods and services, adequate and healthy housing, and healthy economy (SFDPH 2007a, 38).[7]

By starting with a discussion of what is working, rather than a narrow focus on problems and failures, the ENCHIA process aimed to understand, describe, and explain the strengths and assets of the area, its population groups, and existing institutions—the very things that give life and meaning to a place. The ENCHIA process also emphasized that every neighborhood and population group are continually

Table 3.3 Comparison of Environmental, Social, and Health Impact Assessment Processes by San Francisco Department of Public Health

Components	CEQA Environmental Impact Assessment (Planning Department)
Objectives	To identify significant adverse effects of environmental changes; identify and ensure mitigation; identify and evaluate project alternatives with regards to environmental effects
Institutional Setting	Legally required by California law prior to project or plan approval
Scope	Focus is on potentially adverse changes in the physical environment. Scope of the analysis is constrained by procedural requirements and past practice. Eastern Neighborhood EIR proposed analysis includes: (1) Transportation, including a description of existing conditions and estimates of new vehicle, transit trip generation (2) Air quality, including evaluation of the consistency between the plans and regional air quality plans (3) Noise, including evaluation of noise impacts on residential uses (4) Cultural resources, including impacts on landmarks and historical districts (5) Visual quality and shadow (6) Hydrology and water quality, including storm water outfalls (7) Hazardous materials, including an evaluation of permitted and expected hazardous materials uses (8) Land use, including environmental effects from the displacement of business (9) Employment, population, and housing
Research Methods	Checklists; secondary data analysis, quantitative modeling; expert predictions. Will also include some area specific primary data collection and analysis (e.g., traffic counts for transportation analysis)
Role(s) of the Public	Public has opportunities to comment verbally and in writing at specific stages in the assessment process, including public scoping meetings at the start of the environmental review process and comment on the Draft EIR; final EIR must include responses to all comments on the Draft EIR
Role of Experts and Evidence	Experts and consultants do discipline specific research and provide analysis and interpretation

Continued

searching for ways to function better and improve survival, often in the face of dire circumstances, and learning from these strategies could benefit the HIA process.

Debating Objectives for Healthy Policy Making

Once the council created the Healthy City Vision, the process turned to helping participants articulate Community Health Objectives for each element of the vision. Six

Table 3.3 Continued

Socioeconomic Analysis (Planning Department)	HIA of Eastern Neighborhood's Rezoning (SFDPH)
To identify, predict, and document the socioeconomic changes related or influenced by the proposed zoning alternatives	To identify the impacts of proposed rezoning policy on people and communities; to make recommendation for zoning controls, specific plans, and related changes in transportation and public infrastructure in order to protect and promote public health; to increase awareness of urban planning–public health relationships; to test a model practice that may provide lessons for community planning, public involvement, and EIA practice
Discretionary analysis requested by Planning Commission based on public interest	Discretionary analysis based on public and Planning Commission interest; convened by public agency (SFDPH)
Focus on indirect economic, fiscal, and demographic effects of planning; relation of these effects to human health is indirect (e.g., job loss) and scope is determined by planning staff and constrained by available methods and financial resources	Focus on social, economic, environmental determinants of human health; impacts of concern determined by stakeholder council originally selected project planning team. Analyses to include: (1) Housing design and location and indoor/outdoor air quality (2) Vehicle volumes and pedestrian injuries (3) Public transit access and health care utilization (4) Housing adequacy and social cohesion (5) Parks and physical activity (6) Natural spaces and recovery from illness (7) Neighborhood schools and student achievement (8) Building design and violence (9) Social segregation and premature mortality (10) Access to food resources and healthy nutrition (11) Access to child care and child development
Primary and secondary data analysis; limited qualitative methods and focus groups	Literature review; secondary data analysis; quantitative analysis and forecasting; qualitative methods; group deliberative processes; policy analysis; consensus building methods
HIA stakeholders will be tapped to participate in focus groups	Stakeholder Council is established with representatives of public agencies, for-profit and nonprofit organizations; lay residents are also actively recruited and trained for participation on the council; affected populations may be sampled as respondents for surveys and focus groups; council may also hold public hearings
Consultants conduct research and analysis and provide interpretation in partnership with planning staff	Process primarily values experiences of Community Council members as expertise; project staff conducts research and collects data/ evidence for Council to review; where necessary the process uses disciplinary and content experts to respond to stakeholder questions

subgroups were established to match the "healthy city elements," and these groups worked to draft specific health objectives for each element. For instance, a specific objective developed for the healthy city element of "access to goods and services" was "to assure affordable and high-quality child care for all neighborhoods." One objective

Table 3.4 Elements of a Healthy City, ENCHIA Process

Environmental stewardship (1) Clean air and water, (2) renewable and local energy sources, (3) sustainable and green infrastructure, (4) healthy habitats, and (5) sustainable architecture

Sustainable and safe transportation (1) Multiple transportation options, (2) affordable and accessible public transit, (3) safer streets and sidewalks, and (4) fewer cars on roads

Public safety (1) Safe and walkable streets and sidewalks, (2) clean and accessible public spaces, and (3) the absence of crime and violence

Public infrastructure/access to goods and services (1) Quality schools and child care, (2) safe parks, playgrounds, and sports/recreation areas, (3) neighborhood commercial districts to meet daily needs, (4) active street life and uses, (5) healthy and affordable foods, (6) community services and resources for youth and seniors, (7) space for community leisure activities, and (8) disability access

Adequate and healthy housing (1) Affordable, (2) safe from physical hazards, (3) stable and secure, (4) diverse in terms of type and size, (5) located in mixed-income and mixed-race communities of friends and neighbors, and (6) located in close proximity to access to jobs, education, goods and services

Healthy economy (1) Jobs that are safe, pay living wages, and provide insurance and other benefits, (2) diverse employment opportunities for residents and individuals with a range of education, languages, and skill levels, (3) locally owned businesses, (4) a local economy where money is flowing through the neighborhood, and (5) economy does not harm the natural environment

Community participation (1) Active engagement of community members affected by proposed development, (2) community involvement in proposal visioning/planning, allocation of responsibility, appraisal/data collection, decision making, monitoring, and evaluation, (3) opportunities for public comment on proposal,
(4)open and transparent discussion about trade-offs, and (5) accountability and compliance of specific projects with general plans

---

from the "healthy economy" subgroup was to "increase jobs that provide healthy, safe, and meaningful work." During this process participants noted that it was not clear how some objectives could be achieved by land use and zoning changes alone. For example, one participant asked, "How can zoning for a retail use influence the kinds of products offered in the store or the way they treat their workers?" The process of trying to attach objectives to the healthy city vision began to highlight to participants the strengths and limits of HIA (SFDPH 2007a, 41–42).

During the process of assigning specific objectives to elements of the healthy city vision, participants noted that many were linked to one another and could sometimes be in conflict. For example, some participants highlighted that policies that encouraged economically and racially diverse neighborhoods might exacerbate gentrification in existing places. Others noted that requiring "green buildings" could increase the cost of housing construction, and adding more park space might increase property values in an area but also contribute to residential displacement. The complexities and potential conflicts of objectives were recorded, and ENCHIA participants increasingly wanted to attach "hard" data to their newly drafted objectives.

Engaging with Structural Inequalities

ENCHIA participants also debated whether acknowledging conflicts among objectives was enough or whether the ENCHIA ought to take a position on certain objectives. Group members disagreed over which way to proceed, and discussions often highlighted the competing interests represented in the process. Consider this exchange among council members:

Participant 1: What many of the objectives focus on are economics and acquiring more income for health, but what about racism that limits choices even when you have money?

Participant 2: Yeah, I mean, race and class can't be separated, but what I think we are doing is trying to be practical here about what it takes to lead a healthy life, right?

Participant 1: But what you are assuming is that there is a level playing field, that if I get affordable housing, I'll be healthier. But for blacks, Latinos, Asians, people of color, discrimination and racism almost always gets in the way. I'm asking where does white privilege and oppression fit into our objectives?

Participant 2: Of course racism exists, and we want to address it, but that is a value. The objectives are practical ways to address discrimination.

Participant 1: Look, take the objective of increasing bicycling. By increasing bike lanes, you create more safe opportunities to bike. Seems good. But what this ignores is who is riding bikes, why, and where are they going? Latinos use bikes more in this city than anyone else, for work and deliveries, not exercise or leisure. So when we ignore discussing the assumptions behind these objectives and who they are intended for, that ignores that we live in a racialized society.

This exchange was one of many discussions over how and if the ENCHIA process was going to make racism a focus of the assessment process. Some participants wanted race and racism, and the health evidence of racial inequities, to act as the central focus of the ENCHIA. Others, however, wanted to stick to more "tangible" objectives and outcomes. Staff members of the DPH facilitating the process aimed to keep racism part of the discussion, but the group did not reach a consensus that racism should act as the central focus of the assessment.

Some council members, speaking confidentially, feared that the "focus on racism would polarize the group and contribute to participants leaving the process." Others saw the ENCHIA as an opportunity to highlight "that even progressive white-led organizations discount how powerful racism is as a motivator for social action and minimizing the importance of racism by emphasizing cross-racial unity for the sake

Table 3.5 Objectives of the Healthy City

ENCHIA Environmental Stewardship (ES)
Objective ES.1 Decrease consumption of energy and natural resources
Objective ES.2 Restore, preserve, and protect healthy natural habitats
Objective ES.3 Promote food a ccess and sustainable urban and rural agriculture
Objective ES.4 Promote productive reuse of previously contaminated sites
Objective ES.5 Preserve clean air quality

Sustainable Transportation (ST)
Objective ST.1 Decrease private motor vehicle trips and miles traveled
Objective ST.2 Provide affordable, safe, and sustainable transportation options
Objective ST.3 Create safe quality environments for walking and biking

Public Safety (PS)
Objective PS.1 Improve accessibility, beauty, and cleanliness of public spaces
Objective PS.2 Maintain safe levels of community noise
Objective PS.3 Promote safe neighborhoods free of crime and violence

Public Infrastructure/Access to Goods and Services (PI)
Objective PI.1 Assure affordable and high-quality child care for all neighborhoods
Objective PI.2 Assure accessible and high-quality educational facilities
Objective PI.3 Increase park, open space, and recreation facilities
Objective PI.4 Assure spaces for libraries, performing arts, theater, museums, concerts, festivals
for personal and educational fulfillment
Objective PI.5 Assure affordable and high-quality public health facilities
Objective PI.6 Assure access to daily goods and service needs, including financial services and
healthy foods

Adequate and Healthy Housing (HH)
Objective HH.1 Preserve and construct housing in proportion to demand with regards to size,
affordability, tenure, and location
Objective HH.2 Protect residents from involuntary displacement
Objective HH.3 Increase opportunities for home ownership
Objective HH.4 Increase spatial integration by ethnicity and economic class

Healthy Economy (HE)
Objective HE.1 Increase high-quality employment opportunities for local residents
Objective HE.2 Increase jobs that provide healthy, safe, and meaningful work
Objective HE.3 Increase equality in income and wealth
Objective HE.4 Increase benefits to communities impacted by development
Objective HE.5 Promote industry that benefits and protects natural resources and the
environment

Community Participation (CP)
Objective CP.1 Assure equitable and democratic participation throughout the planning process

---

of 'getting things done' might lead to people of color withdrawing from the process."
Eventually the group reached agreement that a commitment to addressing racial privilege through dialogue and policy was necessary, but that this assessment would focus on how racism might be manifested in land use issues, such as transit access, affordable housing, environmental quality, and economic opportunities.

After months of dialogue and subgroup meetings, the ENCHIA reached agreement that twenty-seven overarching Community Health Objectives would be assigned to the elements of the healthy city (Table 3.5). The objectives would also act to direct data gathering, the next stage in the ENCHIA process.

Building a New Evidence Base for Health Assessment

Having worked for almost nine months debating and refining the vision and objectives of the healthy city, the group began gathering evidence to support their objectives. The SFDPH organized data available through municipal agencies and identified additional sources of relevant data, such as those gathered by nonprofit organizations. Public agencies participating in the ENCHIA, from the police department to transit agency, also provided access to data. To help narrow the data-collection process, the council agreed to try and limit "healthy place" indicators to quantitative or qualitative data that was meaningful and valid to ENCHIA participants, regularly collected, reliably measurable and/or observable, actionable, and motivated action.

Using existing data sets, SFDPH staff members analyzed and mapped information at the request of ENCHIA participants, and meetings were used to discuss preliminary findings. Yet conflicts often surface during meetings about the meaningfulness and accountability of different evidence. For instance, the San Francisco Recreation and Parks Department (SFRPD) provided information on the location of parks across the city, and these data were mapped and shown with a quarter-mile buffer around each park (SFDPH 2007a, 45). The map was intended to show the number of residents that had access to a park, defined by those living within a quarter of a mile. Additional analyses using these data suggested that the Eastern Neighborhoods made up 7 percent of San Francisco's land area and 11 percent of the population, but contained only 1 percent of the city's open space (57 of the 6,410 total acres, respectively). During discussions of the map and these data, some participants noted that the quarter-mile distance may be irrelevant if the park was unsafe, occupied by homeless people or drug dealers, and didn't include activity spaces for all groups, such as barbecue pits and playgrounds. Others noted that using linear distance was irrelevant in San Francisco, where "a park can be 500 feet away but if it's straight uphill to get there or on a steep grade, you may never use it." The quality of the resource and whether the data analyses reflected local context—from park users' needs to local topography—was emphasized as a necessary but often overlooked aspect of gathering evidence about healthy places.

The Limits of Quantification and Place-Based Meanings

The discussions over data gathering and analysis also revealed to participants that not all healthy city objectives could or ought to be measured quantitatively. For example, after presenting police department crime statistics for the area around the 16th Street Bay Area Rapid Transit (BART) station in the Mission District, some group members from the mission noted that these data misrepresented the "safety" of the area and may stigmatize the area in a way that may be counterproductive (SFDPH 2007a, 46). Participants offered personal experiences and anecdotes discussing what they interpreted as "racial profiling" in the area, while others suggested that safety couldn't be captured by indicators alone. One member stated, "Feeling safe is about a relationship between you and your surroundings, not counting the number of assaults, how many lights work, or the number of cops on the street. I don't mean to dismiss the statistics, but it's important that we to ask who is being counted, why are people on the street, and how do the users of this space feel about safety and crime?" ENCHIA members expressed a desire to explore the social and political questions that often reside behind statistics and numbers and highlighted that quantitative information can often hide social meanings. While quantitative statistics often act as a tool of public policy by offering a semblance of rationality and objectivity to political decisions, ENCHIA participants requested that the quantitative measures be complemented with interpretive qualitative data.

Community Health Experts: Youth, Elderly, and Workers

Aiming to more systematically capture qualitative information and narratives about health issues, the SFDPH and the ENCHIA Council decided to initiate two new research efforts. The first was a series of focus group meetings and interviews by DPH staff with community members that were not participating in the ENCHIA. The aim of this process was to capture views of the "healthy city" from the direct experiences of community residents. A second research project aimed to gather more in-depth data on the relationships between employment and well-being in San Francisco, a principal concern of ENCHIA participants. This second study would interview day laborers, domestic workers, artists, restaurant workers, and software engineers in the Eastern Neighborhoods. The community study asked participants how they would define the healthy neighborhood and how changes in their neighborhood were impacting their perception of health and safety. The labor study asked participants about their physical conditions at work, sense of job security, whether they received health insurance through work, the amount of control and participation in decision making they had over their job, and the amount of time spent at work versus with family and other activities.

The findings from these research projects were presented to the ENCHIA Council in two reports. The community assessment report was titled *Results from a Community Assessment of Health and Land Use* (SFDPH 2007a, app. 3) and the labor study was compiled into a report titled *Tales of the City's Workers: A Work and Health Survey of San Francisco's Workforce*. The qualitative data findings helped fill information gaps left by quantitative data. For example, while a city-wide database tracked the changing demographics of the Eastern Neighborhoods, the community assessment included interviews and focus group discussions with seniors and revealed that many lived with a great fear of eviction and felt their mobility was increasingly constrained due to increased vehicular traffic. Young people noted that they felt constant stress from overcrowded living conditions, regular gang violence when traveling to school outside their neighborhood, and from a lack of future job opportunities in the area.

The labor study revealed that workers in San Francisco were faced with either very-low-wage, indeterminate, high-stress, and fast-paced jobs that lacked health insurance or highly paid professional positions requiring an advanced college degree that included health benefits and a perceived sense of control. Low-skilled, well-paying jobs that included health benefits and a sense of control over decision making were almost nonexistent in San Francisco. Day laborers and domestic workers emphasized that their lives often revolved around the daily stress of finding work, overcrowded housing conditions, and frequent disruptions to their family life, especially for their children. The findings from these two studies not only provided new data on populations that are often overlooked in health and planning analyses, but they convinced many ENCHIA participants that the process ought to analyze and make recommendations for a much broader set of urban policies for promoting health equity than just those related to land use changes in the Eastern Neighborhoods.

Drafting Healthy Urban Policies

The process of assigning objectives to the healthy city vision and exploring the availability of data that might act as supporting evidence for the objectives increasingly convinced most ENCHIA participants that some healthy city objectives might be best achieved through legislation, rather than administrative decisions or land use plans. For example, during discussions over energy conservation and efficiency, some ENCHIA participants stated that land use rules, such as "green" building requirements in the zoning code, were limited because they only applied to new construction. Other members noted that the Public Utilities Commission and energy purchasing contracts negotiated between state regulators and power generators were a better place to address energy conservation and efficiency than were land use policies. Still others noted that only federal policies were appropriate, such as energy efficiency requirements on consumer products.

These discussions highlighted that ENCHIA participants had many ideas for "healthy public policies" beyond changes to the zoning code. At the same time some city administrators began questioning whether the ENCHIA was only identifying problems and impediments to but not potential solutions for healthy urban policy (SFDPH 2007a, 51). In an effort to be more solution-oriented, the SFDPH built on the knowledge and ideas of ENCHIA participants and began researching possible policy solutions for implementing their healthy community objectives.

The ENCHIA meetings became a forum to vet policy proposals and explore supporting evidence. ENCHIA participants agreed that policy briefs would be drafted

Table 3.6 Policy Briefs Created by ENCHIA

1. Adopt Structural and Operational Requirements for Residential Hotels
2. Amend Inclusionary Housing Ordinance
3. Amend Residential Off-Street Parking Requirements
4. Area-Based Congestion Pricing in the Downtown Business District
5. Charging Market Rates for On-Street Parking
6. Community Benefits Districts/Business Improvement Districts
7. Community Benefits Policy/Community Impact Report
8. Community-Based Mechanisms to Reduce Air Pollution
9. Creating Special Use Districts in San Francisco's Mission District
10. Develop a Healthy Economy Element
11. Develop a City-Funded Program to Aid in Providing Child Care Benefits
12. Develop Food Enterprise Zones
13. Development Impact Fees for Eastern Neighborhoods
14. Establish Housing Development Equity Fund
15. Eviction Prevention
16. Formula Retail Use Restrictions
17. Improve the Effectiveness of Workforce Development Programs
18. Increase Collection Fees for Specialized Adult Recreation Programs
19. Increased Inclusionary Housing for Zoning Incentives
20. Mandatory Paid Sick Days
21. Master Strategy for Affordable Housing Development
22. Neighborhood Schools as Centers of Community
23. Open Space Zoning Requirements
24. Promote Accessory Dwelling Units
25. Reduce Marine Vessel Air Emissions by Requiring Cruise Ships to Use Shoreside Power
26. Regulate Provision of Employee Parking Benefits
27. Strengthen First Source Hiring Program

by the DPH and include a short background, situate the policy within the larger regulatory context, provide case studies or examples of how the policy was drafted and implemented somewhere else, and link the policy to direct and indirect influences on human health. The request reflected the broad scope that the group was willing to take, but also that they increasingly realized the limitations of health analyses and recommendations that were focused only on the Eastern Neighborhoods. As policy discussions moved forward, the tone of the ENCHIA process shifted from an exercise in spatial, often neighborhood scale, analysis to a more general policy discourse. Over the course of three months, SFDPH staff members researched and drafted twenty-seven policy briefs (Table 3.6).

Recognizing the difficulty of shifting the ENCHIA process from a discussion of local land use and zoning to more general policy making, participants devised a process for evaluating and debating each brief that included using small groups that reviewed policy details and then reported back to the larger group. Each small group was tasked with reviewing the evidence base used to draft each brief, evaluating the policy's relevance to San Francisco, and making a suggestion to the larger group over whether or not the policy should be endorsed by the ENCHIA. While some ENCHIA members thought the policy-drafting process would allow the group to address a broader set of issues beyond the rezoning plan, others had concerns about the documents themselves and questioned whether they included a sufficient amount of information that would allow the group to evaluate each policy.

ENCHIA meetings focused on reaching a group consensus on which policies to endorse and propose as part of promoting healthier urban policy and planning. Members often spent more time, however, debating whether they were in a position to make a recommendation than over the content of the policy briefs. One member stated, "I need more time to evaluate the information you have here. Normally our organization would discuss the options and issues with our members before endorsing a possible legislative proposal." Another member stated, "The research behind these policies seems fine, but they are all missing a plan for getting them passed and implemented. As they stand now, I cannot see endorsing any without a more complete legislative plan." After three months of deliberations, the ENCHIA Council was unable to come to any agreement over which policies, if any, to endorse. The ENCHIA process seemed to reach an impasse; frustration over the lack of agreement on the policy briefs was evident in both the DPH and ENCHIA participants. Meeting attendance dropped as organizations that were recruited to work on recommendations for the Eastern Neighborhoods rezoning plan did not want to spend their time on policy discussions.

Sustaining Participation: Moving from the Specific to the General

The DPH struggled to retain interest and met again with the planning department in an effort to reignite the process. In a meeting with Dean Macris, the director of San Francisco's planning department, staff members from the health department reviewed the work of the ENCHIA. The planning director commented that he thought the ENCHIA would be perceived as antagonistic to the interests of developers and viewed by many as a front for progressive movements in the city. He challenged DPH staff to prove that they had political support behind their work by asking, "Does Mitch [Katz, SFDPH director] know what he's getting into?"[8] The DPH responded that they did have their director's support, and Katz would soon thereafter note:

> The ENCHIA is about supporting healthy development and preventing disease for all. It is not about more administrative burdens or another bureaucratic hurdle for private developers. The kinds of issues ENCHIA debates and the connections it makes between land use and human health are not only exciting and relatively new, but the way planning must move to create a healthy economic, social and physical climate for all. We are committed to making planning see that this can be a win-win for them and

not hinder development. I don't see us [health department] going away from this work anytime soon.[9]

Yet the message from the planning department was that the ENCHIA might, at best, be duplicative of existing planning processes and, at worst, a vehicle that highlighted the failure of planning processes to consider human health and an impediment to new development where it was needed most, namely the Eastern Neighborhoods. The SFDPH realized that if the process was going to continue they needed a new strategy to both retain participant interest and better engage with the planning department.

After a year of meetings the ENCHIA process produced a vision of the healthy city, selected seven elements and objectives to attach to the vision, gathered quantitative and qualitative evidence to show how each element promotes health, and drafted twenty-seven non-health-specific policy briefs. Yet the group was in a bind; the planning department had still not issued the final rezoning plan and accompanying environmental and social impact assessments. All the work the group had done was supposed to prepare them for analyzing these documents, but they did not exist.

After discussing disbanding and where the group might go, an idea that was mentioned throughout the process, namely developing a health and land use "scorecard" using data the group had already compiled, resurfaced during council discussions. A scorecard, participants noted, would be a valuable health analysis tool for this and future decision making, and would not be contingent on the final Eastern Neighborhoods' rezoning documents. ENCHIA participants agreed to refocus their efforts to develop this screening tool.

A small group of ENCHIA participants met to strategize on ways to convert all that the group had produced—the healthy city vision, associated elements, supporting data, and policy recommendations—into one screening tool. The group also focused on identifying specific land use and development policies that could promote each of the healthy city elements. With the assistance of DPH staff, ENCHIA participants gathered additional land use and health data specific to different San Francisco neighborhoods in order to help compare conditions and development options in the Eastern Neighborhoods with those in other parts of the city.

This work resulted in a set of healthy development targets; concrete actions that planners, developers, and policy makers could take that would move toward the ENCHIA's specific healthy community objectives. Instead of including one action item, ENCHIA participants suggested a range, from those that were "minimally acceptable" for promoting health to those that were the target or "benchmark," to those that were viewed as the "maximum attainable." This way the group recognized that not all plans and development projects should be held to the same standard and "something was often better than nothing." These concrete project alternatives were added to the goals, objectives, and health-based evidence that the ENCHIA process had already gathered, and together these data became the basis of the group's new screening tool.

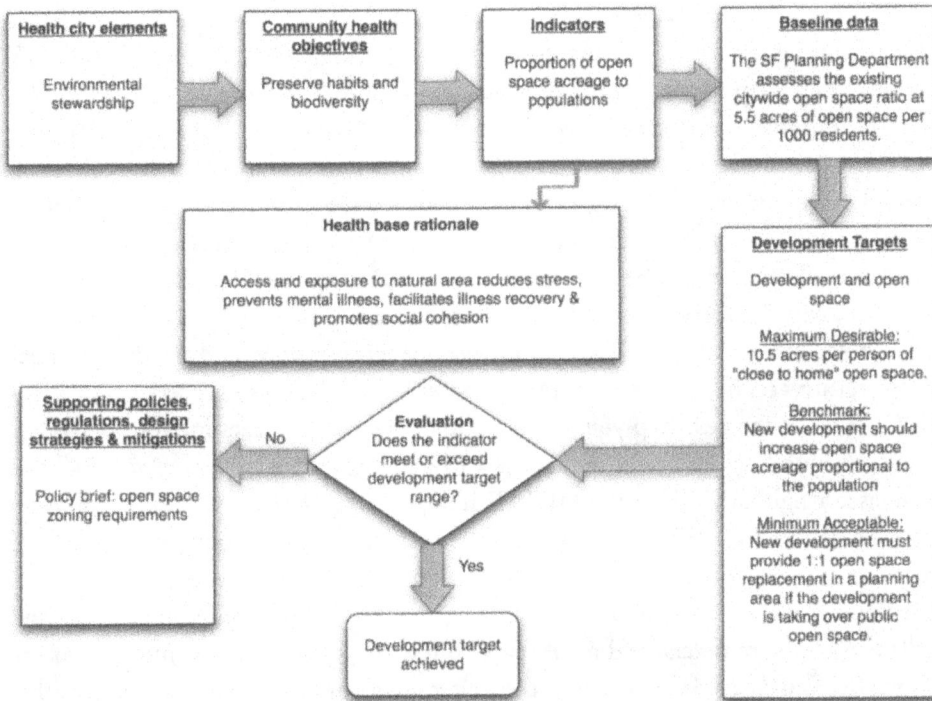

```
┌──────────────────┐   ┌──────────────────┐   ┌──────────────────┐   ┌──────────────────┐
│ Health city      │   │ Community health │   │    Indicators    │   │  Baseline data   │
│ elements         │   │   objectives     │   │ Proportion of    │   │ The SF Planning  │
│                  │   │ Preserve habits  │   │ open space       │   │ Department       │
│ Environmental    │   │ and              │   │ acreage to       │   │ assesses the     │
│ stewardship      │   │ biodiversity     │   │ populations      │   │ existing         │
│                  │   │                  │   │                  │   │ citywide open    │
│                  │   │                  │   │                  │   │ space ratio at   │
│                  │   │                  │   │                  │   │ 5.5 acres of     │
│                  │   │                  │   │                  │   │ open space per   │
│                  │   │                  │   │                  │   │ 1000 residents.  │
└──────────────────┘   └──────────────────┘   └──────────────────┘   └──────────────────┘
```

Figure 3.2 Environmental Stewardship Example of the Healthy Development Measurement Tool (HDMT)

The Healthy Development Measurement Tool

In May 2006 the group finished its first draft of the screening tool, now called the Healthy Development Measurement Tool (HDMT). The draft was reviewed in detail by ENCHIA members and sent to more than a dozen different city agencies and sixty external peer reviewers around the world. The SFDPH spent three additional months incorporating comments and suggestions from reviewers and making revisions to the HDMT. A second draft was completed and an interactive web version (*thehdmt.org*) was released.

The HDMT was organized using the same seven healthy city elements identified through the ENCHIA process, including environmental stewardship, sustainable transportation, public safety, public infrastructure/access to goods and services, adequate and healthy housing, healthy economy, and community participation. Each of the HDMT's seven elements also contained twenty-seven community health objectives that, if achieved, would result in greater and more equitable health assets and resources for San Francisco residents. Also included were measurable indicators with a health-based rationale, along with the most current "baseline data" documenting how well the city—specific population groups and different neighborhoods—was performing with respect to each indicator. A set of development targets and policy recommendations accompanied each healthy city objective. The analytic steps and content of the HDMT for one healthy city element, environmental stewardship, are shown in Figure 3.2.

The objective was to allow anyone with web access to take a land use plan or project they were interested in and to analyze and evaluate it using the criteria offered in the HDMT. For example, imagine you wanted to screen a proposed development in your area for whether it would assure access to daily goods and service needs, including financial services and healthy foods (healthy city, public infrastructure objective 6; see Table 3.5). One measurable indicator for this objective is the proportion of households within half a mile from a full-service grocery store, and the development target for new residential development is that it has a full-service grocery store within half a mile. In the next step you would evaluate the baseline data for your neighborhood, surrounding areas, and the city as a whole. These data are included for all San Francisco neighborhoods in the HDMT. Imagine that there are no grocery stores in your neighborhood. The third step is a close reading and evaluation of the proposed development project and land use plan to see if it includes, in this case, a grocery store. Let's imagine the plan includes new housing for eight thousand new residents and calls for "new commercial and retail space" but does not explicitly mention a grocery store. The fourth step is to explore project alternatives or improvements to ensure that it meets the healthy development target. In this example the HDMT recommends financial, zoning, or political incentives to encourage the project to designate a site for a grocery store or, if a grocery store exists offsite, a plan for improving pedestrian, bicycle, and public transit access to the existing grocery store.

ENCHIA Deliverables

The HDMT emerged as the final deliverable of the ENCHIA, but the process produced a set of tangible outcomes. First, the healthy city vision, created during a public deliberative process, captured specific features and the social meanings of a healthy place. The data-gathering process brought together disparate secondary data sets—including health outcomes, economic and employment statistics, land uses, social services, and transit access—in one place for the first time. The data-gathering process also facilitated spatial and comparative analyses of information that are rarely analyzed in this way, such as grocery stores, poverty, and population density across city neighborhoods. Consequently the public deliberative process allowed community members to challenge and question the local relevance of certain quantitative data, forcing the process to gather original qualitative information revealing local knowledge and understandings highlighting how local people navigate through the physical and social hazards and opportunities in their place.

The flexibility and participatory design of the ENCHIA process allowed both the SFDPH and participants to reshape the objectives and outputs of the process along the way. In the end, the ENCHIA process achieved most of the original objectives defined by the organizers, from identifying and analyzing the likely impacts of land use plans on health determinants to offering recommendations for land use policies and zoning controls that could promote community health. The ENCHIA also demonstrated that a participatory HIA process was feasible and could provide a forum for meaningful public involvement in urban policy making, fulfilling another objective. As I highlight in more detail below, the ENCHIA also provided a space where new interagency and organizational networks could develop and be nurtured, a crucial component of moving toward healthy city planning.

New Issue Framings through Envisioning the Healthy City

This chapter has explored the ways a participatory health impact assessment process can begin to transform urban governance through redefining problems and solutions, collaboratively gathering new evidence, and generating alternatives to entrenched planning and policy-making processes that often fail to consider human health.[10] One of the significant aspects of the ENCHIA, as noted above, was that participants were able to define their own vision of the healthy city and deliberate over the meanings and implications of this vision. The policy framing offered by ENCHIA participants included the broad determinants of well-being, namely economic, social, and physical characteristics of neighborhoods, the region, and beyond. As one ENCHIA participant, reflecting on the visioning process, stated:

> Before this process, I thought of a healthy community as one that lacked disease, didn't have pollution, and people had access to health care. Now [after ENCHIA] I'm more aware that housing is one of the key issues and that you can't consider one thing in isolation. I mean, if you have housing but no other neighborhood life, the place won't be too healthy. If you got a job, but it don't pay enough to live in a community with your family or you got to work two jobs to make good money, this ain't a healthy place either. Measuring unemployment in that situation might make the place look pretty good, but that one measure won't show how people are really living.

Interviews with ENCHIA participants during and after the process suggest that the visioning process and resulting issue reframing also influenced the work of their organizations. According to one ENCHIA member who directs a social service delivery organization, the process opened up his organization to a reframing of its own work:

> I never thought of issues like the design of street intersections, where supermarkets are located, and the mix of commercial activities as public health and equity issues, but now I do. I've been in community-planning

processes before, but not one that involved thinking about health in this broad a way. Our organization is now redefining what we do as promoting health, although we used to think about it as just delivering essential social services of emergency housing and job training for the chronically homeless.

Another ENCHIA member who works for a housing advocacy organization echoed similar sentiments:

Before the ENCHIA we never attempted to make community economic development and housing affordability a public health issue. Yet we always talked about our work as defending "human needs" and "basic living conditions." The ENCHIA has helped us see that we were making public health arguments all along, but just not being explicit about it. Now, by making explicit the connections of our work with health, we have not only seen that [city] supervisors and other elected officials are paying more attention, but it has also helped us expand our organizing base in the neighborhood.

The broad issue framing has also begun to influence the work within the planning department, reluctant for so long to acknowledge the links between human health and land use planning decisions. One planning official stated:

I think we [planning department] always knew land use decisions had some impact on human health, but we just didn't believe it was our role to make these explicit or find ways to incorporate them into our analyses. The ENCHIA process highlighted that the decisions we make on an everyday basis—whether they are directed at housing, transportation, environment, open space, or zoning—have some human health impacts. This insight, combined with unyielding persistence from the DPH and community groups to consider health in our plans, has begun to change the way we think about land use planning processes and who we include in analyses.

Building New Networks

A second lesson from the ENCHIA is that new professional relationships between organizations and agencies unfamiliar with one another is crucial for building the broad knowledge base and political legitimacy necessary for healthy city planning. By bringing together stakeholders from a range of issue areas and city agencies that rarely, if ever, incorporate human health into their work, the ENCHIA facilitated the construction of new "healthy governance" networks. As one ENCHIA member stated:

I see a lot of these same people at other meetings, but now I'm more likely to go talk with them or try and work with them now that I know them better. I never knew some of these groups worked on the same issues that we do and I would have never known who to call. This process has changed this.

Other participants noted that their relationship with city government, particularly the Department of Public Health, was positively altered through the ENCHIA process. An ENCHIA participant described the new relationship with the health department:

My relationships with the DPH have improved through this process. I would have never even thought of calling them about a land use issue before, but now I know how knowledgeable they are about these issues. I trust them more after the commitment they made to this process, and after getting to know them better, they [DPH] have helped us build better relationships with other city agencies.

Another ENCHIA council member echoed these sentiments and reflected on the political power that can come by aligning their planning efforts with the public health agency:

The ENCHIA process has revealed to our organization that when a public health agency says "displacement" or "this land use may cause a health problem, do something else," the government and the public are more likely to listen than when planners say the same thing. I mean when a doctor gets up and says "this plan or project may cause harm to health" who's going to argue with that? After this process we also have the health evidence to support our non-health-specific plans and policies.

The ENCHIA also helped the DPH build new working relationships with organizations beyond the planning department. For example, the ENCHIA process introduced the DPH to the work of the San Francisco Bike Coalition and Transportation for Livable Cities. After the ENCHIA concluded, these organizations approached the DPH and built a partnership to investigate ways to revise the use of vehicle level of service (LOS) analysis in project reviews. The SFDPH is helping these groups use health evidence to make the case that using automobile LOS as a performance measure leads to increased vehicle traffic and travel speeds, resulting in more air and noise pollution and jeopardizing the safety of pedestrians and bicyclists.[11] The SFDPH was asked to participate in the Western SoMa Citizens Planning Task Force and offer health-based technical support. The agency used the HDMT and partnered with community organizations to complete a health analysis of the Executive Park Sub Area Plan in the Visitacion Valley area of San Francisco. Also after the ENCHIA was complete, two participating organizations,

SOMCAN and the Mission Economic Development Association (MEDA), applied for and received funding from the California Endowment to continue their research and activism linking land use, development, and community health issues.

Redefining Expertise and Legitimate Evidence

The deliberative character of the ENCHIA process allowed participants to discuss the merits of different kinds of data for each element of the healthy city vision. When disagreements emerged, ENCHIA members were encouraged and allowed to offer alternative ways to evaluate the issue. The SFDPH recognized that trust in and the credibility of the ENCHIA would not rest solely in the scientific data it used but also in public accountability and transparent evidence gathering and evaluation. To increase the transparency of this process, all documents from the ENCHIA were regularly posted on the web. The public deliberations over evidence further revealed that each participant brought his or her own expertise to the process. The ENCHIA process straddled conventional views of expertise by simultaneously looking to disciplinary professionals for advice and valuing the knowledge of local people.

Yet the broad public involvement and multiple forms of expertise that characterized the ENCHIA also enhanced conflict and alienated some participants. One participant noted after participating in the process for a year:

> The process is still amorphous to me and I'm still not sure where it is going. A few people can push the group off on tangents, and the DPH just agrees to let them all speak and offer ideas. I mean, there is objective data that we should be gathering, not people's opinions.

Other participants disagreed and noted that the openness of the dialogue was rare for a public planning process:

> I've been to many public planning meetings and most often the agencies just sit there shaking their heads and you never get the sense they are taking you seriously. In this process, when it came to talking about homelessness and living in an SRO [single-room occupancy hotel], the doctors, lawyers, and PhDs in the room don't know what I know; I've lived that kind of life and been there, know what I mean? For the first time I felt like the DPH was listening to what community people know and turning that into credible data.

Lydia Zaverukha, a participant in the ENCHIA from the San Francisco Recreation and Parks Department, stated that the participatory process "should become the model for San Francisco's city planning process." Other ENCHIA members, however, suggested that the process spent too much time listening to all points of view and didn't do enough to gather hard evidence that could prove certain land uses were harming community health. One ENCHIA participant noted:

> We need to show the "hard data" that gentrification and displacement makes you sick, I mean diseased. Without that, I don't see this process having much of an impact, since it is already hijacked by city planning and private developers.

Despite the ENCHIA's commitment to meaningful participation and valuing a range of expertise, some controversial issues were left unresolved. For instance, the discussions over whether the process should address racism as a key determinant of health and which policy proposals the group ought to endorse were never resolved.

The participatory and transparent process the ENCHIA used to gather and evaluate a range of evidence and expertise did help the process build and maintain *public trust*. Through their participation in the ENCHIA, community-based organizations recognized that government, especially the health department, could be an ally.

New Institutional Practices

In one of the most significant impacts of the ENCHIA on city planning in San Francisco, the planning department agreed after the conclusion of the process to have the DPH review three area plans, or neighborhood-scale land use plans, using the HDMT. The area plans included the Eastern Neighborhoods of the Mission District, East SoMa, and Showplace Square–Potrero Hill. What began as a skeptical and antagonistic planning department shifted its orientation to human health analyses as evidence was compiled and organized into the HDMT linking land use decisions to human health, and political support for this approach increased. After the final release of the HDMT, the health and planning departments met frequently to review the HDMT and the draft area plans.[12] By December 2007 the SFDPH released its reviews of these three plans, noting the positive and negative impacts of each on community health. In a cover letter for the review, Rajiv Bhatia (SFDPH 2007b) of the health department wrote:

> Over the past year, staff from the SFDPH worked closely with staff from SF Planning to apply the HDMT to Area Plans for East SoMA, Mission and Showplace Square/Potrero Hill. During this time, SFDPH provided SF Planning with many recommendations on draft versions of the plans which have already been integrated into the current version. Following the public release of the December 1st 2007 version of the plans, SFDPH re-evaluated the three Area Plans using the HDMT and documented this "final" evaluation in a document—*Impacts on Community Health of Area Plans for the Mission, East SoMa, and Potrero Hill/Showplace Square: An Application of the Healthy Development Measurement Tool.*

By the end of 2007 the San Francisco planning department, local governments and organizations from across the Bay Area, and private foundations were engaging with health analyses and using the tools developed through the ENCHIA process.

Policy Diffusion across the Metropolitan Region

As noted earlier, healthy city planning cannot be limited to one neighborhood or even within a city; it must become standard practice across entire metropolitan areas since city policies are regularly influenced by other actors within the region (Dreier, Mollenkopf, and Swanstrom 2004; Katz 2007). The ENCHIA process—through its commitment to public participation, transparency, and inclusive data gathering—encouraged other local governments and community-based organizations across the Bay Area to engage with health analyses of land use and urban policy decisions.

In late 2006, the city of Richmond, California, decided to borrow from the ENCHIA, particularly the HDMT, to draft the state's first Health Policy Element as part of the city's general plan update (Johnson 2007). The Health Element was drafted by a group of technical experts and community organization representatives, including some that participated in the ENCHIA, and the SFDPH acted as a key advisor on this project.[13] The drafting of the Health Element is being coordinated by MIG, Inc., a Berkeley, California–based land use planning firm, in cooperation with the Contra Costa County Health Services Department. By August 2007, a Technical Advisory Group had adopted indicators from the HDMT for Richmond and drafted ten healthy community planning objectives (City of Richmond 2007).

Two regional nongovernmental organizations, Urban Habitat and the Transportation and Land Use Coalition (TALC), are also building on the work of the ENCHIA to promote healthy and equitable planning. Urban Habitat, an Oakland-based group that aims to "build power in low-income communities and communities of color by combining education, advocacy, research, and coalition building," is coordinating the Richmond Equitable Development Initiative (REDI). The REDI is working to empower, inform, and share ideas with Richmond residents about land use and development issues and how these decisions can promote social justice (*urbanhabitat. org/richmond*). As part of this work, Urban Habitat is facilitating the REDI's participation in the Richmond General Plan Update and providing help on incorporating the health equity work of groups such as the Asian Pacific Environmental Network's Laotian Organizing Project, Communities for a Better Environment, and Ma'at Youth Academy into the Health Element planning process.

Healthy Regional Planning

TALC is helping to coordinate the Great Communities Collaborative (GCC) (*www. greatcommunities.org*), a regional partnership of four advocacy organizations and two community foundations: the Nonprofit Housing Association of Northern California, Urban Habitat, Greenbelt Alliance, Reconnecting America, the San Francisco Foundation, and the East Bay Community Foundation. This collaborative is focused on regional growth issues, and TALC is coordinating health assessments of three transit-oriented development plans sponsored by the GCC in the Bay Area cities of San Leandro, Santa Rosa, and Pittsburg. One HIA analyzed an extension of the Bay Area Regional Transit (BART) system in Pittsburg, California, and another focuses on improving the San Pablo Avenue Corridor in El Cerrito, California.

TALC is receiving guidance in their "healthy transit planning" from a third regional nonprofit that has benefited from the ENCHIA—Human Impact Partners (HIP). HIP was founded after the ENCHIA, uses the ENCHIA tools to conduct HIAs for its clients, and provides training and mentorship to community-based organizations, governments, and elected officials so that they can perform their own health analyses of planning and policy issues (*www.humanimpact.org*). Human Impact Partners and another regional organization—Communities for a Better Environment (CBE)—are collaborating with West Oakland residents to use the HDMT and health impact assessment methods more generally to screen and analyze a range of development projects in the community.

Regional Health Equity Coalitions

Many of the organizations from the ENCHIA and those working in the region on healthy planning came together to form the Healthy Places Coalition in 2006. The Healthy Places Coalition, coordinated by the Oakland, California–based Prevention Institute, brings together more than thirty different organizations interested in improving health and social justice through policy and planning changes. One of the significant efforts of this coalition was to draft and lobby for the California Healthy Places Act (Assembly Bill 1472) in 2007. This bill proposed to prevent illness and disease, improve health, and reduce health disparities in California by, in part, requiring that a health impact assessment program for land use, transportation, and development policies, modeled largely around the ENCHIA, be established by the state's Department of Public Health by 2010. Under this bill an interagency working group would be established to develop guidelines for conducting HIAs, share information about best practices with local governments, and evaluate HIAs performed under the program.

Finally, the ENCHIA has had a significant impact on the state of California's largest health foundation, the California Endowment (TCE), and on the national research and advocacy group PolicyLink. TCE viewed the work of the ENCHIA as a way to expand its community health and health disparities work and promote the experimentation of a new practice for health promotion, namely HIA (Aranda 2008). Prior to ENCHIA, both TCE and PolicyLink were researching and supporting built-environment and health issues and exploring ways to integrate health equity into planning and land use decisions. After the ENCHIA, TCE became the primary fiscal sponsor of the health assessment work within community organizations in San Francisco (e.g., SOMCAN and MEDA), local government (e.g., the Richmond Health Element planning process), and nonprofit organizations across the region (e.g., HIP, Urban Habitat, TALC, and CBE). PolicyLink has supported this grant making by acting as the fiscal agent for some grants, providing oversight and advice on design and implementation of projects, and convening meetings of Bay Area public health and urban planning professionals, researchers, and activists (Lee and Rubin 2007). A guidebook titled *How to Create and Implement Healthy General Plans* was funded by TCE and drafted by the nonprofit group Public Health Law and Policy and the planning consulting firm Raimi Associates (*www.healthyplanning.org/toolkit_healthygp .html*). Since these are relatively recent reports, their impact on future "healthy regional planning and policy making" remains uncertain. What is clear, however, is that absent financial support from TCE, the diffusion across the Bay Area of ENCHIA lessons, such as innovative assessment practices, coalition-building strategies, and the generation of a new healthy planning evidence base, would not have taken root in so many different organizations and institutions.

The ENCHIA offers an important model for understanding the politics of healthy city planning, from its participatory process for defining the elements of a healthy city to the evidence base and evaluation tool it offered to the new professional networks and trust in local government that it helped build. While the process set out to evaluate the human health impacts of one rezoning plan in San Francisco, the ENCHIA offered insights for building a more general practice of healthy city planning within cities and metropolitan regions everywhere.

Notes

This chapter is the result of a collaborative process involving Rajiv Bhatia, Lili Farhang, and other members of the PHES team at the SFDPH.

1. Personal communication with O. Grande, People Organized for the Defense of Economic and Environmental Rights (PODER).
2. Personal communication with Rajiv Bhatia, director of environmental health, San Francisco Department of Public Health.
3. Rajiv Bhatia, personal communication.
4. Rajiv Bhatia, personal communication.
5. Lili Farhang, personal communication.
6. Lili Farhang, personal communication. This process was very similar to issues of conflict assessment process used in designing consensus-building processes (Susskind and Thomas-Larmer 1999). In a conflict assessment a mediator often conducts interviews with interested parties and those outside the conflict in an effort to understand the substantive issues at stake and historical relationships among stakeholders, and to recruit participants to attend the dispute-resolution process.

7. The vision was later revised and expanded into seven elements by adding transportation and community participation and combining infrastructure with goods and services into one category.
8. Rajiv Bhatia, personal communication.
9. Mitch Katz, personal communication.
10. Much of the data used for this section of the chapter comes from three rounds of confidential interviews with ENCHIA participants and related city agency personnel, observations at most meetings, and content analysis of meeting transcripts. ENCHIA participant interviewees included members of nongovernmental organizations such as Asian Neighborhood Design, Mission Economic Development Association, Mission SRO Collaborative/Mission Agenda, Neighborhood Parks Council, People Organizing to Demand Environmental and Economic Rights (PODER), People Organized to Win Employment Rights (POWER), SF Land Trust, SF Food Alliance, Urban Habitat, and Urban Solutions. In order to preserve confidentiality in what was, at the time of most interviews, an ongoing public process, names of individuals and their organization affiliations are not included here.
11. Rajiv Bhatia, personal communication.
12. Lili Farhang, personal communication.
13. One organization that participated in both the ENCHIA and the Richmond Health Element drafting process was Urban Habitat. There were additional technical advisors that also participated in both processes.

References

Aranda, D. 2008. Personal communication.

City of Richmond. 2007. "Richmond General Plan Update." *Issues and Opportunities Paper 8: Community Health and Wellness. www.ci.richmond.ca.us/DocumentCenter/Home/ View/8579.*

Dreier, P., J. Mollenkopf, and T. Swanstrom. 2004. *Place Matters: Metropolitics for the Twenty-first Century*, 2nd edition. Lawrence: University Press of Kansas.

Fischer, C., L. Leydesdorff, and M. Schophaus. 2004. "Science Shops in Europe: The Public as Stakeholder." *Science and Public Policy* 31 (3): 199–211.

Johnson, C. 2007. "Chevron Looks to Profits, Richmond Looks to Health." *San Francisco Chronicle*, June 8, p. B1.

Katz, B. 2007. *Blueprint for American Prosperity: Metronation*. Washington, DC: Brookings Institute. *www.brookings.edu/projects/blueprint.aspx.*

Lee, M., and V. Rubin. 2007. "The Impact of the Built Environment on Community Health: The State of Current Practice and Next Steps for a Growing Movement." *Policy Link and The California Endowment. www.calendow.org/uploadedFiles/The_Built_Environment_ report.pdf.*

Quigley, R., L. den Broeder, P. Furu, A. Bond, B. Cave, and R. Bos. 2006. *Health Impact Assessment International Best Practice Principles*. Special Publication Series no. 5. Fargo, ND: International Association for Impact Assessment. *www.iaia.org/publicdocuments/ special-publications/SP5.pdf.*

SFDPH (San Francisco Department of Public Health). 2007a. "Eastern Neighborhoods Community Health Impact Assessment." Final report. Program on Health, Equity and Sustainability. *www.sfphes.org/component/jdownloads/viewdownload/12-eastern-neighborhoods-community-health-impact-assessment-final-report/19-enchia-final-report?Itemid=0.*

————. 2007b. "Impacts on Community Health of Area Plans for the Mission, East SoMa, and Potrero Hill/Showplace Square: An Application of the Healthy Development Measurement Tool." December 25. *www.thehdmt.org.*

Scott-Samuel, A., M. Birley, and K. Arden. 2001. "The Merseyside Guidelines for Health Impact Assessment," 2nd edition. International Health IMPACT Assessment Consortium. *www.apho.org.uk/resource/item.aspx?RID=44256.*

Susskind, L., and J. Thomas-Larmer. 1999. "Conducting a Conflict Assessment." In *The Consensus Building Handbook*, ed. L. Susskind, S. McKearnan, and J. Thomas-Larmer. Thousand Oaks, CA: Sage.

Wachelder, J. 2003. "Democratizing Science: Various Routes and Visions of Dutch Science Shops." *Science Technology and Human Values* 28 (2): 244–73.

4

Intramovement Agenda Setting

Nationalizing North Carolina's Fight to Defeat an Anti–Gay Marriage Constitutional Amendment

DANIEL KREISS AND LAURA MEADOWS

> The members [of Equality NC] are all in on this. What we need now is we need to see more national support. I think one of the key things that is unique about North Carolina are key partnerships with the NAACP, and every single major Democratic candidate for governor or lieutenant governor has come out in opposition to the amendment. So I think we are in a very unique position for a Southern state and the amendment which should defeat this amendment and . . . thanks for all you are doing and I really appreciate you joining us in the effort and I would love to take any questions you have.
>
> —Stuart Campbell, National Blogger Call, 3/11/12

■ On a Sunday evening less than two months before a vote on North Carolina's Amendment One—an anti-gay constitutional amendment declaring that "Marriage between one man and one woman is the only domestic legal union that shall be valid or recognized in this State"—Campbell, the executive director of Equality NC, a statewide LGBT advocacy nonprofit, took his appeal directly to a group of bloggers and media producers dispersed around the country. For the next fifty minutes, Campbell, senior online strategist Nation Hahn, campaign manager Jeremy Kennedy, and director of faith outreach Ryan Rowe updated the assembled group on the campaign's progress and fielded questions. Those on the call, a mix of writers for the LGBT movement press, bloggers with national followings who cover gay and progressive issues, in-state and regional advocates, and representatives from civil society groups, offered suggestions to help the campaign and enthusiastically described assisting in the campaign's efforts at wooing national donors and support. One even described "chewing the ear off" a prominent LGBT donor at a fund-raiser in California, urging him to support the effort to defeat North Carolina's ballot amendment.

On Sunday nights throughout the final months of the campaign, this scene played itself out over and over again. Staffers of the Coalition to Protect ALL NC Families working to defeat the amendment innovatively sought to leverage the media platforms and networks of their supporters to gain the attention and support of national LGBT movement donors and organizations. As a social movement coordinating an electoral campaign, the coalition was a hybrid assortment of more than 125 national, regional, and NC-based social movement, political, religious, and civil society organizations and groups. Some of these organizations came from the traditional coalition of the LGBT movement such as the Human Rights Campaign and Equality NC; others, such as the NAACP, are primarily affiliated with different movements for civil and social rights. The campaign relied on their memberships for volunteers and fund-raising, which helped staffers raise the more than $2 million that flowed to its coffers in the months before the election.

But this coalition only took the campaign so far. In order to nationalize the campaign and attract the support and resources of the larger LGBT movement, the campaign used these conference calls as strategic opportunities for "network building," "the creation, cultivation, and maintenance of ties with movement allies that the campaign mobilized for informational purposes" (Kreiss 2012, 205). The campaign's goal was to build far-flung networks of media-producing supporters and leverage these ties to disseminate narratives that were advantageous to the campaign: stories about the progress of the campaign, the new ground it was forging in terms of its diverse coalition, its implications for the national movement, and, above all, its momentum and the possibility for a victory. While these bloggers and media producers at times posed critical questions, for the most part their goals were aligned with those of the campaign in sharing the hope that these narratives would result in increased fund-raising and the campaign would emerge victorious on May 8, 2012.

In some domains, the campaign's strategic work of network building and coordinated messaging seemingly paid off. Online "money bombs" (periods of concentrated fund-raising appeals) promoted through the media producers on these calls helped the campaign raise more than $700,000 in largely small donations online, an extraordinary figure for a state initiative. The other goal those on the call shared with the campaign was the hope that these narratives would spur national movement donors to get involved in North Carolina, enabling it to attract high-dollar donations. The support and resources of national movement elites were by no means guaranteed. Indeed, despite many creative efforts by the campaign, they largely never materialized. Two-thirds of the campaign's fund-raising came from in state. Prominent LGBT donors such as Chris Hughes, publisher and editor-in-chief of the *New Republic*, did not contribute money. Even more symbolically, national organizations kept North Carolina at arm's length, seemingly wary of another loss at the start of an electoral cycle where four other states would head to the polls just six months later.

We refer to this effort to nationalize the North Carolina campaign as an attempt at *intramovement agenda setting*. While previous work has analyzed dynamics between explicitly competing factions within movements (Haines 1984; McAdam 1982), we focus here on processes of attempted influence through strategic communication by an entity at the periphery of a national movement. The campaign convened a far-flung group of media-producing autonomous allies. Staffers then leveraged these ties as the conduits of strategic communications to their networks and publics in the attempt to raise money and shape how actors in the national movement thought about North Carolina. Specifically, the campaign sought to leverage these alternate media producers to add North Carolina to the agenda of national elites, to make the case for the campaign's momentum, and ultimately to create the sense of its potential to be the first state to defeat an anti-gay amendment at the ballot box so donors would be willing to devote resources to the effort. To demonstrate these processes empirically, we present the results of a four-month ethnographic study of the campaign that proceeded from the basic premise that we would construct our field site and research questions inductively in the course of observation. It was a design that led to many surprises, including that the staffers managing the daily operations and social media activities of the campaign routinely engaged in targeted outreach to and hosted a forty-five-to-sixty-minute conference call for national bloggers and alternative LGBT media outlets in the run-up to the election.

In the pages that follow, we analyze intramovement agenda setting, showing how the campaign both built and coordinated networks of media producers in the attempt to create the perception of momentum necessary to gain resources from national LGBT donors. First, drawing on our previous work (Kreiss 2012; Kreiss and Meadows 2013), we provide a discussion of the challenges that movements face when they coordinate an electoral campaign. Second, we detail our ethnographic methods for this study. Third, we discuss our findings, revealing the goals for and implementation of the campaign's strategic communications efforts. We conclude with a general discussion of what this study means with respect to civic innovation for the LGBT movement.

When a Movement Meets a Campaign

Social movements have long engaged in electoral politics to capture public attention and advance their long-term goals (McAdam and Tarrow 2010; Schwartz 2010; Tilly 2004, 1978).[1] Elections are often strategic opportunities for movements to advance their policy objectives and gain influence (Meyer 2003), even as elected officials and candidates seek to harness the energy around movements for electoral, policy, or simply rhetorical advantage (McAdam and Tarrow 2010). Staggenborg and Lecomte (2009) argue that campaigns are "displays of unity" for movements, and enable them to mobilize extant participants and recruit new ones. Movements can use campaigns to forge new networks that grow (Kleidman 1993) or introduce new repertoires and tactics to the movement. Campaigns can help movements create new leaders, strengthen ties between organizations, and shape public discourse; alternatively, they may strain existing alliances or, in the case of failure, undermine movement aims and identity (Staggenborg and Lecomte 2009).

The history of the LGBT movement in the United States is entwined with the politics of ballots. The contemporary Christian right countermovement began during a 1977 campaign against a gay rights ordinance in Dade Country, Florida, and grew into a decades-long electoral effort to limit the rights of LGBT individuals (Fejes 2011; Fetner 2008). The most recent front has been the legislative actions supporting gay marriage in statehouses across the country and ballot measures to ban them, the latter of which have been roundly won by conservatives (Hirschman 2012). Stone (2011, 2012) argues that an explicit strategy of the Christian right was to make gay marriage, and rights more broadly, the subject of popular referendum, which they did almost uniformly successfully until the 2012 electoral cycle.

To date, only a few scholars have conducted systematic research on the actual organization and coordination of ballot campaigns, even though they pose significant challenges for movements that often lack the electoral expertise required to shape strategy, craft ads, raise money, and develop messaging. As Stone (2012) documents, movements often lack the infrastructure of professional staff, institutional knowledge, and organizational resources needed to coordinate highly transactional electoral efforts. To overcome this, Stone argues that over the past decade the national LGBT movement invested in its capacity to engage in electoral politics by developing stable funding resources, organizations that could be mobilized for electoral processes, and trainings for state-level efforts. These national organizations help transfer knowledge across campaigns, for instance through being on the steering committees of local efforts.

While Stone's work details the reasons movements engage in electoral politics and the struggles they face as they do so, we know relatively little about intramovement dynamics during electoral campaigns. For instance, how do state actors interact with national movement elites? How do state initiatives capture the time, resources, and attention of a national movement? And how do the changing technological contexts within which contemporary politics are waged shape these strategies?

The last question is particularly interesting given the proliferation in recent years of media such as blogs, and networked technologies more generally, that have enabled activists of all stripes to coordinate collective action and influence institutional political processes (Bennett 2004; Bimber, Flanagin, and Stohl 2012; Carty 2002; Earl and Kimport 2008). Earl and Kimport (2011), for instance, demonstrate how movements have used networked media to create entirely new modes of online organizing as well as facilitate offline activism. Of all the organizations and movements receiving scholarly attention for their online organizing efforts, none have been more closely studied than the varied bloggers, organizations, and activists mobilizing under the banner of the "netroots" (a portmanteau of "Internet" and "grassroots"). This intraparty social movement often involves organizations that feature "hybrid repertoires" of contentious action, such as MoveOn.org, which has engaged in national political actions including mass, issue-based mobilizations online as well as street protests, candlelight vigils, and lobby days (Chadwick 2007; see also Karpf 2012). Other netroots organizations demonstrate similar hybridity. The heavily trafficked DailyKos group blog, which some of the attendees on the Protect All NC Families conference calls had their primary affiliations with, is a platform for a range of progressive causes and has raised millions of dollars for electoral and advocacy campaigns.

As scholars have found, the audiences, dollars, and activists commanded by the actors in the netroots have fashioned them into a potent force within the extended Democratic Party network in less than a decade (Galvin 2008). For example, in their empirical study of the composition of the networks that make up the two parties, Masket et al. (2011) point out that MoveOn's "rise is especially notable, as its Internet origins and informal organizational structure suggests the increasing centrality of the relatively young 'netroots' as constituency within the Democratic Party" (23). Democratic campaigns have both grasped the netroots' increasing importance and sought to leverage it by building coalitions of netroots bloggers in service of their electoral aims. Campaigns have hired prominent bloggers to serve as liaisons to the netroots and coordinate digital strategy. The "Netroots Nation" conference (formerly known as "YearlyKos") even hosted all the major Democratic Party presidential candidates for a debate in the summer of 2007.

The 2008 Obama campaign leveraged the reach of the netroots for the purposes of strategic messaging and fund-raising (Kreiss 2012). Kreiss shows how new media offer novel resources for strategic actors vying for influence over the goals, direction, and identities of the campaigns, parties, and movements they are a part of. The 2008 Obama campaign strategically engaged in network building, which involved the creation and maintenance of ties with ideologically aligned blogger allies that it mobilized for informational purposes. The campaign then leveraged these ties, providing content to its network of allies and new journalistic online sites in the attempt to gain resources and influence primary voters early in the campaign, and it set the agenda of legacy media outlets to gain access to the wider electorate during the general election. This work shows that new media offer new opportunities for campaigns to gain influence, both symbolically in terms of narratives told about campaigns, and materially in terms of financial and other resources.

Civil society groups in the Democratic Party's extended network now also routinely engage in blogger outreach as part of their communications strategy to mobilize publics, influence key constituencies, and set the agenda for the general public and public officials. For example, a number of scholars have found that blogs play an agenda-setting role vis-á-vis the professional institutional press. Drezner and Farrell (2008) argue that "when key weblogs focus on a new or neglected issue—blogs can socially construct an agenda or interpretive frame that acts as a focal point for mainstream media, shaping and constraining the larger political debate." Others have made similar findings regarding intermedia agenda setting between political blogs and legacy journalistic institutions (Davis 2009; McKenna and Pole 2008; Messner and DiStaso 2008; Treymane 2007). In addition, a number of recent studies have looked closely at intermedia agenda setting in the context of contentious and electoral politics. Anderson (2010) shows how activists leveraged the platforms of bloggers and alternative media outlets to shape professional press coverage about an eviction in Philadelphia. Karpf (2010) shows how the Jim Webb campaign circulated the George Allen "Macaca" video through netroots actors to help generate professional press coverage and favorable framing.

In the pages below, we analyze an analogous process whereby the Protect NC Families campaign sought to strategically shape the agendas and narratives of intra-movement media to nationalize the campaign and secure resources.

Methods

This chapter grows out of a larger ethnographic project (Kreiss and Meadows 2013) that examined the messaging strategy of the Coalition to Protect All NC Families. We conducted a four-month ethnographic study of the campaign and the larger coalition, charting the creation and conduct of this electoral effort from its earliest days to the amendment's eventual passage to develop a rich analysis of the processes through which movements coordinate electoral efforts. Initially invited to observe the work at New Kind, a Raleigh, North Carolina–based consulting firm hired by the steering committee to coordinate the campaign's social media efforts, our research quickly grew to include the entire campaign, including the faith, communication, field, campus, and finance operations. During our four months of fieldwork, we conducted observations at the campaign's headquarters in Raleigh, the offices of steering committee members such as Equality NC, allied civil society organizations and churches, and field offices. We observed weekly campaign staff meetings and attended campaign-sponsored events across the state that targeted myriad groups, including journalists working for legacy outlets and social media producers, faith, rural, college, and LGBT communities, as well as general public audiences.

We draw the data we present here from observations of six weekly conference calls hosted by campaign staffers and consultants on Sunday nights in the weeks before the election for political bloggers, advocates, and specialized movement media outlets. These calls lasted between forty-five and sixty minutes. Campaign manager Jeremy

Kennedy and social media consultant Nation Hahn, who was appointed senior on-line strategist in the final weeks before the election, regularly hosted the weekly calls. A rotating cast of campaign staffers and consultants presented talks about campaign progress and strategy, including faith director Ryan Rowe and field director Chris MacNeil. Several of the campaign's national consultants participated in various conference calls, including media consultants Mark Armour and Chad Griffin of Armour Griffin Media Group, Inc., and pollsters Celinda Lake and Joshua Ulibarri of Lake Research Partners. Other participants included playwright and screenwriter Dustin Lance Black and campaign donor Todd Stiefel. While the audience ranged from five to almost two dozen, a stable core of five to six prominent bloggers consistently took part in the weekly calls.

The Institutional Review Board of the University of North Carolina at Chapel Hill, where we conducted this research, granted this proposal expedited review and approved the study along with a consent form that clearly stated the terms of the participation. Due to the public nature of the ballot measure, the fact that all the campaign's fund-raising and disbursements were matters of public record, and the availability of campaign staff and organizational information through the North Carolina State Board of Elections website, we could not protect the identities of the campaign staff and national consultants. As a result, we do not use pseudonyms in reporting our findings. In keeping with the terms of this study as clearly specified in consent forms, we therefore report data below using the real identities of participants who were part of the campaign and coalition, except in instances when doing so could potentially endanger participants' ongoing working relationships. At the same time, because we only had the formal consent of the campaign and its direct affiliates, we withhold here the names of the approximately fifty external actors who dialed into these conference calls over the course of the campaign.

Findings: Intramovement Agenda Setting

In the pages below, we analyze Protect All NC Families' weekly phone calls with prominent political bloggers on a number of levels. First, these conference calls served as opportunities for network building. Second, Kennedy and Hahn used these weekly calls to both create and propagate a narrative of the momentum of the campaign by leveraging bloggers' networks and publics. All these strategic communication efforts were designed to effect "intramovement agenda setting"—the efforts of the campaign, at the periphery of the national LGBT movement, to extend its messaging through sympathetic bloggers in order to get national donors and elites to pay attention to North Carolina and assist in the effort to defeat the amendment. Finally, we conclude this section by discussing how these bloggers were not simply the passive implements of strategic campaign communications, but autonomous actors whose suggestions and critiques were taken seriously.

Building Networks

Protect All NC Families faced a host of challenges in its fight to defeat Amendment One, none more daunting than historical precedent. As Stone has noted without overstatement, "Direct democracy tends to be devastating for the civil rights of minorities" (2012, 3). From 1974 to 2009, voters rejected LGBT rights in 70 percent of all direct legislative measures (ibid.). From 1998 to 2011, thirty states had attempted to pass constitutional bans against marriage equality via the ballot box, and thirty states had succeeded. Even more challenging from a narrative perspective, North Carolina was the only southern state without a constitutional ban on marriage equality. As one blogger noted, a consistent refrain in his comment section regarding the North Carolina campaign was "why bother?" (National Blogger Call, 3/25/12).

To counter the perceptions that Protect All NC Families' battle was lost before it began, and suggest that a victory was possible in a southern state, the campaign reached out to a core group of prominent LGBT political bloggers and media producers to help them craft a more positive, constructive narrative of the North Carolina effort. Staffers wanted to create the perception that the campaign was *winnable* given its fundraising, diverse coalition, and seeming momentum, and that it had *national implications* at the start of a cycle with marriage referenda on the ballots of four states in November 2012.

To convene these bloggers, the campaign first set up a national conference call in January 2012. Given the aim to create a positive narrative around Protect All NC Families' efforts, a central goal of each week's blogger conference call was to seed new media producers with stories and facts that were advantageous to the campaign. To cultivate ties, the campaign invited political bloggers to become "part of the team," "key members of the blog team," or "part of the family" in e-mail, phone, and social media outreach (National Blogger Call, 3/26/12). Staffers repeatedly made clear that they were available "offline" should any of the bloggers wish to discuss something one-on-one. Additionally, the campaign staff routinely offered to provide relevant photos, graphics, and links to online materials whenever bloggers requested them. In sum, the campaign staff worked to create at least the feel of a decentralized organization, one in which all voices were welcomed and valued.

In keeping with this communicative style, the information shared during the weekly calls was typically delivered under a mantle of transparency. As Kennedy said in March, "I feel like we don't have anything to lose as far as being transparent" (National Blogger Call, 3/18/12). To that end, each call featured an extended update on external polling numbers, fund-raising levels, advertising figures, and field efforts, as well as discussions of upcoming campaign events and key endorsements. Many of these updates featured specific numbers that bloggers could use as evidence of the campaign's progress. For instance, in March Hahn noted, "We're over 4,000 individual donors who've made over 5,500 contributions" (National Blogger Call,

3/26/12). Later in April, he announced, "We have surpassed the 1.6 million dollars raised mark" (National Blogger Call, 4/15/12).

In addition to information, staffers consistently provided bloggers with on-the-record access to key campaign actors, including national consultants and large donors. For instance, pollster and message strategist Celinda Lake provided a detailed discussion of the campaign's messaging strategy, which focused on the unintended harms the amendment's broad language could have on families, children, and victims of domestic violence. A few weeks later, media consultants Chad Griffin and Mark Armour spoke at length about their production decisions in crafting the campaign's television ads. During another call, philanthropist Todd Stiefel explained his reasons for donating $100,000 to Protect All NC Families.

Transparency was not, however, the same as full access or disclosure. Regardless of the affiliation of the speaker, the staffers, consultants, and donors papered over many internal, backstage debates and uncertainty and spoke with one voice regarding the campaign's public messaging. Bloggers received poll numbers from the campaign that portrayed it in the best possible light and were not privy to wrenching internal discussions over the lack of resources and hard decisions regarding outlays. Lake policed the message even among this network of autonomous supporters, reminding a blogger that "We're voting 'no' because this harms, this is so poorly written it harms people in North Carolina" (National Blogger Call, 3/26/12). Independent donors paraded on the conference call were on message, as when Stiefel stated he was motivated to donate "because of the harm" and not his broader interest in advancing the separation of church and state (National Blogger Call, 4/15/12). Griffin claimed that the campaign was winnable, if we "let the voters of the state know the harmful impacts of the measure to all North Carolina residents" (National Blogger Call, 4/22/12).

Creating a Momentum Narrative

In other words, concrete, detailed information and on-the-record access to these message-disciplined campaign actors was designed to deliver selective, positive news to bloggers advantageously positioned as both movement actors and media producers. This seeming good will and insider access was designed to seed these outlets with advantageous frames about the campaign. For instance, staffers made consistent appeals to the unprecedented progress of the North Carolina campaign, particularly through demonstrations of its fund-raising capacities. Typical of such assertions, Hahn noted in one March call, "We raised more money online this week than we have any other week to date for the campaign, which is fantastic!" (National Blogger Call, 3/18/12). On a number of calls, Hahn and Kennedy noted that Protect All NC Families had raised more money than any southern state except the much bigger and wealthier Florida, that it had outraised every previous progressive campaign effort in North

Carolina, and that it had launched an online store that more closely resembled the website of a presidential candidate than a statewide ballot referendum.

Staffers also highlighted the uniquely diverse nature of their coalition, which included not only the NAACP, but also a substantial number of faith communities. For instance, faith director Ryan Rowe spoke of the campaign's efforts to forge partnerships with the state's churches and congregations. As Rowe said, "You really can't engage a coalition in the South without engaging churches and houses of worship. . . . We really want to mobilize an army of people of faith" (National Blogger Call, 3/11/12). It is a truism that religion is central to southern culture. Aware of this fact, and perhaps in an effort to turn a perceived weakness into a strength, staffers often highlighted to the assembled bloggers the coalition the campaign built with the state's faith communities. For example, near election day, Hahn noted, "More than 400 clergy members signed an open letter against the amendment, including Episcopal and Methodist bishops. We're just really, really pleased with everyone who's speaking out" (National Blogger Call, 5/7/12).

Staffers also consistently made statements regarding the numerous endorsements the campaign received from a variety of celebrities and public figures. Emblematic of such communicative work was a statement by Hahn near election day: "So, again, high-profile surrogates across the spectrum continue to be very outspoken against this amendment. The Democratic governor is likely to continue to campaign against the amendment in the closing weeks, which is very helpful for us and somewhat unprecedented, particularly in a southern state" (National Blogger Call, 4/15/12). These types of statements often included details about specific endorsers. For instance, on April 15, Hahn and Kennedy focused bloggers' attention on Duke Energy's Jim Rogers, who was the first Fortune 500 CEO to oppose the amendment. By doing so, the campaign was able to simultaneously create the perception of momentum and highlight a story that they wanted circulated.

All this added up to a theme that ran throughout these calls and through the campaign more generally: staffers working to create a perception of momentum. This was not simply subterfuge to gain resources. Many staffers believed that this momentum was not only tangible, but that the campaign had a real shot at achieving victory on election day. The mood in the war room on election night was one of cautious optimism, tempered by an underlying sense that it could all fall apart. Indeed, if staffers did not at some level believe in the possibility of victory themselves, no matter how unlikely, it would have been hard to have the energy to sustain the round-the-clock work that went into the campaign.

For example, nearly every conference call opened with staffers and consultants highlighting several campaign milestones. Within the first few minutes of one illustrative March call, Kennedy and Hahn announced that "We have over 500 donors to ActBlue," "We've raised $150,000 in the last 48 hours," and "We will be announcing publicly that we are at the $1.1 million raised mark" (National Blogger

Call, 3/26/12). In addition to referencing these fund-raising milestones, Hahn announced that Freedom to Marry, Human Rights Campaign, and Minnesota United had all agreed to send e-mails to their lists on behalf of Protect All NC Families. Kennedy followed these announcements by contending that "I think we just might have one of the largest upsets in the country on our hands this year" (National Blogger Call, 3/26/12).

As evidenced by bloggers' statements during these weekly calls, staffers' efforts to legitimate the campaign and create a sense of momentum were effective. One blogger noted, "I'm up here in D.C., but it sure feels like there's momentum" (National Blogger Call, 3/26/12), and weeks later another said, "It's just really palpable, remarkable energy" (National Blogger Call, 5/7/12). These perceptions often led to blog posts that reflected the perceived momentum. For instance, in a representative post published days after a call, one blogger wrote:

> Polling shows that we can win—if we can get the resources. I have been very impressed with the team running the NC team. They are playing to win. And, playing hard. Their newest hashtag on twitter is #FirstinFight, a very clever play on the state's motto—and an indication of the key role NC has for the equality debate in 2012. Winning in North Carolina will keep up the momentum.

In conjunction with the bloggers' continued participation on the weekly calls throughout the campaign, their willingness to circulate campaign messages, and their general lack of contention in regards to campaign strategy, it appears the campaign succeeded in convincing these media producers of the electoral prospects of Protect All NC Families.

In addition to creating a perception that the campaign to defeat Amendment One was winnable, campaign staffers and consultants consistently positioned the North Carolina effort as crucial to the larger LGBT movement in the attempt to attract the resources and support of the broader movement. In March, Kennedy contended that "I think that this is really going to set the stage for the other ballot fights that we have coming up in November" (National Blogger Call, 3/26/12). Similarly, earlier in the month, Rowe referenced the fact that the campaign's faith efforts and strategies were being shared with national organizations such as the Human Rights Campaign and statewide campaigns like Minnesotans United for All Families, and that North Carolina's efforts could serve as a model for subsequent LGBT referenda efforts. In discussing the campaign's messaging strategy, national consultant and prominent progressive pollster Celinda Lake stated that:

> It is so nice to actually be in a place where we're seizing the offense on the children's message rather than just dreading the day when two princesses

come up on the air or whatever. And we think that this can really, being aggressive on this message and getting this out, can change, frankly, not only results in North Carolina, but change the context in which we operate in every single other state this year and beyond (National Blogger Call, 3/26/12).

Lake's position, as a veteran of many progressive campaigns who was active in previous LGBT referenda campaigns, presumably afforded her words a heightened importance and lent legitimacy to Protect All NC Families' claims to national significance.

Autonomous Actors

That the campaign staff was disciplined in being on-message during these weekly calls is not to suggest that all the information flows operated in a top-down direction or that these bloggers were simply dupes of the campaign. On multiple occasions, the assembled bloggers were used for their expertise with regard to online fund-raising and blogging best practices. For instance, as the exchange below makes clear, staffers deferred to several bloggers when planning a weeklong online fund-raising effort:

KENNEDY: Nation thinks I am too optimistic about this, but I think that I am going to get there. Do you think that it is unrealistic to put out that goal right up front or do you think that we should stick to something like $50,000?

BLOGGER 1: I think that $250,000 sounds a little high to lead with. . . . So, you can always, like I said in an earlier call, you can always, if it looks like your bomb is going really well and you started with a goal of $100,000 and you know you have $250,000, you can announce a change.

KENNEDY: The most that we have raised in one week online is $50,000.

BLOGGER 2: This is where I think context matters . . . if people understand that you have already raised $850,000, then getting to that million is $150,000 and that seems more relative and it's probably doable . . .

HAHN: What do you think about saying we have the donor stepped up and gave us $50,000 and offered to match the next $100,000 online . . .

BLOGGER 1: That is terrific. I think that is the best way to do this . . .

BLOGGER 2: It also takes the edge off. . . . I normally find myself resenting donors and going look, either just give the goddamn money or don't but don't hold it hostage for a lot of other people.

HAHN: My instinct is that we announce a funded donor and announce that they are going to match a certain amount from there . . .

BLOGGER 1: That sounds great.

As is true with most statewide ballot referenda, many staffers had little or no experience on electoral campaigns, and the campaign itself had a limited budget. In this case, Kennedy was a first-time campaign manager and Hahn had limited experience as a junior staffer on John Edwards' 2008 presidential primary bid. Due to these resource and knowledge constraints, and coupled with the fact that new media campaigning is a relatively new area of campaign practice, the expertise of political bloggers who had previously conducted online fund-raising was welcomed and valued, as was the support they gave the campaign on their blogs. As the following post reflects, the call participants leveraged their blogs to support the campaign's fund-raising efforts:

> That our team is fast closing in on the million dollar mark and 92% of their donations are in-state is a strong sign the campaign is prospering in the Tarheel state. But it's also a sign that nationally, the community has not rallied around North Carolina the way they did California in 2008, which saw a flood of money pouring in. Some have written this fight off as hopeless. But I don't buy that North Carolinians are just too southern and can't be reached and educated.

The fund-raising drive mentioned above raised more than $170,000, due in large part to the expertise and support of the blogging community.

At other times those assembled on these conference calls actively questioned the campaign's strategy. These bloggers were not simply passive implements of campaign strategy; they were autonomous actors who at times questioned and challenged the official campaign (although always within the general context of an alignment in the goal of winning). For example, the following is an exchange about the campaign's television advertisements:

BLOGGER: I have a question. This is SPEAKER. Can you hear me?
GRIFFIN: Sure, go ahead.
BLOGGER: OK, according to this 2010 site, the black population in this state is 21.5%, and congratulations to the campaign because they've found unprecedented public support from the NAACP and many black pastors on this issue, so I was wondering why that didn't make the cut for the TV ads given the opposition has been clear in both web ads and in local events, they have no intention of using people of color to make their case.
KENNEDY: I think my first answer to that would be, as Mark said, in the beginning we wanted to make sure we were telling real stories and an intimate story, and when I initially started this campaign I had hoped that we could run a $3 million campaign. And if we had had another million dollars like Mark said, we would love to make five or six ads that tell a whole lot of stories. And the two stories we are going forward with tomorrow were the best

and the most impactful stories that we could find of people that are willing to share their stories in this way, I think would be my first answer to that. So, and I think the research before the ads and after the testing of the actual ads themselves bore out the fact that our demographic voters do respond to the messages and the stories that we put forth here.

BLOGGER: Sorry, that didn't really answer the question. Just to follow up, since we already know we have plenty of people in state who are willing to go on camera and have spoken on web ads, I was wondering why we couldn't integrate that somehow into a message since we know the kind of vote that we're after.

GRIFFIN: Well, I mean a couple of things. First, we did want to create actual stories of people harmed, and we found a domestic violence victim who was willing to go on television and create risk to her own personal safety. Not so easy to actually ask someone who has beaten almost to death by someone to go on and share a story. Secondly, we created an ad based on a child who's losing her health insurance, and that ad has people of color in it for sure. I want to be clear, the messages that we use work with African-American voters and they work well, and in fact, in the ad tests, they move African-American voters, and I'm sure Josh can speak more to that.

This was, however, an extraordinary incident; in general there was convergence in the orientations and objectives of these autonomous actors. For example, in the final press conference before the vote, the assembled bloggers asked about the preparations for the day of and after. They also asked what they could do to help. The following exchange makes clear the tone of these calls and the campaign's perceptions of the value of these calls and the bloggers more generally:

BLOGGER: What specifically do you want us to do as bloggers and reporters, what are you looking for in addition to putting your new video out?

HAHN: I think as bloggers what you have been doing I don't know if I can even ask you to do any more than that. I think that you really have been telling the narrative of this campaign in a way that has been truthful, honest; I think that you have really been able to tell our story on a national level in a way that resonates with how I feel the campaign inside . . . I think that you can continue to do that for the next 48 hours and I think that although the drum beat has continued to be the polls are still tough and there is still a gap. I am not just blowing smoke when I say that I really do think that there is room for an upset, it's not impossible. Yes, I think continuing that narrative that we are fighting to the very last minute and you will see that, that is the last quote in the video that we just sent around is we are not going to go without a fight and that is really our theme for the next 48 hours (National Blogger Call, 5/7/12).

Conclusion

The case of Protect All NC Families suggests how new media have offered new opportunities for civic innovation. Although the Protect All NC Families campaign ultimately came up well short of its goal, it spurred massive amounts of participation in the campaign, from supporters having conversations about gay marriage with their extended social networks and canvassing their communities, to online donors helping fuel an impressive funding effort for a state campaign. Along the way, the campaign helped broker a set of new relationships with organizations such as the NAACP that has been replicated in states around the country, and it gained national visibility that may have influenced President Obama to announce his support for gay marriage the day after North Carolina's vote.

The extensive efforts at network building that the campaign engaged in throughout the months leading up to the election were certainly a factor in this success. The campaign created a distributed national network of media producers made up of professionals and amateurs, and people in the movement and outside of it. To some extent, this civic innovation was successful. The campaign mobilized hundreds of new donors, and there was a palpable sense of possibility and momentum that permeated both the campaign and the broader culture in the final weeks before the vote. There was, in other words, hope that a long-shot state could buck the southern trend of inequality.

While these efforts came up short, the campaign's innovative varieties of civic action will no doubt leave their legacy. The campaign was dismantled soon after the vote, but its primary actors went on to further the new civic and progressive networks they had crafted in North Carolina, in the South, and nationally. Meanwhile, other referenda in the months after North Carolina's vote and rulings in other courts turned the arc of history towards LGBT equality.

Note

1. This section is adapted from Kreiss 2012 and Kreiss and Meadows 2013.

References

Anderson, C. W. 2010. "Journalistic Networks and the Diffusion of Local News: The Brief, Happy News Life of the 'Francisville Four.'" *Political Communication* 27: 289–309.

Bennett, Lance. 2004. *Communicating Global Activism: Strengths and Vulnerabilities of Networked Politics*. In *Cyberprotest: New Media, Citizens and Social Movements*, ed. W. van de Donk, B. D. Loader, P. G. Nixon, and D. Rucht, 123–46. New York: Routledge.

Bimber, Bruce, Andrew J. Flanagin, and Cynthia Stohl. 2005. "Reconceptualizing Collective Action in the Contemporary Media Environment." *Communication Theory* 15: 365–88.

Carty, Victoria. 2002. "Technology and Counter-Hegemonic Movements: The Case of Nike Corporation." *Social Movement Studies* 1: 129–46.

Chadwick, Andrew. 2007. "Digital Network Repertoires and Organizational Hybridity." *Political Communication* 24: 283–301.

Davis, Richard. 2009. *Typing Politics: The Role of Blogs in American Politics.* New York: Oxford University Press.

Drezner, Daniel W., and Henry Farrell. 2008. "The Power and Politics of Blogs." *Public Choice* 134: 15–30.

Earl, Jennifer, and Katrina Kimport. 2008. "The Targets of Online Protest: State and Private Targets of Four Online Protest Tactics." *Information, Communication & Society* 11: 449–72.

———. 2011. *Digitally Enabled Social Change: Activism in the Internet Age.* Cambridge, MA: The MIT Press.

Fejes, Fred. 2011. *Gay Rights and Moral Panic: The Origins of America's Debate on Homosexuality.* New York: Palgrave MacMillan.

Fetner, Tina. 2008. *How the Religious Right Shaped Lesbian and Gay Activism.* Minneapolis: University of Minnesota Press.

Galvin, Daniel J. 2008. "Changing Course: Reversing the Organizational Trajectory of the Democratic Party From Bill Clinton to Barack Obama." *The Forum* 6: 1–21.

Haines, Herbert H. 1984. Black Radicalization and the Funding of Civil Rights: 1957–1970. *Social Problems* 32: 31–43.

Hirschman, Linda. 2012. *Victory: The Triumphant Gay Revolution.* New York: Harper.

Karpf, David. 2010. Macaca Moments Revisited . . . Electoral Panopticon or Netroots Mobilization? *Journal of Information Technology and Politics* 7: 143–62.

———. 2012. *The MoveOn Effect: The Unexpected Transformation of American Political Advocacy.* New York: Oxford University Press.

Kleidman, Robert. 1993. *Organizing for Peace: Neutrality, the Test Ban, and the Freeze.* Syracuse, NY: Syracuse University Press.

Kreiss, Daniel. 2012. *Taking our Country Back: The Crafting of Networked Politics from Howard Dean to Barack Obama.* New York: Oxford University Press.

Kreiss, Daniel, and Laura Meadows. 2013. "Campaigning from the Closet: The Contexts of Messaging During the Campaign to Defeat North Carolina's Amendment One." Presented at the annual Association for the Education in Journalism and Mass Communication conference, Washington, DC, August 2013.

Masket, Seth E., Michael T. Heaney, Joanne M. Miller, and Dara Z. Strolovich. 2011. "Networking the Parties: A Comparative Study of Democratic and Republican Convention Delegates in 2008." Paper presented at the conference on the State of the Parties: 2008 and Beyond, Ray C. Bliss Institute of Applied Politics, University of Akron, Cuyahoga Falls/ Akron, OH, October 2009. Retrieved from *opensiuc.lib.siu.edu/pn_wp/33.*

McAdam, Doug. 1982. *Political Process and the Development of Black Insurgency, 1930–1970.* Chicago: University of Chicago Press.

McAdam, Doug, and Sidney Tarrow. 2010. "Ballots and Barricades: On the Reciprocal Relationship Between Elections and Social Movements." *Perspectives on Politics* 8: 529–42.

McKenna, Laura, and Antoinette Pole. 2008. "What Do Bloggers Do: An Average Day on an Average Political Blog." *Public Choice* 134: 97.

Messner, Marcus, and Marcia W. Distaso. 2008. "The Source Cycle: How Traditional Media and Weblogs Use Each Other as Sources." *Journalism Studies* 9: 447–63.

Meyer, David S. 2003. "Political Opportunity and Nested Institutions." *Social Movement Studies* 2: 17–35.

Schwartz, Mildred A. 2010. "Interactions Between Social Movements and U.S. Political Parties." *Party Politics* 16: 587–607.

Staggenborg, Suzanne, and Josee Lecomte. 2009. "Social Movement Campaigns: Mobilization and Outcomes in the Montreal Women's Movement Community." *Mobilization* 14: 163–80.

Stone, Amy. 2011. "Dominant Tactics in Social Movement Tactical Repertoires: Anti-Gay Ballot Measures, 1974–2008." *Research in Social Movements, Conflicts, and Change* 31: 141–74.

———. 2012. *Gay Rights at the Ballot Box*. Minneapolis: University of Minnesota Press.

Tilly, Charles. 1978. *From Mobilization to Revolution*. Reading, MA: Addison-Wesley.

———. 2004. *Contention & Democracy in Europe, 1650–2000*. New York: Cambridge University Press.

Tremayne, Mark. 2007. *Blogging, Citizenship, and the Future of Media*. New York: Routledge.

5

Civic Communication in a Networked Society

Seattle's Emergent Ecology

LEWIS A. FRIEDLAND

■ Throughout the history of the American republic, there has been a close relationship between the organization of communication and the form of civic life. From the newspapers and committees of correspondence of the colonial era to the strong relationship between newspaper reading and civic voluntarism, communication and civic life have formed an interlocking system of relationships (Brown 1991; Pasley 2003).

Our democratic and civic institutions and the forms of communication that hold them together shape and constrain each other. This balance is strongly affected by two traditions that run through American history and are sometimes at odds. The first is government support for building communication infrastructure (starting with the roads and postal system of colonial America) and the widespread understanding that we need to regulate communication to ensure fair and equal access (Starr 2004). The second is civic voluntarism, the idea that democratic action best emerges from the community level, and that accomplishing community goals is (sometimes) better done through association than through government action (Putnam 2000; Tocqueville 2004). While these traditions are often posed as being at odds with each other, they are in fact two poles of the same "ecosystem" of communication and civic life in the United States.

The purpose of this chapter is to explore this balance in relation to what I call the civic communication ecology, or the relationships between civic life and local communication. This relationship is rapidly spiraling out of balance. The era of civic life in the United States from roughly 1930 to 1975, the decline of which has been chronicled by Putnam and others, is reaching a point of breakdown because the social conditions of life that underpinned the forms of civic engagement characteristic of that era no longer predominate (Dahlgren 2009; Couldry 2012). At the same time, a networked communication system has emerged in the past two decades, with breathtaking speed and worldwide scope, that is fundamentally changing the lifeworld of all Americans but particularly those under thirty (Bennett 2007, 2008; Friedland and Morimoto 2005; Mindich 2005; Morimoto and Friedland 2011, 2013).

In the previous era, arguably, there was mutual support between the civic and communication ecologies. The linchpin of both was the daily newspaper, which chronicled civic life and provided critical information on government and community that, in turn, made decision making possible. Whether good citizens made for strong newspapers or vice versa is a debate that has never quite been settled. But that the two together drove both local democratic politics and civic association on the one hand, and the identification of citizens with local community on the other, is quite clear.

Now we see those systems moving apart. As the older system of civic life erodes, particularly in local communities, the new system of networked, online communication is rapidly becoming a parallel world, although one that pervades and remains pervaded by local community. As newspapers continue to economically decline and frantically scramble for a foothold in the online world, a range of civic communication alternatives have started to emerge. These hybrids are a mixture of old media and new, nonprofit and for-profit, professional and amateur (Anderson, Bell, and Shirkey 2013; Deuze 2007; Robinson 2007).

It is too early to know which of these forms will succeed, or indeed whether any will. But this chapter looks closely at the actual alternatives. It begins with the decline of newspapers and how this old system did or did not serve local civic life, then moves to a review of the range of alternatives to the newspaper-driven system that are starting to emerge and explains why we use the term "ecology" and what it means.

I then move to examine the civic communication ecology in Seattle, one of the most advanced in the United States. In particular, I examine three interlocking sets of institutional processes and their relationships: government support for civic communication; communication support in local civil society; and the interplay of the older and emerging media systems. The main claim is that for local civic community to thrive there must be a rich layer of communication capacity at the grass roots, in neighborhoods and the "civic spaces" of a community, and in the media system itself. Further, these two sets of institutions—civic and media—reinforce each other in the new media world, just as they did in the old, but in different and more complex ways. Finally, I point to the role of government in helping make this happen, both directly and indirectly, showing that civic communication ecologies are not just "natural" but they are built through institutions and therefore can be changed and grown.

Before examining the older system of news and civic life, I look briefly at "civic communication ecology" and why I use this term. In sociology, the attempt to understand urban communities as "environments" goes back to Robert Park (1923) and the Chicago School in the 1920s. In this older usage, communities were studied in terms of space and territory to try and understand how this larger environmental pattern of development affected both smaller spatial units (e.g., neighborhoods) and social insti-tutions within the city (e.g., families, occupational patterns, etc.). Amos Hawley (1950) advanced the study of human ecology to include the study of both spatial patterns and social processes, the perspective of "collective life as an adaptive process consisting of an interaction of environment, population, and organization" out of which emerges the ecosystem (Hawley 1986, 3–4). Beginning in the 1970s, students of communities' interorganizational networks (Galaskiewicz 1979; Laumann and Pappi 1976) examined how the interlocking network structures of communities depended on and shaped each other. Communication scholars (Monge and Contractor 2003) began to examine how networks of communication coevolved with organizational and social structures in a more formal way and to look at how "networks of networks" in local communities made some kinds of civic action possible (Friedland and McLeod 1999).

This chapter applies this theory to the problem of the interacting systems of civic life (the ways that citizens in local communities band together to engage in democratic and public life) and the local communication system (the sum of local media, and the networks of communication that have grown up with the rise of the Internet). These structures have evolved over time: the form of local governments, schools, and associations in the demo-cratic and civic sector, the institutions of newspapers and television, and now emerging social media have changed, and these take on a life of their own. That means that local community members may choose to act together but that first they have to act within the "containers" of these social structures, and second they can only act on the information that they have, which is shaped by both local social and communication networks.

The Older Civic Communication Ecology

The era of the modern newspaper runs roughly from 1900 to 2000. It is rooted in the Progressive Era, in the ideal of providing rational citizens with the information they need to make the decisions (particularly voting) to govern themselves. Since Walter Lippmann's (1922) devastating critique of the ideal of the rational citizen in a modern republic, we have understood that most citizens navigate the informational world looking for what they need to know within the restricted sphere of their daily lives. Further, as Schudson (1978) and Hamilton (2006) have demonstrated, this rational ideal of objective coverage, and the corollary separation of fact and opinion, is rooted in the competitive needs of the newspaper for advertising. No potential reader should be alienated so that no advertiser is left behind.

Despite these limitations, newspapers in the traditional civic ecology did fulfill core functions that allowed civic and democratic life to thrive in the local community. First, newspapers provide a *common information environment*, one that was, in principle, pub-licly accessible to all citizens. The newspaper "surveilled" the broad range of local institu-tions—government, business, and nonprofit—and allowed any citizen willing and able to buy a newspaper to indirectly monitor their activities (Lasswell 1948).[1]

By gathering the broad civic environment into a public report, newspapers also created possibilities for action, both direct and indirect. Citizens could intervene directly by expressing their views in elections, phone calls and direct contact with public officials, and letters to the editors. They could intervene indirectly through local associations and by activating civic, community, and interpersonal networks in response to news in order to influence decisions through the medium of associational influence, or through collective action (Katz and Lazarsfeld 1955; Laumann and Pappi 1976).

The results of reporting sometimes became a stimulus to public discussion. The agenda setting through which the newspapers (and also local television) established what was most salient at any given time in the local community was the most powerful mode of framing local issues. Agenda setting, in its classical formulation, established that the media don't tell people what to think, but what to think about (McCombs and Shaw 1972). In this way they effectively set the boundaries for local discussion: what issues would be discussed by whom and through what sorts of groups or networks.

The newspaper has also functioned to *integrate* the local community directly and indirectly. First, the newspaper has played a central role in creating a *local identity*, or an *imagined community* (B. Anderson 1991). As great cities emerged, the newspaper wove together the stories of multiple neighborhoods into a larger narrative of the city. Later, during and after postwar suburbanization, the newspaper was the central institution that created the narrative of the metropolitan area from the patchwork of regional suburbs. The newspaper was the primary medium that made different groups—across racial, ethnic, and class lines—*visible* to each other, even if often through a distorted mirror, and created the possibility for a broader civic identity with others. Newspaper coverage, at its best, was a catalyst for civic solidarity with both like and unlike groups by enabling citizens to visualize a common fate (Friedland and McLeod 1999; Janowitz 1952; Kaniss 1991).

Beyond social integration, the local media helped generate and sustain (but also at times commercialize and homogenize) local culture and tradition. Local cultural identities were transmitted through many different regions of social life, within ethnic and racial communities and neighborhoods. But to the extent that these were generalized, made visible, and sustained over time, local media played an important role in their transmission.

Finally, and not least, the local newspaper functioned to *entertain* not only through nationally syndicated features like comics and advice columns, but also through its coverage of sports at all levels, of local food, restaurants, and lifestyles, and of the arts. Even when local reporters wrote on nationally distributed movies, television, and books, they helped generate a distinctively local discussion and opinion.

This picture certainly understates the role of conflicting interest, exclusion, and hierarchy. To be sure, the local newspaper was most often an elite institution, whether in the town or city. Publishers were, of necessity or choice, businessmen (and almost all were men) who actively sought the formal and informal support of local elites, and vice versa. While a broad literature exists debating the extent to which editors and reporters exercised news judgment autonomously from the wishes of publishers and local elites, the setting of public agendas has been largely a top-down affair, in which authority resided with a combination of institutional and political elites and experts. Reporters and some editors might have circumvented these strictures some of the time, but the overall institutional routine reflected elite dominance (Gans 2004; Schudson 2003; Tuchman 1978).

Further, the integrated local narrative also reflected the interests of elites, whether through commercial boosterism, initiatives for "urban renewal" (that devastated some neighborhoods for the sake of suburbanization), or the commercial interests of local sports teams. The local narrative generated by the media may have served integrative functions, but this integration was certainly not always in the equal interest of all citizens, and in some cases it benefited some to the direct detriment of others (Logan and Molotch 1987; Molotch and Lester 1974).

Finally, local television amplified and extended all these processes. Newspapers are and always have been engines of local reporting at the multiple layers of urban and metropolitan life. In the heyday of the metropolitan newspaper, through the 1990s, even a moderate-sized city of 250,000 might have a newspaper editorial staff in the hundreds, while a television news operation in the same city might have had a dozen to twenty. Television news always has relied on the newspaper to do the bulk of local reporting, while providing a visual narrative to (some) stories that were still deemed to be of some public significance. Most air time, however, was filled with a mixture of episodic tragedy—crime, car crashes, fires—and feel-good stories and soft news, weather, and sports. To the extent that a public agenda existed, it was largely *set* by the newspaper but on television more people saw that agenda *portrayed*, even if only in a few voice-overs sandwiched in between more dramatic visuals. So the local media ecology, in its mid-to-late twentieth-century form, has been driven by newspapers for most serious news coverage and public policy agenda setting, and visualized, episodically, by television for a majority of local viewers (Kurpius 1997; McManus 1994).

This *media ecology* in the latter half of the twentieth century, then, represented at best an incomplete, partial, and skewed *civic ecology*; at worst, a distorted and elite-driven one, further reduced to the banal and visual on local television. Nonetheless, this media ecology did intersect with the existing civic infrastructure to enable *some* degree of civic capacity building and civic mobilization, however imperfect. Further, it was a *necessary* component of civic life and democratic participation in the form of community that dominated through the latter part of the twentieth century.

Beyond the effects of media on local civic life, in a federal republic the generation of an activist civic culture, social integration, and cultural tradition at the local level ramifies upward. That is to say, civic and democratic identity and action are not, for the most part, generated at the state or federal level, but are built up out of the repertoire of habits and routines learned and reproduced in local communities. This is particularly true in the United States with its strong cultural-political legacy of voluntarism and localism. So, in a real sense, elements of national and state civic identity also rest on the generative ability of local civic culture. Because this is true, the role of *local* communication in generating civic identity remains critical to the regeneration of a vibrant national civic life.

The Decline of the Newspaper Business Model

Despite the centrality of the newspaper in maintaining civic life for most of the twentieth century, it is unquestionably in decline and some would say endangered. The causes for decline are complex, but we can point to two major trends. The first is the long-term decline of readership. The second is the failure of the newspaper business model.

Newspaper readership in the United States as a percentage of the population began to peak as early as the 1950s, but this was masked by the continuing growth of absolute numbers as more citizens received higher levels of education. By the 1970s, however, circulation began a steady absolute decline that continues today. In 2007, weekday circulation in the United States fell to its lowest point since 1945. Between 2008 and 2010, eight major newspapers and chains, such as McClatchy and Lee, in the United States filed for bankruptcy (although subsequently reorganized) or were being kept alive by their creditors (Meyer 2009). US newspapers derive more of their revenue from advertising than their European counterparts (73 percent to 57 percent) and so have been more vulnerable to both secular declines in readership and the severe economic downturn that began in 2008 (Pew Research Center Project for Excellence in Journalism 2011).

There are many reasons for the decline of readership. The shift from an industrial to postindustrial economy and the rise of television, along with growing suburbanization and car commuting killed afternoon newspapers. Television news made the morning newspaper less timely for most event-driven news. As discussed, the decline of traditional social capital in local communities both drove and was driven by declining readership in a vicious cycle.

But the greatest blow to newspaper readership is undoubtedly the Internet for (at least) two reasons: the shift to online reading (without pay) and the related destruction of the newspaper business model. First, younger age cohorts, those thirty and below, have all but abandoned readership of the news in paper form. Even those socialized into newspaper reading now read almost exclusively online. So while news readership has not declined anywhere near the extent of news*paper* readership, those reading the journalism produced by newspapers are increasingly more likely to find it through search or social media.

This might be a positive step toward a new journalism model *if* newspapers, still the primary producers of news, received either the brand recognition for their product or the bulk of the revenue. But online readers rarely associate news found through search or social media content with its original published source, and advertising rates for online news are in the range of 10 percent of print rates and falling. Further, newspapers have traditionally relied on three legs for revenue: subscribers, advertising, and classified advertising. Classified revenue imploded with the growth of Craigslist starting in the late 1990s. So even if *readership* holds steady or even grows, advertising and classified revenues are in a downward spiral. The current business model of local newspaper journalism is untenable (Kirchhoff 2009).

Newspapers, then, are caught in a trap. The changing structure of local community, disinvestment in traditional local social capital, and shifts in consumption and advertising patterns alone would have severely challenged the business model of the twentieth-century newspaper. But the rise of the Internet, the shift to online reading among those under thirty-five, the shift of revenue to search and social media, and advertising rates at 10 percent or less of print have killed it.

Is there a form of local journalism that can replace the traditional newspaper while remaining connected to the civic life of local communities? The news industries themselves are, not surprisingly, concerned primarily with their survival as profit-making institutions. So if news consumers demand less news about local civic and public life, and an alternative product can be profitably supplied (e.g., more local sports, lifestyle, etc. without as much (or any) local reporting), then for corporations whose mission is to sell information to consumers at a profit, the radically reduced local newsroom is an acceptable substitute.

But critics have suggested that news is too important to leave to private enterprise, which may skim the profitable information cream while leaving communities without journalism. The major responses to this "news as information commodity" model treat news as a *public good*, that is, something that the public needs but which cannot be produced profitably by the private sector. Former *Washington Post* editor Len Downie and scholar Michael Schudson have called for a large increase in funding for news from the nonprofit sector (Downie and Schudson 2009). They argue that philanthropies should step into the void left by the commercial and technological retreat *and* that they are capable of doing so. Robert McChesney and John Nichols (2010) argue that only the government is capable of providing the capital necessary for adequate news provision for democracy. They have proposed a federally funded $35 billion voucher program to separate federal funding from potential control.

Both proposals are important and innovative, and would have extraordinarily positive effects on civic and public life if adopted. But the current cost of producing daily local journalism in the United States can be *conservatively* estimated at $6 billion (Friedland and Konieczna 2014). Much of this cost (almost 50 percent) goes to the costs of print and distribution, so if we assume that this number is closer to a bare minimum of $3 billion for maintaining current operations in an online environment, this is what would be required from the philanthropic sector. However, *total* philanthropic giving in the United States in 2007 (before the recession) was $309.7 billion, and giving for news and communication that year (minus public broadcasting) was about $100 million. It seems unrealistic to assume that charitable giving could grow to fill this gap. The McChesney-Nichols proposal faces other obvious difficulties. Amidst economic downturn, political dysfunction, and Republican control of Congress, it is nearly unimaginable that a $35 billion allocation for a new journalism program, or even the $3 billion barest minimum that we estimate, would be enacted in the next decade.

So we are left with a hard dilemma. Is there any way that the current news industry might transition to an online business model while maintaining, or even growing, its commitments to local, civic, and public reporting? And if so how might foundations and nonprofit organizations, and, perhaps governments, realistically contribute to this process with the limited funds they have in a transition period?

There are no simple answers to these questions, but there are some emerging models that combine local media ecologies and robust civic ecologies to begin to create new forms of local journalism with civic focus and outcomes. There are still relatively few that are effective in both journalistic and civic terms and economically sustainable. Those that exist tend to be in communities that have robust local media, a strong civic life, or both. So the new models may be suitable for their specific niches (cities with high social capital and strong media), but not elsewhere. We'll return to this problem in the conclusion. But even if these models are not replicable elsewhere, they offer one realistic vision of what a new civic communication ecology might look like.

New Civic Communication Ecologies

One thing we know about the emerging civic communication ecology is that despite the rapid growth in new forms of online community news, and the steadily declining coverage in traditional outlets, traditional news institutions remain the primary original source of local news in the United States, although the stream of news from these same institutions is in a steady and rapid decline.

The most comprehensive study to date of a single city media ecology, Baltimore, by the Pew Center for Excellence in Journalism (2010) found that the *Baltimore Sun* in 2009 produced 32 percent fewer stories on any subject than in 1999 and a full 73 percent fewer than in 1991, when there were two competing newsrooms. Although there were fifty-three news outlets (from blogs to talk radio), 83 percent of all stories on the six topics researched were repetitive. Of the 17 percent that did contain new information, virtually all came from traditional media, and of these half came from the *Sun*. The study finds that new media have mainly served as an "alert system and way to disseminate stories from other places." A 2010 J-Lab study (Schaffer 2010) of Philadelphia's media ecosystem finds a 17 percent decline in public affairs stories from 2006 to 2009 in the *Inquirer*, although it also found more than 260 active blogs, public policy, or niche web sites, with 60 having "some journalistic DNA, in that they report on the news, not just comment on it." The Philadelphia study, however, still finds the same paradox amidst a rapid deterioration of the traditional media: old media are still the wellspring of much city coverage. Hindman (2011), in a systematic study of one hundred markets, found that local news sites are overwhelmingly online posts or reposts of local newspapers and television stations.

Making sense of this new environment is not easy. New sites proliferate daily and even new *types* of sites are emerging every six months or so. Furthermore, there are different configurations of old and new media types, and the pattern of their connections can be very different. Still, it is worth cataloguing the kinds of sites that are emerging to understand what elements are beginning to combine in specific communities.

This classification moves from the "top" of the ecosystem, the most comprehensive levels of local community coverage, to the most micro- and niche-focused types of sites (Friedland 2001; Schaffer 2009).

Local newspapers online. Local newspapers, especially their online editions, remain at the top of the local media ecosystem, providing much of the content repurposed by others. Local newspapers also remain at the center of the civic ecology, connecting disparate networks and groups across community, city, and metropolitan boundaries. Powerful local online newspapers collaborating with other media are the most powerful examples of how a new civic ecosystem might work. The *Seattle Times* offers among the best examples.

Local comprehensive news sites. These sites are generally run by traditional journalists who have made the move to a pure online model by choice or necessity (often after layoffs or buyouts). They seek to provide a comprehensive account of local news and public policy, but not the complete daily report of a newspaper. They are "second reads," providing depth and enterprise that the daily newspaper can or does not (Konieczna 2014). Local comprehensives generally are nonprofit or mixed models, often heavily supported by foundations, especially the Knight Foundation. Leading examples include the *MinnPost, Voice of San Diego, Texas Tribune, New Haven Independent,* and *St. Louis Beacon.* The local comprehensives are thriving with local publics, but to date none is independently sustainable, and all rely on national or local foundation and philanthropic support.

Local comprehensive civic sites. Similar in structure to the local comprehensives, these sites are also city-wide and sometimes engage in policy reporting, but are more focused on community issues and questions, whether urban or ethnic. They have paid staff at their hub, but usually smaller numbers of reporters. They act more as editor/aggregators of local civic news, drawing from smaller micro-local sites, neighborhood or ethnic sites, newspapers, and newsletters. Leading examples include the *Gotham Gazette* and *Twin Cities Daily Planet.* Some, like the *Madison Commons,* are located in journalism schools.[2]

City region sites. Often run by professional journalist-entrepreneurs, city region sites cover more than a single neighborhood or cover large neighborhoods in major metropolitan areas. City region sites function much like traditional community newspapers online, specializing in urban regions or towns that lie below the ability of the metro newspaper to cover well, and they often include significant government, community, and policy reporting on their neighborhood or region. Leading examples are the *West Seattle Blog*, discussed below, and *Oakland Local*.

Micro-local, hyperlocal, or neighborhood sites. Often run by one or two individuals, usually working as citizen journalists, these are rarely economically self-sustaining (although many make some money). Micro-local sites concerned with civic and public issues generally focus on neighborhood schools, development issues, business, and community events. Some have grown or merged into city region sites.

Niche sites. These sites concentrate on single issues or clusters like schools or politics. More frequently, they discuss local lifestyle options, at the community-wide, city region, or neighborhood level.

Corporate local news systems. These are local (city or town) news sites set up by national news corporations that both generate and aggregate local news that can generate advertising revenue (e.g. Patch/AOL). They may originate some news and so contribute to the civic ecosystem indirectly, but they are not a major source of original content.

The challenge in understanding the emerging civic media ecology is in capturing the configuration of these elements in different communities and understanding the dynamics of these patterns. For example, while almost all newspapers now have online editions, fewer have made the transition to a robust online edition that has many connections to other online resources in their local communities. Fewer still have done this in a way that is oriented toward civic or public life. There are clear ecological constraints as well: local comprehensive, comprehensive civic, or city regional sites are less likely to exist in smaller cities because they lack the density of resources or demand to support them (although there are some exceptions). Similarly, niche sites can only emerge where the niche is large enough to support them, whether civic (e.g., about local schools) or lifestyle-oriented (e.g., sailing, local brewing). Right now, we have a poor understanding of either the distribution of the types across different communities, or their interaction, so generalizations about emerging patterns are premature (Kurpius, Metzgar, and Rowley 2010).

The case study that follows is an attempt to demonstrate what a sustainable civic media ecology looks like at the level of a single metropolitan case, what sorts of patterns or combinations of the above elements it would include, and how would they be connected and sustainable.

The Case of Seattle

The city of Seattle provides something of an ideal type, at least in current terms, of what a civic communication environment might look like. It begins with a rich civic environment, which in turn has made successful government support for civic life in the neighborhoods possible. Seattle's traditional media (newspapers and to a lesser extent TV) are making a successful transition to the new media ecology in ways that encourage and benefit from this civic environment. Beyond traditional media, the city has an extraordinary range of online media addressing broad and niche audiences. Its broad city regional sites, covering large sections of the city (e.g., West Seattle) are among the best in the nation; they gather news from neighborhoods under their umbrella and support the thriving micro-local neighborhood coverage that is diverse and rooted in community. Taking all these elements together points toward what a sustainable *civic media economics* would look like: a mix of government support, civically engaged media, traditional commercial media economics, entrepreneurial startups, new local advertising models, and national and local foundation support.

These very strengths mean that Seattle is not a "typical" US city. Still, it provides one of the best cases of a broad range of civic communication and tells an important story of what might be possible in other cities given the right conditions.[3]

First, Seattle has a thriving, postindustrial economy centered on information, which in turn both produces and draws a population that is more educated, prosperous, literate, and technically oriented than the United States as a whole. Second, Seattle has a rich history of the use of public policy at the municipal level to develop civic engagement and address social inequalities of resources, training, and opportunity. Third, this public policy has been explicitly and systematically applied to the domain of communication and information, so the city itself has sought to develop information equity, transparency, and positive civic communication as a foundation of governance. Fourth, Seattle has a long history of independent journalism and communication activism that has spawned an independent media culture. Fifth, and not least, each of these four conditions feed a rich new media ecology at every layer of civic life: individuals and small groups, neighborhoods, communities of interest, "regional" media (covering city sectors), and the larger canopy of the existing commercial media system.

This case concentrates primarily on the city's investment in civic communication and the emerging media ecology before finally evaluating what Seattle may tell us about the more general challenges involved in developing a democratic communication system in the digital environment of the twenty-first century (Durkin, Glaisyer, and Hadge 2010).[4]

Economy and Population

Seattle is the major city of the US northwest, with a 2011 population of 608,660 in a metro area of almost 3.5 million, making it the fifteenth-largest metropolitan area in the United States and the twenty-third largest city. It is among the most wired cities in the

United States based on broadband access, usage, and wi-fi availability, and in 2009 ranked second behind only Silicon Valley among US high-tech centers. Among its internationally known companies are Microsoft, Amazon, Expedia, Boeing, Nintendo, and T-Mobile.[5]

Beyond these large companies, Seattle has what the city's chief technology officer Bill Schrier calls an "ecosystem of technology startups. Folks who got tired, left Microsoft, made money and started their own companies" (personal communication, October 7, 2011). Eighty-eight percent of Seattle residents have computers at home. Seattle residents, by city percentage, are among the most highly educated in the United States, with 47 percent of those twenty-five and older having a BA or higher and almost 90 percent holding a high school degree. In 2010 it was ranked America's second most literate city among those with populations over 250,000, based on six key indicators: newspaper circulation, number of bookstores, library resources, periodical publishing resources, educational attainment, and Internet resources. According to data collected in 2000, approximately 70 percent of residents are white, 8.5 percent African American, 13.5 percent Asian or Pacific Islanders, and 5.3 percent Latino; percentages of nonwhites have risen consistently over the past decade ("America's Most Literate Cities, 2010").[6]

On the whole, then, Seattle is more wired, better employed, more highly educated, and whiter than the nation as a whole. At the same time, it has working-class, ethnic, and immigrant populations that are both geographically concentrated and, in some cases, lack resources. Through systematic public policy, Seattle has attempted to address questions of equity among neighborhoods, including information inequity, as a problem of governance that affects the city as a whole, which makes it distinct, if not unique, in the nation. So the story of public policy and governance is essential to understanding its civic communication infrastructure.[7]

Seattle Governance Policy for Civic Communication

Seattle demonstrates that public policy and civic governance make a major difference in whether communication opportunities are extended to all citizens and, if so, whether these opportunities lead to a richer *civic* communication infrastructure. In Seattle, systematic public policy for neighborhood governance, begun almost twenty-five years ago, has significantly shaped the possibilities of broader civic communication participation, beginning with attempts to forge new relations between citizens and government. This policy rests on three distinct pillars: a general policy of neighborhood governance, community technology for neighborhood development and equity, and information governance for equity.

Neighborhood Governance

Seattle's efforts to develop neighborhood-based governance began in 1987–88, when "district councils" were formed to represent independent community councils in its then twelve major neighborhoods. An Office of Neighborhoods was established, along with a city-wide Neighborhood Council consisting of representatives from each district council (Sirianni 2007, 2009). For almost two decades, this citizen-led, neighborhood-based planning grew through an active Department of Neighborhoods, led starting in 1988 by long-time community organizer Jim Diers, who had worked in the south side neighborhood of Rainier Valley in the 1970s. Among the core design principles were "building relationships and partnerships, citizen coproduction of public goods, deliberative civic democracy, and asset-based community development" (Sirianni 2009).[8]

Two key programs developed by the Department of Neighborhoods (DON) laid the foundation for *common civic space* throughout the community. First, in 1989 a neighborhood matching fund was established, which grew from $150,000 to $4.5 million by 2001 before it was slowly cut back for budgetary reasons. The city awarded grants to neighborhood-generated projects that committed to matching in-kind contributions, cash, and labor from citizens. Among the many types of projects developed over the decade were community playgrounds, arts, and gardens; neighborhood environmental projects; and community learning centers, the latter often computer-equipped. In this way, the DON and matching fund contributed to the development of (1) a city-wide civic culture of collaboration and public work with broad equity and diversity, (2) common civic spaces, and (3) *community-wide communication infrastructure*, more evenly distributed than in many US communities. This in turn laid the foundation for a broader, common communication infrastructure as new media blossomed in the 2000s.

Also, the Department of Neighborhoods established neighborhood service centers in all twelve (later thirteen) Seattle neighborhood districts. The centers have served individuals in the tradition of "little city halls," providing a place to pay taxes and utility bills, traffic violations, etc. But they also provide applications for neighborhood matching grants and free public access to the Internet. The neighborhood service centers also engage in civic convening designed to add democratic capacity to Seattle governance. Service center coordinators act as organizers, staff members for the district councils, and elected leaders.

The neighborhood governance system has suffered some erosion since its peak under Mayor Paul Schell from 1998 to 2002 (Sirianni 2007, 2009), but it has nonetheless contributed to a framework within which specific civic communication initiatives can flourish.

Community Technology Program: Extending Neighborhood Governance to Civic Communication

The Community Technology Program (CTP), located within the city's Department of Information Technology (DOIT), lies at the heart of Seattle's effort to build and sustain neighborhood civic communication. CTP is headed by David Keyes, who joined the city in 1997 with a background in social work and communications. Since 1998, the CTP has run a Technology Matching Fund, separate from but inspired by the Department of Neighborhoods Matching Grants. A total of $1.9 million has been disbursed for 139 community communication projects. Civic and community groups can apply for up to $20,000 in matching funds. There is a focus on underserved and diverse communities, and a citizen board guides the awards.

The CTP has actively leveraged neighborhood contributions: Keyes estimates a three-to-one return on its investment. In 2007–08 more than $230,000 was disbursed in matching funds. Thirteen funded projects served more than 1,343 individuals at twenty funded locations including 81 seniors, 751 young people, 870 immigrants and refugees, and 775 low-income individuals. Of those, 46 percent gained technology-based employment skills and 55 percent completed ESL and citizenship education. Public terminals were placed in ten neighborhood service centers, two police stations, and ten community learning centers. Free broadband access was provided at 130 locations at more than 500 computers. Beyond wi-fi in community centers, the CTP helped provide free public wi-fi to more than 16,000 users in 2008, expanding access to citizens in parks and other open spaces (Keyes 2009).[9]

The range of grants awarded in 2010 offer a strong picture of the role that the Technology Matching Fund grants play in bridging the digital divide in Seattle, expanding access and inclusion, and stimulating civic communication. Twenty-four grants totaling $300,000 were awarded, including for expanding low-income access and training in the South Lake Union neighborhood center and public housing. Low-income women were taught basic life and computer skills. Computer resources for the homeless were expanded through the Plymouth Housing Group. Young women in the juvenile justice system learned the media skills to tell their personal stories at the Reel Grrls media boot camp, and Native American youth were funded to build dance arcade games compatible with their culture. The Vietnamese Friendship Association is creating a media lab for Vietnamese youth that includes resume building and college application training, and the New Horizons Ministries helps homeless and street youth to get off the streets. Seniors in the Central Area Senior Center received upgraded computer labs and skills instruction. Assistive technology evaluation centers were built by the Alliance of People with Disabilities and Provail. And to increase civic engagement directly, the Rainier Beach Community Empowerment Coalition 2.0 began training and support for an innovative team of "information stewards" to manage an online "information and exchange commons" to improve the flow of communication among Rainier Beach neighbors. As part of this mission, in 2010 the Rainier Beach Coalition established "Seattle Freedom Net," which encourages and trains young people to become citizen journalists using cell phones, iPads, cameras, and social media, contracting with Ken Gilgren, a Seattle community media veteran for training. The Knowledge as Power Citizen Seattle Outreach developed an online civic engagement portal that helps residents track legislation on civic issues. Each of these projects met real information needs of distinct and specific communities, bridged the digital divide, and provided essential skills, all of which are preconditions for civic participation in an online community. The Rainier Beach Coalition and Knowledge as Power more directly advanced citizen use of information and communication for civic engagement.[10]

Beyond the provision of core skills, technology, infrastructure, and civic skills, the Community Technology Program launched the Seattle Communities Online Project (SCOP) in 2009 to help neighborhood groups actively engage community members by teaching them to use Web 2.0 online tools, including wikis, blogs, Facebook, iPhone Apps (as language translators), and other social media. Led by Amy Hirotaka, then a student at the Evans School for Public Affairs at the University of Washington and a CTP intern (now graduated), SCOP was founded after the CTP realized that community and neighborhood groups were actively seeking to use new technology to increase civic participation beyond face-to-face meetings.

District coordinators interviewed about the needs in their communities unanimously felt it was necessary for "neighborhood groups to build capacity for the use of online tools to communicate" (Hirotaka 2010, 24). SCOP trained district coordinators in the use of online social networking tools. The projected long-term outcomes of SCOP are to (1) engage more people to participate in neighborhood groups through online discussions, (2) have groups share information, tips, and advice on SCOP blogs, (3) increase knowledge about neighborhood-specific information, and (4) increase the number of groups using online tools (Hirotaka 2010, 14).

An important step toward meeting these goals is the SCOP Neighborhoods on the Net project, designed to make it easier for residents by listing virtually all online resources in their communities—blogs, Twitter feeds, neighborhood lists—by neighborhood, in one place, with addresses, by both neighborhood and district.[11] Neighborhoods on the Net has developed a citizen curriculum, teaching citizens and neighborhood leaders how to choose web tools for specific community communication-building purposes, use them better, and get help and training. It has also posted instructions on how to host a locally filtered version of Neighborhoods on the Net on neighborhood websites or blogs and how to subscribe to official city blogs via RSS.

Critically, SCOP has taken an inventory of all local and neighborhood-based online activity in Seattle and has identified more than 250 online modes for hyper-local, neighborhood, and neighborhood-regional (e.g., West Seattle) communication. Although there is some duplication of sources (e.g., for a given source Twitter and Facebook feeds are counted independently), there are still more than 150 unique sources.[12] While no systematic comparisons exist, this suggests that Seattle is among the more dense local communication environments in the nation.

The CTP also supports Puget Sound Off, an innovative partnership with the Center for Communications and Civic Engagement at the University of Washington, headed by Professor Lance Bennett, the YMCA, and One Economy. Launched in September 2008, Puget Sound Off encourages youth civic engagement through its online portal and skills training in blogging, storytelling, and Web 2.0 tools. As of late 2009, the site had more than 1,100 users, who started 620 events, posted 330 videos, started 90 groups, and administered 68 youth polls.[13]

Taken together, these programs demonstrate the extraordinary, perhaps unique commitment of Seattle government to support *citizen-led* efforts for civic communication in every neighborhood in Seattle, and for many groups that otherwise would not have access to local computers or training. The civic commitments go beyond simple access, important as this is as a prerequisite to participation, to begin to outline a positive vision of digital inclusion, which encompasses the development of active communication skills and social and physical infrastructure for civic participation.

City of Seattle Information Governance

Parallel to its broader civic infrastructure, Seattle has one of the most robust city communication infrastructures in the United States, led by its Department of Information Technology (DOIT). Specifically, the Seattle infrastructure is oriented toward government *provision of necessary information* (not only infrastructure) through various means, including clear information transparency goals, as well as the civic communication goals discussed above.

DOIT has outlined a series of "Goals for a Technology Healthy Community," including furthering educational opportunities, solving social issues, fostering civic participation, relationship building and community development, sustainability, and ensuring that technology is affordable and equitably distributed. The DOIT goals line up with both the governance culture of civic participation and the broader culture of healthy communities and sustainability.

DOIT has been led by chief technology officer Bill Schrier since 2003. Schrier describes the Community Technology Program matching grants as "extraordinarily important," because "access to education, good jobs, information, and quality of life" depend on the ability of individual citizens to access and use technology. "Some people can afford computers or have access to broadband; some can't. This is a way to level the playing field for a whole set of people, those who are low income or speak English as a second language."[14]

Finally, the city maintains a large, common data site at *data.seattle.gov*, which includes information from almost every city agency, up to 150 data sets on police, neighborhood crime, potholes, schools, water consumption, museums, neighborhood fishing, and the mayor's visitation logs, to list just a few. These data are being widely used. Beyond the data sets themselves, DOIT is leading the development of an "ecology of applications," through public-private partnerships, in which private developers are encouraged to develop useable interfaces for government data. One example is the "Public Data Ferret," a resource to summarize data in clear language, provide analysis, and increase usability for citizens and journalists, created by Matt Rosenberg, former journalist and former director of the King Countywide Community Forums.[15]

Seattle's infrastructure of civic and neighborhood governance, as well as its specific civic communication investments, is extensive and deep, reaching down to every neighborhood, including those traditionally excluded, and up throughout the governance process. Although there will almost certainly be some retrenchment as the city, like others, faces massive budgetary problems in the decade ahead, the governance structures established in the 1990s and 2000s give both the traditional media and the new online media ecology roots in the neighborhoods upon which to build.

Seattle's Media Ecology

The media ecology of Seattle has been both a driver of civic communication and an effect of its civic life. Seattle's traditional media—its newspapers, TV, and radio—have a history of strong local coverage and have paid particular attention to civic and public life for decades. They were also quicker to adapt to the changing online media ecology than most, with several innovative partnerships. And, in turn, the new media ecology is quite dense, layered, and linked to civic life. We discuss each in turn.

Traditional Media

Seattle has historically been a strong newspaper city, consistent with its high levels of education, literacy, and civic engagement. Seattle had two dailies for more than a hundred years, the afternoon *Seattle Times*, locally owned by the Blethen family (with a 49.5 percent stake held by McClatchy, acquired in 2006), which went to a morning edition in 2000, and the Hearst-owned *Post-Intelligencer*, known as the "PI," which became online-only in 2009 after years of declining circulation.

The *Times* has a history of participation in the public journalism movement. Rosen (1999), Friedland (2003), and Haas (2007) provide substantive overviews of the public journalism movement.[16] From 1994 to 1999 the *Times* teamed with public radio stations KPLU and KUOW in the "Front Porch Forums," part of a national NPR project in public journalism (more below). It covered elections in a "citizen-centered" way, as well as the issues of transportation, property taxes, and more general quality of life issues under the leadership of executive editor Mike Fancher (now a participant in Journalism that Matters–Pacific Northwest).

By the 2000s, the paper, like most, was de-emphasizing its formal public journalism efforts, but it continued to invest heavily in local news coverage, winning four Pulitzer Prizes in that decade, including one in 2010 for its breaking news coverage of the murders of four Seattle police officers and the manhunt that followed. The *Times* also invested heavily in the online transition, partnering early with the *West Seattle*

Blog published by Tracy Record (more below) and other neighborhood publications. After the PI ceased paper publication in 2009, the *Times* circulation rose temporarily, not surprising given the demise of its major competitor, although it has fallen every year since.

In 2007, the *Times* editorial pages published a series of essays, titled "The Democracy Papers," that examined the role of media in a democracy, with an eye to this century's increasing media consolidation and the effects of online media on traditional media. Owner Ryan Blethen continues to discuss these issues in his blog on the *Times* website. The *Times*, under the executive editorship of Kathy Best, continues to invest heavily in the local communication ecology, serving as an umbrella for much of the regional and local online activity that thrives at the neighborhood level (discussed below).

Television

All three major Seattle television stations have had national reputations (at times) for high quality and independent production extending back to the 1950s. While these have declined significantly (paralleling local television more generally), during the last three decades, their (varied) emphasis on community and special projects has continued to place them above the national trends. For decades, KING was the leading television station in the city, and it developed an early tradition of in-depth coverage of civic news and public affairs. In 1979–1980, it sponsored the KING City Fair, for which Anne Stadler, a legendary local activist and television producer, was engaged as the assistant director of public affairs to form a "People Power" coalition that assembled 2,500 volunteers to gather best civic practices in six areas including food, energy, and waste management. In 1992, the station was sold, eventually becoming part of the Belo Broadcasting chain of Dallas, and its investment in politics and community affairs contracted significantly.

The other two commercial stations, KIRO and KOMO, competed with KING to provide local coverage, setting off a virtuous cycle (at least in the lowered expectations of local television) for the last several decades of the twentieth century (former mayor Norman Rice was a KOMO reporter). This legacy continues in a higher-than-average level of community coverage in local television today. In contrast, public television station KCTS-TV has long seen itself as a national producer. Although it has partnered with the *Seattle Times* for some local coverage, today it is seen as distanced from local public affairs.

Seattle Radio

Seattle public and noncommercial radio has a long-time engagement with democracy, civic life, and alternative politics and culture. KUOW, affiliated with the University of Washington, is the flagship NPR affiliate in Puget Sound, with almost 400,000 listeners. It is the number two ranked radio station overall in the region, making it one of the more locally influential NPR affiliates in the United States. KUOW was a key partner in the "Front Porch Forum" in the 1990s, which it helped initiate along with KPLU, a second strong NPR affiliate located at Pacific Lutheran University in Tacoma. It was among the most significant public service projects in both stations' history. The project was part of a national NPR–Poynter Election project, which was funded by the Pew Center for Civic Journalism. The *Seattle Times*, under Mike Fancher as executive editor, joined the project, in part because it was free to find an independent path. KUOW continued with a strong program of civically oriented programming.[17]

Beyond exceptionally strong public radio, Seattle has an unusually vibrant community, alternative, and micro-radio scene. Today, there are at least ten public and student radio outlets in the region, including colleges and high schools. KRAB, founded in 1962, was one of the first of a new crop of alternative community radio stations in the United States that began to emerge in the 1960s and 1970s (the Pacifica radio network began after World War II), organized by radio pioneers Lorenzo Milam and Jeremy Lansman. The National Federation of Community Broadcasters, founded in 1975, grew from this effort. KRAB was a hotbed of alternative music and culture and laid the groundwork for Spanish-language KDNA, "La Voz del Campesino," which began in 1977 and evolved into community station KSER. KRAB's general manager Sharon Maeda went on to found "Reclaim the Media" and provide training in media for at-risk youth in South Seattle. And there are at least eight low-power and micro-radio stations in the Puget Sound region, some, like Central Seattle Grassroots Radio, with explicit social movement and democratic missions (Lawson n.d.).

Alternative and Community Press

Seattle is also served by a number of other alternative and niche print publications. The *Stranger* is Seattle's alternative newsweekly, founded in 1991, which combined satire with serious city and state news coverage. There are three weekly neighborhood publications owned by Robinson Newspapers: The *Ballard News-Tribune*, *West Seattle Herald*, and *Highline Times*, as well as alternative weeklies and monthlies covering many other Seattle neighborhoods. There are weeklies serving African American, Spanish, Asian, Vietnamese, Chinese, and Japanese communities, the gay community, business, and the homeless, among others, a much richer and denser mix than we would expect from a metro area of Seattle's size.

Seattle's traditional media, then, have a stronger orientation toward civic life, public participation, and overall news quality than most other cities. Until recently it was a two-newspaper city, and the *Seattle Times*, the surviving paper, has both a history of public journalism and a continuing commitment to local reporting at all levels, as well as an innovative orientation toward collaboration with neighborhood online media. The leading commercial television broadcaster, KING, had an explicitly civic orientation for decades, and although this has become attenuated under chain ownership, some legacy of local reporting remains. Public radio is a central local news source and also has a history of civic engagement, and a vibrant community radio scene continues to enliven grassroots media from the bottom up. Clearly there was a vibrant civic media ecology that preceded the growth of online media, but that also helped prepare the groundwork for the explosion of local, community-based online media in the 2000s.

The New Media Ecology

The new media ecology in Seattle is a work in progress, but it is already seen by national observers as a laboratory for the rest of the United States. It encompasses at least five identifiable layers. The first is the intersection of the new media ecology with the traditional media system, in particular the *Seattle Times'* new media efforts. The second is the layer that we are calling "city regional" new media, referring to reporting ventures that aggregate multiple neighborhoods, for example the *West Seattle Blog*, which covers an area of seventy thousand residents and functions effectively like a large online community newspaper. These regional media are particularly robust in Seattle and are among the first in the United States to have established deep roots and developed a plausibly sustainable economic model. The third layer consists of the neighborhood-level blogs, sometimes called micro- or hyper-local reporting. Some of these are quasi-commercial ventures, which are either owned by or affiliated with regional or traditional media, and of these some focus more on neighborhood issues, others on specific lifestyle issues or communities (music, food, arts). Others, as in those supported through the Community Technology Program's Seattle Communities Online, are noncommercial, written by citizens or city district coordinators or their staffers, and have a directly civic purpose. The fourth layer consists of city-wide online ventures. There are many of these, particularly in lifestyle areas, but we limit our discussion to those that are specifically civic or political. Finally, a fifth layer consists of several national online organizations (AOL, Yahoo, MSN) seeking to build a local media presence through aggregation, which may affect the longer-term development of Seattle's new media ecology.

The *Times* New Media

After a decades-long history of civic reporting, the *Seattle Times* is expanding to every layer of the new media ecology, becoming a central hub through both its own internal efforts and a series of agreements with regional bloggers, called the *Seattle Times* partner network, that began in 2010. Bob Payne, a thirteen-year *Times* veteran, is the director of communities and is responsible for the project. He says that the *Times* had been looking for a way to cooperate for several years, recognizing that the regionals were doing important work. A grant from J-Lab, then a Knight-funded project headed by Jan Schaffer (former director of the Pew Center for Civic Journalism) was an impetus, giving a "little bit of money, enough to charter five partner sites," and hire a half-time person to coordinate the network. The five key partners were the *West Seattle Blog*, *Rainier Valley Post*, *Next Door Media* group, *Capitol Hill/Central District*, and *Local Health Online*. As of 2011, the five partners had grown to thirty-three, twenty-three neighborhood sites and ten topical sites, ranging from health to sailing to beer.

The inclusion of the partnerships is changing some of the *Times* workflow. Stories are flowing back and forth among the partners, often with a spot news story starting in the blogs, then being reported more systematically by the paper, whose report is then linked back to the blogs. Photos are also being shared freely, although Payne stresses that the paper is careful to make sure that permissions are given in order to ensure proper credit and payment.[18]

Probably the richest civic collaboration to date, reminiscent of civic journalism, is a joint series on the homeless, "Invisible Families."[19] The project began when a freelance photographer who worked with *BloggerFriend Aurora* (a *Times* partner) wanted assistance from the paper with a project on the homeless. That didn't work out, but it evolved into a partner-wide collaboration, with support from the Gates Foundation and Seattle University, including stories on African immigrants, refugees, fathers, and children, as well as possible solutions to some of the problems they faced. The final project involved three regional partners, local neighborhood blogs, and freelancers, and it continues to influence debate in the city. Payne stresses that "we're not trying to tell the blogs what to do; it's completely up to them. We're a partner, not the flagship of a network. They are completely autonomous." In 2010 the *Seattle Times* won the Associated Press Managing Editors "Innovator of the Year" award for its social media efforts as well as its partnerships with neighborhood blogs in the Network Journalism Project.[20]

This networked approach is changing the *Times* itself. In early 2011, the *Times* underwent a complete reorganization to become a fully digitally integrated publication, with two managing editors, one for content creation and the other for curation and distribution, reflecting a growing awareness that the primary task of news organizations is to gather and add value to the best local reporting, rather than to be the sole owner and originator of content. Kathy Best was made the managing editor for content creation; she had been managing editor for digital innovation since 2007. Best believes that community partnerships are necessary for survival as a community-oriented news organization: "As resources shrink, if we're going to continue serving the community on *any* platform, we can't do it by ourselves anymore. This was a need we couldn't meet and a recognition of reality. Hyper-local sites are springing up, some very good. Why not partner with them and let them provide us with content?"[21]

But Best believes that while partnering is the future, it has to be intentional: "There is a fundamental threshold for partnering. We only partner with people who share our journalism values . . . we want to create a network of journalism that can be trusted in an environment where there's a lot of journalism and not all of it *can* be trusted."[22]

Beyond the *Times* partnership efforts, the *Seattle Post-Intelligencer* began online-only publication in March 2009, but has cut its staff from 165 to 20. It features neighborhood blogs in Seattle and collaborates with KOMO-TV in news sharing. But its reporting online lacks the depth of the *Times* and its partnerships are much weaker. It is allied with KOMO/Fischer Broadcasting, which connects it to the network of KOMO Communities blogs, but these are also small efforts without, to date, the depth of coverage of the *Times* partner network.

City and Regional Civic and Public Sites

Beyond the partnership hub centered on the *Times*, several news sites reach across Seattle and the Puget Sound region, with explicit civic and political aims. All three are a mix of the local comprehensive and civic types discussed above.

PubliCola: Seattle's News Elixir (named after the alias of the authors of the Federalist Papers) was formed in 2009 by Josh Feit, former news editor and state reporter for the alternative weekly *The Stranger*. Feit became the first online-only reporter to get state capitol news accreditation. He was joined by *Stranger* Seattle city hall reporter Erica Barnett, who had covered city politics since 1998. *PubliCola*, which mixes daily political reporting from city hall and the statehouse, has won wide praise and readership. The site sees itself as nonpartisan and balanced, albeit with an "urban green politics." It serves as an aggressive watchdog, similar to the function the *Stranger* previously played.[23]

Crosscut began in 2007 as both a daily guide to local and Northwest news and a forum for writers and citizens from many points of view to report and discuss local news. Originally a for-profit, in 2008 it became nonprofit entity with a civic board and a mission "to produce journalism in the public interest." Revenue comes from memberships, grants, and donations in a "public radio" model. It focuses on news analysis, rather than breaking news, by highlighting the "best local journalism" and commentary, whether from large news organizations or micro-bloggers, and it selects all links by hand. *Crosscut* also publishes its own journalism and commentary. Its primary editorial stand is "to encourage and strive for good journalism that is accurate, fair, civil, and transparent. Our political disposition is to encourage communities to create sustainable solutions to major issues." *Crosscut* compares itself to other mixed new journalism sites, including the *Voice of San Diego*, *MinnPost*, and *St. Louis Beacon*, discussed above.

Finally, *InvestigateWest* is focused broadly on the Pacific Northwest and West.[24] It's one example of a new type of nonprofit investigative organization supported primarily by foundations and memberships, as discussed by Friedland and Konieczna (2010).

City Regional Sites

The four major regional online news producers in the Seattle area have diverse approaches and organizations. At their best, they are independent news organizations, with a deep community connection.

The *West Seattle Blog* (*WSB*), which has garnered the most national attention, was started in 2005 by Tracy Record, a journalist with more than thirty years' experience in newspapers, television, radio, and online news, and her husband, Patrick Sand. Originally, they wrote anonymously about news around the neighborhood, in which they had lived since 1991. In 2006, a large windstorm hit the Puget Sound region, and the *WSB* gathered news, informal notes, and posts, becoming a critical hub for the entire neighborhood. By 2007, readership had built to the point where local businesses asked whether *WSB* would consider selling ads, and Record and Sand (who had a young son) decided to make a go of it. Record describes the *WSB* as developing organically; for example, when people started reporting lost pets on the site, the *WSB* posted a dedicated pets page. The *WSB* is a serious news organization (albeit of only two and a half people; their son also takes pictures and creates graphics); it was the first online news site in the region to get police credentials. Record says that she is "not looking for free labor," so they pay freelance writers and photographers.

Record says the "advertising business model is not dead." The question is whether new organizations can evolve and adapt. Creating large news infrastructures to aggregate, as in Patch (discussed below), is, she believes, an ineffective strategy. Further, the loss of news from the decline of traditional media is overstated: "[W]hen the *Post-Intelligencer* stopped printing, everyone was lamenting the loss of investigative journalism. The truth is, there wasn't a whole lot of that happening anyway. In some cases, a lot of civic issues are getting more coverage [now]" (Leadingham 2010, 10–11).

The *WSB* coverage of the "California Park Place" on March 6, 2009, by Record, a controversy over three design changes in a proposed park in the North Admiral neighborhood, lays bare the intersecting lines of regional coverage and the civic ecology. This is not a remarkable or exceptional story, but one that shows how the day-to-day cumulative coverage of civic and public life can have a small effect.

First, Record advances the story of a public meeting, letting citizens know twenty-four hours in advance what the three designs will be, and also notifying them that they *can* participate and showing them *how* to get involved. This technique goes back at least to the public journalism practice of the Norfolk *Virginian-Pilot* in the 1990s (Friedland 2003). It was developed by then managing editor Dennis Hartig and public life editor Tom Warhover. There's no evidence that Record is drawing from this earlier precedent. Rather, it shows an elective affinity between public journalism and certain practices of the newer media ecology.

The group that ordered the designs, Friends and Neighbors of North Admiral (FANNA), had obtained a $15,000 city matching grant from the Department of

Neighborhoods for the designs and public workshops. Record reports on the history of the planning process by FANNA, as well as efforts by opponents to block the change. She carefully reports on challenges to the facts presented by FANNA and publishes the opponents' document, which to that point had not appeared online. She carefully reconstructs the back-and-forth and asks readers to comment on whether she has missed anything, with a promise to follow up. She examines *each claim* carefully, with a response "What we found," not simply stating claims and counterclaims, but trying to adjudicate the facts themselves to give citizens a more firm foundation for decision making. Comments from readers/citizens both thank Record for her "superb point-by-point analysis" and for being a "diligent and fair source for neighborhood information" and ask her for further coverage, such as video from the upcoming meetings.[25]

Record is practicing an exemplary civic journalism (although she herself does not use this label) in the new media environment. Not only has the *WSB* covered the community closely but it has (1) aired conflict systematically, in a way designed to give voice fairly to all sides such that they could recognize themselves in her writing, (2) provided actionable civic information that would not otherwise be available and aggregated it in a nonpartisan manner, (3) presented the story in a way that does not downplay conflict but offers multiple parties access to the underlying facts in a way that makes civic solutions possible, and (4) opened up its pages as a voice for sometimes strident but nonvituperative civic and public dialogue. This particular case also shows how the new neighborhood media, when handled with the care, sensitivity, and thoroughness of a professional and careful reporter, can amplify other governmental civic efforts.

Finally, the *West Seattle Blog* demonstrates how this new regional neighborhood media serves as an essential bridge, gathering civic information from "below," but also channeling it upward and outward. The *WSB* is a core partner of the *Seattle Times*, and through the *Times*, the kind of in-depth coverage discussed above becomes available to other citizens, neighborhood leaders, and government decision makers (of course, they could read the *WSB*, but the *Times* curates content from across the partners to make them easily accessible).

Other major regionals include the *Rainier Valley Post*, run by Amber Campbell, covering the southeast region of Seattle. It blogs on neighborhood issues, but taken as a whole is a more typical micro-blogging site, with a strong emphasis on local community and lifestyle. *Next Door Media*, founded in 2008 by Kate and Corey Bergman, began with *My Ballard*, a blog about the neighborhood of Ballard, and has since expanded to eight additional neighborhoods covering the north central region of Seattle. *NDM* claims to be the "most-visited network of neighborhood newsblogs" in Seattle and has won two national online journalism awards. The Bergmans' tagline is that the sites are edited by trained journalists, but "powered by the neighborhood." *Capitol Hill Blog/Central District News* began when Justin Carder moved to the Capitol Hill neighborhood in 2006, one he describes as the center of nightlife, gay culture, and the music scene. But as a resident, he found that many things "just weren't covered, so I began to focus more on its geography." Eventually, the *Capitol Hill Blog* attracted advertising, and he took on the *Central District News* (now defunct) to the south. Carder had worked at Microsoft in analytics but had a background in journalism, and the new venture was a natural merger of the two.[26]

An analysis of regional bloggers shows many stand-alone regional bloggers (including pioneers in 2005–2006 like *West Seattle Blog*, *My Ballard*, and *Capitol Hill*) are now being integrated into content and ad sales networks, suggesting that by 2011 a new media ecology had emerged. Regional networks are the most important "meso-layer" of this ecology (Friedland and McLeod 1999). They allow for (even demand) close contact with all the micro-bloggers in a region: civic blogs stimulated by the Community Technologies Project and Seattle Communities Online, small neighborhood independents, and commercial and lifestyle blogs. The daily bread and butter of the regionals is to report, gather, and aggregate micro-content, and then repurpose it in a variety of ways. This allows for a channel upward, primarily to the *Seattle Times*, but also through the KOMO-TV-driven network. Our discussion of the Seattle Communities Online Project (above) referenced some 150 independent voices (aggregating for Twitter and Facebook streams under the same editorial control).

This stream of small neighborhood voices at the micro-level helps bring the ecological framework into focus. Some micro-blogs "naturally" occur, that is, independently of higher-level stimuli (such as the Community Technology Office or ad-driven support networks), as individuals decide they want to speak out on some neighborhood issues, voice opinions, or simply write about lifestyle or personal issues. Many of these die quickly, within days or weeks, but some of these micro-blogs take hold with micro-level publics, networks that are large enough to extend beyond a relatively small, personal circle of friends but that do not capture the attention of a larger region or network. These become a source of energy for the regional blogs, which thrive on either aggregating the successful micro-blogs or on adding significant value to them through new reporting (e.g., West Seattle). This evolution is critical. Without the regionals, the micro-blogs would stay small and hyperlocal and would die out fairly quickly. Without the micro-locals, the regionals would be overextended and would find it more difficult to add new journalistic value, either to the meso-region, or to the larger macro-region.

This new media ecology is not, of course, necessarily civic. The analytical difference between community and civic media ecologies often becomes blurred. But community media ecologies help like-minded communities to thrive by networking them together, as the example of the regional–micro-blogging relationship makes clear. At this level, Seattle is an extraordinary, perhaps unique, example of how information flowing across the macro-meso-micro-layers of the communication ecology helps create new forms of information and new kinds of advertising support. This kind of community ecology is a prerequisite for a civic communication ecology, but it is not in itself sufficient. The Community Technology Office and Seattle Communities Online have systematically tried to address equity and skills gaps in the community ecology, while also raising the *civic skills* of communication: deliberative discussion, problem solving, and decision making. The *West Seattle Blog*, driven by the journalistic orientation of its owners, has taken some of the routines and ethics of both traditional and civic journalism and applied them to the meso-regional level.

To what extent will the continual generation of micro-blogging take on (however partially) this civic dimension? Is it necessary for government-sponsored programs like the Community Technology Program and Seattle Communities Online to generate civic content that would not be spontaneously produced otherwise? And if so, is this even possible over the long run? The strength of the community ecologies is that micro-blogs do emerge organically from below, reflecting the specific interests and passions of their writers. It's unclear whether a top-down framework, however rooted in the neighborhood, could continue to generate the civic dimensions.

The Civic Communication Ecology of Seattle

Seattle has a robust civic communication ecology, one of the strongest in the nation. It generates a significant amount of autonomous communication by citizens at every layer of the city and, of equal importance, it allows communication from lower layers (neighborhoods and regions) to travel upward so they can affect the interactions of key actors and groups at higher levels. Individual citizens and small groups can express themselves with a reasonable chance of being picked up by neighborhood bloggers. Neighborhood bloggers can be picked up to shape the discussion on issues and policy in regions like West Seattle. Regional bloggers have a range of alliances with each other and with traditional media, most of all the *Seattle Times*, which has put together a working network of autonomous regional bloggers, initially with the assistance of the national journalism incubator J-Lab. Not least of all, the city has taken a long and proactive role in ensuring that the conditions exist in every neighborhood for citizens to have access to both communications technology and skills, including, through CTP-funded programs like the information stewards in Rainier Valley, skills of finding relevant, actionable, civic information.

Multiple layers of a rich civic communication ecology are present in Seattle. First, the citizenry itself is highly engaged. Some of this is predicted by the high levels of education and literacy that correlate strongly with traditional measures of civic engagement. But it is also driven by a long history of movement activism, including activists in the sphere of communication itself. Further, the city government has a unique commitment to the active development of civic communication capacities in its neighborhoods, particularly to those who are historically underserved. This commitment extends to both *technology* and *skills,* and skills training itself moves beyond how to use technology generally to training in *civic skills* of community expression (Hargittai and Walejko 2008). This latter commitment is partly responsible for the lower levels of disparity in communication infrastructure among neighborhoods (although they still exist). While the city's commitments are markedly atypical in the United States, they offer a clear path for emulation for those cities that wish to increase civic communication and engagement. Indeed, while many recommendations for building civic communication focus largely on technology training and the nonprofit civic sector, Seattle shows that government investment is essential if the civic communication playing field is to be leveled. Further, there are a large number of important intermediary civic institutions, funded in part by government (neighborhood service centers, district councils, an engaged public university, public libraries) that stimulate ongoing civic engagement and boundary crossing.

Second, Seattle has a number of unusual characteristics that add to its civic communication capacity. It has a high base of technology use, driven by its high-tech economy, and widely accessible broadband, in both city-supported spaces (district and neighborhood centers) and commercial places, particularly coffee houses. While the economic aspects of Seattle's high-tech base may not be easily replicable, one key lesson is that widespread broadband access as a policy goal is integral to both economic development *and* to civic life in the twenty-first century and this, too, is a legitimate and attainable goal of government.

Third, there is a history of strong, competitive, community-oriented journalism across many of the traditional media, which has created a deep foundation of civic communication in the city. While the historical civic role of newspapers in communities is declining, the future of newspapers in some form will almost certainly play a critical role in fostering community-wide, civic problem solving. Public policy to support newspapers, in the interest of local democracy and not the special interests of newspaper owners, was discussed in Congress and at the Federal Trade Commission and Federal Communication Commission in 2009–2010 (2009 FTC Workshop, n.d.; Knight Commission on the Information Needs of Communities 2009; Waldman 2011). While a policy of public support for newspapers is almost certainly on hold through at least 2016, given divided government, the example of the *Seattle Times* and its partner networks points toward one possible avenue of reinvention for newspapers elsewhere, as hubs of civic networks, partners in content creation, and curators of the best and most important content locally.

Fourth, Seattle demonstrates the ongoing role of a base of journalists and "parajournalists," with the skills and incentives to gather and aggregate the news as entrepreneurs, citizens, and freelancers. While it is unclear what policies would stimulate this pool (as the debate over the role of the "creative class" in urban economic growth demonstrates) the examples of the *Gotham Gazette*, the *Twin Cities Daily Planet*, and Seattle itself show how important this pool can be in feeding the middle and lower layers of a civic media ecology. The examples of Deerfield, New Hampshire (and to some extent the *Twin Cities Daily Planet*) also show how associated citizens can play a similar role (Schaffer 2009).

Lessons for the (Very Near) Future

Civic communication in the twenty-first century is inevitably a networked affair (Friedland, Hove, and Rojas 2006). Despite lingering nostalgia about traditional media and the superiority of face-to-face communication for civic action, the new civic communication environment will inevitably combine large-scale news organizations, entrepreneurial efforts, existing civic networks, expanded online civic communication networks, and the individual efforts of citizens to express themselves about issues large and small. Seattle has shown how important government policy for democracy can be in creating an equitable civic communication infrastructure. To move forward, we need to answer (at least) two questions: What configurations of these elements are most likely to work, and what can policy do to support the growth of new civic ecologies?

Seattle is both an ideal case and a hard case: ideal because all these elements are present and offer a vision of how they might work together, hard because it seems to be too demanding. We might ask: Which of these elements are necessary for a new civic ecology to emerge and which are sufficient? Answering this question with greater certainty would demand a broad and comparative investigation of many cases of civic ecologies, centered on their successful outcomes in multiple dimensions: sustainability, reach across diverse neighborhoods and communities, and, most important, evidence of stimulating civic engagement (Kim et al. 2013). But Seattle offers some hypotheses.

First, a robust, healthy local newspaper, with a strong online presence that is central to its mission, is necessary. As we have seen, the newspaper remains the central connector and source of news in local communities. But that role is changing rapidly. The newspaper of the future, if it is going to play a role of civic catalyst, will be a hub of connection, rather than the single authoritative fount of knowledge. Rather than trying to cover all the news (and inevitably falling short), the online *civic* newspaper will recognize its shortcomings and reach out to others—regionals, micro-locals, and individual citizens—to include them as full partners. At this writing, the *Seattle Times* may play this role better than others in the United States.

Second, it is necessary that a civic communication network be equally accessible to everyone. As a minimal condition of civic communication, this means that the city is wired for all, that broadband access is not restricted by ability to pay, and that citizens have access to skills, training, and assistance (Hargattai and Walejko 2008). Here too, Seattle comes closer than many cities, in no small part because of systematic public policy put into place almost two decades ago. There are different paths to accessible broadband, but if some parts of the community can access the new civic media ecology and others cannot (or can only do so at slower speeds), then the formal conditions for equality are not being met.

Third, a larger civic communication ecology must rest on the foundation of a (minimally) robust micro-ecology, among individuals, niches, groups, and neighborhoods, that generates information from below. This need not be "civic" in any formal sense. Just as Putnam's account of associational life posits that social capital can emerge from groups that have no formal civic or public intent, civic life in the networked environment rests on a foundation of networked communication among many different types of individuals and groups, most of which will *not* be formally civic. The knitting group, the mother's group, the beer "community," as well as loose informal networks of people communicating via Facebook, Twitter, FourSquare, or other social media about the best place to hang out, hear music, or find tacos all contribute to the minimal conditions of integration that are necessary for trust to emerge in any civic environment. This is the element most likely to emerge spontaneously from the way individuals are increasingly integrating their lives with and through new media.

Each of these conditions—community integrating, online professional journalism, equal access to the new media environment, and robust micro-ecological networks—are necessary for an emergent civic ecology. It is too early to know whether they are sufficient.

A more difficult question concerns the meso- or middle layers of the civic ecology: Are they necessary to connect the most local layers with larger governance issues, and are they supportable? This is likely to depend on scale. The case of the *West Seattle Blog* shows that in a larger city, there is a need for an intermediary journalism that both reports and aggregates. This contemporary case displays functions similar to those described in Janowitz's (1952) study of community newspapers. Without it, much of what goes on at the micro-level will not be shared with the broader community, since it will be lost in the daily online noise. We simply don't know yet what the tipping point of scale is. But it seems likely that any community in the range of 150,000 to 200,000 is likely to need this middle layer to function well, a hypothesis supported by the Madison Commons experiment, which has shown both a need for civic news in the "middle layer" and the capability of providing it under the right conditions (Robinson et al. 2011).

To this point, we have discussed aspects of the media ecology. But it is also reasonable to ask: Does a robust civic media ecology require a strong *civic* infrastructure? If it does, then perhaps we have not advanced much beyond Putnam's questions about social capital in new media guise. If a strong civic infrastructure *is* necessary for the civic communication ecology to function, then causality would only work in one direction; the media system would be a secondary effect of a robust civic life. Seattle's strong civic history certainly contributed to its robust civic communication ecology, and, in this case, it's impossible to separate the two. One of the key premises of the public journalism movement was the idea that strong civic and public media *can* give rise to stronger civic and democratic engagement (Friedland and Nichols 2002; Nichols et al. 2006). Unfortunately, the Seattle case alone does not shed much light on this problem.

But we can imagine cases in which weak but minimally significant civic communication ecologies give rise to stronger trust, common visibility, and community problem solving, including some briefly noted above. The *Oakland Local* is driven by a small group led by Susan Mernit, a dedicated editor who through sheer effort of will has managed to connect many parts of a community divided by race and class. In a different vein, *Baristanet* has helped tie together a community of northern New Jersey and become commercially viable.[27]

Beyond a strong civic infrastructure, Seattle clearly demonstrates the powerful effect that local collaborative governance can play in building civic communication and how that might be used to leverage *some* greater equality of unequally distributed skills and resources. Seattle is a work in progress, and the foundation on which that progress was built, neighborhood governance, the Neighborhood Matching and Community Technologies Programs, will almost certainly be cut back as the fiscal crisis of local government continues into the next decade. The larger question is whether such a governance structure might be implemented elsewhere. Others in this volume have addressed the question of new collaborative governance structures, and their plausible advancement in an era of fiscal retrenchment is beyond the scope of this chapter. But it does seem clear that public policy for civic communication is a step that *can* be taken, as part of the tool kit of both governments and funders in the field, and that formalizing the lessons of Seattle for other governments, and comparing Seattle to other cities in this regard, would be an important first step.

The major funder of civic communication has been the Knight Foundation, which has put several hundred million dollars into the field in the past decade (Friedland and Konieczna 2010). It has launched a major communities initiative, in partnership with local community foundations, which has been successful in raising millions of dollars for local civic communication. But there has been very little work in collaborative governance for civic communication among the funding community or the federal government. The federal government would be best positioned to invest in the kinds of experiments in collaborative governance for civic communication that we find in Seattle, in ways that would allow them to diffuse across a broader landscape, but this seems unlikely in the next decade. Seattle, for now, will serve as a model of what could be if collaborative governance, robust local digital journalism led by a forward-looking newspaper, and robust neighborhood journalism can combine in the same community, alongside citizens deeply engaged in producing all sorts of new media content related to their daily lives.

Notes

1. Lasswell (1948) named three functions of media: surveillance, correlation, and cultural transmission across generations. Surveillance creates a common information environment that can be scanned by citizens, elites, and organization.
2. *Gazette*: www.gothamgazette.com; *Twin Cities Daily Planet*: www.tcdailyplanet.net; *Commons*: madisoncommons.org.
3. Charles Ragin's method of Qualitative Comparative Analysis (QCA) offers a promising method for exploring the possibility space of civic communication ecologies (Ragin 2008). In brief, Ragin allows us to ask what are the necessary and sufficient conditions under which a civic media ecology would thrive across the range of variables identified in the Seattle case, a necessary first step in the direction of a formal comparison. For an early application see Kim et al. (2013).
4. A case study of Seattle for the New America Foundation, by Durkin, Glaiyser, and Hadge (2010), was developed in parallel with this one but was published earlier, which gave me the benefit of lead researcher Jessica Durkin's research and knowledge of the city. I gratefully acknowledge her assistance in identifying some key partnerships that I had not previously discovered. Also after this research was completed, former *Seattle Times* executive editor Mike Fancher published "Seattle: A New Media Case Study" (Fancher 2011), which was also an important resource. For a comprehensive comparative analysis of Seattle's ecology as of 2014 see: Powers, M, Baisnee, O. and Zambrano, S. V. "Comparing Metropolitan Journalism: An Analysis of Newsmakers in Toulouse, France, and Seattle, USA." In *The Uncertain Future of Local Journalism*, edited by R. K. Nielsen. Oxford, UK: Reuters Institute for the Study of Journalism
5. *www.seattle.gov/dpd/Research/Population_Demographics/Seattle_at_a_Glance*.
6. Bill Schrier, phone interview, October 7, 2011; John Miller, "America's Most Literate Cities 2010," Connecticut Central University, *www.ccsu.edu/page.cfm?p=8140*.
7. Wired city: Forbes, 2009; Rank as high tech: Milken Institute, June 2009; US Census Bureau, Quick Facts: *quickfacts.census.gov/qfd/states/53/5363000.html*.
8. Jim Diers, interview, January 7, 2010.
9. David Keyes, telephone interview, October 11, 2010.
10. For a complete list, description, and funding see *seattle.gov/tech/tmf/projects2010.htm*; Gregory Davis, board chair, Rainier Beach Community Empowerment Coalition, telephone interview, February 20, 2013.
11. Amy Hirotaka, telephone interview, October 5, 2010.
12. *www.seattle.gov/communitiesonline/neighborhoods.htm*.
13. For Puget Sound Off, see Keyes (2009) and *www.pugetsoundoff.org*.
14. Bill Schrier, telephone interview, October 7, 2010.
15. For Seattle city data, see *data.seattle.gov*; for Public Data Ferret, see *socialcapitalreview.org/public-data-ferret*.
16. Public journalism was a movement in the 1990s and early 2000s that attempted to change the fundamental routines of journalistic practice and reach out to citizens in more direct way, listening to and writing about their concerns. It included newspapers and commercial television as well as public media.

17. For a complete account see *www.cpn.org/topics/communication/frontporch.html.*

18. Bob Payne, telephone interview, January 26, 2011.

19. *seattletimes.nwsource.com/flatpages/local/invisiblefamilies.html.*

20. *www.apme.com/news/51325/The-Seattle-Times-Wins-APMEs-Innovator-of-the-Year-Award.htm.*

21. Kathy Best, telephone interview, February 4, 2011.

22. Kathy Best, telephone interview, February 4, 2011.

23. *publicola.com.*

24. *invw.org.*

25. *westseattleblog.com/2009/03/california-place-park-controversy-the-no-change-documents.*

26. Justin Carder, telephone interview, November 19, 2010.

27. *oaklandlocal.com, baristanet.com.*

References

2009 FTC Workshop: New Media Workshop. N.d. Retrieved March 28, 2013, from *www. ftc.gov/opp/workshops/news/index.shtml.*

Anderson, Benedict. 1991. *Imagined Communities: Reflections on the Origin and Spread of Nationalism.* London: Verso.

Anderson, C. W., Emily Bell, and Clay Shirkey. 2013. "Post Industrial Journalism: Adapting to the Present." Report, Tow Center for Digital Journalism, Columbia University.

Bennett, W. Lance. 2007. "Changing Citizenship in the Digital Age." The John D. and Catherine T. MacArthur Foundation Series on Digital Media and Learning, 1–24.

———. 2008. *Civic Life Online: Learning How Digital Media Can Engage Youth.* Cambridge, MA: The MIT Press.

Brown, Richard D. 1991. *Knowledge Is Power: The Diffusion of Information in Early America, 1700-1865.* New York: Oxford University Press.

Couldry, Nick. 2012. *Media, Society, World: Social Theory and Digital Media Practice.* 1st ed. Cambridge: Polity Press.

Dahlgren, Peter. 2009. *Media and Political Engagement: Citizens, Communication and Democracy.* 1st ed. Cambridge: Cambridge University Press.

Deuze, Mark. 2007. *Media Work.* Digital Media and Society series. Cambridge: Polity Press.

Downie, Leonard, Jr., and Michael Schudson. 2009. *The Reconstruction of American Journalism.* New York: Columbia University Press.

Durkin, Jessica, Tom Glaisyer, and Kara Hadge. 2010. *An Information Community Case Study: Seattle.* No. Release 1.1. Washington, DC: New America Foundation.

Fancher, Michael. 2011. "Seattle: A New Media Case Study" State of the Media. Retrieved March 28, 2013, from *stateofthemedia.org/2011/mobile-survey/ seattle-a-new-media-case-study.*

Friedland, Lewis A. 2001. "Communication, Community, and Democracy: Toward a Theory of the Communicatively Integrated Community." *Communication Research* 28: 358–91.

———. 2003. *Public Journalism: Past and Future.* Dayton, OH: Kettering Foundation.

Friedland, Lewis A., Tom Hove, and Hernando Rojas. 2006. "The Networked Public Sphere." *Javnost-the Public* 13.

Friedland, Lewis A., and Magda Konieczna. 2010. "The Field of Nonprofit Funding of

Journalism in the United States: A Report to Active Philanthropy." Berlin; Madison WI: Active Philanthropy.

———. 2014. "The Costs of Journalism in the U.S.: An Estimate." Center for Communication and Democracy, University of Wisconsin-Madison Working Paper No. 1 (forthcoming).

Friedland, Lewis A., and Jack M. McLeod. 1999. "Community Integration and Mass Media: A Reconsideration." In *Mass Media, Social Control, and Social Change*, edited by David Demers and K. Viswanath, pp. 197–226. Ames: Iowa State University Press.

Friedland, Lewis A., and Shauna Morimoto. 2005. "The Lifeworlds of Young People and Civic Engagement." In *Youth Civic Engagement: An Institutional Turn*. College Park, MD: Center for Information and Research on Civic Learning and Engagement.

Friedland, Lewis A., and Sandra Nichols. 2002. "Measuring Civic Journalism's Progress: A Report Across a Decade of Activity." A study conducted for the Pew Center for Civic Journalism.

Galaskiewicz, Joseph. 1979. *Exchange Networks and Community Politics*. Beverly Hills, CA: Sage Publications.

Gans, Herbert J. 2004. *Deciding What's News: A Study of* CBS Evening News, NBC Nightly News, Newsweek, *and* Time. Evanston, IL: Northwestern University Press.

Haas, Tanni. 2007. *The Pursuit of Public Journalism: Theory, Practice and Criticism*. New edition. London: Routledge.

Hamilton, James T. 2006. *All the News That's Fit to Sell: How the Market Transforms Information into News*. Princeton, NJ: Princeton University Press.

Hargittai, Eszter, and Gina Walejko. 2008. "The Participation Divide: Content Creation and Sharing in the Digital Age." *Information, Community and Society* 11 (2): 239–56.

Hawley, Amos H. 1950. *Human Ecology; A Theory of Community Structure*. New York: Ronald Press Co.

———. 1986. *Human Ecology: A Theoretical Essay*. Chicago: University of Chicago Press.

Hindman, Matthew S. 2011. "Less of the Same: The Lack of Local News on the Internet." Prepared for the FCC. Retrieved from *www.fcc.gov/document/media-ownership-study-6-submitted-study*.

Hirotaka, Amy. 2010. "Seattle Communities Online: Building Capacity for Web Tool Use by Neighborhood Groups." MA thesis, University of Washington.

Janowitz, Morris. 1952. *The Community Press in an Urban Setting: The Social Elements of Urbanism*. Chicago: University of Chicago Press.

Kaniss, Phyllis. 1991. *Making Local News*. Chicago: University of Chicago Press.

Katz, Elihu, and Paul F. Lazarsfeld. 1955. *Personal Influence: The Part Played by People in the Flow of Mass Communication*. Glencoe, IL: Free Press.

Keyes, David. 2009. "Digital Opportunities: Lessons from Community Technology Programs & Practices." Presentation to National Association of Telecommunications Officers and Advisors, Nov. 9.

Kim, Nakho, Magda Konieczna, Ho Young Yoon, and Lewis A Friedland. 2013. "Contributors to Sustainability of Emergent, Civic News Sites: A Qualitative Comparative Analysis." Presented at the Association for Education in Journalism and Mass Communication, Washington, DC.

Kirchhoff, Suzanne M. 2009. "The US Newspaper Industry in Transition." Congressional Research Service 7-5700 Federal Publication 634.

Knight Commission on the Information Needs of Communities. 2009. *Informing Communities: Sustaining Democracy in the Digital Age*. Washington, DC: Aspen Institute.

Konieczna, Magda. "Do Old Norms Have a Place in New Media: A Case-study of the Nonprofit MinnPost." *Journalism Practice*. 8 (1): 49–64.

Kurpius, David. 1997. "Commercial Local Television News and Public Journalism: A Case Study of the Range of Organizational Routines of Coverage." Ph.D. dissertation, University of Wisconsin-Madison.

Kurpius, David, Emily T. Metzgar, and Karen M. Rowley. 2010. "Sustaining Hyperlocal Media: In Search of Funding Models." *Journalism Studies* 11 (3): 359–76.

Lasswell, Harold D. 1948. "The Structure and Function of Communication in Society." In *The Communication of Ideas*, ed. Lyman Bryson, 37–51. New York: Harper, 1957.

Laumann, Edward O., and Franz U. Pappi. 1976. *Networks of Collective Action: A Perspective on Community Influence Systems*. New York: Academic Press.

Lawson, Jonathan. N.d. "Principle, Not Profit: Seattle's History of Alternative Media." Reclaim the Media. Retrieved from *www.reclaimthemedia.org/grassroots_media/principle_not_profit_seattles_history_of_alternative_media*.

Leadingham, Scott. 2010. "Tracy Record." *The Quill: Society of Professional Journalists* (December).

Lippmann, Walter. 1922 (1992). *Public Opinion*. New Brunswick, NJ: Transaction Publishers.

Logan, John R., and Harvey L. Molotch. 1987. *Urban Fortunes: The Political Economy of Place*. Berkeley: University of California Press.

McChesney, Robert Waterman, and John Nichols. 2010. *The Death and Life of American Journalism: The Media Revolution that Will Begin the World Again*. New York: Nation Books.

McCombs, Maxwell, and Donald Shaw. 1972. "The Agenda-Setting Function of the Mass Media." *Public Opinion Quarterly* 36: 176–87.

McManus, John H. 1994. *Market-Driven Journalism: Let the Citizen Beware?* Thousand Oaks, CA: Sage Publications.

Meyer, Philip. 2009. *The Vanishing Newspaper: Saving Journalism in the Information Age*. Updated 2nd ed. Columbia: University of Missouri Press.

Mindich, David T. Z. 2005. *Tuned Out: Why Americans Under 40 Don't Follow the News*. New York: Oxford University Press.

Molotch, Harvey, and Marilyn Lester. 1974. "News as Purposive Behavior: On the Strategic Use of Routine Events, Accidents, and Scandals." *American Sociological Review* 39: 101–12.

Monge, Peter R., and Noshir S. Contractor. 2003. *Theories of Communication Networks*. Oxford: Oxford University Press.

Morimoto, Shauna A., and Lewis A. Friedland. 2011. "The Lifeworld of Youth in the Information Society." *Youth & Society* 43 (2): 549.

Nichols, Sandra, Lewis A. Friedland, Hernando Rojas, Jaeho Cho, and Dhavan Shah. 2006. "Examining the Effects of Public Journalism on Civil Society From 1994 to 2002:

Organizational Factors, Project Features, Story Frames, and Citizen Engagement." *Journalism & Mass Communication Quarterly* 83.

Park, Robert E. 1923. "Natural History of the Newspaper." *American Journal of Sociology* 29: 80–98.

Pasley, Jeffrey L. 2003. *"The Tyranny of Printers": Newspaper Politics in the Early American Republic*. Charlottesville: University of Virginia Press.

Pew Research Center Project for Excellence in Journalism. 2010. "How News Happens: A Study of the News Ecosystem of One American City. Project for Excellence in Journalism." Retrieved from *www.journalism.org/analysis_report/how_news_happens*.

———. 2011. "Why U.S. Newspapers Suffer More than Others | State of the Media." Retrieved August 15, 2011, from *stateofthemedia.org/2011/mobile-survey/international-newspaper-economics*.

Putnam, Robert D. 2000. *Bowling Alone: The Collapse and Revival of American Community*. New York: Simon & Schuster.

Ragin, Charles C. 2008. *Redesigning Social Inquiry: Fuzzy Sets and Beyond*. Chicago: University of Chicago Press.

Robinson, Sue. 2007. "Someone's Gotta Be In Control Here: The Institutionalization of Online News and the Creation of a Shared Journalistic Authority." *Journalism Practice* 1 (3): 305–21.

Robinson, Sue, Cathy DeShano, Nakho Kim, and Lewis A. Friedland. 2011. "Madison Commons in Wisconsin: Experimenting with a Citizen-Journalism Model." In *Public Journalism 2.0: The Promise and Reality of a Citizen-Engaged Press*. New York: Routledge.

Rosen, Jay. 1999. *What Are Journalists For?* New Haven, CT: Yale University Press.

Schaffer, Jan. 2009. *New Media Makers: A Toolkit for Innovators in Community Media and Grant Making*. Washington DC: J-Lab: The Institute for Interactive Journalism.

———. 2010. *Exploring a Networked Journalism Collaborative in Philadelphia*. Washington, DC: J-Lab: The Institute for Interactive Journalism.

Schudson, Michael. 1978. *Discovering the News: A Social History of American Newspapers*. New York: Basic Books.

———. 2003. *The Sociology of News*. New York: Norton.

Sirianni, Carmen. 2007. "Neighborhood Planning as Collaborative Democratic Design: The Case of Seattle." *Journal of the American Planning Association* 73 (4): 373–87.

———. 2009. *Investing in Democracy: Engaging Citizens in Collaborative Governance*. Washington, DC: Brookings Press.

Starr, Paul. 2004. *The Creation of the Media: Political Origins of Modern Communications*. New York: Basic Books.

Tocqueville, Alexis de. 2004. *Democracy in America*. New York: Library of America.

Tuchman, Gaye. 1978. *Making News: A Study in the Construction of Reality*. New York: The Free Press.

Waldman, Steven. 2011. "Information Needs of Communities: The Changing Media Landscape in a Broadband Age." Federal Communications Commission.

6

Accounting for Diversity in Collaborative Governance

An Institutional Approach to Empowerment Reforms

CAROLINE W. LEE

■ In his famous essay "The Trouble with Wilderness," William Cronon (1995) argues that the idealization of wilderness as a space untainted by civilization prevents environmentalists from recognizing the inextricability of wilderness from culture. For Cronon, the danger of wilderness is in the creation of an ahistorical, acontextual place apart—a sacred, "ultimate landscape of authenticity," which allows us to "forgive ourselves the homes we actually inhabit" (25). "Wilderness poses a serious threat to responsible environmentalism," because it prevents us from attending to a more complex, morally ambiguous nature profoundly entangled with everyday human activities, "all around us if only we have eyes to see it" (38). In this chapter, I argue that deliberative democrats have made a similar mistake in framing collaborative governance innovations as cherished spaces apart, uncontaminated by ordinary politics.[1]

Rather than testing whether deliberative outcomes like enhanced social capital or local empowerment are achieved as theorized, I investigate how stakeholders themselves assess the ambiguity and complexity they faced in the design of three multistakeholder collaboratives formed in the late 1980s and early 1990s. Instead of asking *whether* these particular collaboratives live up to deliberative ideals, I ask in this chapter *how* the implementation of those ideals varies in actual practice, and *why*. For these actors, tensions among competing logics of organization and pressure to differentiate social ties among involved and uninvolved stakeholders often drove institutional design decisions and produced unintended consequences over the long term. Each of the partnerships departed from deliberative democrats' ideals in some ways and at some times, but these departures were agentive choices made by process organizers, often in spite of their knowledge of how such choices compromised a particular logic of virtue. According to many process leaders and participants, a conscious focus on making processes look good at the expense of their substantive meaning or value to participants was not only destructive to ultimate environmental goals, but to social acceptance within the larger community. Rather than representing a fall from grace to ordinary politics, I argue that efforts to adapt collaborative institutions to their larger social and political contexts—and the variety of choices, competing values, and nuanced interactions they reveal—are a necessary and critical aspect of innovations' political functioning and long-term social survival. I conclude by summarizing the key differences in the partnerships and what these suggest for a more comprehensive appreciation of the diversity of collaborative institutions in local decision making.

Ideals and Realities in Collaborative Environmental Problem Solving

The last three decades have seen a flowering of innovative approaches to environmental problem solving, engaging companies, environmentalists, recreational users, and local citizens in substantive decision making on issues ranging from habitat conservation to fisheries management and infrastructure planning (Cortner and Moote 1999; Kraft and Mazmanian 2009; National Research Council 1999; Wondolleck and Yaffee 2000). This new openness to multistakeholder collaboration has been the result of a variety of converging trends: greater devolution of environmental decision making to state and local governments and increasing coordination of environmental planning at regional scales such as watersheds and ecosystems; a promising new era of "civic environmentalism," involving more demand for citizen involvement in local environmental issues; and the failure of top-down federal regulatory approaches, often mired in litigation and inadequate to protecting valued resources. Collaborative reforms have attracted more attention from students of politics than they have from those studying organizations. Political scholars were some of the first to herald these new initiatives—variously called deliberative democracy, collaborative governance, or empowered participation—as promising innovations for resolving governance challenges around shared resources (Fung and Wright 2003; John 1994; Sabel, Fung, and Karkkainen 2000; Sirianni and Friedland 2001).

By bringing traditional public and private opponents such as regulators, environmentalists, and developers to the same table for extended discussions, new multistakeholder partnerships on environmental issues have been promoted as democratic alternatives to "command and control" and "decide-announce-defend" politics as usual. Organizers promise participants that state-sponsored spaces for cooperative decision making will reduce costly litigation, produce better quality environmental decisions, and enhance community capacity for continuing engagement. The social capital generated through reasoned discussion and more networking with diverse others will produce healthier environments and healthier communities. Celebrated examples testify to just how dramatic such changes can be. In the Pacific Northwest in 1993, timber companies and spotted-owl lovers called a truce and met in a county library to try to find a way out of the "timber wars" (Terhune 1998). For veterans of bloody endangered species battles, these new political institutions have signaled a revolutionary shift. Judith Layzer notes a veritable "euphoria that accompanied the explosion of collaborative, place-based, environmental problem-solving in the 1990s" (2008, xi).

Understandably, many researchers and practitioners have sought out guidelines for how to design these multiactor, time-intensive new institutions, which typically involve convening new groups that meet on a continuing basis over a number of years. A vast scholarly literature in political science, communications, and political sociology seeks to use successful case studies and normative theory to shape guidelines of institutional design and formal principles of democratic engagement to guide new initiatives (Gastil and Levine 2005; Glock-Grueneich and Ross 2008; Sirianni 2009). Evangelists seek to diffuse best practices in collaboration more broadly by enshrining participatory requirements for transparency, collaboration, and participation in government agencies (National Research Council 2008), most recently in the Obama administration's Open Government Initiative.

Over the past decade, however, many researchers have begun to question whether even recognized models of collaborative environmental governance are actually producing their promised benefits. On the environmental side, many activists and organizations have withdrawn their support (Blumberg and Knuffke 1998; Hibbard and Madsen 2003). Critics fear process capture by development interests and little improvement in environmental outcomes despite the substantial money, time, and energy invested; Layzer (2008) finds ample evidence for this pessimism in a comparison of environmental outcomes of collaborative decisions to those made from the top down. In contrast to the optimism of proponents, Coglianese (1998) finds that collaborative decisions were actually more likely to produce litigation, often from former participants. Fifteen to twenty years on, the verdict on many of these innovative institutions is that they have fallen short of their collaborative, inclusive, and deliberative goals (Abel and Stephan 2000; Cohen and Rogers 2003; Irvin and Stansbury 2004). While this new literature seeks to define where collaborative partnerships deviated from the model, the normative orientation of political scholars, and the model of institutional homogeneity and collective rationality on which it relies, hinders their ability to explain what has transpired. If sought-for outcomes are not achieved, local initiatives must not have measured up to the ideal set by model institutions, according to these scholars; in the words of Cohen and Rogers (2003, 239), "we have a problem in the circumstances, not in the ideal that condemns them."

It is high time for scholars of organizations to assist in explaining how new collaborative institutions have shifted, but not revolutionized, the political landscape of resource management in the United States. Such a project can assist the cause of political scholarship by illuminating the limits of formal institutional design in fomenting political change. But it can also enhance the study of contemporary politics by shedding light on the diffusion of fashions in organizational reform in the past three decades—in this case, for top-down "empowerment projects" (Eliasoph 2009, 294). This is a particularly rich field of investigation, since research indicates that there is substantial variety in the organization of contemporary collaborative environmental partnerships and in the kinds of participation they favor (Ansell and Gash 2008; Bidwell and Ryan 2006; Koontz et al. 2004; Margerum 2008; Moore and Koontz 2003, Wondolleck and Ryan 2007). But even when this variety is recognized by scholars, it is typically seen as incidental to measuring how well innovations "fit" the model and to extracting structural principles of good governance that can be replicated universally (Thomas 2003, 150).

A comparative institutional analysis of this kind offers new ways of understanding heterogeneity in the development of collaborative institutions, just as scholars have discovered surprising variety in the development of political and market institutions (Haydu 2008; Berk and Schneiberg 2005). Turning to an institutional analysis of collaborative organizations and the political cultures they have sustained requires abandoning normative perspectives on collaborative ideals as alternatives to normal politics and instead comparing the perspectives espoused by participants and organizers in situ. The creation of distinct political spaces for innovative collaborations often produces substantial anxieties within communities about a new and uncertain terrain for contention, which may divert attention from community problem solving to claim making about procedural fairness (Hendriks 2006; Walker and Hurley 2004). The stakes for new institutions that promise so much are high, and potential failure may permanently alter the risk aversion of community members to other collaborative initiatives (Lee 2007). Once bitten participants may be twice shy about future innovations, even if they have little relationship to the failures of prior efforts (Nyce 2000). According to Berk and Schneiberg (2005, 46), this type of collaborative learning over time is key to understanding variance in institutions; "making room" for institutional diversity also involves making room for "actors' capacities for reflexivity and learning."

Far from being constituted by legible routines, structures, and rules, institutions encode complex, ambiguous, and often competing logics of value that must be negotiated (Hirsch and Lounsbury 1997; Hallett and Ventresca 2006). Actors must creatively decide which rules and values can be constructively adapted to particular contexts or problems on a regular basis, such that "scrambled moments" arise frequently (Eliasoph and Lo 2011). In the case of collaborative institutions, the logics of deliberative dialogue, transparency, and inclusion may conflict routinely, as when, for example, a participant in a collaboration may change her mind over the course of an open meeting, but may not want to be seen as having changed her mind in public. In this case, the value of transparency—often held up as incontestably virtuous—may militate against the value of preference change, a key indicator of authentic deliberation (Naurin 2007). How local organizers choose to locate such transformations or to enable their occurrence has far more to do with culturally specific tolerances for shame, disagreement, and trust than with theoretically complementary abstract principles of deliberative process design. By investing a particular structure of relationships with moral value, we may neglect the content and texture of those relationships.

In addition, those specifically investigating the social capital developed through new institutions have questioned the overinvestment of political theorists in the metaphor of capital as a "product" (or by-product) of organization. For the new collaborative institutions studied here, social capital outcomes are typically seen by deliberative democrats as instrumentally valuable to community purposes, and the circumstances of their development through social ties are treated as amenable to intentional design: getting opponents to talk together around a table is half the battle, and new understandings and relationships should emerge over time from the camaraderie of ineluctable togetherness. This application of rational logics to social capital production, however, neglects the fact that those relationships or interactions that are most valuable to participants—unusual alliances with diverse others—are often valuable *because* they were not developed instrumentally (Fishman 2009). Social capital is far harder to accumulate according to rational logics of institutional design than is financial capital.

Not only can institutional designs produce unintended consequences, but instrumental outcomes may only be possible if they are perceived as emerging from serendipitous contingencies of social context wholly unrelated to intentional design. Fishman observes "considerable causal force" in "those ties that are valued as intrinsically worthwhile interactions and that are not primarily seen by their participants as brokerage-like avenues to influence and power-based resources" (Fishman 2009, 80)—not surprising given the derogatory connotations of terms like "social climber." New collaborative institutions may create relationships that are less rich and productive by virtue of participants' conscious investment in leveraging those relationships. On the flip side, new institutions are also designed in contexts of rich pre-existing networks that were not developed instrumentally but may be of paramount value to making collaboration work as intended. Such nuances of local reception and organizational design have been given recent attention in the work of scholars observing the "enduring influence of local communities" on organizations (Marquis and Battilana 2009; Marquis, Glynn, and Davis 2007; McQuarrie and Marwell 2009).

The approach of Fagotto and Fung in this volume is to emphasize that success depends on embedding reforms in communities where experts, civic organizations, decision makers, and publics routinely embrace deliberative norms and have the capacity to do so based on supportive culture, resources, and networks; according to this view, deliberation may fail to take root in communities due to "weak social fabric" and "fundamental shortcomings of the structures of local democratic governance" (Fagotto and Fung 2009, 3). A comparative institutional approach to collaborative governance can give us new perspectives on how empowerment reforms are always and necessarily implemented over time within particular communities with varying enthusiasm for and sensitivities to abstract political ideals, differences that do not make such communities pathological or deficient. Comparing the development of collaborative institutions across cases that do not fit preconceived notions of deliberative norms and habits allows for a better appreciation of actors' capacities for deliberation about competing values not only within forums, but as they structure them.

Comparing Multistakeholder Collaborative Partnerships

There is ample reason to attempt a better understanding of the relationship of reforms to their larger social worlds, not least because participants in collaborative institutions have multiple institutional affiliations, and because the range of options available to potential participants is so complex. The contemporary social context of political life in the United States is one of hybrid, multilayered forms of activism, organization, and politics (Armstrong and Bernstein 2008; Eliasoph 2009; Eliasoph and Lo 2011; Heaney and Rojas 2011), and civic innovations typically blend public and private organizational structures and are nested in institutional domains of different scales and sectors. Public-private collaborative partnerships for regional habitat conservation planning, the subject of this chapter, take place in multijurisdictional regulatory, legislative, and political landscapes. The current era is also one of "hybrid events" and "blended forms of social action" (Sampson et al. 2005, 673) in which individual citizens and organizations face a vast range of strategic options for civic engagement, protest, lobbying, cultural change, or some combination of the above. According to Briggs, "because 'joint action' can include so many stages and levels, the key decision makers, decisions, and opportunities multiply exponentially" (2008, 311). Scholars have also noted that the recent era has produced "awkward" forms of collective action, in which nontraditional challengers or "social entrepreneurs," including elites or insiders, employ movement frames and adapt insurgent tactics to accomplish institutional change (Duffy, Binder, and Skrentny 2010; Polletta 2006; Walker 2009). In all three sites studied below, different categories of elites provided the initial impetus for collaborative innovation.

That scholars of collaborative innovations have for the most part neglected to compare the variety of civic strategies or hybrid institutional types in such a complex landscape is completely understandable. Studying just one of these institutions involves mastering a daunting number of events, perspectives, and documents over an extended period of time. Layzer, who compares six large-scale environmental management initiatives, notes that they are "extraordinarily complicated. . . . Because each is invented in its own place, comparison among them can be hazardous" (2008, xi). Studying those adaptations that make particular collaboratives unique or awkward is especially challenging, inasmuch as these features are obstacles to controlling for variance (Cohen and Rogers 2003; Thompson 2008).

Given these difficulties, how can we compare unique cases in order to assess the institutional diversity represented by collaborative partnerships? In the analysis, I compare three collaborative partnerships for conservation planning along three pa-rameters: the formation and administration of the partnerships; their outreach to lo-cals, both likely and unlikely participants; and their ability to sustain and build on collaborative efforts outside the group—the last a critical indicator of the social capital outcomes deliberative democrats predict in collaborative partnerships. The three cases in this study are home to multistakeholder collaborative partnerships that engaged local residents and community organizations in ecosystem-scale planning about how best to protect natural resources and habitat areas in coastal regions facing severe de-velopment pressures.

In order to control for variance in partnerships based on type or scale of the re-source problems involved, or the national administrative and legislative contexts of their development, I focus in this chapter on three collaborative resource conserva-tion partnerships in the coastal United States that addressed habitat conservation and development planning over similarly sized areas established during the late 1980s and early 1990s (see Table 6.1). San Diego's Multiple Species Conservation Program Working Group collaborated from 1991 to 1997 to develop a habitat conserva-tion plan safeguarding endangered and threatened species for nearly 200,000 acres within San Diego County in Southern California. Portsmouth, New Hampshire's Great Bay Resource Protection Partnership (RPP) was formed in 1994 to develop a habitat protection plan to guide conservation efforts in a unique inland estuary of 272,000 acres centered around the Great Bay on the New Hampshire seacoast. The South Carolina Lowcountry's ACE (Ashepoo, Combahee, and South Edisto Rivers) Basin Task Force, south of Charleston and north of Beaufort, organized in 1988 to coordinate conservation efforts for the watersheds of three undammed blackwater rivers, home to a number of endangered and threatened species. These case studies are based on fieldwork and 103 in-depth interviews conducted in 2001 and 2003 with twenty-six to forty regional, state, and local interviewees for each site and an additional nine national-level decision makers. Reflecting the multi-institutional, multiscalar nature of contemporary environmental decision making, interviews took place in eight states, with federal, state, and local officials, representatives and volunteers for national, regional, and local organizations, corporate spokespersons, and private citizens.[2]

Each collaborative partnership has received generous federal subsidies for a complex of interconnecting preserves and research units that anchor their larger land-protection efforts. Each site has a National Estuarine Research Reserve (a part-nership system of reserves sponsored by the National Oceanic and Atmospheric Administration) and a National Wildlife Refuge run by the US Fish and Wildlife Service. These federal investments indicate the maturity of conservation efforts and the national and international value of the ecosystems in each site, in addition to the success each site has had compared to its adjacent neighbors in winning federal funding for local projects.[3]

Table 6.1 Comparison of Multistakeholder Collaborative Partnerships

Collaborative regional conservation partnership	Multiple Species Conservation Program San Diego, CA	Great Bay Resource Protection Partnership Portsmouth, NH	ACE Basin Task Force Charleston, SC
Duration	1989–present (Working Group: 1991–1997)	1994–present	1988–present
Scope	194,318 acres	272,000 acres	350,000 acres
National Estuarine Research Reserves and National Wildlife Refuges	Tijuana River Reserve (1982) and San Diego Refuge Complex (1970s–1990s)	Great Bay Reserve (1989) and Great Bay Refuge (1992)	ACE Basin Reserve (1992) and ACE Basin Refuge (1990)

Involving stakeholders in each of these cases meant inviting them to an ongoing series of discussions entailing substantive deliberation over project goals and recurring consideration of conservation- and development-relevant issues. These might take place in a hearing room with a dais in a public building, as in San Diego's MSCP working group, or in the party room of a local pizza parlor, as in the Great Bay Partnership, or in the dining room of a restored plantation house, as in the ACE Basin Task Force. In each of these different venues, potentially adversarial or competitive stakeholders met face to face on a repeated basis in the company of assorted public officials. Meeting duration and frequency ranged from two- to three-hour gatherings during the working day once a month, with time for public comments at the end, as in California, to a half-day affair every quarter, as in South Carolina, to four-hour bimonthly get-togethers, as in New Hampshire. All three projects involved far more investment in labor and time for participants than the standard-issue council hearing or public meeting—many stakeholders participated in hundreds of hours of meetings.

Because each partnership plans coastal conservation at the ecosystem scale, they have substantive similarities in relevant stakeholders. Federal and state wildlife agency employees are involved, in addition to state and county officials from wildlife, planning, and parks departments. Those with an interest in urban land use, such as environmentalists and developers, are central stakeholders in each case, whether or not they are official participants. Land use interest groups, civic organizations, and recreational clubs play active roles as well. Group representatives across the sites often hold parallel positions within analogous organizations (as in the case of directors of local native plants groups), or as regional or local chairs of the same national organization. More than half of the interviewees in the sample had direct counterparts in the other two sites. Actors in the same organization or in organizations within the same institutional field may be expected to have similar values and norms; the perspectives collected in this project revealed drastically different roles and perspectives even among those working in the same position for the same organization (Lee 2011). These differences can be ascribed both to sources of institutional variance within organizations and to variance in the local contexts within which those organizations act.

Organizing Collaboration: Governance in Formal and Informal Processes

Because of the ways observers have critiqued multistakeholder partnerships for falling short of participatory, collaborative, and deliberative ideals, this analysis begins by exploring the variety of choices made by process organizers regarding inclusion and governance in the collaboratives. Scholars of landscape-scale resource management partnerships have tended to focus on formal, public processes at the local level as processes most in line with the goals of participatory governance and deliberative democracy, and the Multiple Species Conservation Program (MCSP) Working Group in San Diego, California, represents a case of habitat conservation planning tied directly to these principles (Kaye 1997; Thomas 2003; Layzer 2008). Even though the MSCP was intended to diminish the role of the federal government in land use planning in San Diego, the actual impetus for the MSCP came from a variety of decidedly nonlocal federal and state agency leaders and behemoth developer the Irvine Company, all wary of the impending listing of one threatened species, the California gnatcatcher, and willing to experiment with collaborative alternatives. Regulatory protection of California gnatcatcher habitat would have meant expensive setbacks for development in Southern California, as its habitat covered a wide swath of desirable and developable unbuilt land in the region (Hogan 2003).

San Diego planners and officials welcomed the infusions of outside money and assistance for acting as a conservation plan "test case" and were eager to try out the new plan, particularly as they were facing a mandate to do an environmental assessment and watershed planning effort as part of a Clean Water Act judgment against the city (county planner, interview, January 2004). As interior secretary Bruce Babbitt's chief assistant on the MSCP plan describes, the MSCP "really carved out the role nationally of being a leader on approaching these environmental challenges in a different and bold way" (interview with author, March 2004). The new MSCP regime seemed promising to local parties but was uncertain territory as well for environmentalists, planners, and developers used to engaging in contention on individual development projects. If the habitat conservation plan worked, it would mean prioritizing the most important lands, setting them aside permanently as habitat through acquisition, and letting the rest be developed (and mitigated as specified in the plan), rather than having constant standoffs on each new development or road project that came down the planning pipeline.

In order to negotiate such agreements, developers and environmentalists would have to sit at the planning table together, and a working group was formed of representatives from public wildlife agencies, local jurisdictions, a selection of local environmental non-profit groups and chapters of national environmental organizations, a builders industry association, a landowners' group, individual development companies, the regional association of governments, the transportation and water districts, the local energy company, hired environmental and financial consultants—a much larger planning table than most participants were used to. Despite its size, some participants in retrospect lamented that the table had not been big enough. The working group did not include representatives from the EPA or the Army Corps of Engineers, an oversight that many regretted later when they realized that the guarantees in the comprehensive plan resulting from the MSCP could potentially have also focused on wetlands and thus included exemptions from Clean Water Act permitting from these agencies (Merrick 1998).

By contrast, the organization of the ACE Basin Task Force and the Great Bay Resource Protection Partnership was intentionally informal and private, with no authority to determine where development could or could not occur. When they have considered informal collaboration at all, theorists typically have understood informal strategies as subversive or destabilizing forces for comprehensive planning, typical of the collusion and exclusionary politics of growth machines—the ultimate in politics as usual. This is even though noted longstanding collaborations, including the Quincy Library Group, are informally organized and have rejected government institutionalization. In a typology of collaborative environmental partnerships, Margerum (2008, 487) found that ten out of thirty-six cases studied were private (not institutionalized in the public sector), revealing substantial "differences in the role of government and the decentralization of power" that collaboratives enact. Whereas the San Diego MSCP task force was dedicated to producing a plan that would be legally binding and implemented by government officials, the ACE Basin Task Force and the Great Bay Resource Protection Partnership, while involving federal and state agencies as members, were not administered or managed by their public sector partners, and they oriented their efforts simply to coordinating land and easement acquisition (see Table 6.2).

Far from indicating capitulation to machine politics as usual, organizers of the Great Bay and ACE Basin collaboratives intentionally pursued this style of organization as most effective for protecting shared environmental resources. Whereas the San Diego working group was seeking to reconvene the usual players on a new playing field with a different form of governance, the ACE Basin Task Force and the Great Bay Resource Protection Partnership were seeking to use a traditional form of backstage politics for a nontraditional purpose, with particularly resistant elite actors explicitly excluded. Leaders of the ACE Basin Task Force and the Great Bay Resource Protection Partnership credit a key element of their success to the fact that they are relatively invisible, unofficial, and informally organized, and therefore make difficult targets. Kay Truitt, the leader of the New Hampshire partnership, laughs about this element of the partnership:

Table 6.2 Governance and Inclusion in Multistakeholder Collaborative Partnerships

Regional conservation partnership	Multiple Species Conservation Program, San Diego	Great Bay Resource Protection Partnership, Portsmouth	ACE Basin Task Force, Charleston
Governance	Deliberative, public, run by public planner	Deliberative, private, run by private planner	Authoritarian, private, run by private citizen
Inclusion of interested parties and usual suspects	Yes, citizen working group with decision-making authority, public workshops and hearings	Yes and no, open group of community partners, limited group of decision-makers, developers not included	No, limited group of decision-makers, developers and local jurisdictions not included
Inclusion of uninterested parties and unlikely participants	No	No	Yes, informal participation welcome

We're a nonentity. You know, someone was telling me, "We were a virtual organization. We only existed when we got together." Which has become kind of a joke with us, you know? That we don't really exist. (Interview with author, August 2003)

Philip Rhodes, the leader of the South Carolina partnership and a private landowner whose family has owned property in the watershed for four generations, elaborated on how his partnership's lack of structure made it easy to avoid capture by powerful interests in the community:

I mean the Task Force is nothing. It's a group of people that come together. There's no budget, there's no constitution, there's no bylaws, it's just a meeting that occurs whenever we set the next meeting at the meeting we're at. So there's nothing for anyone to even—there's no way to get at it. . . . And because it doesn't exist there's no way for anyone to try to take over. You know, you can't buy it. (Interview with author, November 2003)

Certainly, these partnerships are much more than "a group of people coming together," especially since, as in San Diego, they have both managed to change the development status of thousands of acres of ecologically significant habitat.

But the joking nature of these claims indicates that participants are aware of the paradoxes of their strategic "nonexistence"; on the one hand, they have avoided becoming a convenient target for stakeholders resistant to the idea of government or interest group interference in local development issues, but on the other, their invisibility departs from the ideal of open, transparent governance and looks more like backstage maneuvering of the "we never had this conversation" variety. Researchers have tended to be skeptical of the ability of such partnerships to accomplish much, even as they have noted that informal collaboration is a key factor for successful elites in urban regimes (Stone 1989). Korfmacher (2000, 549), who explores a similar partnership in the Darby Creek watershed, asserts that while an informally structured watershed partnership demonstrates that "loose coordination is not pointless," "a stronger institution may be needed." However, Briggs argues that in a multi-institutional political field, where government activity is limited, effective problem solving requires community action "beyond government. . . . Too many . . . mistake . . . institutional designs for consensus-building . . . for the more complex and elusive resource of civic capacity" (2008, 298).

Negotiating Inclusion: Varieties of Participation

Because the San Diego process was public and was going to result in a formal, legally binding plan, the stakes of inclusion were high: either a stakeholder was a member of the working group or not. Stakeholders struggled prior to making the substantial commitment to be involved, a decision that was not without anxiety. Iris Greene, from the environmental consulting firm engaged in developing the plan, reports:

> In 1991, that was just really a new notion, and it was hard for developers to
> agree to. It was very contentious, and it was really a stressful time for a lot
> of people in San Diego. But what came out of that really was an incredible
> partnership of developers, environmental groups, different federal state and
> local agencies, and not as many cities as probably would have liked to have
> been involved. But it was a partnership that realized that land use planning is
> going to be different from now on and these are the partners that have to be
> involved. (Interview with author, January 2004)

While the ACE Basin Task Force and the Great Bay RPP organized informally in order to exclude potential enemies like developers, the MSCP was designed to bring developers and environmentalists together to deliberate on difficult tradeoffs. Developers were not the only ones who had trepidations about joining the program. Jeffrey Ecker, the former director of the county planning department, describes how a national environmental organization, despite being far more involved than any of the other national organizations with local chapters, still couldn't figure out how to engage in the process while preserving integrity among members:

> [The national group] tried to get involved, but they never really were
> successful. It was partly they weren't quite sure what their role was. Should

they be an advocate and keep very clean or did they want to get involved
and be a little closer with people, you know? (Interview with author, January
2004)

Because of wariness about potential contamination from association with a messy
process, signing on developers and environmental groups was a slow and difficult
process for Jeffrey:

> There were other people that were there on the building side that were
> willing to see this as something that would have benefits for them if it was
> successful even though they wanted to negotiate the best deal possible.
> There were some environmental people on the environmental side, that were
> also willing to do that, which was, that was probably equally as hard as the
> building side . . . finding environmental people that were willing to take a
> leap of faith and try to negotiate the best deal on their side was also hard.
> (Interview with author, January 2004)

Nevertheless, some environmental groups welcomed the invitation for inclusion in
a formal collaboration. Virginia Reade, the executive director of a small chapter of a
birding group, claims, "The more formal a role, the better off you are. . . . It's much
better to get in the process earlier if possible" (interview with author, March 2004).

Some less moderate environmental groups were not willing to collaborate and
did not join the MSCP process, and property rights advocates on the right felt that
the cooperation encouraged within the MSCP was sinister. Ecker half-jokes, "When
this was first approved, there were a lot of property rights types down here that sort
of viewed us as being the new world order, the United Nations coming in with blue
helmets on" (interview with author, February 2004). Descriptions of the comprehensive planning in the MSCP as "socialism" and "communism" from property-rights-
oriented stakeholders who did not participate were typical (Chase 1997, 30). From
Ecker's standpoint, self-interest from those attempting to assert themselves within the
working group was a far bigger threat. His own mindset for producing deliberative
decisions was drawn from the corporate negotiation bible, "Getting to Yes" (interview
with author, February 2004).

Once groups had committed to the process, the simple fact of demonstrated commitment to grueling meetings provided a huge incentive to make conclusive decisions
on particular issues that seemed intractable at the beginning, as predicted by deliberation scholars. Bobby Goode, the head of a regional environmental group formed
to engage in the MSCP, claimed that a lot of the working group's success could be
attributed to "Just being in the trenches with a number of people for years . . . at some
point you realize that the mutual goal can serve several different objectives. It can
serve their objectives, it can serve your objectives, and the cliché is you start rolling

together" (interview with author, April 2004). Such turning points from strategic ne-gotiation to collaboration are an ideal goal for proponents of deliberative structures within institutions (Gastil 2008). One participant noted in a public report that par-ticipants actually got along "suspiciously well" (Merrick 1998).

By contrast, the fact that the East Coast partnerships were organized informally meant that there was much less scrutiny of their decisions about who should partici-pate and how decision making would proceed among multiple parties. Organizers in both sites turned away willing participants who wanted to be involved. Neverthe-less, the ways they decided on inclusion and governance in their "virtual" collabo-ratives differed in crucial ways. The partnership in New Hampshire was much more concerned with deliberation among members, impartial administration, and power sharing. The original organization of the partnership is typical in this respect, where Truitt, who was an independent consultant unaffiliated with any of the organiza-tions at the time, reports on how she came to be a part-time paid coordinator of the partnership:

> And we just kind of put everybody's thoughts together and we talked about it and decided on this somewhat loose framework but the framework that we came up with was I was to have nine bosses, that it was better that way because we didn't know how much competing interests there was going to be. (Interview with author, August 2003)

With Truitt's professional background in community planning, there were many dis-cussions about who should be invited to participate and what was the most productive group size:

> When we were talking about "What is this partnership? How should we organize it?" the question became, "How big should this table get?" . . . And again going back to group dynamics and my leanings on that. I didn't want this huge table, no more than twelve people per meeting, somewhere between eight and twelve I thought was a good group size, that was one piece of it. (Interview with author, August 2003)

Keeping potential participants out of the tight collaborative group was not necessarily difficult; one principal partner noted that towns "were certainly indifferent in the beginning" (interview with author, September 2003). In fact, the New Hampshire partnership actually approached three state agencies about participation and only one accepted the offer. Nevertheless, there were concerns about discussing sensitive property deals and the need to limit meetings to participants who could be counted on—and this led to the exclusion of potential participants like other landowners or local groups:

There was a high degree of confidentiality and professionalism that we
needed at that table. And it was really important, we had come to this point,
and the partners we all discussed, that we have a forward motion, that we
have this professional level, that we have confidentiality insured at all our
meetings so we could be talking about landowners and money and not have
to worry. (Interview with author, August 2003)

In order to rectify this apparent exclusion of locals, the New Hampshire RPP came up
with a plan to call the professional partners "principal partners" and the local partners
"community partners," who would be involved and have their own meetings four
times a year with Truitt but would not be privy to the negotiations of state and federal
agencies and state and national conservation groups. Truitt describes the process of
deciding on the right strategy for dealing with these "included" members who would
be excluded from the actual negotiations:

However, we didn't want to, we went back and forth on this, we had a
number of people who wanted to become principal partners and we said
no. Recognizing that the community and the regional component was
an important one, we needed a way of including them in the process but
making it basically manageable, so we came up with this idea of community
partners. (Interview with author, August 2003)

In this sense, the New Hampshire partnership, while recognizing the importance of
grassroots involvement and deliberation, nevertheless resisted empowering local participants at the same decision-making level as national and state NGOs at the start.
As the partnership has developed, it has adapted the intermediate participant category
of "community partners" to two separate groups: "associate partners," higher-capacity
organizations with a regional focus, and "community partners," local municipalities
and organizations. In addition, principal partners noted an evolution in the attitudes
of initially skeptical local jurisdictions: "they started to get on board and they turned
around and they're raising their own money for land acquisition" (interview with
author, September 2003). For the Great Bay RPP, an exclusive starting group has
gradually garnered greater local support and embraced deeper forms of participation
and local empowerment.

By comparison, the formation of the South Carolina collaborative and its decisions on the best governance format involved far less concern about impartiality,
confidentiality, or power sharing than in New Hampshire, and more interest in a
top-down authority structure. Instead of hiring an independent professional planner
with "nine bosses" to forestall organizational competition, a local property owner has
been installed in the partnership as volunteer chairperson from the very beginning, as
Philip Rhodes, the current task force leader and a local businessman, describes:

> What we've done is set up a system where the leadership of the task force is always to be drawn from private landowners. These other organizations are not going to be in positions to be chairmen of the task force and the reason for that is because they compete with each other. (Interview with author, November 2003)

These landowners do not play subservient roles to the public or third-sector partners, and they are not paid for their work. A lawyer in his family's firm, Will Reidel founded the task force and was its first leader in his capacity as a local landowner, in a process much faster and less reflective than the gradual, sensitive consensus building of the New Hampshire approach:

> We said if we're going to do this, we need a plan. And that's where that little sheet came out about, "We're going to have to do easements and all this kind of stuff." And I wrote it and had the other members edit it and they elected me chairman at that thing. And that was our first task force meeting and that was how it started. And it's interesting that we never really changed from that. The formula worked, and the formula worked essentially because the people who were involved were local people who understood the sensibilities and the politics of the area. (Interview with author, August 2001)

Reidel's legitimacy as an unpaid local property owner in touch with local priorities is unquestioned, which in turn legitimizes the goals and governance structure of the task force. Reidel describes his own philosophy of leadership:

> We're organized like the Politburo was in Russia. I'm chairman, and as long as everybody likes me, I have authority, but I could be pushed out at any one time. And I just made a lot of unilateral decisions, but I always built consensus, because I'm a diplomat, and not a—I'm very diplomatic, I make sure that everybody agrees on everything and I've never pushed something down. (Interview with author, August 2001)

Reidel understood himself to be responsible for consensus building, but for his own "unilateral decisions." The ability to be "pushed out" is not limited to the task force chair, however. If participants do not respect the confidentiality of the proceedings, Rhodes relates that there are harsh consequences: "If someone isn't on the program, they git gone. Period" (interview with author, November 2003).

While on their own, these quotes might produce an alarmingly authoritarian picture of participation in the South Carolina case, it is critical to remember that the New Hampshire partnership does not allow local citizens, or even local or regional group representatives, into the principal partners' meetings at all—which could explain why there was so much more concern in the New Hampshire case about the appropriateness of deliberative processes and the construction of the "community partner" role. As compared to San Diego, the boundaries for appropriate participation in the task force are determined far more narrowly and punitively—no doubt possible because the balance of the partnership is far more heavily weighted to its private rather than its public side. The ability to dismiss recalcitrant members would have severely compromised the legitimacy of the working group in San Diego, where members had taken on considerable risks in joining and were more likely to (and did) threaten abandoning the process than to be banned from it (Layzer 2008).

Due to their explicit exclusion from the process, local and county governments were often hostile to task force activities at the beginning. Rhodes states frankly, "I would say the county has been largely unsupportive. Both with their regulations and with their pocketbooks. It's been done in spite of the county" (interview with author, November 2003). He acknowledges that this is not particularly admirable, but that it is unavoidable because local government support proceeds at a much slower pace than land deals:

> I mean, I'm just speaking plain, now I know I'm being recorded, I'm just telling you, you know, what I think, is that it isn't about how people on the outside are thinking, it's about how people on the inside are working with each other. You don't get the inside part right the outside part will never work. (Interview transcript, November 2003)

For the task force, the content of stakeholders' substantive commitments and the substance of their potential contributions was far more important than superficial collaborations that looked good, even if those were among traditional allies like environmental groups. Far from being a dirty secret, this exclusiveness was actively and openly discussed by task force members and even promoted in the local press (Lee 2009). Deliberative theorists would argue that the collaborative spirit that evolved over the course of the MSCP process would have been impossible in the task force, since members excluded potentially disagreeable opponents from the start. Despite this intentional exclusion, Rhodes notes that the perspective of unincluded stakeholders changed over time: "The outside part, over a period of time, they start to get it more and more and even in [the county] they're starting to get it a little bit better than they used to" (interview transcript, November 2003). By demonstrating successful collaborative efforts within the smaller group, the task force managed to garner the support of those stakeholders they had initially excluded.

This ability to win over antagonistic, disinterested, or uninvolved stakeholders without requiring their collaboration at the outset does not accord with the ideal of maximal inclusion of all parties with a potential stake in planning processes. Nevertheless, the governance and inclusion choices made by task force and RPP organizers were pursued intentionally, and, when compared to each other, reveal very different choices with respect to the level of inclusion and the type of reception anticipated by organizers. Xavier de Souza Briggs notes that alternation of roles and the use of strategic intermediaries and private discussions of the sort recounted here is critical to democratic problem solving: "informal civic space matters. . . . One can thwart democracy's basic purpose . . . with a rigid attachment to well-intended protections" (2008, 304, 313). Similar endorsements of the strategic advantages of limiting inclusion in the early stages of collaboration are emerging among some researchers of governance design (Johnston et al. 2011).

Building Instrumental Ties:
The Subjective Meanings of Participation

Cooperation qua cooperation in the massive planning effort of the MSCP did yield substantial collective benefits for the players in ways that deliberative democrats might expect. At the conclusion of seven years of difficult negotiation, Ecker in San Diego reports that leveraging consensus among unlikely allies when lobbying for federal funding allows organizers "to use that social capital and go back and pitch [to legislators] that this is all something that everybody agrees with" (interview with author, February 2004). On a special segment profiling the MSCP on the *Newshour* with Jim Lehrer, the mayor of San Diego at the time crowed, "Everybody wins!" (Kaye 1997). From the outside, this cooperation in long-term deliberative process is impressive to legislators and agencies with their hands on the purse strings, as well as to newsmagazines. For researchers of empowered deliberative democracy like Craig Thomas, the habitat conservation planning model's weaknesses are countered by these potential gains in social learning that can accrue over the course of deliberation: "In deliberative HCPs with broad participation, participants typically design a preserve system with other social benefits in mind. . . . In doing so, they also develop social capital, including skills for deliberative practice" (2003, 163–64).

Despite the success of San Diego's process organizers in bringing a wide number of groups to the table and producing a plan that represented the outcomes of their deliberative collaboration, the long nature of the process ended up wearing down stakeholders with less resources and capacity and generating substantial skepticism and bad will after the process concluded. Time was an obstacle to continuing to sustain the project and the participating groups' belief in the worth of the process. When asked about difficulties, Ecker responds, "Just change in people and administrations. You're always having to re-educate people as to what you've done and sometimes it's a lot more difficult than you would hope it would be" (interview with author, February 2004). Simply participating in so many concurrent, extended initiatives (other simultaneous regional planning processes were also occurring throughout the 1990s) is exhausting for all but the most engaged players. Environmentalist Bobby Goode describes this as "the self-limiting reality": "There's only a handful of people that are involved with the MSCP that have had a continuum of engagement. It's just different jobs and moving on and so on, just life. In San Diego, I know there's less than ten people that have been in there since the beginning [1991]" (interview with author, April 2004).

State officials and those working for NGOs that facilitate and fund public conservation land purchases see the MSCP as largely irrelevant to both conservation and their ongoing work acquiring properties. Veronica Tanner, an official with the state coastal commission, says, "I'm not an expert but I haven't been all that impressed that much has changed" (interview with author, May 2004). Christopher Sigler and Joshua Guertin, two project directors for a national conservation NGO, openly admit, "We didn't go to a lot of meetings since we're involved with purchase." Sigler reports that "another meeting to attend" does not get the job done on the ground: "It's a lot of feel good, not a lot of deals" (interview with author, April 2004). Despite their belonging to a national NGO engaged in inking major deals to finance habitat purchases, for Christopher and Joshua, "getting to yes" must take place outside of the MSCP negotiating table. Essential property purchases required for land conservation in San Diego do not revolve around partnership tables and "usual suspects." Even Virginia Reade of the birding group, who had such enthusiasm for the leverage her group could gain by participating at the formal negotiating table, openly admits, "The MSCP is a last gasp. It's not the answer for conservation—too little, too late" (interview with author, January 2004).

Participants in the working group were all aware that sensitive negotiations often took place on a smaller scale in closed-door sessions. Although these more intimate negotiations were supposed to be referred back to the larger group, one report on the results of the MSCP describes disagreement on the way these negotiations were perceived: "Some interviewees indicated that the process was not such a collaborative negotiation as it was portrayed to be by the media, and one participant expressed frustration with the 'behind the scenes' decisions that made the working group process appear to be 'window dressing'" (Merrick 1998; also see Layzer 2008). The preceding comments on the limits of the MSCP are a window on the pragmatism of those who engage with land use planning in Southern California. For environmental groups, participation might yield future leverage for the group as an organization, but they realize that it will probably effect only minor improvement for species in the region. For those looking to make the biggest mark in terms of assembling viable habitat before it's too late, the politicized negotiations that go on at the planning table for recognition in the decision-making community are time-consuming and simply irrelevant to the property-oriented deal making and negotiation with funders and individual property owners that take place outside collaboratives and have more immediate and substantive impacts.

Finally, it seems that the trust building produced through MSCP deliberations was relatively superficial in that it did not produce smoother cooperation outside the MSCP, as deliberative democracy theorists predict. Ecker, who was so proud of how much cooperation the groups in the MSCP planning could show when they lobbied in Washington for federal funding, acknowledges that when the issue is deciding how organizations will contribute their own money to regional funding sources, stalemate is common: "There's a regional funding source requirement which is how [funding is] supposed to happen, by the way, but that has never come together because it takes a lot of cooperation" (interview with author, February 2004). A court judgment on a suit brought by environmentalists against the MSCP has borne out the skepticism of conservation deal makers regarding the environmental outcomes of the process, which Judge Rudi Brewster ruled "violates both the spirit and the letter of the ESA" (*Southwest Center for Biological Diversity v. Bartel* 2006).

Most disappointing for those who see the MSCP as a flawed but promising start for collaborative decision making on habitat conservation, Ecker confesses that those at the top have advised the county in its own planning efforts for current and future habitat conservation planning processes to avoid formal deliberative groups: "We did not—at the direction of our board and this is something that we were just told by the board members—they didn't want to have an ongoing stakeholder group" (interview with author, February 2004). Instead, the board advised that the county planners revert to an older model of episodic public consultation, where the planners could deal with gatherings of common stakeholding interests like environmentalists on their own turf:

JEFFREY ECKER: They [the board] said you go out and do ad hoc . . .
INTERVIEWER: Charrettes?
JEFFREY ECKER: Yeah. . . . So we're trying to do it that way rather than have a formal set of folks that are at the table and I think it's working but we'll find out at the end of the day. (Interview with author, February 2004)

While the San Diego MSCP working group began with a groundbreaking new commitment to collaboration, the ultimate effects of that collaboration have been disappointing, inasmuch as environmentalists reverted to—and won—lawsuits challenging MSCP implementation, and stakeholders were not able to leverage their collaboration into new funding institutions to support the plan they approved. Major players still meet, but stakeholders with lesser capacity withdrew from subsequent processes, which no longer involve a formal, public collaborative group. San Diego has thus been criticized as a case that does not measure up to deliberative ideals—results typically explained in terms of the failure of organizers to counterbalance development interests effectively (Hogan 2003; Layzer 2008).

By contrast, the processes that began far less promisingly as far as inclusionary and deliberative ideals in New Hampshire and South Carolina have gained ground toward realizing those ideals in more participatory formats and more deliberative de-cision making as the processes have evolved. While scholars have documented other similar cases of evolution toward, rather than away from, collaboration (Briggs 2008), the institutional starting point for deliberative democrats interested in harnessing the social capital and more informed decisions of deliberative democracy is, understand-ably, open, inclusive, deliberative structures. Deliberative democrats often lament that communities that don't have capacity are unlikely to be able to carry out the delib-erative processes that might build it (Mansbridge 2003). But the findings described here reflect those of scholars who have studied evolution and learning in institutions over time (Lyon et al. 2009), in that communities may be able to build deliberative or more open structures out of initially unpromising, closed, or authoritarian structures: "history is not a curse," according to Briggs (2008, 298).

In fact, the least deliberative, least open case studied here demonstrates that non-deliberative or exclusionary processes have potential to engage participants highly re-sistant to collaboration, specifically because they are less threateningly political and more informal than well-publicized models of collaboration. The Great Bay Partner-ship in New Hampshire, closer to the ideals of inclusion of likely participants than the ACE Basin Task Force, finds reaching out to adversarial or resistant stakeholders difficult. Truitt, who has the most contact with the community partners, reports that dealing with low-capacity stakeholders is extremely time-consuming. The community partners are the most difficult and challenging part of her job, despite her professional and personal commitment to democratic process: "To me, you have to have a commu-nity partner. I'm a firm believer in that but it is a messy process. It's like democracy is messy, but it works. We've partnered over here, huge mess, but it's a great property and it works" (interview with author, August 2003). Truitt acknowledges that community partners are "important, they bring money to the table, and they bring buy in and they help us identify properties and they're our voice in the community and all that's critical" (interview transcript, August 2001).

Nevertheless, they are difficult for her to manage for reasons other than the extra time and effort involved in having so many parties involved in a land transaction: "The thing for me, I don't know about the other partners, for me, it's the commu-nity partner piece. I always feel there's somebody not happy at any given time. . . . It's like having your kids, you know, I don't mean to demean it. I'm just saying that sometimes there's a—the community partners is much more territorial" (interview with author, August 2003). Undoubtedly, the newly minted "associate" partners have grown in capacity through their participation and have earned a different type of role in the process. But what about involving stakeholders wholly outside of the partnerships that do not necessarily want to or have the capacity to participate? The Great Bay RPP has a light-handed approach to those landowners they anticipate resisting conservation, despite their surprising experience with local governments, according to Truitt:

> There are properties on our list on this stretch of the [creek], incredible
> habitat, we've identified it. They're never going to sell until hell freezes over.
> They're on our list, and I'll contact them, but, you know that, they just,
> they're not going to do it. It doesn't mean I don't contact them, but then
> you have a backup. . . . When hell does freeze over someone else will buy
> it from 'em. I say this tongue in cheek, but we talk about the likelihood of
> the personalities involved, of them working with us. (Interview with author,
> August 2003)

In contrast, despite their exclusion of community organizations they perceive as
peripherally relevant to the tasks at hand, task force leaders in South Carolina seem
less conflicted than Truitt in New Hampshire about the important role of the local
partners they do include and view as equally capable negotiating partners. Rhodes
asserts the importance of the national organization but segues into a discussion of the
value of local groups in the mix:

> If you were trying to protect something somewhere and all you had was the
> local groups, I think you'd be missing something. If you didn't have the local
> groups, you'd be—I mean, we function fine with local landowners, but local
> conservation groups offer an enormous amount. I mean some people just
> want to deal with the local people. . . . It's just, you've gotta have *lots* of tools.
> *Lots of tools.* (Interview with author, November 2003, emphasis his)

Both partnership leaders recognize that local organizations involved in land conservation are eager to participate and can be useful to the partnerships' overall goals
because of the depths of their connections and legitimacy in the local community.
The task force in South Carolina even involves local organizations and private citizens in decision-making capacities far more substantively than in New Hampshire or
than was ultimately achieved in the San Diego deliberations, given that lesser-capacity
players exited following the process. But what makes the South Carolina case unique
for this study is the extent to which it actively seeks out unlikely stakeholders who do
not want to or have the capacity to participate.

In fact, in South Carolina, the task force is proud of the strong pressure it exerts
on landowners whose interest in environmental conservation on their own property
falls in the "cold day in hell" category that the Great Bay Partnership writes off. Chair
Reidel gets visibly animated when discussing the variety of methods the task force
uses: "We never stop asking. . . . We're down to where if we can't get this guy, we work
the children. Hell, we work the grandchildren! We connect every day. We sit down
and say whoever got the most connections [should approach the landowner]. . . .
We will never stop until the day—and they will feel the pressure from every end . . .
until finally one day you're just going to have to do it because all your neighbors are

doing it" (interview with author, August 2001). The South Carolina partnerships' tactics seem aggressive and blunt, but the chair's pride in this sort of pressure is doubly remarkable due to South Carolina's proud resistance to public interference in private property matters. Reidel does not indicate any embarrassment about pressure as a legitimate course of action. The partnership uses two ways to persuade locals to conserve in a region filled with property owners who would not identify themselves as environmentalists.

First, the task force leverages personal social networks not just for information as in the New Hampshire case, but for actual influence. Second, the task force provides many different opportunities to get involved through organizations with varying missions and potential liaisons. Contrary to Skocpol's assertion (2003) that national organizations diminish local civic participation, for the South Carolina task force, the cooperation and variety of national partner organizations with seemingly opposed interests like birding and duck hunting is crucial to involving those locals unlikely to become involved. Philip puts this in plain terms: "If someone hates land trusts maybe they like killing ducks, they can go to Ducks Unlimited, if they don't like DU, they can do the Nature Conservancy, and you know, well maybe they're really rich, so they create their own foundation. There's all kinds of ways" (interview with author, November 2003).

In San Diego, by contrast, membership in the MSCP working group itself was frighteningly stigmatizing for those who would like to avoid perceived association with partners claiming opposing values. In the South Carolina partnership, those who typically "avoid politics" or hate "tree huggers" can simply make a show of support for another cause they favor, like a hunting group, with no presumption that they endorse an overarching, comprehensive community plan for environmental conservation—even though they have played a small but significant part in making it happen. As a result, annual "landowner appreciation" events for the South Carolina project area often involve useful seminars on deer management or other common challenges that the easement donors share as property owners, not as activists for environmental conservation.

The South Carolina task force paradoxically manages to include some participants who might reject even being associated with their activities. Not least, the interest group representatives who make up their inner circle often act to advance task force goals not in their capacity as task force members or professional organization staff, but by wearing other hats such as family member, friend, neighbor, and volunteer (see Lee 2011 for more on participants' strategic use of multiple professional and volunteer affiliations). This evidence suggests that informal, nondeliberative collaboratives might be superior at initiating dialogue and soliciting reluctant participation from strongly opposed stakeholders. Nevertheless, the less deliberative partnership in South Carolina also spends far less time soliciting support from the "usual suspects" like local governments or environmental groups whose "buy-in" it anticipates will not be of any immediate help. Ironically, despite the emphasis on socializing in the South Carolina task force (Lee 2007), members have a particular disdain for involving agencies or organizations just to keep them abreast of goings on and supportive, because these sorts of forums are seen as venues for the protection and advancement of purely political rather than environmental interests.

The ability to build reluctant cooperation from people who are either resistant to or disinterested in comprehensive conservation is out of reach of even the most inclusive formal habitat conservation planning process. As we saw in the San Diego case, professional public and private planners have great difficulty maintaining consensus around collaboratively developed plans between developers and other interest groups. Similarly, the ACE Basin task force members faced challenges scaling their model across to other focus areas along the coast. The consensus-based format that had worked so well in the first task force did not coalesce in other regional task forces in the same way—personal investments and connections among group members had been far more important than the organizational form of regional meetings organized around watershed boundaries. Like those in San Diego, the burden of constructing additional collaborations proved to be too taxing and distracted from substantive conservation work, and participants refocused their priorities on working at the statewide level for conservation planning (see Lee 2007 for more on this phenomenon).

Assessing Heterogeneity in Multistakeholder Collaboratives

The comparison above sketches three areas where the administration of these conservation decision-making bodies differs: in their approach to official public status, in their authoritarian or deliberative governance, and in their inclusion of interested and disinterested parties. The informal organization of the collaboratives in South Carolina and New Hampshire was just as deliberately designed as in the formal working group in San Diego, but the concern of organizers in these cases were oriented less on restructuring politics than on accomplishing habitat conservation whether the process looked good to outside observers or not. These organizers did care in theory about how the process "looked," but they believed that the substantive accomplishments of collaboration would be better proof of their good faith and would win over more converts in the long term than making the process transparent from the start. In San Diego, the substantial investment of organizers and some participants in producing a process that was fair and transparent did not forestall criticisms from outside observers that the process was rigged to benefit the powerful, and it did not create bonds strong enough to sustain the involvement of low-capacity stakeholders or to produce new collaborative institutions.

While the South Carolina task force on its face seems exclusive and authoritarian, it is led by local stakeholders, manages to elude capture by developers, and does include many politically conservative stakeholders (whether through informal channels or through mediating organizations) who might resist its goals otherwise. But its exclusive approach to allowing participation only of those who have an obvious stake in the outcomes of its proceedings doesn't allow for the inclusion of local governments. The New Hampshire partnership is skilled at soliciting participation from local governments, but runs into trouble negotiating local politics among these partners. As a result, it has limited their decision-making role far more than in the South Carolina partnership. The New Hampshire approach, while certainly exhibiting many of the qualities of an exclusive regime, nevertheless approaches governance, planning, and grant seeking with consultative strategies based on the experience of a professional planner—a welcome relief for representatives of strapped state agencies with very little planning capacity (interviews with author, October 2003).

The experience of participants in the San Diego MSCP gives cause to question whether the "sage scrub revolution" that has produced a fragmented system of subregional planning processes (Feldman and Jonas 2000) stands to produce the civic engagement benefits that have largely been assumed thus far. While even critics of deliberation see potential for participation in state-centered deliberative processes if these are a complement to other forms of social action (Fung, Young, and Mansbridge 2004), the ways in which formal participation in the San Diego MSCP was framed as a comprehensive solution presumed that participating groups would cease using other access points to decision makers and the public and suspend indefinitely other strategies such as litigation. Such agreements are fragile and unstable at best and put tremendous burdens on strapped ground-level administrators (Koontz et al. 2004; Wondolleck and Ryan 2007).

Solutions based in state-centered governance privilege local, state, and federal governments with a stability and solidity they may not have—an assumption belied by regular executive turnover, limited or cyclical time frames for accomplishing legislative mandates, and internecine bureaucratic struggles over policy making and administration. With these findings in mind, we might design and manage processes very differently than deliberative democrats concerned with best practices and universal principles. We might try to ensure that participation was sufficiently malleable to meet participants' conflicting senses of what participatory ideals should look like. Instead of attempting to "lock in" social capital benefits and reinforce bonds formed in collaborative groups, we might even design processes that have plenty of opportunities for participants to disengage. Paradoxically, fluidity of roles and responsibilities, the informalization of government involvement, and the avoidance of legal rules and obligations can make participants' commitments to collective enterprise stronger, not weaker.

The Trouble with Deliberative Democracy

When deliberative democracy is attempted on the ground, it tends to be judged by its capacity to create a space for a rare kind of politics to blossom and perpetuate itself, generating stores of social capital that will re-energize sojourners from our fallen world. Just as Cronon describes the paradox of creating intensively managed habitats to sustain a single species, this kind of hothouse approach to "perpetual participation" (Fung and Wright 2003, 32), in which deliberative democracy may bloom continuously in a few well-managed environments, risks making participatory innovations exotic and untenable. It also risks reducing the variety of political possibilities that exist to an ideal type that has little relationship to the messy, turbulent landscape of political collaboration as actually practiced. As this analysis has shown, two cases that both depart from the public, formal model of inclusive collaboration can actually look quite different from each other in the way they incorporate concerns about deliberation, inclusion, and local legitimacy in their design.

By critiquing the celebration of collaborative innovations as "real utopias" (Fung and Wright 2003), I am not arguing, as other scholars have, that deliberative democracy is morally suspect or should be condemned (Sanders 1997; Young 2000; see Kadlec and Friedman 2007 for a review of these critiques). Indeed, the transformative effects of deliberative democracy in collaborative governance, like those of stunning wilderness landscapes, are sublimely compelling for good reason (Fung 2004). Rather, I argue that we can gain a much richer understanding of politics as it currently is and politics as it might be if we suspend moral distinctions in favor of deeper empirical investigation of the relational content and diverse institutional contexts of civic innovations—if, like good conservation biologists, we pay just as much attention to edge effects and nonnative species as we do to indigenous biomass within a preserve.

This approach recognizes that all political institutions are adaptive and adapting, constantly transformed by and transforming their participants (Clemens and Cook 1999). New participatory innovations are not simply a route to the real business of community deliberation; they encode claims about the belonging of participants, the fairness of process, and the saliency of topics, claims that are inherently political and often contested. These conversations about the politics of collaboration and participation occur before, during, and after the process, within the process and outside it, in public and private, among participants and nonparticipants, and are themselves subject to contestation. In the process of institutionalization, different environmental projects and political institutions become "localized" in diverse ways as they shape and are shaped by their social environments.

This chapter argues that we should take new institutions for collaborative governance seriously as institutions and not simply as political innovations. By understanding these institutions not just through the prism of scholarship on governance, we can appreciate the dimensions of their heterogeneity, but we can also interpret their challenges through the vast body of research on common processes in the development of twenty-first-century institutions. While some scholars have begun to do so with respect to civic projects and urban organizations (Eliasoph 2009; McQuarrie and Marwell 2009), far more research is needed to place collaborative environmental institutions within the context of a comparative institutional history of the last three decades of neoliberal governance reforms.

I propose in this study that advocating for collaborative, participatory, and deliberative ideals without comparing how they are transformed and interpreted within complex multi-institutional contexts has caused scholars to neglect important aspects of how participation, collaboration, and deliberation in these new institutions actually work. The push in the 1990s both academically and practically was to formalize collaboration—meaning to embed it in government according to universal principles of good governance. Because of their belief in institutionalizing collaboration, scholars and reformers have tended not to consider whether collaboratives can be successful in settings that do not seem to accord with inclusive or transparent ideals. I find that attention to the ambiguous and multivalenced meanings of institutional contexts for participants reveals counterintuitive possibilities for expanding and perpetuating political change.

Notes

1. I use deliberative democracy as an umbrella term here because it is the most fully developed theoretical model representing a number of related reforms that include collaborative governance (Sirianni 2009), empowered participatory governance (Fung and Wright 2003; Fung 2004), ecosystem-based management (Layzer 2008), and others. While there are significant differences in these models, the general ideals of inclusivity, deliberative learning, and social capital building are widely shared.

2. Stakeholders in the conservation and development community who were not members of the partnerships were identified through a number of methods, including network sampling, analysis of local press, conservation and development directories, and annual reports. At the conclusion of interviewing, continued investigation returned very few new names. Interviews were transcribed, entered into a fully searchable electronic database, and inductively coded for emergent themes and concepts. I also coded publicly available organizational documents, websites, newsletters, and annual reports. The need to identify context and location, and to recognize the authors of publicly available documents, has been balanced with the use of pseudonyms to identify individuals and local organizations. The historical importance of national organizations—parties to the development of federal conservation policies and administration—justifies their identification in the study. For a more detailed discussion of methodology, see Lee (2007).

3. All three projects were successful in attracting substantial investments in large-scale, high-value conservation acquisitions during the periods studied. From 1991 to 2005, the ACE Basin conserved 31,000 acres of wetlands with $8 million of North American Wetlands Conservation Act (NAWCA) funding administered by the US Fish and Wildlife Service; this was matched by $16 million from partners (Watson 2005). From 1994 to 2005, the Great Bay Resource Protection Partnership received $12 million in NAWCA grant and matching funds for conservation of 7,500 acres (Milliken 2005); current figures are available at: *www.greatbaypartnership.org*. From 1999 to 2004, public

and foundation grant funding for acquisition, management, and monitoring of MSCP lands in the county totaled $21.1 million (1999–2004 MSCP Annual Report data). Federal agencies had acquired 6,800 acres, state agencies had acquired 14,300 acres, and the county had acquired 4,100 acres for conservation under the MSCP by 2004 (County of San Diego 2004). For detailed studies of long-term environmental outcomes in Southern California and South Carolina, see Layzer (2008) and Halfacre (2012).

References

Abel, Troy D., and Mark Stephan. 2000. "The Limits of Civic Environmentalism." *American Behavioral Scientist* 44: 614–28.

Ansell, Chris, and Alison Gash. 2008. "Collaborative Governance in Theory and Practice." *Journal of Public Administration Research and Theory* 18: 543–71.

Armstrong, Elizabeth A., and Mary Bernstein. 2008. "Culture, Power, and Institutions: A Multi-Institutional Politics Approach to Social Movements." *Sociological Theory* 26: 74–99.

Berk, Gerald, and Marc Schneiberg. 2005. "Varieties in Capitalism, Varieties of Association: Collaborative Learning in American Industry, 1900 to 1925." *Politics and Society* 33: 46–87.

Bidwell, Ryan D., and Clare M. Ryan. 2006. "Collaborative Partnership Design: The Implications of Organizational Affiliation for Watershed Partnerships." *Society & Natural Resources* 19: 827–43.

Blumberg, Louis, and Darrell Knuffke. 1998. "Count Us Out." *Chronicle of Community* 2: 41–44.

Briggs, Xavier de Souza. 2008. *Democracy as Problem Solving: Civic Capacity in Communities Across the Globe.* Cambridge, MA: MIT Press.

Chase, Carolyn. 1997. "Multiple Species Planning Marches On." *San Diego Earth Times*, April.

Clemens, Elisabeth S., and James M. Cook. 1999. "Politics and Institutionalism: Explaining Durability and Change." *Annual Review of Sociology* 25: 441–66.

Coglianese, Cary. 1998. "Assessing Consensus: The Promise and Performance of Negotiated Rulemaking." *Duke Law Journal* 46: 1255–1350.

Cohen, Joshua, and Joel Rogers. 2003. "Power and Reason." In *Deepening Democracy: Institutional Innovations in Empowered Participatory Governance*, ed. Archon Fung and Erik Olin Wright, 237–47. New York: Verso.

Cortner, Hanna J., and Margaret A. Moote. 1999. *The Politics of Ecosystem Management.* Washington, DC: Island Press.

County of San Diego. 2004. "MSCP 2003 Annual Report." San Diego: Multiple Species Conservation Program, Department of Planning and Land Use, County of San Diego. *www.sdcounty.ca.gov/pds/mscp/docs/SCMSCP/2003AnnualReport.pdf*.

Cronon, William. 1995. "The Trouble with Wilderness; or, Getting Back to the Wrong Nature." In *Uncommon Ground: Rethinking the Human Place in Nature*, ed. William Cronon, 69–90. New York: Norton.

Duffy, Meghan M., Amy J. Binder, and John D. Skrentny. 2010. "Elite Status and Social

Change: Using Field Analysis to Explain Policy Formation and Implementation." *Social Problems* 57: 49–73.

Eliasoph, Nina. 2009. "Top-Down Civic Projects Are Not Grassroots Associations: How The Differences Matter in Everyday Life." *Voluntas* 20: 291–308.

Eliasoph, Nina, and Jade Yu-Chieh Lo. 2011. "Broadening Cultural Sociology's Scope: Meaning-Making in Mundane Organizational Life." In *The Oxford Handbook of Cultural Sociology*, ed. Jeffrey C. Alexander, R. Jacobs, and P. Smith. New York: Oxford University Press.

Fagotto, Elena, and Archon Fung. 2009. *Sustaining Public Engagement: Embedded Deliberation in Local Communities*. East Hartford, CT: Everyday Democracy and the Kettering Foundation.

Feldman, Thomas D., and Andrew E. G. Jonas. 2000. "Sage Scrub Revolution? Property Rights, Political Fragmentation, and Conservation Planning in Southern California under the Federal Endangered Species Act." *Annals of the Association of American Geographers* 90: 256–92.

Fishman, Robert. 2009. "On the Costs of Conceptualizing Social Ties as Social Capital." In *Social Capital: Reaching Out, Reaching In*, ed. Viva Ona Bartkus and James H. Davis, 66–83. Northampton, MA: Edward Elgar Publishing.

Fung, Archon. 2004. *Empowered Participation: Reinventing Urban Democracy*. Princeton, NJ: Princeton University Press.

Fung, Archon, and Erik Olin Wright. 2003. "Thinking about Empowered Participatory Governance." In *Deepening Democracy: Institutional Innovations in Empowered Participatory Governance*, ed. by Archon Fung and Erik Olin Wright, 3–41. New York: Verso.

Fung, Archon, Iris Marion Young, and Jane Mansbridge. 2004. "Deliberation's Darker Side" [Interview]. *National Civic Review* 93: 47–54.

Gastil, John. 2008. *Political Communication and Deliberation*. Thousand Oaks, CA: Sage Publications.

Gastil, John, and Peter Levine, eds. 2005. *The Deliberative Democracy Handbook: Strategies for Effective Civic Engagement in the 21st Century*. San Francisco: Jossey-Bass.

Glock-Grueneich, Nancy, and Sarah Nora Ross. 2008. "Growing the Field: The Institutional, Theoretical, and Conceptual Maturation of 'Public Participation.'" *International Journal of Public Participation* 2: 1–32.

Halfacre, Angela. 2012. *"A Delicate Balance": Constructing a Conservation Culture in the South Carolina Lowcountry*. Columbia: University of South Carolina Press.

Hallett, Tim, and Marc J. Ventresca. 2006. "Inhabited Institutions: Social Interactions and Organizational Forms in Gouldner's *Patterns of Industrial Bureaucracy*." *Theory & Society* 35: 213–36.

Haydu, Jeffrey. 2008. *Citizen Employers: Business Communities and Labor in Cincinnati and San Francisco, 1870–1916*. Ithaca, NY: Cornell University Press.

Heaney, Michael T., and Fabio Rojas. 2011. "Hybrid Activism: Social Movement Mobilization in a Multi-Movement Environment." Paper Presented at the 2011 Annual Meeting of the American Political Science Association, Seattle, Washington, September 1–4.

Hendriks, Carolyn. 2006. "When the Forum Meets Interest Politics: Strategic Uses of Public Deliberation." *Politics & Society* 34: 571–602.

Hibbard, Michael, and Jeremy Madsen. 2003. "Environmental Resistance to Place-based Collaboration in the U.S. West." *Society & Natural Resources* 16: 703–18.

Hirsch, Paul M., and Michael Lounsbury. 1997. "Ending the Family Quarrel: Toward a Reconciliation of 'Old' and 'New' Institutionalisms." *American Behavioral Scientist* 40: 406–18.

Hogan, Richard. 2003. *The Failure of Planning: Permitting Sprawl in San Diego Suburbs, 1970–1999.* Columbus: Ohio State University Press.

Irvin, Renee A., and John Stansbury. 2004. "Citizen Participation in Decision Making: Is It Worth the Effort?" *Public Administration Review* 64: 55–65.

John, Dewitt. 1994. *Civic Environmentalism.* Washington, DC: Congressional Quarterly Press.

Johnston, Erik W., Darrin Hicks, Ning Nan, and Jennifer C. Auer. 2011. "Managing the Inclusion Process in Collaborative Governance." *Journal of Public Administration Research and Theory* 21: 699–721.

Kadlec, Allison, and Will Friedman. 2007. "Deliberative Democracy and the Problem of Power." *Journal of Public Deliberation* 3: Art. 8. *www.publicdeliberation.net/jpd/v013/iss1/art8.*

Kaye, Jeffrey. 1997. "Peaceful Co-Existence?" [Transcript]. *Newshour* with Jim Lehrer. July 14.

Koontz, Tomas M., Toddi A. Steelman, JoAnn Carmin, Katrina Smith Korfmacher, Cassandra Moseley, and Craig W. Thomas. 2004. *Collaborative Environmental Management: What Roles for Government?* Washington, DC: Resources for the Future Press.

Korfmacher, Katrina S. 2000. "What's the Point of Partnering? A Case Study of Ecosystem Management in the Darby Creek Watershed." *American Behavioral Scientist* 44: 548–64.

Kraft, Michael E., and Daniel A. Mazmanian, eds. 2009. *Toward Sustainable Communities: Transition and Transformations in Environmental Policy.* Cambridge, MA: MIT Press.

Layzer, Judith A. 2008. *Natural Experiments: Ecosystem-Based Management and the Environment.* Cambridge, MA: MIT Press.

Lee, Caroline W. 2007. "Is There a Place for Private Conversation in Public Dialogue? Comparing Stakeholder Assessments of Informal Communication in Collaborative Regional Planning." *American Journal of Sociology* 113: 41–96.

———. 2009. "Conservation as a Territorial Ideology. *City & Community* 8: 301–28.

———. 2011. "The Politics of Localness: Scale-Bridging Ties and Legitimacy in Regional Resource Management Partnerships." *Society & Natural Resources* 24: 439–54.

Lyon, Alexandra, Michael Bell, Nora Swan Croll, Randall Jackson, and Claudio Gratton. 2010. "Maculate Conceptions: Power, Process, and Creativity in Participatory Research." *Rural Sociology* 75: 538–59.

Margerum, Richard D. 2008. "A Typology of Collaboration Efforts in Environmental Management." *Environmental Management* 41: 487–500.

Marquis, Christopher, and Julie Battilana. 2009. "Acting Globally but Thinking Locally? The Enduring Influence of Local Communities on Organizations." *Research in Organizational Behavior* 29: 283–302.

Marquis, Christopher, Mary Ann Glynn, and Gerald F. Davis. 2007. "Community Isomorphism and Corporate Social Action." *The Academy of Management Review* 32: 925–45.

Mansbridge, Jane. 2003. "Practice-Thought-Practice." In *Deepening Democracy: Institutional Innovations in Empowered Participatory Governance*, ed. Archon Fung and Erik Olin Wright, 175–99. New York: Verso.

McQuarrie, Michael, and Nicole Marwell. 2009. "The Missing Organizational Dimension in Urban Sociology." *City & Community* 8: 247–68.

Merrick, Jennifer. 1998. "The San Diego Multiple Species Conservation Plan." In *Improving Integrated Natural Resource Planning: Habitat Conservation Plans* [Web page]. Knoxville, TN: National Center for Environmental Decision-making Research. *www.ncedr.org/ casestudies/hcp/sandiego.htm*.

Milliken, Andrew. 2005. "Atlantic Coast Joint Venture: New Hampshire." Hadley, MA: US Fish and Wildlife Service. *www.acjv.org/Fact_Sheets/NH_11.pdf*.

Moore, Elizabeth A., and Tomas M. Koontz. 2003. "A Typology of Collaborative Watershed Groups: Citizen-based, Agency-based, and Mixed Partnerships. *Society & Natural Resources* 16: 451–60.

National Research Council, 1999. *New Strategies for America's Watersheds*. Washington, DC: National Academies Press.

———. 2008. *Public Participation in Environmental Assessment and Decision Making*. Washington, DC: National Academies Press.

Naurin, Daniel. 2007. *Deliberation Behind Closed Doors. Transparency and Lobbying In The European Union*, Colchester, UK: European Consortium for Political Research Press.

Nyce, Chris. 2000. "Improving Public Outreach and Education for Natural Community Conservation Planning." Sacramento: California Department of Fish and Game. *www. dfg.ca.gov/nccp/pubs/outreach.pdf*.

Polletta, Francesca. 2006. "Awkward Movements." *Mobilization* 11: 475–500.

Sabel, Charles F., Archon Fung, and Bradley Karkkainen, eds. 2000. *Beyond Backyard Environmentalism*. Boston: Beacon Press.

Sampson, Robert J., Doug McAdam, Heather MacIndoe, and Simón Weffer-Elizondo. 2005. "Civil Society Reconsidered: The Durable Nature and Community Structure of Collective Civic Action." *American Journal of Sociology* 111: 673–714.

Sanders, Lynn M. 1997. "Against Deliberation." *Political Theory* 25: 347–64.

Sirianni, Carmen. 2009. *Investing in Democracy: Engaging Citizens in Collaborative Governance*. Washington, DC: Brookings Press.

Sirianni, Carmen, and Lewis Friedland. 2001. *Civic Innovation in America*. Berkeley: University of California Press.

Skocpol, Theda. 2003. *Diminished Democracy: From Membership to Management in American Civic Life*. Norman: University of Oklahoma Press.

Southwest Center for Biological Diversity v. Bartel. 2006. US Dist (SD CA). 98-CV-2234-B (JMA). October 13.

Stone, Clarence N. 1989. *Regime Politics: Governing Atlanta, 1946–1988*. Lawrence: University Press of Kansas.

Terhune, George. 1998. "The Quincy Library Group Case Study." Presented at the

Engaging, Empowering, and Negotiating Community: Strategies for Conservation and Development Conference, West Virginia University. *www.qlg.org/pub/miscdoc/casestudy. htm.*

Thomas, Craig W. 2003. "Habitat Conservation Planning." In *Deepening Democracy: Institutional Innovations in Empowered Participatory Governance*, ed. Archon Fung and Erik Olin Wright, 144–72. New York: Verso.

Thompson, Dennis F. 2008. "Deliberative Democratic Theory and Empirical Political Science." *Annual Review of Political Science* 11: 497–520.

Walker, Edward T. 2009. "Privatizing Participation: Civic Change and the Organizational Dynamics of Grassroots Lobbying Firms." *American Sociological Review* 74: 83–105.

Walker, Peter A., and Patrick T. Hurley. 2004. "Collaboration Derailed: The Politics of 'Community-Based' Resource Management in Nevada County." *Society and Natural Resources* 17: 735–51.

Watson, Craig. 2005. "Atlantic Coast Joint Venture: South Carolina." Charleston, SC: US Fish and Wildlife Service. *www.acjv.org/Fact_Sheets/SC_11.pdf.*

Wondolleck, Julia M., and Clare M. Ryan. 2007. "What Hat Do I Wear Now? An Examination of Agency Roles in Collaborative Processes." *Negotiation Journal* 15: 117–33.

Wondolleck, Julia M., and Steven Lewis Yaffee. 2000. *Making Collaboration Work: Lessons from Innovation in Natural Resource Management.* Washington, DC: Island Press.

Young, Iris Marion. 2000. *Inclusion and Democracy.* New York: Oxford University Press.

7

Networks and Narratives in the Making of Civic Practice

Lessons from Iberia

ROBERT M. FISHMAN

■ Early in 2006 a group of poor immigrants, mostly of African origins, were evicted from their formally illegal houses in Amadora, a large municipality just outside Portugal's capital city, Lisbon, and their dwellings were demolished. That event marked not just a personal tragedy for those who lost their homes but also the beginning of an important example of civic practice. Television newscasters reported the events live from Amadora and carried the voices and perspectives of those affected to television viewers throughout the country. The immigrants and their advocates organized a march on the parliament several weeks later and spoke with representatives of all the political parties represented in Portugal's Assembly of the Republic. These actions by the immigrants, and the interest the news media had manifested in their plight, provided much of the basis for subsequent public efforts to address their concerns.[1]

Two years later, in 2008, in the larger country situated alongside Portugal, a group of immigrants dwelling in formally illegal houses just outside Spain's capital, Madrid, were also evicted and their homes demolished, but the political and public ramifications of their plight were remarkably different. Advocates of the Madrid-area immigrants lamented their inability to establish useful channels of conversation with public authorities.[2] Given the absence of adequate public attention to their plight, many of those evicted spent more than a month living inside the church ministered to by the activist priest Javier Baeza in southern Madrid. The problems faced by the Madrid immigrants were left largely outside Spain's officially recognized civic arena of discussions with—or within—elective institutions. Yet during that same year, 2008, immigrants in Amadora were invited to participate in comprehensive policy conversations with Portugal's leading housing official, João Ferrão, with the aim of regularizing many dwellings while providing in other ways for those residing in housing not to be regularized. Similar people facing similar challenges—and residing in the neighboring countries which share the Iberian Peninsula at the western end of continental Europe—experienced vastly different encounters with political authorities. This fundamental contrast afforded the immigrants dwelling just outside the capital cities of Portugal and Spain thoroughly dissimilar opportunities to seek attention and assistance through civic action. For some reason the Portuguese political system proved far more open to meaningful civic action by poor immigrants than did the Spanish system. In this chapter I offer an explanation for this and other instances of divergence in the capacities of people to forge creative avenues of civic action.

One decade earlier, miners in the Asturias region of northern Spain were threatened with the loss of their jobs and way of life. HUNOSA, a large state-owned coal company, drew up plans to permanently close mines employing thousands of workers in the Nalón and Caudal valleys of that northern region. The two Asturian coal valleys, separated by only twelve kilometers of winding mountain highway, were remarkably alike in most respects, yet valley residents responded to this threat in fundamentally different ways in the two cases. In the Caudal valley miners and their supporters organized large campaigns focused entirely around the goal of keeping open existing mines such as the Barredo pit in Mieres, the Santa Bárbara mine in Turón, and others. Through mine occupations, demonstrations, and other forms of mobilization, they defended their direct local interests. Their plea, as a banner hung on one of these mines in the mid-1990s put the matter, was quite simple: "For our future, Don't close it."[3] But a few kilometers away, in the Nalon valley, leaders and activists largely rejected the defensive localism underpinning the exclusive focus on efforts to keep existing mines open. Instead, both their diagnosis of the problems they faced and their proposals for the future were *global* in scale—extending well beyond the confines of their valley and its mines. Their civic discourse looked well beyond their locality, addressing processes and engaging actors situated far away. Once again similar people facing similar challenges responded in vastly different ways. The Asturian miners working in the region's neighboring coal valleys made thoroughly dissimilar claims on the civic space of mobilization, debate, and political action.

These paired instances of *similar* people making *dissimilar* uses of civic channels and mechanisms to address important difficulties that they face speak to two dimensions of civic life, which I argue to be extraordinarily important in the contemporary world. These two great contemporary challenges for civic life can be briefly summarized as follows: (1) engaging the increasing *global scale* of economic and political phenomena, and (2) enabling the poor and disadvantaged to become meaningful political actors. In a world scenario increasingly characterized by the global nature of processes shaping local experience and by the growth of inequalities, the capacity of civic life to engage the global arena's distant horizons and to incorporate the poor assumes growing, indeed inescapable, significance. Yet the ability and commitment of political forces—and ordinary citizens—to meet these contemporary civic challenges rests on their capacities, innovative potential, and a variety of factors shaping the contexts in which they dwell. In this chapter I identify ways in which two factors located *outside* the specialized political terrain of elections and official institutions can powerfully contribute to enhancing or discouraging opportunities for civic action of the sort here emphasized.

I draw both on work by fellow sociologists (as well as sociologically minded political scientists) and on my own research to specify various ways in which *networks* and *narratives* can help to invigorate civic endeavors, thus providing ordinary citizens with crucial tools for enlivening public life without fully committing themselves to fulltime or officially political activity. I focus heavily on my extensive research in the Iberian Peninsula neighbors of Portugal and Spain, pioneers in both the late twentieth-century worldwide expansion of democratic rule (Fishman 1990; Linz and Stepan 1996) and centuries earlier in the European colonization of the world. The civic initiatives to be found in the recent history of the Iberian Peninsula include some that generated extraordinary success along with others culminating in "dead ends" or other disappointments. I will examine various examples, some of them rooted in collective protest and in the unfolding of negotiation or *conversation* between institutional office holders and actors lacking any institutional source of power.

Strategies and initiatives intended to foster civic creativity and inclusion often focus on what can be done *inside*, or through governmental structures and other political institutions. That emphasis has yielded many important results (Fung 2004; Baiocchi 2005; Sirianni 2009), but in this chapter I examine other venues and mechanisms for enriching citizenship practice. Indeed, I argue that much of the energy generating civic innovation and inclusion, and many of the settings in which creative citizenship practices *show up* in the world, are to be found *outside* formal political institutions. A large body of work by sociologists, and sociologically minded political scientists, specifies how processes and mechanisms located outside the most overtly political realm end up facilitating—or blocking—robust and satisfying forms of civic activity. This perspective is not intended to question the importance of the more conventional focus on formal political institutions but rather to complement it: My argument does not attribute *priority* to societal sources of citizenship action, but I do focus analytically on such factors, seeking to identify crucial mechanisms underpinning the interplay between broadly *social* underpinnings of civic initiative and those strategies and institutional designs that take their form in unmistakably, and often proudly, political endeavors. The experiences I relate in this chapter are rooted in important episodes of collective action in Portugal and Spain, but they—and their implications for how we understand civic life—can only be fully understood by framing these experiences in the conceptual and theoretical debates of social scientists concerned with networks, narratives, and civic life. The episodes I examine carry global significance.

This chapter's dual focus on networks and narratives—on both the broad structure of social ties connecting individuals and the stories that are told about a nation and its history—may strike some readers as an odd combination of two dissimilar phenomena, despite their shared location *outside* the self-consciously political arena of parties and elective or governance institutions, but in fact a growing body of scholarly work has sketched out various ways in which the cultural sphere of discourse, narratives, meanings, and practices is tightly interconnected with structures of acquaintance and social interaction among individuals (Bearman 1993; Emirbayer and Goodwin 1994; Somers 1994; Eliasoph and Lichterman 2003; Fishman 2004; Lizardo 2006; Perrin 2006; Polletta 2006; Mische 2007). From this perspective, and for reasons that I develop below, social networks and culture can be understood, in the recent formulation of Pachucki and Breiger, as "mutually constitutive" (2010, 209). Culturally rooted understandings, meanings, and practices do shape the emergence and significance of social network ties, but those networks, in turn, strongly influence the extent to which cultural innovations and assumptions can spread. As this chapter elaborates, social ties and *stories* are woven together in the social fabric in ways that enrich, but render quite complex, the societal underpinnings of lively civic endeavors.

The identification of ways in which networks and narratives can enhance civic practice—in complementarity with institutional innovations and explicitly political initiatives—has the effect of broadening the playing field for those committed to enhancing the practical meaning of citizenship. This chapter's exploration of this theme takes us beyond civic strategies that are explicitly or consciously political and into the micro-level realm of personal biographies as well as the macro-level sphere of national history and large collective movements. It takes us into the terrain of friendships and cultural expression. The phenomena that shape the possibilities for civic engagement and innovation among ordinary citizens extend well beyond those deployed by political "specialists," be they professional politicians or extraordinarily dedicated activists. Partly thanks to the major contributions of Robert Putnam (1993, 2000), the social underpinnings of democracy's energy and successes have attracted growing interest among social scientists and the general public, but specifying *how* social ties and culturally embedded stories can activate civic life and enhance its quality is a far greater challenge than simply demonstrating that some sort of effect exists. This chapter takes up that challenge.

I argue below that one of the keys to the large impact of social ties and narratives—or related cultural phenomena—on civic vitality lies precisely in the development of synergies between these two elements and their positive engagement with the sphere of formal political institutions. Students of social ties and networks place a great deal of emphasis on the overall structure of connections in a population (White, Boorman, and Breiger 1976; Degenne and Forse 1999; Wasserman and Faust 1994), and on the important differences in the nature and effect of different types of ties (Granovetter 1974; Burt 2005; Wellman 1992; Centola and Macy 2007). I build on that work but, drawing from the scholarship on culture and social networks (Emirbayer and Goodwin 1994; Mische 2011) and my own research findings, I also elaborate how the impact of social connections on civic practice is strongly shaped by the cultural or *subcultural* meaning placed on those ties.

Some important scholarship argues that the structural form of network connections is strongly related to the actual content of social ties and that dense ties within communities are likely to be treated by those involved as strong connections of intrinsic meaning, while less common "cross-boundary" connections among individuals embedded in different collectivities are more likely to be weak and instrumental (Baldassari and Diani 2007). I instead contend that structurally quite *similar* social connections can actually be given very *different* meanings by their participants for reasons rooted in the actors' subcultural understandings. How we think about our connections to others, and their broader placement in extensive complex networks, is powerfully shaped by our cultural assumptions. From this perspective, the impact of ties on civic practice and their ability to encourage important types of innovation in public life is partly rooted in the subcultural moorings of actors that lead them to develop (or leave largely untapped) the potential carried by their connections to others. My argument places considerable weight not only on networks but also on the ideas and understandings actors hold about their social ties. In what follows, I turn first to a discussion of national narratives and the politics of inclusion before proceeding to an examination of network ties and globalizing civic action.

Narratives of Freedom and Political Inclusion: Evidence from Portugal

Portugal's 1974 Carnation Revolution dramatically brought to a sudden end nearly five decades of right-wing authoritarian rule and initiated a period of mass mobilization in the streets, wide-ranging social upheaval, and democratic institution building. On April 25 of that year, rebellious army captains, and others organized in the clandestine Armed Forces Movement, marched on Lisbon, where to the delight of growing crowds in the streets, they managed to quickly overcome resistance from defenders of the authoritarian Estado Novo (Maxwell 1995). It is crucial to note that the leadership role middle-level officers collectively assumed in the democratizing coup required the captains to act in direct disobedience to commands issued by their erstwhile hierarchical "superiors." This overturning of institutional discipline ushered in a period characterized by the *partial inversion of hierarchies* inside numerous social and political institutions as well as the emergence of new forms of cultural expression and practice (Fishman 2010, 2011). Portugal's unsuccessful colonial wars in Africa and the fundamental challenge to discipline within the armed forces that took shape in April 1974 together produced a growing crisis of the state, making possible not only democratization but also social revolution (Bermeo 1986; Fishman 1990; Durán Muñoz 2000; Palacios Cerezales 2003). Crucially, an important feature of Portugal's revolution was the political empowerment of workers and the poor, who became important actors in their places of work and residence during the country's turbulent passage from dictatorship to democracy (Hammond 1988). I argue that such events established a historical and cultural foundation for the emergence of a distinctive form of democratic practice, rooted in Portugal's social revolutionary pathway to democracy (Fishman 2011). The story of April 1974 and its relevance for contemporary democracy form the subject of a great deal of discourse—and narration—in the new political system, with important consequences for the shape of the civic arena and its ability to incorporate relatively poor and powerless actors.

The Portuguese experience speaks to the significance of themes and processes that have been extensively theorized in recent work. The contribution of stories and storytelling for politics of all sorts—including protest movements as well as more institutionally anchored forms of political activity—has attracted a great deal of attention from prominent social scientists (Tilly 2002; Polletta 2006) as well as contemporary political actors and commentators. Much of that work is focused on the narration of either micro-level individual experiences thought to hold political significance, or the meso-level endeavors and experiences of larger groups such as immigrants and farm workers. I examine instead the way in which narratives about a collective *national* experience (Spillman and Faeges 2005), such as Portugal's political passage to democratic freedoms, hold important consequences for contemporary civic practice, thus making use of an approach that has yielded important results in the comparative analysis of culture and politics (Berezin 2009).

In contemporary practice, the Portuguese devote enormous energies to telling the story of their revolutionary liberation from dictatorship in the captains' coup of April 25, 1974, and the period of social mobilization and cultural renewal that followed. Narratives of the Carnation Revolution, as the events beginning in April 1974 came to be known, and reflections on its significance are articulated in books, poems, movies, concerts, demonstrations, and an annual commemorative session of the parliament. The anniversary itself is a national holiday and the occasion for an extraordinary array of commemorative activities organized by civil society and political associations as well as government institutions. The most widely viewed telling of the story of April, Maria de Medeiros's film *Captains of April*, has been shown repeatedly on Portuguese television, in movie theaters, and in many schools in the years following its initial release in 2000. The publicity trailer for the movie shows Maia, one of the rebellious captains—and the film's hero—refusing the orders of a superior officer and initiating the uprising in the base where he was stationed. In the words captured by the trailer, Maia dismisses the call to obedience, insisting that sometimes it is necessary to *disobey*. This celebration of disobedience stands as only one of many politically potent messages carried by the narrations and commemorations of April 25th. A common theme in this large cultural enterprise has been the commitment to tell the revolution's story to children too young to have experienced it directly. Various books, such as the text written by a team under the direction of theorist Boaventura de Sousa Santos (2004), attempt to tell the story to schoolchildren in easily accessible ways. On the revolution's thirtieth anniversary in 2004, one of countless commemorative activities—a gathering of immigrants on Lisbon's Largo do Carmo, where the rebellious captains won the surrender of dictator Marcelo Caetano in 1974—culminated in an extraordinary celebratory spectacle. A large birthday cake was brought onto the stage that presided over the gathering, and the young children of immigrants were called forward to lead those assembled in singing happy birthday to April 25th—and the democracy it brought into being.[4]

That Portugal's democracy has devoted great cultural energy to celebrating and telling the socially empowering story of April is undeniable, but what is the broader civic significance of those endeavors? What structural or institutional factors have acted in consonance with narration in helping to build the basis for the country's distinctive civic life? Those questions are of considerable relevance not only for scholars, but also for political actors and ordinary citizens in Portugal. Although the revolution's most ardent enthusiasts are for the most part located somewhere on the political left, the embrace of April 25th and its presumed message has been broad-based. In 2007 in a large town north of Oporto, a local leader of the country's largest center-right party offered telling words on the significance of the Carnation Revolution: "To exercise citizenship is to fulfill April. . . . Democracy only really exists when it assures everyone, without exception, the possibility to exercise in absolute fullness their rights and duties." He directly linked this perspective to the memory of the revolution: "For me, the best way to commemorate and respect the spirit of April 25th is creating mechanisms to consolidate a truly participatory democracy."[5] Numerous statements by other political leaders, as well as the broader character of ongoing practice, underscore the tendency of Portuguese political actors to understand democracy in ways that emphasize both inclusion and a certain openness to initiatives that challenge authority. I argue that remembrances of April 25th, and the collective experiences of the revolutionary period itself, contribute to making possible a form of *democratic practice* more open to the voices of the poor and the relatively powerless than that of many other contemporary democracies (Fishman 2011).

In what follows, I show that the story of this country's revolutionary passage to democracy helps to generate both a distinctive form of civic practice and a series of societal or policy outcomes shaped by that practice. Yet in making this argument I do not intend to privilege the causal weight of the revolutionary narrative itself, or any other cultural phenomena. Instead, my aim is to show that the cultural efforts that have gone into elaborating and conveying the story of April 25th form part of a broader ensemble of factors—many of them institutional or structural in nature—which together shape political and social outcomes in Portugal. The story and its message do not act alone in producing the revolution's distinctive legacy in contemporary democracy, but at the same time the broader macro-historical pattern cannot be understood without attributing a significant role to the cultural efforts involved in telling the story of April 25th.

The most distinctive feature of Portugal's postrevolutionary democratic practice is the relative openness of institutional office holders, and the broader democratic political sphere, to the voices of poor and relatively powerless actors including demonstrators protesting one or another element of official policy (Fishman 2011). The experience of residents of formally illegal housing in Amadora, just outside Lisbon, described in this chapter's introduction, offers a telling instance of this pattern. This episode of social protest, with its ultimate focus on the republic's center of institutional power, appears to have influenced political debate and policy making on housing issues; leaders of the immigrant movement insist that they succeeded in reorienting the country's broader political agenda on housing issues.[6] The country's leading housing official at the time subsequently engaged in negotiations with residents of informal housing in Amadora, searching for a solution that would regularize their status and offer them acceptable conditions.[7] To a remarkable degree, poor immigrants who sought the attention of elected parliamentarians and policy makers—and the general public—succeeded.

The incorporation of economically disadvantaged actors, such as the immigrants of Amadora, into political processes that set the public agenda and make policy is of broad theoretical relevance. Despite the normative arguments in favor of such broad democratic inclusion, it is not a common occurrence. Theorists such as Robert Dahl (1998) insist on the principle of full political equality among citizens as fundamental to democracy, while recognizing the extraordinary difficulty of attaining that end, especially in the terrains of agenda setting and policy making. Indeed, genuine political equality has proved difficult to attain *even* in democracy's institutional core, namely the act of voting itself, given the relative disinclination of many low-income citizens to participate in elections in a variety of historical and contemporary contexts as well as the obstacles placed in the way of their participation in some settings (Mansbridge 1980). At the conceptual level, political equality among citizens is central to the idea of democracy, and it continues to be emphasized in theories of citizenship (Somers 2008) as well as in the literature on the deepening of democracy (Roberts 1998; Heller 2000; Fung and Wright 2003), but in empirical reality it is very difficult to fully attain. Herein lies the special significance of Portugal's narrative of the April 25th delivery from dictatorship: it has encouraged the poor and powerless to see themselves as potentially relevant political actors while also providing institutional office holders with a powerful argument in favor of inclusion. At both ends of the dimension differentiating between the politically powerful and powerless, the story of April has encouraged practices that promote broad inclusion.

The principles of political inclusion and of resistance to domination are frequently articulated in contemporary Portugal in ways that explicitly link those commitments to the underlying message of the Carnation Revolution. The words of a municipal leader of the center-right in a town north of Oporto, quoted above, stand as just one instance of that broader pattern. In the 2008 commemorative session of the parliament held on April 25th, it was a deputy of the left-socialist Bloco de Esquerda,

José Soeiro, who remarked, "Democracy is the strongest answer against all forms of domination—in the space of enterprises, schools, families, sexuality. . . . If there is one thing that April 25th teaches us it is that it is always possible to change everything."[8] This insistence on the possibility of change, and of success in resisting domination, is echoed—or anticipated—in the practice of Solidariedade Inmigrante, the association that helped to mobilize the residents of informal dwellings in Amadora. Timóteo Macedo, leader of the association, enjoys leading members and supporters in chanting "change *is* possible" and he makes explicit reference to the story of April in conveying that message.[9] Other urban protesters, such as the residents of the Lisbon neighborhood of Amendoeiras, have also drawn explicitly on memories and narratives of the Carnation Revolution to provide their initiatives with encouragement and legitimation.[10] The Amendoeiras protesters won official recognition—indeed restoration—of their control over houses initially seized during the revolution.

The inclusionary tendencies in Portuguese democratic practice are manifested in numerous ways, including in the behavior of institutional power holders and the news media. When the Portuguese parliament commemorated the thirtieth anniversary of the country's democratic constitution in 2006, the exhibit assembled for the occasion gave considerable prominence not only to the constitutional text but also to numerous demonstrations, protesting decisions made by the parliament itself. In this and numerous other ways Portuguese office holders have conveyed their sense that demonstrations—many of them led by relatively poor actors such as the immigrants of Amadora—play a recognized and legitimate role in democratic politics. The approach of the press is captured well by the declarations of journalist Estrela Serrano, who wrote in 2006 that "on the balance and variety of voices expressed in the media depends also the quality of democracy" (Serrano 2006, 193). My fieldwork in Portugal confirms the predominance of an inclusionary approach to news coverage that is congruent with Serrano's remarks, but what is the connection between narratives of revolution and the practice of inclusion on the part of both the press and elected politicians? If—as I argue—the voices of relatively poor and powerless actors, including demonstrators, are incorporated within the space acknowledged as legitimate by institutional office holders and reported in the news media, what role does the story of revolution play in generating that effect? Central to the revolution was the active participation of crowds in the streets, first simply cheering on the insurgent movement led by the captains and later carrying numerous social demands, old and new, into the public arena. Economist Mário Murteira, a government minister during the revolutionary period, captured this component of the Portuguese story when he remarked, "Several times when I was engaged in important conversations with [prime minister] Vasco Gonçalves, in his office, we would go to the window to see those who were passing by in demonstrations. In the end and to a great extent we were more spectators in a grand popular movement than actors" (Silva et al. 2006, 105). The political significance of crowds and protesters in the streets is captured not only in narrative histories and social science analyses of the revolution (Maxwell 1995; Palacios Cerezales 2003), but also in pictorial and poetic representations of the period as was reflected by two widely disseminated posters that proclaimed, "A Poesia está na Rua" (The Poetry Is in the Streets).[11] The Portuguese have not only recognized, but also celebrated, the contributions to democracy made by popular voices in the streets.

The Portuguese democratic culture was forged in the context of a pervasive challenge to hierarchies inside both state and social institutions. A wave of purges swept the country in the year and half following the country's liberation by revolution in 1974. Loyalists of the old regime were removed from government ministries, private firms, and even schools, where students themselves led this effort in large assemblies (Costa Pinto 2001, 2006). Farm workers, industrial workers, and urban residents all joined in challenging existing hierarchies—whether in their workplaces or their neighborhoods—thus reshaping various facets of the country's collective life (Bermeo 1986; Hammond 1988; Durán Muñoz 2000). Portugal's political transformation was socially inclusive, incorporating the poor and other relatively disadvantaged actors into the mainstream of democratization. The demonstrations, which the Portuguese understood as a major part of the process that brought democracy to their country, included protests of actors who would have been seen as marginal to political life in many other societies. The evocations of participatory inclusion and of the challenge to domination in commemorations of April 25th—and on other occasions during the year—thus resonate with widely recognized elements of the revolution's story.

But without organizational or institutional support, the narrative of April 1974 would not be capable of generating the effects identified here, namely the fostering of a type of democratic civic practice which is highly inclusionary, recognizing the legitimacy of the voices of poor and relatively powerless actors. Organizations such as Solidariedade Inmigrante, political parties that organize the institutional life of the Assembly of the Republic, and various official endeavors and policies, such as the annual program of commemorations of April 25th, all play a crucial role in providing opportunities, substance, and weight to the story of the Carnation Revolution. The cultural efforts involved in telling the story of liberation by revolution are central to contemporary Portugal's sense of democratic politics and civic life, but those efforts gain their strength and impact through their thorough interweaving with routine political life, organizational efforts, and institutional design. The narrative of revolution helps to enable an extraordinarily inclusive form of civic practice—welcoming into the public square actors who would be largely marginalized in many other national settings—in part because of its synergies with the organizational and institutional components of politics, which also owe their contemporary configuration to the process initiated on April 25, 1974. My emphasis in this chapter on contributions to civic initiative and inclusion made by actors operating outside the official political sphere—such as authors, painters, poets, musicians, protest leaders, and others involved in telling the story of April—helps to identify the significance of narratives of revolution for contemporary civic life. We now turn to an examination of social connections that cross social boundaries, another potential source of strength for the objectives under discussion here.

How Boundary-Crossing Social Ties Can Enable a Globalized Civic Perspective

Many scholars have shown that both direct social connections and patterns of indirect connection within populations help to shape political participation by individuals as well as the broader contours of public life and discourse (Bearman 1993; Zuckerman 2005; Fishman 2004; Mische 2007), but this point of fairly wide agreement leaves us with the need to specify *how* networks can enhance democracy. I am especially concerned here with two questions, which I consider to be interrelated: (1) What consequences follow from the growth or decline of boundary-crossing ties—such as "town-gown" connections between university students and residents of the towns where they study, bonds between recent immigrants and families who have lived in a locale for generations, close relations between middle-income individuals and those substantially above or below them in the income hierarchy, or links between intellectuals and workers? (2) Can the network ties and conversations of ordinary citizens help *enable* civic life to effectively engage the *global scale* of economic and social dynamics affecting the lives of citizens? The severing or withering of cross-class and boundary-crossing ties (such as those I mention above by way of example) is a feature of contemporary social life that has attracted the concern of social analysts such as Christopher Lasch (1995), and which is closely related to the decline of cross-class mass-membership organizations persuasively documented by Skocpol (2003). Given the theorized decline of boundary-crossing or cross-class social connections, it makes good sense to examine whether the presence of such connections—where they *are* to be found—contributes to the quality of civic life. After all, if boundary-crossing connections are in decline but nonetheless *do* enhance civic life in one fashion or another, that finding would identify both a significant threat to the civic sphere and a way in which concerned individuals' simple choice of conversation partners and associates might hold surprisingly large implications for the evolution of civic life.

For reasons to be explained in what follows, I argue that the ability of civic actors to successfully address the global scale of contemporary economic and social phenomena in their discourse is related to their networks and more specifically to their boundary-crossing ties. Indeed, I provide evidence that the capacity of public actors to defend their interests in ways that cognitively and discursively *globalize* is strongly rooted in the nature of their social ties. Whether activists, leaders, and ordinary citizens think of their own interests, and articulate them in the context of political life, in ways that look to the global horizons of the contemporary world or in ways highly constrained by the blinders of localism is largely a function, I argue, of the network dynamics presented here.

I make use of a concept designed to capture the capacity of leaders and activists to look beyond their immediate context and to engage the increasingly global arena of contemporary economic and social processes. On the basis of extensive field research, discussed in *Democracy's Voices* (Fishman 2004), I argue that the points of reference and the policy remedies articulated in the political discourse of community leaders can either focus consistently on the thoroughly local arena or extend well beyond it. I conceptualize the result—in the political language, initiatives, and proposals of civic leaders—as constituting either *globalizing discursive horizons* or *narrow localism*, typically of a defensive nature. Based on fieldwork in Spain, I show how certain sorts of network ties (such as friendships between miners and university professors, shared political work linking activists to authors and engineers, and other cross-class connections) have enabled those local leaders and activists shaped by them to promote their community interests in ways that address both national and broadly global concerns—rather than simply those preoccupations most powerfully bounded by locality.

The *discursive horizons* articulated by local leaders in their efforts to promote employment and other straightforward material concerns of local communities may be thoroughly bounded by the confines of locality, or expansively focused on crucial processes, challenges, and potential solutions located far beyond the local context and, for that reason, of meaning to a broad national or even international audience. The discursive horizons of local communities, such as the industrial towns where I conducted extensive fieldwork in Spain, may be expansively global or irredeemably local, with large consequences for the ability of community civic life to engage extralocal actors and audiences in dialogue and with equally large implications for the capacity of those same local actors to successful identify genuine causes of local problems, and potential remedies for them, anchored in large dynamics transcending their immediate context. One of the most crucial dimensions of civic innovation in the contemporary world is precisely the ability of local actors to connect their challenges and aspirations to geographically distant realities and processes.

In the Spanish industrial towns where I conducted interviewing and fieldwork, leaders and activists whose civic discourse was thoroughly bounded by localism limited their demands and initiatives to the (often unsuccessful) efforts to keep their towns' factories, mines, and facilities open. In the 1990s, the militant mobilization of the Andalusian town of Linares offered a clear instance of such limited discursive horizons in the campaign intended to keep Santana Motor from closing the plant located in the town. In the wave of demonstrations, road and rail line blockades, building occupations, and so forth initiated by town residents, two of the central slogans of Linares' activists were "2,400 jobs and not one less" and "Linares," the name of their municipality. The impact of national, European, and global economic dynamics, the global policies of multinationals, and the plight of workers in similar situations in other towns, as well as potential remedies articulated around district-wide, regional, or broader policy initiatives, were *all* absent from the discourse and demands of Linares protesters. Their efforts, protests, and disruptions were all about their concrete and bounded local interests—and nothing else. "2,400 jobs and not one less." Social protest in this instance was thoroughly lacking in civic imagination or innovation and could hardly be thought to contribute to any public goal lying outside the immediate context of the town. Many other towns and industrial areas have shared the political or discursive style of Linares, limiting their demands and proposals to the narrow effort to secure or maintain local interests. As was discussed in this chapter's introduction, the mining valley of the Caudal in the northern region of Asturias—where towns such as Mieres or Turón focused their mobilizations on attempts to keep specific mines open—offers some of the clearest examples of this same pattern.

Other towns or districts with socioeconomic structures—and problems—similar to those of Linares or the Caudal valley, however, instead articulated their analyses and objectives through globalizing discourse that linked the local to the regional, national, and global arenas. The Nalón coal valley of Asturias, adjacent to the localistic Caudal, provides one of the clearest instances of such a contrast. The Nalón valley defended its interests through globalizing discourse that informed numerous campaigns and endeavors launched in the 1990s. Leaders in the Nalón pushed not simply to keep specific mines open but instead to reindustrialize the entire area; their statements in support of that objective clearly linked their valley's employment crisis to multilevel economic trends and dynamics of global scale (Fishman 2004, ch. 3). They criticized regional, national, and European policies while warning of the dangers of extraordinarily high unemployment as manifested by the rise of the Nazis in the 1930s. The Nalón's leaders and activists delivered public statements and produced publications replete with references not only to their valley but also to distant places—and times—in Spain, other European countries, and beyond. A speaker in a seminar organized in San Martín, one of the valley's towns, asked rhetorically in 1990 whether the problems of that town could be resolved *exclusively* within San Martin and offered the obvious answer in the negative, rejecting the blinders of localism. Leaders and activists constantly looked beyond their valley and its towns for solutions to the problems they faced. A variety of industrial areas in other regions of Spain shared the globalizing "frame" of the Nalón. Workers and unionists in Catalonia's Baix Llobregat district, located just outside Barcelona, and in the old textile town of Alcoi in Alicante province, provide instances of a globalizing approach to politics and civic life in areas structurally quite unlike the Nalón valley. Whether the issues at play involved environmental conditions, corporate behavior, or employment policy, leaders and activists in the globalizing towns looked to distant horizons articulating positions consonant with the global scale of the problems being felt in their towns. In all these cases—and others that I studied in *Democracy's Voices*—leaders of industrial towns showed a noteworthy ability to conceptualize and articulate their towns' interests, and remedies intended to address those interests, in broadly global terms, whereas their counterparts in numerous nearby and economically similar communities focused instead on simple defensive localism of the narrowest sort.

What accounts for these great differences in the degree to which communities manage to address the genuinely global scale of the problems that are felt locally? Why are the civic endeavors of local activists informed by globalizing perspectives in some settings and localistic blinders in others? Remarkably, in the field settings I studied, the distinction between globalizing discourse and defensive localism is essentially un-correlated with variation on the more conventional dimension of politics differenti-ating between radicalism and moderation. Both globalizing and localistic leaders and activists may be either moderate *or* radical. Yet the horizons adopted by discourse do match up with a fundamental difference among local leaders, namely the extent to which their social connections cross important social boundaries. Boundary-crossing social ties proved capable of generating globalizing discourse—and thus a crucial type of civic innovation—whereas their absence was typically associated with narrow local-istic discourse and political initiatives.

Both a face-to-face survey of more than three hundred local union and political leaders and my extensive in-depth qualitative interviewing with many of the same lead-ers showed a strong association between intellectual-worker connections—a prime ex-ample of boundary-crossing social ties—and the predisposition of leaders to articulate their political objectives through globalizing discourse. The local leaders in the towns I studied were primarily either industrial workers or others clearly committed to speak-ing on behalf of such workers. Their linkages to intellectuals—defined in the study as university professors or authors of general works intended for an educated public—took many forms including friendships formed in childhood (before the individuals involved followed one or another career path), joint work inside a political party or association, participation in a public forum or symposium, and visits to a university to consult with scholars. Connections between intellectuals and workers took many forms, but in the data collected (and discussed in *Democracy's Voices*) one important type of variation made little or no difference in the impact of the ties. Friendship ties between intellectuals and workers, rooted in individual biographies, proved neither stronger nor weaker in their effects than more institutionally defined ties forged by joint work in a political or labor organization. The prevalence of interchange between intellectuals and workers proved predictive of the local leaders' predisposition toward globalizing discourse, but the genesis of those social connections in personal friend-ship or institutional work exerted no impact at all on the frequency with which local leaders articulated globalizing discourse. On the other hand, leaders who enjoyed *mul-tiple* ties to intellectuals were even more inclined to articulate globalizing discourse—with its innovative framing of public issues—than leaders enjoying only one tie to an intellectual. Several ties thus matter more than one lone cross-boundary connection, but the difference between connections that emerge inside formal institutions such as political parties and others that take shape in the personal realm of friendship—or other forms of acquaintance enabled by the twists and turns in personal biographies—appears to be unimportant for our purposes.

Another dimension of variation, itself a matter of considerable theoretical significance, proves decisive. The leaders interviewed belonged to two historically quite different subcultures, one of them socialist and the other initially communist but now postcommunist. The quantitative evidence generated by my survey of local leaders shows that ties between intellectuals and workers exerted a thoroughly dissimilar effect in these two subcultures. Whereas within the postcommunist subculture local leaders tied to intellectuals were more than twice as likely as their unconnected counterparts to articulate globalizing discourse, among leaders of the socialist subculture ties to intellectuals exerted no meaningful impact on the prevalence of globalizing discourse. This large empirical disparity in the capacity of boundary-crossing social ties to foment civic discourse commensurate with the new challenges of a globalized world offers us a puzzle worthy of considerable attention: What determines whether boundary-crossing social ties will carry great power to remake civic life—or instead none at all? The implications of this question are of broad significance. The ties in question involve substantial effort on the part of those who expand their social connections and conversations to include people of dissimilar circumstances or group membership, but what determines whether efforts to build all sorts of boundary-crossing ties—from town-gown connections to conversations between musicians and miners or immigrant workers and their professional neighbors—will yield a large civic impact or none at all?

From the standpoint of a structural network analysis of social relations that theorizes social ties on the basis of their placement in a holistic pattern of direct and indirect network connections—or disconnections—among individuals, the ties between workers and intellectuals would appear to be similar in the two Spanish subcultures. In both instances, two quite separate social worlds are connected by the ties in question. A great deal of excellent scholarship, such as Ronald Burt's deeply insightful *Brokerage and Closure* (2005), provides a strong rationale for the structural approach to social ties, with its emphasis on ways in which any given dyadic tie takes on one or another significance as a function of its placement in larger network structures that—precisely through the accumulation of individual ties—may either isolate tightly knit social communities from one another or, instead, connect those communities to one another even if only through a very few structurally crucial boundary-crossing ties. That perspective offers a plausible approach for thinking about how intellectual-worker connections may influence collective outcomes, structurally connecting two social worlds that are largely isolated from one another. That structural perspective is not, however, the only possible prism for conceptualizing the substance and significance of social ties. Social networks and their structural composition actually rest on a large set of direct (and often two-way or dyadic) conversations and interactions (Mische 2003), a fact that offers an alternative perspective for understanding social connections (Fishman 2009): ties can be understood through a prism emphasizing the direct two-way, or dyadic, conversations and connections themselves, instead of the large structural pattern of indirect connections to distant others highlighted by some network analysts. I argue that the purely structural analysis of social ties that searches for the key to their impact in the placement of any given tie within larger complex networks (of indirect connections to distant others) is useful for many purposes, but not for others. After all, in the Spanish industrial towns I studied, intellectual-worker ties played essentially the same structural or network role in the two subcultures, linking the disparate social worlds of intellectuals and workers to one another, but the ties made a large impact on civic discourse in one subculture and no impact in the other. Clearly something other than the network structure itself was at play.

I argue that this large disparity in the impact of intellectual-worker ties on the discourse of local leaders is strongly rooted in subculturally embedded meanings attached to the ties (Fishman 2004, 25–28, 145–66). Both closed-ended survey research findings and qualitative interviewing suggest that whereas the postcommunist subculture has seen intellectual-worker linkages as intrinsically meaningful and valuable, the socialist subculture has tended to view the ties in instrumental fashion as a means to an end. At the time of the field study, the Spanish Socialist Party (PSOE) was firmly located in government in Madrid and a primary utility of the ties was to increase local leaders' access to distant office holders and institutions in the country's capital, Madrid. In this sense the ties performed the function of *brokerage*, potentially offering tangible forms of advantage. In contrast, in the postcommunist subculture the ties were conceptualized as intrinsically meaningful—as being valuable on their own even if they generated no concrete benefit external to the experience itself—and in that sense they can be understood to constitute *conversation*. In the socialist subculture the intellectual-worker linkages are best understood as representing *brokerage*, offering those involved access to distant sources of power, influence, and resources centered in the PSOE government in Madrid. The intellectual-worker ties that emerged among Spanish socialists are best understood by adopting the theoretical prism of scholars such as Burt, who view ties through their structural placement in large and complex networks; many of the participants in these ties understand them to constitute opportunities to gain access to distant sources of power or resources, precisely the perspective suggested by Burt's theory of brokerage. But for those who take the direct dyadic—and thus conversational—content of their ties to be intrinsically meaningful, as appears to be the case in the postcommunist subculture, the structuralist network gestalt proves quite unproductive. The power of the ties in such contexts is carried by their experiential effect, by conversation itself, rather than through distant resources and content newly made available by network connections.

Thus if boundary-crossing ties, such as connections between intellectuals and workers, are to generate powerful civic results, they must be embedded in cultures that afford them meaning and purpose. The socially rooted sense that conversation across societal boundaries is of value matters as much as the accumulation of social relations that traverse class or identity frontiers. To put the matter differently: the meaning placed on social interaction helps to determine its effects, and that meaning is strongly conditioned by the subcultural milieu in which social ties are embedded. I take as especially significant the extent to which ties are seen by those involved as a means to an end—and in that sense as instrumentally useful—or as an end in and of themselves, which is to say intrinsically meaningful. Whether one spends time with given people because one sees the experience itself as enjoyable and meaningful or because one thinks that the connection to those people will likely prove useful for other purposes is the crux of the matter. I assume that both circumstances are quite common, but that the consequences of human ties seen in these two very different lights are quite dissimilar. This claim holds important implications of both a practical and theoretical nature, but before examining them it will be useful to briefly consider additional support for the claim.

The work of various scholars offers much evidence that the social ties that carry the greatest impact on civic behaviors are indeed those seen by their participants as intrinsically meaningful, as constituting *conversations* of value in and of themselves, just as this chapter argues. Paul Lichterman's important analysis of how some church groups that are engaged in civic endeavors manage to tie together socially diverse actors shows that the style or culture of group interaction decisively shapes the prospects for attaining the goal of civic togetherness (Lichterman 2005). Those church groups that approach their own interactions reflexively—valuing social connections and conversation as intrinsically meaningful and discussing how to improve them—were far more successful at generating civic togetherness than those groups that lacked a cultural commitment to the intrinsic value of their own interactions. In a similar vein, Sirianni and Friedland found that cultural change enabling a genuinely civic journalism rested heavily on participating journalists' capacity to *listen* and to their related willingness to take time to value direct conversation (Sirianni and Friedland 2001, 202–20). In another significant contribution, Eiko Ikegami's important historical analysis of cultural and aesthetic bonds in Japan—and their carryover relevance for the political sphere—argues that boundary-crossing ties that were valued on the basis of the cultural activity that constituted their very content ended up exerting a large impact on the network structure of the larger society and its political endeavors (Ikegami 2005). Ikegami shows that the Japanese stitched together social connections crossing hierarchical lines of division because participants valued their aesthetic activities and cultural interactions with diverse others as *intrinsically meaningful*. The expressive enjoyment of joint cultural activity rather than an instrumental search for useful connections to distant holders of power and resources remade network structures and thus the groundwork for broad-based political activity.

The power of network ties in all of these instances was unleashed by an approach to social connections that valued direct interactions among diverse actors as inherently meaningful and valuable. The power of network ties was quite real, but it was contingent on a culture of social interaction that valued human relations, expressiveness, and interaction as an intrinsic good instead of viewing them instrumentally as a vehicle to construct "useful" contacts with distant others. Networks and social ties were able to forge an infrastructure supportive of civic life because they were constituted within a cultural framework valuing direct human interactions instead of conceptualizing them only as a means to other ends. This theorization of *how* network ties shape civic activity challenges some common approaches to networks such as those exclusively focused on the search for individual advantage, but it is strongly congruent with a central finding of established scholarship in this field, namely the claim that different types of ties generate different sorts of effects (Granovetter 1974; Wellman 1992; Centola and Macy 2007). Instrumentally conceived network ties, which conceptualize direct two-way interaction as useful only insofar as it affords access to distant resources, certainly also exert effects, but not—I argue—in the making of an innovative and high-quality civic life. The analytical "preference for selfish preferences" (Sanchez-Cuenca 2008) that characterizes a great deal of social science, that is to say the assumption that essentially all social life is driven by individual self-interest, fits some human action but not *all* human action given the importance of altruistic and other nonselfish motivations.

Thus social ties to diverse others help to nourish civic life by encouraging political actors to articulate a global discourse that addresses concrete local problems in ways that look well beyond their localities. But the ability of boundary-crossing ties to elicit this outcome is, in turn, a function of the culturally rooted beliefs and understandings that actors hold about their interactions. For ties to diverse others to realize their civic potential they must be enabled by a perspective that values interactions with others as an intrinsic good rather than simply as an instrumental "means to an end." Various systems of belief and of meaning may accord that status to social interactions, but others do not and thus may lead actors to an understanding of their interactions that encourages them to pursue benefits accruing from their network-based access to distant others but to undervalue the potential benefits of their direct conversations and interactions with immediate others.

Conclusion: Tying Together the Significance of Networks and Narratives for Civic Innovation

I have sought to show that cultural phenomena such as narratives of national political events as well as relational phenomena such as networks and social ties can work together with the institutional infrastructure of politics to foster innovative and inclusionary forms of civic practice. This claim rests on the sort of multicausal and configurative analysis that constitutes Weberian methodology (Fishman 2007). My argument implies that those constellations that underpin innovative civic outcomes are sustained by viable forms of *complementarity*, convincingly embedded in national and local histories, rather than being copied from one or another external model in template form. In the large project required to stitch together the synergy of networks, narratives, institutions, and other facilitating conditions for a lively and inclusive civic life, many different types of effort and creativity are surely needed. My contribution in these pages does not attempt to provide a comprehensive map for that large effort but instead seeks to underscore the breadth of the venues and forms of action that can contribute to civic innovation commensurate with the challenges of a globalized and highly unequal contemporary context. Despite the political and institutional nature of much that needs to be done to enliven and renew civic life, this chapter has identified meaningful and important contributions that can be made by those who largely eschew specialized or explicitly political work. My analysis highlights the significance of the selection of others with whom one speaks and associates—the choice of one's friendships and social ties—and the importance of the stories one tells or, better yet, elaborates. Cultural and associative work—including conversation itself—can make a huge contribution to enabling a country's civic life. The patience to listen—an essential part of conversation—and both the energy and expressive imagination needed to construct compelling narratives, play an enormous role in the successful civic experiences I have related. The ability of civic-minded political actors on the Iberian Peninsula to construct new ways to address the global scale of contemporary challenges and to incorporate the poor into the public square offer us hope that much can be done and accomplished not only by redesigning institutions but also by applying the best civic spirit to our associative, conversational, and cultural efforts.

Notes

1. Fieldnotes, Lisbon, January and April 2006.
2. Javier Baeza, interviews.
3. The exact phrase in Spanish was "*Por nuestro futuro, no al cierre.*" This and other elements of the story of the Asturian coal valleys are related in detail in Fishman (2004).
4. Fieldnotes, Lisbon, April 23, 2004.
5. The complete statement by Oliveira de Silva, the leader of the center-right PSD in Maia, can be found at *www.scribd.com/doc/38862/Discurso-evocativo-do-25-de-Abril* Accessed on May 22, 2009.
6. Timoteo Macedo, interviews, Lisbon, April 27, 2006; February 7, 2008; June 20, 2008; January 12, 2009.
7. Joao Ferrao, interview, Lisbon, January 13, 2009.
8. I am grateful to Jose Soeiro for making available the full text of his remarks.
9. Timoteo Macedo, interviews.
10. Pedro Soares, interview, Lisbon, January 14, 2009.
11. Many of the political posters of the revolutionary period are reproduced in a volume published by a Lisbon daily newspaper on the revolution's thirtieth anniversary in 2004 (Diário de Noticias 2004).

References

Baiocchi, Gianpaolo. 2005. *Militants and Citizens: The Politics of Participatory Democracy in Porto Alegre.* Stanford, CA: Stanford University Press.

Baldassarri, Delia, and Mario Diani. 2007. "The Integrative Power of Civic Networks." *American Journal of Sociology* 113 (3): 735–80.

Bearman, Peter. 1993. *Relations into Rhetorics: Local Elite Social Structure in Norfolk England, 1540–1640.* New Brunswick, NJ: Rutgers University Press.

Berezin, Mabel. 2009. *Illiberal Politics in Neoliberal Times: Culture Security and Populism in the New Europe.* Cambridge: Cambridge University Press.

Bermeo, Nancy. 1986. *The Revolution within the Revolution.* Princeton, NJ: Princeton University Press.

Burt, Ronald S. 2005. *Brokerage and Closure.* Oxford: Oxford University Press.

Centola, Damon, and Michael Macy. 2007. "Complex Contagions and the Weakness of Long Ties." *American Journal of Sociology* 113 (3): 702–34.

Costa Pinto, Antonio. 2001. "Settling Accounts with the Past in a Troubled Transition to Democracy: The Portuguese Case." In *The Politics of Memory: Transitional Justice in Democratizing Societies,* ed. Alexandra Barahona de Brito et al. Oxford: Oxford University Press.

———. 2006. "Authoritarian Legacies, Transitional Justice and State Crisis in Portugal's Democratization." *Democratization* 12 (2).

Dahl, Robert A. 1998. *On Democracy.* New Haven, CT: Yale University Press.

Degenne, Alain, and Michel Forse. 1999. *Introducing Social Networks.* London: Sage.

Diário de Noticias. 2004. *A Poesia Está na Rua: 25 de Abril. 30 Anos. 100 Cartazes.* Lisbon: Diário de Noticias.

Durán Muñoz, Rafael. 2000. *Contención y trangresión: Las movilizaciones socials y el Estado en las transiciones Española y Portuguesa.* Madrid: Centro de Estudios Políticos y Constitucionales.

Eliasoph, Nina, and Paul Lichterman. 2003. "Culture in Interaction." *American Journal of Sociology* 108 (4): 735–94.

Emirbayer, Mustafa, and Jeff Goodwin. 1994. "Network Analysis, Culture and the Problem of Agency." *American Journal of Sociology* 99: 1411–54.

Fishman, Robert M. 1990. "Rethinking State and Regime: Southern Europe's Transition to Democracy." *World Politics* 42 (3): 422–40.

———. 2004. *Democracy's Voices: Social Ties and the Quality of Public Life in Spain.* Ithaca, NY: Cornell University Press.

———. 2007. "On Being a Weberian (After Spain's March 11–14): Notes on the Continuing Relevance of Weber's Methodological Approach." In *Max Weber's 'Objectivity' Revisited,* ed. Laurence McFalls. Toronto: University of Toronto Press.

———. 2009. "On the Costs of Conceptualizing Social Ties as Social Capital." In *Social Capital: Reaching Out, Reaching In,* ed. Viva Ona Bartkus and James H. Davis, 66–83. Northampton, MA: Edward Elgar.

———. 2010. "Rethinking the Iberian Transformations: How Democratization Scenarios Shaped Labor Market Outcomes." *Studies in Comparative International Development* 45 (3): 281–310.

———. 2011. "Democratic Practice after the Revolution: The Case of Portugal and Beyond." *Politics and Society* 39 (2): 233–67.

Fung, Archon. 2004. *Empowered Participation: Reinventing Urban Democracy*. Princeton, NJ: Princeton University Press.

Fung, Archon, and Erik Olin Wright, eds. 2003. *Deepening Democracy: Institutional Innovations in Empowered Participatory Governance*. London: Verso.

Granovetter, Mark. 1974. *Getting a Job*. Cambridge, MA: Harvard University Press.

Hammond, John L. 1988. *Building Popular Power: Workers' and Neighborhood Movements in the Portuguese Revolution*. New York: Monthly Review Press.

Heller, Patrick. 2000. "Degrees of Democracy: Some Comparative Lessons from India." *World Politics* 52 (4): 484–519.

Ikegami, Eiko. 2005. *Bonds of Civility: Aesthetic Networks and the Political Origins of Japanese Culture*. Cambridge: Cambridge University Press.

Lasch, Christopher. 1995. *The Revolt of the Elites and the Betrayal of Democracy*. New York: Norton.

Lichterman, Paul. 2005. *Elusive Togetherness: Church Groups Trying to Bridge America's Divisions*. Princeton, NJ: Princeton University Press.

Linz, Juan, and Alfred Stepan. 1996. *Problems of Democratic Transition and Consolidation: Southern Europe, South America and Post-communist Europe*. Baltimore: Johns Hopkins University Press.

Lizardo, Omar. 2006. "How Cultural Tastes Shape Personal Networks." *American Sociological Review* 71 (5): 778–807.

Mansbridge, Jane J. 1980. *Beyond Adversarial Democracy*. Chicago: Chicago University Press.

Maxwell, Kenneth. 1995. *The Making of Portuguese Democracy*. Cambridge: Cambridge University Press.

Mische, Ann. 2003. "Cross-talk in Movements: Reconceiving the Culture-Network Link." In *Social Movements and Networks: Relational Approaches to Collective Action*, ed. Mario Diani and Doug McAdam, 258–80. Oxford: Oxford University Press.

———. 2007. *Partisan Publics*. Princeton, NJ: Princeton University Press.

———. 2011. "Relational Sociology, Culture and Agency." In *Sage Handbook of Social Network Analysis*, ed. John Scott and Peter Carrington. London: Sage.

Pachucki, Mark A., and Ronald L. Breiger. 2010. "Cultural Holes: Beyond Relationality in Social Networks and Culture." *Annual Review of Sociology* 36: 205–24.

Palacios Cerezales, Diego. 2003. *O Poder Caiu na Rua*. Lisbon: Imprensa de Ciencias Sociais.

Perrin, Andrew. 2006. *Citizen Speak: The Democratic Imagination in American Life*. Chicago: University of Chicago Press.

Polletta, Francesca. 2006. *It Was Like a Fever: Storytelling in Protest and Politics*. Chicago: University of Chicago Press.

Putnam, Robert. 1993. *Making Democracy Work: Civic Traditions in Modern Italy*. Princeton, NJ: Princeton University Press.

———. 2000. *Bowling Alone*. New York: Touchstone Books.

Roberts, Kenneth. 1998. *Deepening Democracy? The Modern Left and Social Movements in Chile and Peru*. Stanford, CA: Stanford University Press.

Sánchez-Cuenca, Ignacio. 2008. "A Preference for Selfish Preferences: The Problem of

Motivations in Rational Choice Political Science." *Philosophy of the Social Sciences* 38 (3): 361–78.

Santos, Boaventura de Sousa. 2004. *25 de Abril: Uma Aventura para a Democracia*. Porto: Afrontamento & Coimbra: Centro de Documentação 25 de Abril.

Serrano, Estrela. 2006. *Para Compreender o Jornalismo*. Coimbra: Minerva.

Silva, Manuela, et al. 2006. *Memorias de Economistas*. Lisbon: Exame.

Sirianni, Carmen. 2009. *Investing in Democracy: Engaging Citizens in Collaborative Governance*. Washington DC: Brookings Press.

Sirianni, Carmen, and Lewis Friedland. 2001. *Civic Innovation in America*. Berkeley: University of California Press.

Skocpol, Theda. 2003. *Diminished Democracy: From Membership to Management in American Civic Life*. Norman: University of Oklahoma Press.

Somers, Margaret R. 1994. "The Narrative Constitution of Identity: A Relational and Network Approach." *Theory and Society* 23 (5): 605–49.

———. 2008. *Genealogies of Citizenship*. Cambridge: Cambridge University Press.

Spillman, Lyn, and Russell Faeges. 2005. "Nations." In *Remaking Modernity: Politics, History and Sociology*, ed. Julia Adams, Elisabeth Clemens, and Ann Shola Orloff. Durham, NC: Duke University Press.

Tilly, Charles. 2002. *Stories, Identities and Political Change*. Lanham, MD: Rowman & Littlefield.

Wasserman, Stanley, and Katherine Faust. 1994. *Social Network Analysis: Methods and Applications*. Cambridge: Cambridge University Press.

Wellman, Barry. 1992. "Which Types of Social Ties and Networks Give What Kinds of Social Support?" In *Advances in Group Processes* ed. Edward Lawler, Barry Markovsky and Cecilia Ridgeway, 207–35. Greenwich, CT: JAI Press.

White, Harrison C., Scott A. Boorman, and Ronald L. Breiger. 1976. "Social Structure from Multiple Networks. I. Blockmodels of Roles and Positions." *American Journal of Sociology* 81: 730–80.

Zuckerman, Alan S., ed. 2005. *The Social Logic of Politics: Personal Networks as Contexts for Political Behavior*. Philadelphia: Temple University Press.

8

Turning Participation into Representation

Innovative Policy Making for Minority Groups in Brazil

THAMY POGREBINSCHI

■ Brazil holds a particular position in the national consolidation and international dissemination of participatory democratic devices of governance. The most well-known of such devices, the participatory budget, has become a model after being originally created in Porto Alegre in 1989, and since then it has been replicated all over the world, regardless of the different levels of success it has achieved in each context (Sintomer, Röcke, and Herzberg 2010). Participatory budgeting's positive outcomes, especially for the redistribution of public goods (Baiocchi 2003), is certainly one of the causes of the increased institutionalization of participatory mechanisms, along with the enforcement of the democratic constitution enacted in 1988, which contains strong directives for the improvement of political participation in the country (Abers 2001; Avritzer 2009).

Since the Workers Party (Partido dos Trabalhadores, PT) took hold of the presidency in 2003, it has been applying at the national level the same programmatic participatory commitments that allowed its former administration in Porto Alegre to become known worldwide. Lula's government has, over its two subsequent periods in office and now that of president Dilma Roussef (also PT), been responsible for activating and institutionalizing at the federal level a participatory innovation that has been altering the way public policy is designed, implemented, and monitored in Brazil: the national public policy conferences.

Today the national public policy conferences are doubtless Brazil's major participatory innovation. There are at least three reasons why such experiments both confirm the country's prominent role in designing democratic practices of social empowerment and its potential to envisage new forms of inclusive governance. First, the national conferences are, as implied by their name, nationwide, and thus challenge the myth that participation is possible only at the local level. Not only do national conferences transcend geographic boundaries of local space, they also overcome the limits imposed on their substance and content. By enabling participation to be exercised at a national scale, national conferences favor interests that are national, which ensures that participatory procedures will lead to the formulation of guidelines for federal public policies. Yet the local level is where citizens meet and is therefore the site from which demands sprout, and national conferences are but the culmination of a process that begins in municipalities, based on municipal conferences, where the delegates are elected in an open poll of participants. Delegates then meet in state conferences, with further linkages that transcend any geopolitical division, such as so-called free and virtual conferences, both entirely open for participation. The open and elective nature of the municipal conferences not only allows for any local issue to get channeled through to the national level, it also allows any citizen to potentially become its representative at the highest level. The national conferences thus can elevate local problems into national solutions.

Second, the national conferences consist of participative experiences that originate, develop, and unfold within representative institutions. Thus they defy the myth that participation and representation are concepts opposed to each other or entail incompatible or even antagonistic democratic models. Summoned by the executive branch through its ministries, secretariats, or national councils, and organized jointly with civil society through commissions, forums, or working groups, the national conferences come full circle at the moment they direct their demands to the executive and legislative branches in the form of administrative or legislative guidelines. In choosing public deliberation as its mechanism of participation, the national conferences are converted into representative entities, providing voice to ideas, preferences, ideals, and opinions, therefore bypassing the limits of formal representative institutions and directly communicating demands to those who, elected by the ballot, have the power to turn them into law and policies. In becoming more responsive to the guidelines presented by the national conferences, the executive and legislative branches are strengthened and fulfill the role of political representation more democratically. The purpose of national conferences is to enrich formal representative institutions through complementary forms of popular participation, not to replace it.

Third, the national conferences enable the direct participation of social and cultural groups in making their minority interests better represented as they are converted into public policies, thus challenging the myth that citizens can only represent their collective interests through elections or through lobbying and interest groups. Because women, indigenous people, and blacks can all voice their own demands, the national conferences enable representation that is more just by providing a form of presence that is often not possible through political parties or quotas in parliaments. By enabling indigenous women to deliberate on health policies as women and as indigenous citizens, or by allowing young black citizens to deliberate on educational policies as young and black citizens, the national conferences diminish the chances of representation being reduced to the need to bargain, with their interests as a tradable commodity, vulnerable to cooptation. By allowing women, indigenous peoples, or blacks to affirm their identity as groups, by the sharing of experiences, perspectives, and values that transcend divisions of class or ideology, the national conferences redefine the meaning—and practice—of political equality. The national conferences thus have the potential to turn the aggregation of individual preferences into social choices and, furthermore, by dethroning pluralism in favor of multiculturalism, to turn historically excluded groups into bearers of rights and transform particular interests into universal policies.

The national public policy conference resembles a form of participatory democratic governance (Fung 2003), although it is much larger than most minipublics tend to be, and it mainly provides for the representation of groups and not merely of individual citizens. It is precisely this feature of such democratic innovation that will be addressed in this chapter. My aim is to take Brazilian national conferences as a case study that enables me to argue that the institutionalization of participatory mechanisms of deliberation within representative institutions may actually enhance the political inclusion of minority groups, advance their preferred policies, foster their rights, and consolidate their identities. Moreover, this chapter aims to present empirical evidence on how participation and deliberation may be turned into representation, or more specifically how minority groups can improve their political representation in the legislative branch through channels other than the formal mechanisms of electoral democracy. The Brazilian case shows how a participatory innovation can reduce some of the known flaws of representative democracy, such as representational deficit and political inequality. Minority groups can be effective in having favorable policies adopted by the government without having been directly successful in electing their favorite parties or representatives. Institutional practices of social participation and deliberation may not only provide further accountability and legitimacy to electoral democracy and its traditional institutions. They may also indicate a shift in representative government. The Brazilian case may thereby provide a step forward in making participation and deliberation enhanced features of political representation itself, and not as opposed models of democracy.

The National Policy Conferences on Minority Groups

The national policy conferences are designed to allow for more democratic policy making. Instead of formulating policies by itself through a formal process that might at best involve the technical aid of expertise, the government permits civil society to join the task of designing new policies and while doing so revising old ones. Brazil's federal government summons a national conference to convene, and the president's decree to initiate the process may either follow an internal governmental perception that a certain area is in need of new (national) policies or an external claim coming

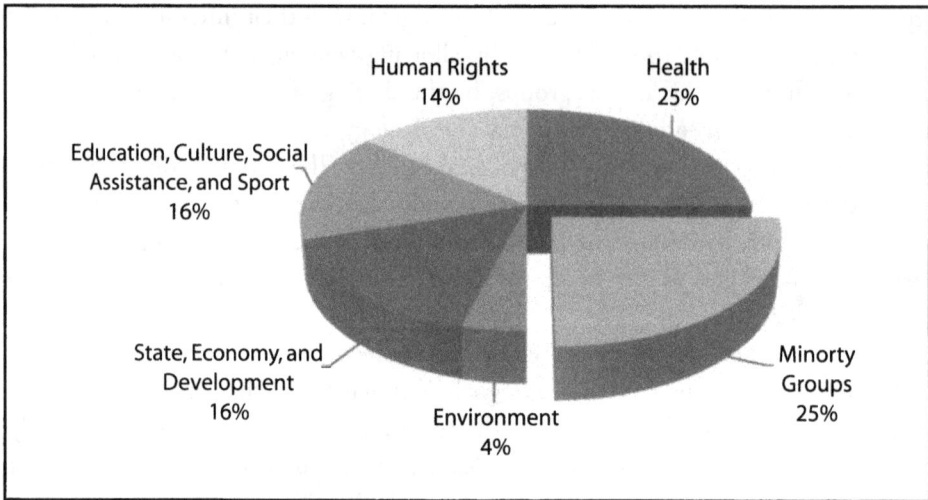

Figure 8.1 Policy Areas Deliberated in the National Conferences (1988–2009)

from civil society. In general, both parts in the national conference process, government and civil society, join each other early on as partners in the task of organizing these new venues for democracy.

No matter the origin of the claim that initiates the process, it usually sheds light in one area of public policy, focusing on diverse policy issues. In their historical origin, the national conferences arose from the health reform movement, which has traditionally been strong and organized in Brazilian civil society long before the re-democratization in 1985. That is why before then—though not during the military dictatorship—the first national conferences were organized to deliberate on health and health-related policies. It was only after the enactment of the new constitution in 1988, however, that other policy areas began being discussed in the national conferences, although these were still limited before Lula took office in 2003.

Between 1988 and 2009, eighty national public policy conferences, all of which were deliberative and normative in scope, were held in Brazil.[1] Depending on the substantive convergence of the policy issues, these national conferences can be classified into six thematic sets: (1) health, (2) environment, (3) state, economy, and development, (4) education, culture, and social assistance, (5) human rights, and (6) minority groups. As illustrated by Figure 8.1, the fraction of national conferences related to policy issues concerning minority groups corresponds to 25 percent, that is, a fourth of all conferences held in the country in twenty-one years.

The twenty national conferences that make up this minority-related policy area are further subdivided into nine policy issues, each one corresponding to a social or cultural group that has been historically excluded from the political decision-making process in Brazil. The nine policy issues from which twenty national conferences were

Year				
1997	Children and Adolescents			
1999	Children and Adolescents			
2001	Children and Adolescents			
2003	Children and Adolescents			
2004	Women			
2005	Children and Adolescents	Racial Equality		
2006	People with Disabilities	The Elderly	Indigenous People	
2007	Children and Adolescents	Women		
2008	People with Disabilities	GLBTT	Youth	Brazilian Communities
2009	Children and Adolescents	The Elderly	Racial Equality	Brazilian Communities

Figure 8.2 Evolution of National Conferences on Minority-Related Issues

organized are "elderly people," "people with disabilities," "gays, lesbians, bisexuals, transvestites and transsexuals," "indigenous peoples," "public policy for women," "youth," "children and adolescents rights," "promotion of racial equality," and "Brazilian communities abroad." Of these nine policy issues that address the rights and interests of social and cultural minority groups, eight were not deliberated in national conferences until 2003, which coincided with the beginning of Lula's first presidential term. The sole exception are the conferences on rights of children and adolescents—to be sure, a quite institutionalized national conference—which were first held in 1997 and since then occur every two years.

Figure 8.2 indicates the evolution of national conferences on policies for minority groups since the first national conference on the rights of children and adolescents took place in 1997. Furthermore, it indicates a strong pull after 2003 toward the broadening of minority-related issues as subjects of national conferences, the diversification of policies formulated according to this participative mechanism, and the increase in the numbers (both relative and absolute) of conferences designed for the deliberation of policies for minority groups.

In just seven years, national conferences for deliberating minority-related policy reached 25 percent of the total of all conferences held since 1988. When considering national conferences held during the seven first years of Lula's government (2003–2009), conferences related to the interests of minority groups account for 31 percent of the fifty-five national conferences held, as shown in Figure 8.3.

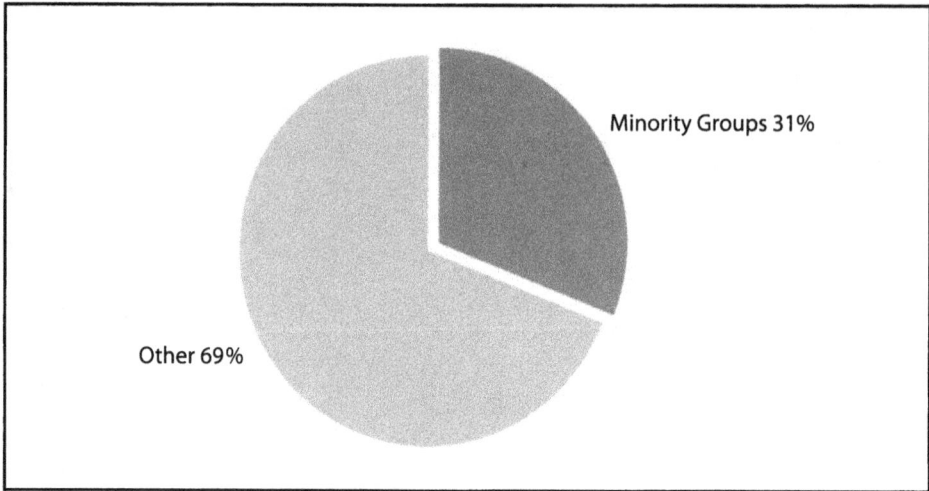

Figure 8.3 Conferences on Policy for Minority Groups

Lula's government was alone responsible for introducing twenty-two new policy areas into the deliberative process of the national conferences, which corresponds to 67 percent of a total of thirty-three areas of public policy that the government has been deliberating, along with civil society, through such participative mechanisms up to the end of 2009. Going beyond the obvious implication that the policy areas subject to public deliberation became more numerous, as well as more diverse, after Lula took office, what also becomes clear is the central role conferred on minority groups, which started taking on a prominent role in the newly created national participative spheres. During the Lula government, not only did minority group conferences increase in number, assuming a higher profile in the overall context of national conferences held during his two terms, but the very conception of minority group also was broadened to encompass a larger and more heterogeneous set of social and cultural groups, which from then on found a channel through which demands for specific policies could be voiced on their political, social, cultural, and legal inclusion.

At least nine are groups whose specific policies have begun to be deliberated in national conferences in which they have the chance to directly participate alongside government representatives. I said at least nine, since in the case of the "national conferences for the promotion of racial equality," for example, although blacks constitute the main group targeted, other racial, ethnic, and religious minorities are also included: gypsies, African descendants, practitioners of African religions, Jews, and Arabs, as well as indigenous people and women. Still within this same group targeted as "black" in the "national conferences for the promotion of racial equality," there are specific policies for black youth, black women, and the *quilombolas* (the surviving descendants of runaway African slaves).

In this same direction, the national conferences for the rights of children and adolescents focus on groups whose specific policies can be further subdivided into actions and specific programs for two subgroups: children and adolescents. It is worth remembering that this latter designation does not perfectly coincide with the group designated "youth," the specific policies for which did not become the object of national conferences until 2008, with precisely the aim to broaden the scope of the group benefited by policies formulated until then, thus including those aged over eighteen and below twenty-nine. Furthermore, the "national conferences for the rights of children and adolescents" deliberate upon policies specifically targeted at "children and adolescents with disabilities" and "black children and adolescents." In addition, the "First National Conference for Youth" in 2008 deliberated upon specific policies for "black youths," "youths with disabilities," "young women," and "GLBT youths." The same occurs with the "national conferences for public policies for women," when there is deliberation upon specific policy guidelines for "black women," "indigenous women," and "young women," among others. Similarly, the "national conferences on rights of people with disabilities" deliberate upon inclusive policies for the blind, deaf, mute, physically impaired, and, within this latter group, the wheelchair-bound.

The examples above indicate that, first, policies for minority groups deliberated in the national conferences tend to crosscut as to their content. The policies tend to favor more than one group simultaneously, respecting overlapping identities. Second, the national conferences on minority policies constitute spaces of deliberation for specific policies for certain minority groups defined according to their unique identity-traits, but also for specific policies that are inherently crosscutting among minority groups since they all somehow seek inclusion. While claiming to have their differences respected, minority groups frame their identity as a minority. Third, each minority group participates and makes itself represented not only in those national conferences designed to deliberate policies targeted at them, but also in others that prioritize policies aimed at other social and cultural minorities. The groups have decisively learned how to use such democratic innovation to shape their own demands and to successively reiterate them until the government converts them into policies.

Besides all national conferences that specifically address policy for minority groups, the main participative arena in which cultural and social minorities have been able to express their demands are the national human rights conferences. Eleven such conferences have occurred from 1996 to 2008, almost one per year. Until 2003, the human rights conferences were the only policy conferences in which minority groups found their demands specifically deliberated. This makes sense when one keeps in mind that up to then, policies addressing minority groups' interests were usually part of larger national policies, such as human rights, and that it was only during Lula's government that each of the minority groups became the subject of a broad national policy program. Indeed, if one looks at the demands made by minority groups in the national conferences on human rights, one realizes that they mostly call for specific actions and programs to be adopted by the federal administration (such as "the elaboration of a massive, systematic, and permanent campaign, to be disseminated in all types of media, against any form of prejudice, and stimulating diversity—including religious and cultural—as something to be respected and as a value") or enacted as more generic and abstract law by the legislature (as for example "creating a National Program Against Religious Intolerance and Racial and Ethnic Discrimination").

Minority groups also make themselves heard in national conferences addressed to other policy areas, whose deliberations are not targeted at minorities or human rights issues. This explains why, for example, in the "I National Conference on Education," held in 2010, deliberations upon guidelines included policies aimed at the inclusion of blacks and the indigenous in universities and the extension of the national educational system to incorporate *quilombola* populations, among other sectorial policies aimed at promoting the inclusion of minority groups. Another national conference on a general policy area that also systematically approves guidelines that incorporate the demands of minorities is the health one. Since 1992 the health conferences have emphasized policies that, for example, aim at promoting the reconsideration of professional curricula to adjust them to the ethnic and cultural profile of the population, especially in the case of the indigenous. This group, it must be added, has been the target of specific conferences within the health and education policy areas: the national conferences for indigenous health (which has existed since 1986) and the national conferences for indigenous schooling (the first of which was held in 2009).

The guidelines approved in national conferences that are aimed at the deliberation of universal policies such as education (and its several categories: "elementary education," "professional and technological education," "education for the indigenous," in addition to the national conference for education) and health (and all of its categories: "mental health," "oral health," "workers' health," "environmental health," "health for the indigenous," in addition to the general national conferences for health) have during the past years incorporated an increasing number of specific policies aimed at the inclusion of social and cultural minorities (as, for example, in the two abovementioned cases, promoting the access of such minorities to the national education system and the unified public health system). This can be explained by referring to the broadening and strengthening of civil society entities for the rights of minorities, as well as to their greater experience acquired in national conferences in which specific policies are deliberated upon and that allow them to voice their demands in other participative arenas that deal with issues of their concern.

If minority groups demand their inclusion in deliberations concerning general universal policies such as health and education, then what is the nature of the demands voiced in the national conferences that are aimed at providing guidelines for the design of policies specifically addressed to them? After analyzing the policy guidelines approved in the final assembly that closes each national conference, summoning the results from the deliberation and consent of all participants, it can be said that in terms of their substance, they can be classified into three types: (1) guidelines for the inclusion in general area policies (*inclusive* policy guidelines that aim for the inclusion of groups within the scope of general universal policies, which in many cases already exist, as for example: "creating a law providing for the teaching of indigenous culture in public schools" or "creating health programs, awareness and prevention campaigns for diseases, aimed at black women and communities traditionally victimized by violence), (2) guidelines for the broadening of specific policies (*specific* policy guidelines that aim to promote or broaden specific interests of minority groups such as "creating quotas for black, indigenous and *quilombola* populations in civil service" or "instituting November 20, the National Black Awareness Day, as a national holiday"), and (3) guidelines for general public policy (*general* policy guidelines, expressing demands that go beyond the interests of the group as a group, such as "promoting the preservation of the natural environment and the decontamination of water springs" or "mandatorily including computer classes in elementary and high school"). Besides their inclusion on supposedly universal policies such as education and health, minority groups seem to seek in the participatory space of the national conferences their recognition as a group through the claim of rights, but as well as citizens concerned with general policies not necessarily connected to their group identity.

Enlarging Participation: Minority Groups' Claims

The national conferences are organized by the government with the explicit intent of deliberating on public policy along with civil society. Although the results of the conferences are not binding, the government has been strongly relying on this participatory practice to draft its policies. And this is how minority groups manage to have their interests further represented and taken into consideration in political decision making. Civil society has incentives to participate in the national conferences once it knows its claims will potentially be heard. And the government has incentives to take the conferences' results seriously once it counts on the support of civil society, both at election time and between elections. The result is a more participative government, a more fully represented civil society, and more responsive political institutions, and therefore a deeper democracy.

Several are the civil society entities—from more organized NGOs to less organized social movements—that represent minority groups' interests in the national conferences. The II National Conference on Women's Policy, held in 2007, for instance, gathered together dozens of entities representative of women's interests, plus many other civil society associations that represent diverse interests, among which are those of women. If one also takes into account the women's associations that participated in the local and state conferences but have not managed to elect delegates to the national-level conference, this number increases significantly—especially if one bears in mind that 690 local conferences on women's policy were organized, and that all twenty-seven states also had their own conferences preceding the national one. There were 2,306 participants in the 2007 National Conference on Women's Policy, of which 60 percent were civil society representatives and 40 percent members of the government.

One can therefore assume that even considered as a group united by common features (such as common identity, experience, memory, narrative, values, needs, and interests), and distinct from others by the shared differences that distinguish them as a minority, women (as other minority groups) have diverse positions regarding their own demands and thus have diverse claims. There is no such homogeneous group as "women," and although internal diversity is part of the group's identity, a minimal homogeneity must be reached regarding the political claims; otherwise, lack of consensus among the group's members may result in lack of policies enacted by the government. Therefore, the national conferences provide a deliberative space in which not only civil society and government are able to openly negotiate policies to be drafted, but also the groups themselves have a chance to frame their own claims and thus shape their identity as a group.

The new institutional venues for participation, and the increased chances to channel claims to the government, stimulates civil society. New associations, NGOs, and social movements have been created; old ones have been reformulated or have been joined by new members. Participation does increase when there is an increase in the participatory spaces, and mostly when those prove themselves effective. Civil society entities begin to organize themselves long before a national conference takes place. They are generally responsible for negotiating with the government the call for a new conference, as well as its date, format, and other organizational aspects. Once the president decrees that a national conference convene, which occurs on average twelve to sixteen months prior, the social organizations begin to internally discuss their claims and choose their representatives. Therefore, the national conferences have a positive impact on civic association and political mobilization.

The local-level conferences allow social organizations to meet and deliberate along with similar social organizations from neighborhoods and municipalities. Together they frame their claims, negotiate with representatives from local governments, and elect delegates to the subsequent stages. The same procedure occurs at the state conferences, this time involving the representatives from all local conferences and state government. When the national conference takes place, the social organizations that participated and elected delegates in all states, which includes national organizations that may have participated in several municipal and state conferences, already have their demands better framed and are more ready to make their claims. They will be able to negotiate with other representatives, civic and government, to have their claims included in the final document that will contain all approved policy guidelines.

As the aim of the national conferences is to have those policy guidelines later converted into real policy by the government, they are framed in such a way as to be followed by either the executive branch or the legislature. Hence the policy guidelines that come out of the national conferences can be classified in two types, administrative and legislative. Administrative guidelines express demands whose fulfillment falls within the powers of the executive branch, while legislative guidelines require a normative act by the legislative branch, even if the initiative for proposing a law comes from the executive. Let's look at examples for each type of policy guideline, both taken from the II National Conference on the Promotion of Racial Equality, held in 2009. One of the hundreds of approved administrative guidelines reads: "producing orientation material concerning racist behavior, attitudes and acts in order to inform the population at large of the Anti-Racism Statute and its application and of the federal and state-level prosecution's offices and local public safety authorities in charge of enforcing it." One legislative guideline says: "proposing state and municipal-level legislative branches the elaboration of statutes creating state and municipal councils for the Racial Equality Promotion Policies, linked to executive bodies responsible for developing said policies," or, furthermore, "approving the bill creating the Racial Equality Statute." The first contains a directive for a policy that must be enacted by the executive, and the second is clearly addressed to the lawmaking power of the legislative branch.

What is deliberated in the national conferences aimed at policy for minority groups? What do approved policy guidelines consist of and to whom are they addressed? I will answer those questions by looking into data I have collected concerning all conferences aimed at deliberating on policy for minority groups that took place between 2003 and 2010, that is, during the two terms of Lula's government. This data sums up a total of fifteen national conferences, distributed into eight minority groups: women (I and II national conferences on women's policy, respectively held in 2004 and 2007), elderly (I and II national conferences on rights of the elderly, respectively held in 2006 and 2009), people with disabilities (I and II national conferences on rights of people with disabilities, respectively held in 2006 and 2008), gays, lesbians, bisexuals, transvestites, and transsexuals (I national conference on gays, lesbians, bisexuals, transvestites, and transsexuals, held in 2008), indigenous people (I national conference on indigenous people, held in 2006), children and adolescents (IV, V, VI and VII national conferences on the rights of children and adolescents, held respectively in 2003, 2005, 2007, and 2009), black and other racial and ethnic minorities (I and II national conferences on the promotion of racial equality, held in 2005 and 2009), and youth (I national conference on youth, held in 2008). Taken together, those fifteen conferences approved 3,428 policy guidelines, which can be divided into administrative and legislative ones.

The data reveal that the executive branch is the main addressee of the guidelines approved in the national conferences aimed at the deliberation on policy for minority groups: 68.7 percent of all deliberations originating from minority groups' national conferences since 2003 demanded some kind of direct response from the executive branch. To this percentage should be added a total of 23.4 percent of mixed guidelines, that is, guidelines that contain demands that could be fulfilled by both executive and legislative branches. Only 7.9 percent of all approved guidelines specifically addressed the legislative branch.

Interestingly enough, the results for groups that only very recently became the subjects of specific public policies—such as the youth, the elderly, the GLBT, and the people with disabilities—display a higher number of legislative guidelines than the average. This clearly reveals the greater need for recognition of those groups as legal subjects, that is, as recipients of rights and bearers of judicial protection. They certainly need as much policy as the other minority groups do, but they also need to be first recognized as groups, and as such they claim a legal benchmark of their own. More than having their political inclusion granted, those groups expect to have their social and cultural identity recognized. Women, blacks, and children have been for a longer time protected by law in Brazil, even though they still lack basic policies that meet their needs and interests. Indigenous people present an exception here. Although this group has been considered by state policies for a longer time, such policies have always proven insufficient in recognizing indigenous cultural diversity, and although indigenous people were included in the democratic constitution of 1988, they still lack basic rights and they mostly still lack legal protection. Part of this protection is a territorial one, required due to continued land ownership conflicts. And these are issues that must be addressed by law, which explains the high number of legislative guidelines among those approved in the "I National Conference on Indigenous Peoples," held in 2006. Table 8.1 displays the data on the nature of the guidelines approved in minority group's national conferences.

This apparent bias toward administrative guidelines should not lead one to infer that it denotes a stronger preference among delegates of national conferences for punctual and specific policies rather than generic and abstract laws. Neither should one infer that national conference participants simply consider that the executive can potentially respond more effectively and rapidly than the legislature. Beyond the fact that consensus on policies takes longer to consolidate in the legislature (due not only to the many procedures required in the course of the legislative process, but also to the need of forging coalitions able to approve the policies, in addition to other variables), one should also remember that many demands that are administrative in nature require the implementation of policies that have been previously established by law.

With regard to minority groups, the proposition above seems all the more true. It is no casual coincidence that national conferences on minorities are often referred to as "conferences for rights," something which, not surprisingly, some of their names carry: national conference on the *rights* of elderly, national conferences on the *rights* of people with disabilities, national conference on the *rights* of children and adolescents. Many of these rights—such as those concerning the elderly, the children, and people with disabilities—already are declared in the constitution, but they are social

Table 8.1 Nature of Guidelines Approved in Minority Groups' National Conferences

National Conference	Year	Legislative Guidelines	Administrative Guidelines	Mixed Guidelines	Total
Rights of the Elderly	2006	49 (23%)	97 (45.5%)	67 (31,5%)	213
	2009	0 (0%)	1 (14.3%)	6 (85,7%)	7
Rights of People with Disabilities	2006	5 (2.7%)	67 (35.8%)	115 (61,5%)	187
	2008	9 (18.4%)	40 (81.6%)	0 (0%)	49
Gays, Lesbians, Bisexuals, Transvestites, and Transsexuals	2008	29 (23.2%)	68 (54.4%)	28 (22.4%)	125
Indigenous Peoples	2006	93 (49.2%)	73 (38.6%)	23 (12.2%)	189
Women Policy	2004	5 (6.3%)	21 (26.3%)	54 (67.5%)	80
	2007	0 (0%)	251 (66.4%)	127 (33.6%)	378
Rights of Children and Adolescents	2003	8 (5.9%)	120 (88.2%)	8 (5.9%)	136
	2005	0 (0%)	37 (61.7%)	23 (38.3%)	60
	2007	0 (0%)	14 (58.3%)	10 (41.7%)	24
	2009	1 (1.6%)	12 (19.4%)	49 (79%)	62
Promotion of Racial Equality	2005	33 (3.1%)	874 (83%)	146 (13.9%)	1053
	2009	16 (2.1%)	646 (84.9%)	99 (13%)	761
Youth	2008	23 (22.1%)	34 (32.7%)	47 (45.2%)	104
Total		271 (7.9%)	2355 (68.7%)	802 (23.4%)	3428

and cultural rights that, due to their legal nature, imply a greater number of obstacles standing between their specification, implementation, and enforcement. This explains why often what administrative guidelines call for is the actual fulfillment of rights that have already been granted but whose implementation depends on policies that wait to be drafted. Therefore, once able to rely on laws that guarantee their rights and preserve their interests, minority groups tend to eventually prioritize the approval of administrative guidelines rather than legislative ones. This, however, does not prevent them from demanding that the implementation of certain policies be one way or the other guaranteed by law.

The points made in the previous paragraphs suggest yet another proposition: for as much as the main objective of the national conferences consists of providing guidelines for the *formulation* of public policies, they have also demonstrated their potential as both sources of guidelines for the *implementation* of previously formulated policies and arenas for the *monitoring* of already implemented policies. The national conferences thus have an impact in several stages of the public policy cycle. Furthermore, since 2003 such a participatory mechanism has been responsible for a major change in the way political decisions are made and the way public policies are made in Brazil.

Improved Representation: Governmental Responses

To what degree are the executive and the legislative branches in Brazil responsive to civil society's demands, as voiced in the national conferences? How much are the guidelines deliberated in such participatory spaces followed in the government's drafting of policies and laws? To what measure have minority groups been further included in the political decisions and proved to be the final beneficiaries of policies and laws that advance their interests and guarantee their rights?

In order to answer these questions, I have built up a database with all the policy guidelines that have been approved in the national conferences on minority groups, plus all those approved in the human rights national conferences that deal with minority group issues. Those policy guidelines have been classified into administrative and legislative according to the branch of the government that is institutionally competent to fulfill them. Each policy guideline has been entered as a search term in the databases of the federal executive branch and of the Congress, according to the nature of the guideline. Those searches were made taking into consideration the date of each national conference whose guidelines were searched, and they cover the entirety of Lula's government (2003–2010), except for its two final months. All search results were then analyzed to verify precisely which ones matched the policy guidelines. Naturally, one presidential decree or law may match more than one policy guideline, and in the results I will mention below those that have been counted only once. Certainly the fact that a decree or law matches the national conference guidelines is not enough, on its own, to draw the conclusion that the guidelines resulting from the social participation processes have led to the creation of such a decree or law. But such fact is certainly enough to support the argument that the national conference guidelines operate as an informative basis that somehow influence the policy making by the executive and lawmaking by the legislature. That seems even truer when one notes not only the substantive congruence between the contents of conference guidelines and those of the law and policies enacted by the government, but also the temporal coincidence between them.

Let's first look at the presumed impact on the executive branch. Considering only the presidential decrees issued from 2003 onwards, one can note a significant increase starting in 2006. As we have already seen in Figure 8.2, with the exception of children and adolescents, the first specific minority group national conference was held in 2004 (women's policy), the second in 2005 (promotion of racial equality), and then in 2006 three national conferences on minority groups were held (elderly, people with disabilities, and indigenous people). This average of three conferences per year on minority

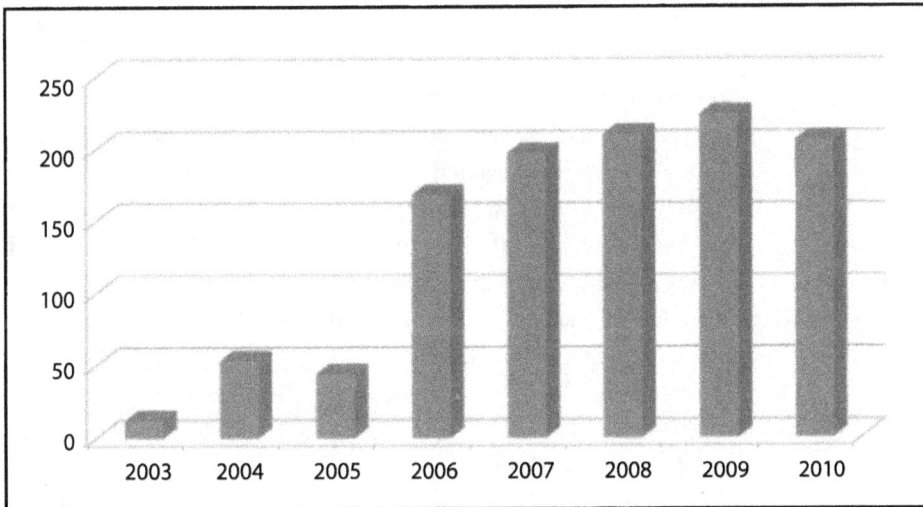

Figure 8.4 Presidential Decrees on Minority and Human Rights Issues (2003–2010)

group issues was maintained until 2009. Figure 8.4 displays how policy making by the executive branch has increased following the increase of the national conferences focusing on minority groups' issues. In 2003, when only the regular national conferences on human rights and children and adolescents took place, 12 presidential decrees relating to those issues were issued. In 2009, after each minority group had had its own specific national conference, the number of presidential decrees that matched such conferences' administrative guidelines rose to 224.

The major impact of the national conferences on policy making is, however, qualitative and not merely quantitative. While it is harder to rigorously evaluate the presumed impact of the national conferences on the legislature due to the many variables that may be at stake when a bill is proposed or a law enacted, in the executive branch policies were made in Lula's government with the clear and explicit intent of fulfilling civil society's demands contained in national conference guidelines. One of the most well-known examples is the so-called National Program for Human Rights 3. This long national plan, which contains among other things policies for all sorts of minority groups, became binding after the publication of a presidential decree in the end of 2009. As it is written in the policy itself, its twenty-five guidelines, eighty-one strategic objectives, and hundreds of actions reflect the demands of about fifty-five national conferences held during the Lula presidency, and especially those related to minority group's and human rights issues.

Several other important presidential decrees were issued, many of them bringing to life for the first time national policy plans in areas that had never before been specifically addressed by federal policy making. This is the case, for example, of women. Although women have in one way or another been contemplated in different policies over the years, they have never had a specific policy that addressed them as a group and that intended to provide them with a national framework to be implemented in each and every state of the country. Most importantly, apart from never having had a full policy agenda of their own, women had also never taken part in the drafting of such a policy. That was until the enactment in March 2005 by presidential decree of the "1st National Plan for Policies for Women," which explicitly states in its introduction that it was the result of the 1st National Conference on Women's Policy "that in July 2004 established itself as a watershed in the affirmation of the rights of women, and mobilized throughout Brazil approximately 120,000 women, who directly participated in debates and presented proposals for the elaboration of a National Plan of Policies for Women." As participation began to be institutionalized in Brazil and women's movements received a new impetus, a second national plan on women's policy was issued by presidential decree in March 2008. The Second National Plan for Policies for Women declares in its introduction that it is the "result of the mobilization of almost 200,000 Brazilian women, who participated throughout the country in the municipal and state Conferences, and elected 2,700 delegates to the II National Conference on Women's Policy that took place in August 2007."

As with women, national policy plans were drafted for black people, people with disabilities, and the elderly. These examples are just a small sample of the potential that administrative guidelines formulated at national conferences have of being converted into public policies formulated and implemented by executive branch at the federal level. Even though the main scope of national conferences consists of providing content for the formulation of *national* policies, the national plans and programs that incorporate the demands voiced by minority groups are complemented by several other decrees regulating them, and their scope has been both broadened and specified by a wide array of normative acts of the federal public administration, which privilege policies and specific actions that aim to turn the deliberations of the national conferences into reality.

The exact measure of how much national conferences are able to shape the public policy agenda in Brazil certainly requires a more rigorous analysis. There is no doubt, however, that, based on data presented in the preceding pages, these nationwide participative practices strongly impact the actions of the executive branch, which has become increasingly responsive to the demands of minority groups and, equally important, has been redesigning itself institutionally, particularly with regard to the way it formulates, implements, and monitors public policies.

Let's now turn to the presumed impact on lawmaking in the legislative branch. We already know that the final deliberations of the national conferences on minority group policy tend to approve more administrative than legislative guidelines. But the volume of legislative guidelines, although smaller, is significant.

As shown earlier in this chapter in Table 8.1, legislative guidelines approved by the fifteen specific national conferences on minority group policy make up an average of 7.9 percent of the total, but to this percentage should be added the 23.4 percent of mixed

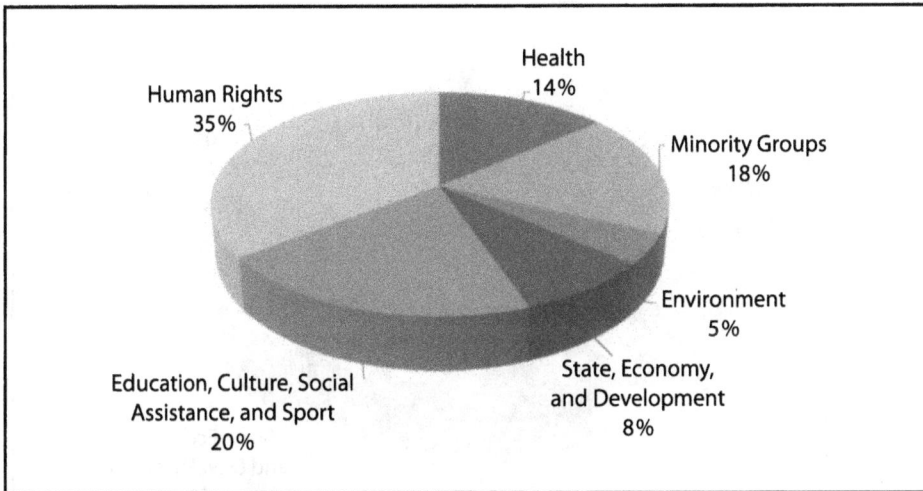

Health
14%

Human Rights
35%

Minority Groups
18%

Environment
5%

Education, Culture, Social
Assistance, and Sport
20%

State, Economy,
and Development
8%

Figure 8.5 Bills in Congress in 2009

guidelines that contain demands addressed to the legislative as much as to the executive branch. Since 2003, total of 1,073 guidelines thus envisaged a response from the legislature. Therefore, while minority groups and national conferences tend to demand more from the executive than from the legislature, their demands to the legislature indicate, first and foremost, that regardless of how avidly groups might pursue actions and programs from the executive, the need for formal inclusion and the legal guarantee of many rights, in addition to the conversion of temporary government policies into permanent state policies, remains unfulfilled. This leaves us with the task of examining how the parliament has responded to the demands submitted by minority groups.

If one looks at the presumed impact on the legislature of all eighty deliberative national public policy conferences that took place in Brazil from 1988 to 2009, one arrives at the conclusion that conferences dealing with minority groups stood out either because of the rising number of occurrences, the high number of legislative guidelines deliberated upon, or the presumably significant effect of these guidelines on the Congress's lawmaking activities. Such conclusions can be derived from a comparison between the results achieved in the legislature by the minority group conferences and the results achieved by all others. Those results concern both the bills introduced by the representatives and those laws and constitutional amendments effectively enacted by the Congress. Looking at bills is as important as looking at approved legislation, because they reflect the eventual informational basis provided by the national conferences to the elected representatives. Some representatives may not be successful in having their bills approved by the Congress and converted into law, but the fact that they have proposed bills congruent with national conference demands suggests that they are representing those demands.

Figure 8.5 displays the distribution of all bills that cover national conference demands that were, by the end of 2009, active in the Brazilian Congress, waiting to be

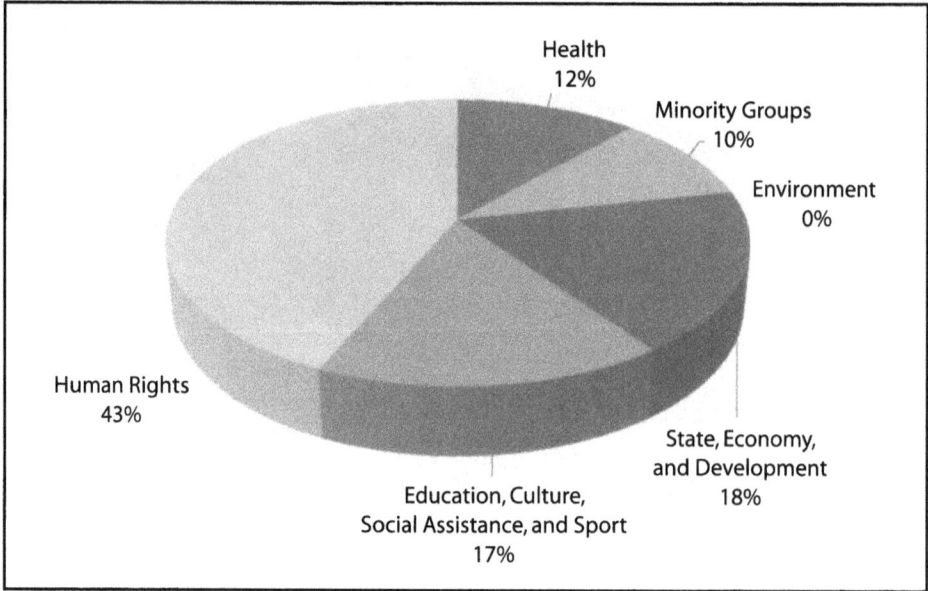

Figure 8.6 Laws and Constitutional Amendments

voted on and converted into law. One can note that of all national conferences held since 1988, the twenty dealing specifically with minority group issues were alone responsible for 18 percent of the total of bills and constitutional amendment proposals whose subject involved guidelines approved in national conferences. Adding the 35 percent of proposals that correlate to the national conferences on human rights, one comes to the conclusion that more than half of all bills proposed aimed at fulfilling the demands of minority groups.

With regard not only to the legislative activity, but also to the actual output of the Brazilian Congress, Figure 8.6 shows that minority groups are also successful in converting bills that relate to their interests into statutes and constitutional amendments: 10 percent of all laws and constitutional amendments identified as congruent with the legislative guidelines of the national conferences incorporated, to some degree, the demands expressed by minority groups at the national conferences. Although this proportion is smaller that the one found for the bills, when one adds the laws and amendments congruent with the guidelines of the conferences on human rights, one finds the same 53 percent reached in Figure 8.5 concerning the bills not yet voted upon. Nevertheless, the fact that the number of bills congruent with the guidelines from the national conferences on minority groups is smaller than the number of laws actually enacted by the Congress is absolutely to be expected. When compared to the other policy areas, the national conferences on minority groups were the latest to occur (mostly beginning only after 2003), and the average time required to have a bill converted into law must be taken into consideration.

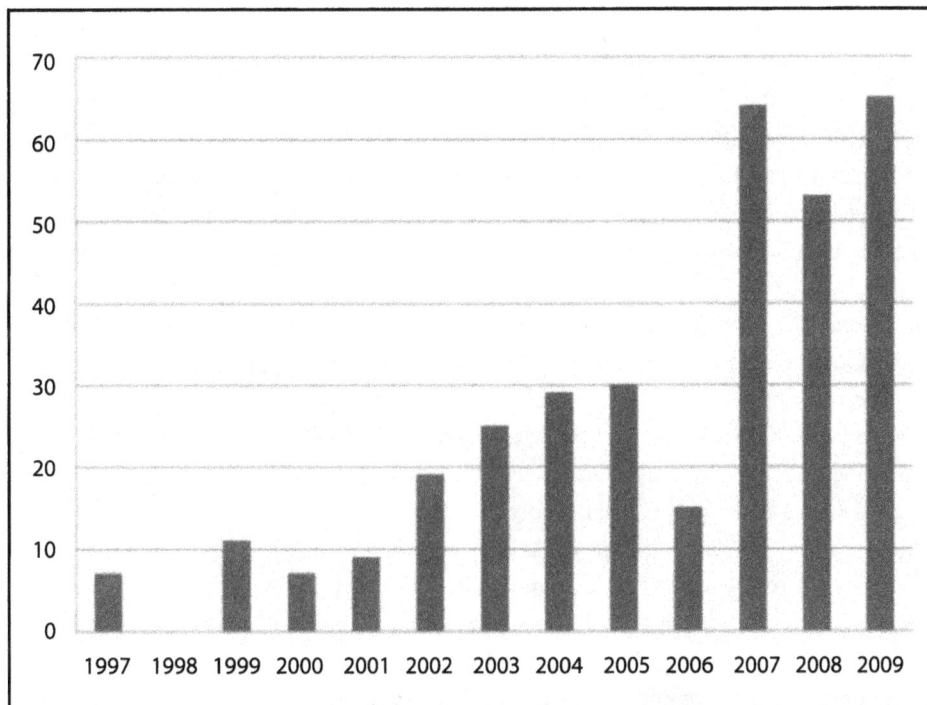

Figure 8.7 Bills on Minority and Human Rights

Unlike the bills and proposals to amend the constitution, which correspond to those active in the Congress by the end of 2009, the statutes and constitutional amendments displayed in Figure 8.6 encompasses all those enacted between 1988 and 2009. Since the national conferences for minorities did not begin until after 2003, there are still unanswered questions: How were they capable of generating as many responses by the legislature in so little time? How capable are the national conferences for human rights in absorbing and representing the demands of minorities?

Figure 8.7 can provide some tentative answers to these questions. It presents the distribution over time of bills and constitutional amendment proposals congruent with the guidelines of the national conferences for minorities and human rights. The period under scrutiny spans from 1997, when the I National Conference on the Rights of Children and Adolescents took place, until 2009. One notices that, save for a slight dip in 2006, the number of projects has been increasing steadily and considerably since 2003, when the first of the eight new specific national conferences on minority groups were put into practice by Lula's government. In 2007, the year following the I National Conference on the Rights of Elderly, the I National Conference on the Indigenous People, and the I National Conference on People with Disabilities, one can notice that the number of bills presented pertaining to minority groups increased sixfold compared to 1997.

The year 2008 presents a slight decrease from 2007, and it is interesting to notice that it follows a year in which, in addition to the VI National Conference for the Rights of Children and Adolescents, which was taking place every two years since 1997, there was only one new specific conference for minority groups, the I National Conference on Women's Policy. This indicates that the decrease of the number of national conferences on minority groups held in a year, no matter how small, is related to a decrease in the number of bills pertaining to minorities the following year. The relationship between the number of national conferences and the number of bills shows that (1) the national conferences are a driving force behind legislative activity of the Congress, and (2) national conferences shape the agenda of the Congress.

The year 2009 also seems to confirm these two hypotheses; since there is an increase over 2008, it is likely that this was caused by the holding of four minority group conferences in the previous years. Since the national conferences take a few months to announce publicly their final reports and approved guidelines, it is reasonable to expect that any potential effects would only be felt months later. It is thus advisable to wait a year or two year for this kind of analysis. The year 2008 set new records for national conferences for minority groups and brought three new policy issues to public deliberation. Also, during the two preceding years new policy issues had become the object of national conferences. This can perhaps explain the high success rate achieved in 2009 and allows me to advance one further hypothesis: (3) national conferences succeed in placing *new* items in the agenda of the Congress.

Converting Participation into Representation

The data discussed in the previous pages suggest that Brazil's national public policy conferences have established themselves as spaces in which social and cultural minority groups are able to successfully convert themselves into political majorities. If this claim is true, then institutionalized participation and deliberation may in fact strengthen political representation.

As we have seen, the national public policy conferences have become not only broader and more frequent since 2003, they have also become more wide-ranging and inclusive with the beginning of Lula's government. Since then, an increasing number of policy areas have been submitted to public deliberation, and an impressive portion of them have dealt with issues aimed at minority groups. The contours of the public policy are thus to be defined to a large extent by the particular nature of the groups that participate in those public deliberations. Demands formulated through the national conferences on women's policy, indigenous people, the elderly, people with disabilities, gays, lesbians, bisexuals, transvestites and transsexuals, children and youth, and different races and ethnicities inevitably touch other nonparticular public policy areas, such as health, education, social assistance, and culture. Therefore, in addition to increasingly including more diverse and heterogeneous interests usually represented by civil society (dispersed among NGOs, social movements, worker unions, business entities, and other professional or nonprofessional entities), such Brazilian democratic innovations operate as spaces that allow minority groups to represent their hitherto fragmented and scattered interests and advance a policy agenda of their own.

Minority groups have therefore not only been able to rely on an increasing number of participatory spaces in which public policies targeting them are the specific object of deliberation within the government. They have also been effective in articulating a considerable number of administrative and legislative guidelines addressed respectively to the executive and the legislative branches. Although such policy guidelines, formulated through participatory deliberation, are not binding, it is reasonable to suppose that they do actually inform policy making and lawmaking. A high percentage of their informational basis passes on to the executive branch and the legislature and deal with demands made by minority groups.

The data discussed in this chapter suggest that the two main branches of representative government have been responsive to those demands. Such responsiveness, in turn, may lead to the increase of the representativeness of groups whose interests are not directly taken into account in electoral and party politics. Minority groups' interests have been reaching the government through new channels. To put it in another way, these interests have been generated within government through new forums of participation and deliberation, and ultimately might be able to reconfigure how political parties mediate interests.

The institutionalization of participatory experiments such as the national public policy conferences in Brazil may not only give minority groups a voice, but they also may make that voice effectively heard in the government. Even when minority groups eventually are not able to elect their preferred candidates, institutional democratic innovations may provide them with an opportunity to have their interests represented in the traditional institutions of representative government.

The effect of a law or policy backed up by the guidelines deliberated in the national policy conferences may operate as a form of "retrospective representation" (Mansbridge 2003), since elected representatives may be presented with strong incentives (which eventually transcend party agendas or the priorities of traditional constituencies) to endorse the demands voiced by minority groups and thereby gain new voters or re-establish severed ties with former ones. Democratic participatory innovations are thus capable of achieving political representation for political minorities that would otherwise not be able to build party majorities.

The institutionalization of democratic innovations may therefore allow for the political representation of minority groups even when, in the first instance, their preferences are not envisaged in party programs and platforms. The public policy guidelines contained in the deliberations of the national conferences stimulate governmental activity, offering elected representatives a broad menu of demands directly shaped according to the preferences of civil society's groups in a nonelectoral setting, one that is therefore free from party influences, media appeal, or any other form of interference in the formation of citizens' opinion and will. Once institutionalized, democratic participatory deliberations are imbued with a strong claim to legitimacy, which allows minority groups to overcome the traditional logic of interest distribution. This is what can eventually enable a major party to decide to represent a previously unrepresented interest, one hitherto not represented by any other party or perhaps weakly supported by a minor party.

Brazil's national public policy conferences therefore function as a form of political mediation that runs parallel to elections and party politics but that is nonetheless capable of converging to achieve democracy through representative institutions. The participation of civil society organizations, and the deliberation they engage in with government, yield more representative institutions, insofar as such participatory deliberation is able to include broader and more inclusive interests. The process bolsters political representation by creating new incentives for elected representatives to perform their activities in ways that are better aligned with preferences in civil society.

The concrete impact of such bolstered political representation in the actual inclusion of minority groups is, however, an issue yet to be addressed, as is the redistributive effects of the policies designed accordingly to the demands brought up by those groups in the national policy conferences in Brazil. Nevertheless, the way such institutional innovation has been serving the interests of minority groups evidences how democracy is able to express itself as representation in yet another way through participation and deliberation.

Note

1. There were, in fact, ninety-two national conferences organized in this period, but only eighty of those satisfy what I call a deliberative and normative scope, that is, a previously arranged deliberative procedure consisting of various stages and resulting in the approval by all participants of a document containing the policy guidelines resulting from the entire process.

References

Abers, Rebecca. 2001. *Inventing Local Democracy: Grassroots Politics in Brazil.* Boulder, CO: Westview.

Avritzer, Leonardo. 2009. *Participatory Institutions in Democratic Brazil.* Baltimore: Johns Hopkins University Press.

Baiocchi, Gianpaolo. 2003. "The Porto Alegre Experiment in Empowered Participatory Governance" In *Deepening Democracy: Institutional Innovations in Empowered Participatory Governance*, ed. A. Fung and E. O. Wright. London: Verso.

Fung, Archon. 2003. "Survey Article: Recipes for Public Spheres: Eight Institutional Design Choices and Their Consequences." *Journal of Political Philosophy* 11.

Mansbridge, Jane. 2003. "Rethinking Representation." *American Political Science Review* 97 (4).

Sintomer, Yves, Carsten Herzberg, and Anja Röcke. 2010. *Der Bürgerhaushalt in Europa: Eine Realistische Utopie.* Wiesbaden: VS Verlag.

9

Bringing the State Back In through Collaborative Governance

Emergent Mission and Practice at the US Environmental Protection Agency

CARMEN SIRIANNI

■ Can an agency of the federal administrative state enable productive engagement by citizens themselves to help solve public problems and thereby take a rightful, even noble place in a democratic theory and practice of self-governance for the twenty-first century?

American founders—everyday revolutionaries as well as those who attended the Constitutional Convention of 1787 and the state ratifying conventions that followed (Maier 2010)—invoked the ideal of republican self-government, though they never completely agreed upon what this meant, nor did the "multiple traditions" from which they drew—liberal, civic republican, Protestant, commonwealth, Scottish common sense (Kloppenberg 1987; Gibson 2006). Within a few short years, James Madison and Thomas Jefferson were signaling support for nongovernmental Democratic-Republican "societies" (though they remained ambivalent) and then the first political "party" to restrain top-down "aristocratic" tendencies they saw at work in administrative agencies and policy designs, especially in the Treasury Department, headed by Alexander Hamilton (Brooke 1996). In effect, they were questioning policy feedback effects on the capacities, virtues, and interests of self-governing citizens. A very imperfect Jeffersonian Revolution of 1800 cemented the ideal of a self-governing republic even further, though primarily for white males, and various kinds of civic associations began to flourish, thus further enriching and pluralizing a public sphere rhetorically linked to ideals of self-government. Soon associations were created by women as well as men, free blacks as well as whites, and they came to constitute the first antebellum social movements, such as antislavery, temperance, and women's rights, in some cases with pragmatic, collaborative, and partnership practices (Boylan 2002; Robertson 2010).

The creation of a broad array of associations, of course, is exactly what impressed

Tocqueville when he visited the United States for nine months in 1831–32 and then famously memorialized in *Democracy in America:* "Each time a new need arises, the idea of association comes immediately to mind. The art of association then becomes . . . the fundamental science; everyone studies it and applies it" (de Tocqueville 2004, 606). But, as various scholars of American political development have shown (John 1997; Novak 2001; Skocpol 2002; Campbell 2005, 2012; Mettler 2005, 2011), government institutions and policy designs have often had a major impact on the development, capacities, and roles of civic associations, even in Tocqueville's time, and certainly since the New Deal. Administrative and policy design can have positive or negative civic feedback effects, thereby enabling or disabling, enlightening or obscuring, civic action in various ways. The question posed in the opening lines of this chapter is thus not new. It simply takes different forms when we are speaking of the far more elaborate array of civic associations, as well as institutions of the administrative state and, indeed, many other kinds of institutions of the late twentieth and early twenty-first centuries. In this chapter, I discuss policy design and feedback as place-based (community, ecosystem), in contrast to most discussions of policy feedback and mass publics in individual-benefit-based social welfare programs. Both types are essential and there are, of course, hybrids.

In 2008, the National Advisory Council for Environmental Policy and Technology (NACEPT) issued a report that called upon the US Environmental Protection Agency (EPA) to *"reframe its mission with stewardship as the unifying theme and ethic and strive to become the world's premier stewardship model"* (original italics). Because the EPA can be "only one piece of the overall systemic solution . . . collaborative governance . . . is a key strategy," and will "require continuing EPA management attention and a long-term sustained investment" (NACEPT 2008, 1). NACEPT serves as the main nongovernmental advisory council to the EPA and was referencing practices of public engagement that were becoming increasingly prevalent in the agency. The EPA's own Innovation Action Council (IAC), composed of senior civil servants with a mandate to generate cross-agency innovation, had prepared the groundwork for NACEPT with a technical report reviewing prior practice and persistent problems (IAC 2005).

The National Environmental Justice Advisory Council (NEJAC), with a narrower mission but considerably more representation from leading social movement actors than NACEPT, issued several reports just prior to this, with much the same theme: addressing deep patterns of environmental injustice will require collaborative models that enable empowered community groups and associations to work with public agencies at all levels of government, as well as with multiple stakeholders from business and trade associations, universities and health care institutions, professional and trade union groups, academic and scientific institutions (NEJAC 2003, 2004). Contentious social movement frames and action repertoires, while often necessary, are simply not adequate when it comes to enabling effective voice and sustained action in low-income communities of color, where place matters, risks are cumulative and inter-active, people want to see visible improvements in areas of priority set by the community itself, and where there are genuine opportunities to meld local and professional knowledge in a much richer blend of "street science" to create healthier communities (Corburn 2005, 2009). The National Academy of Public Administration (NAPA), the most prestigious body in its field with a charter from Congress, urged much the same in several earlier reports, beginning in 1995 (NAPA 1995, 1997, 2000; see also John 1994; Dietz and Stern 2008), as had several internal agency reviews and framing documents (US EPA 1999, 2000, 2003).

Each of these reports is saying, in effect, that a federal administrative agency, even with explicitly delegated powers from Congress (representative government) and sophisticated regulatory tools based on science and expertise, cannot solve public problems without a more robust role for citizens, associations, and partnerships of many varieties (Innes and Booher 2010; Booher 2008; Sirianni and Girouard 2012; Sørensen and Torfing 2007; O'Leary and Bingham 2009; Weber and Khademian 2008; Kettl 2002; Goldsmith and Eggers 2004). Each is saying that the problems are too complex and the publics too diverse for administrative action alone to be sufficiently effective and democratically accountable (Smith 2010; Weber 2003; Stivers 1990). None of the reports are part of a deregulatory, promarket agenda, though each recognizes limits of the command-and-control regulatory regime—pollutant by pollutant, bureaucratic silo by bureaucratic silo—and each sees a role for market incentives and for transforming corporate cultures and institutional fields in ways that can help to green business practices (Fiorino 2006; Hoffman 2001; Vasi 2011). Nor is the EPA alone among federal environmental and conservation agencies in the United States in investing in collaborative models of problem solving, nor to have continued learning through turnovers in Democratic and Republican administrations in Washington (Weber 2003; Kemmis 2001; Wondolleck and Yaffee 2000). Our polarized politics obscures this learning and may eventually squander it if we cannot reinvent democracy more broadly, though this is a topic for another occasion.

None of the models for collaborative environmental and natural resource governance are institutionalized in a robust fashion or without normative deficits in terms of deliberation, equal voice, or democratic anchorage of networks (Sørensen and Torfing 2007; Fung 2004). I will return to these problems in the conclusion and suggest some ways forward. My focus in this chapter is how a federal agency, operating largely with command-and-control mandates contained in laws passed by Congress over a forty-year period, has managed to learn as an organization within larger institutional and social movement fields (Fligstein and McAdam 2012; Young, Schroeder, and King 2008; Davis et al. 2005; Clemens and Minkoff 2004; Ostrom 1990, 2005; Greenwood et al. 2008; Klandermans 1992), so that collaborative problem solving and governance with empowered community groups, as well as intermediary and social movement networks, become increasingly possible.

While such innovation is significant in its own right, its import is potentially much broader. As I argue in *Investing in Democracy: Engaging Citizens in Collaborative Governance* (Sirianni 2009), the increasing complexity of public problems, diversity of publics, and forms of lay and professional knowledge for solving public problems, *require* the administrative state to become a key catalyst for collaborative governance as an essential component of our broader and most fundamental normative ideals of self-governance. An administrative state that erodes or displaces links to citizens, communities, and networks motivated and capable of helping to deliberatively frame and actively solve public problems is highly problematic from the point of view of democratic self-government (Landy 1993; Landy, Roberts, and Thomas 1990; Ingram and Smith 1993; Richardson 2002). A new New Deal cannot be built on such foundations, not only in the environmental arena, but also not in many other policy areas. An administrative state stripped of its regulatory powers in favor of the supposed magic of the market, however, is even further from our ideals of democratic self-governance. Yet there are alternatives that can combine the tools of the administrative state and markets with deliberative and pragmatic problem solving among citizens, communities, and a diversity of relevant publics in a way that rescues the democratic pragmatism of John Dewey for the far more complex and information-based society of the twenty-first century (Ansell 2011; Briggs 2008), and that permits citizens to combine and switch among various forms of democratic action, as appropriate (Mansbridge 1980). A relative but significant shift toward more robust forms of collaborative self-governance would reconfigure the overall constellation of democratic forms (elected representatives, movement contestation, face-to-face consensus, initiative and referenda, interest group and public interest lobbying, among many others), but would not likely displace any, since each serves a variety of important purposes and all have become institutionally layered and intertwined over decades, in some cases several centuries. While the US EPA is certainly an imperfect case of how this might be done, it is nonetheless instructive in several significant ways. Some of the principles and practices it has employed resonate profoundly with our founding ideas of self-government and Jeffersonian democracy, as implausible as it may seem that a large bureaucratic agency might also be able to learn how to catalyze, enable, and support the democratic work of ordinary citizens.

My empirical focus here is on two program and cross-program areas—watersheds and environmental justice—within the EPA that have demonstrated significant capacity to innovate by engaging citizens and multistakeholder partnerships. Several programs also elicit federal interagency collaboration (e.g., from the National Oceanic and Atmospheric Administration at the Department of Commerce and the Centers for Disease Control at the Department of Health and Human Services), as well as collaboration with state and local government. My analysis draws upon semistructured interviews, between one and two hours in length, with ninety-three current and former EPA personnel (headquarters and regional), as well as leaders and staff members of various environmental groups and movement networks that have partnered with or contested the agency. Interviews were conducted primarily at three points in time, in conjunction with three distinct research projects: 1994 to 2000, 2001 to 2002, and 2004 to 2007, though I draw primarily from the most recent. Unless otherwise noted, quotations come from this round of interviews. Interview data were supplemented by review of agency documents and tools, strategic planning and project reports from watershed associations and intermediaries, as well as secondary research. As academic advisor to the headquarters team of one specific cross-media program (Community Action for a Renewed Environment), I also participated in team meetings and training of staff and grant recipients, as well as an overall review conference (October 2011), in addition to three agency-wide national community involvement conferences over a ten-year period that included other program areas where public participation models have been utilized. In March 2009, I also benefitted from an extended discussion with the Innovation Action Council, where I presented some of these findings and received useful feedback, as well as from a conference in April 2010 at the Brookings Institution, sponsored by the EPA, Brookings, and the Ash Institute for Democratic Governance and Innovation, Kennedy School of Government, Harvard University, where I served as faculty fellow and conference co-organizer. This latter conference included contributions from leading watershed and environmental justice and health movement organizations, five other federal agencies, four White House offices, local government officials, and a team of scholars (Partnering with Communities 2009). I draw upon field notes taken at all of these trainings and meetings.

After briefly examining the limits of command-and-control regulation, I turn to how the EPA has helped build civic capacity within broader institutional fields, especially in the watershed and environmental justice movements, respectively. I then turn to some broader questions on limits and possibilities for strengthening the potential synergies between federal administrative agencies and civic associations.

Limits of Command-and-Control Regulation

The US Environmental Protection Agency was set up by an executive order of President Nixon in 1970, and its structure was pieced together from more than a dozen units in several federal agencies, each operating under pre-existing, media-specific statutes. These statutes, along with a spate of new laws soon to follow, established a relatively clear regulatory paradigm of command and control. Congress would outlaw certain activities, set quantifiable limits and temporal deadlines for reducing specific pollutants, and mandate the use of specific technologies over others. The EPA would bear responsibility for enforcing some of these mandates directly and also delegate some authority to the states, while helping to build the capacity of their environmental agencies. Should polluters fail to meet requirements and deadlines, the EPA could impose penalties. Citizens, in turn, could sue polluters and the EPA itself should the intent or letter of the law not be carried out. Of course, in practice all this proved a much more complicated affair (Landy, Roberts, and Thomas 1990; Harris and Milkis 1996; Scheberle 2004).

There are many reasons that favored the choice of command and control as a regulatory regime. The federal government was the only level of government with significant countervailing power to large polluters; Congress had earlier hoped that states might be effective on their own, but they quickly proved inadequate. Command and control could also demonstrate significant and fairly quick results from regulating point-source pollution, such as smokestacks and outflow pipes (the low-hanging fruit), thus legitimating the new regulatory regime in the eyes of the public, which clearly favored action but whose support was still uncertain for the longer run. In addition, national environmental groups, including those with commitments to participatory democratic ideals from the 1960s, and even earlier (e.g., Sierra Club), chose to deploy their relatively limited organizational resources strategically to maximize their impact, especially through lobbying and litigation at the federal level. Public participation mandates in many of the new laws were interpreted to favor well-organized and well-resourced national groups (Boyer 1981–1982). Signals of resistance or delay by industry, or by the ambivalent administrations of presidents Richard Nixon (1969–1974) and Gerald Ford (1974–1977), further reinforced the preferences for command and control by the large environmental advocacy groups. The new opportunities for substantive policy and rule making, as well as procedures of public participation, provided by the Carter administration (1977–1981), reinforced such preferences even further (Sirianni and Friedland 2001, 86–91; Berry, Portney, and Thomson 1993, 42–43; Fiorino 2006).

Mainstream environmental organizations, however, have been repeatedly challenged from below by various groups in the name of greater democratic participation and of relative effectiveness in addressing persistent problems, such as ecosystem degradation and environmental injustice, that do not lend themselves as well to the kinds of command-and-control tools and action repertoires preferred by most of the national advocacy organizations. Agency professionals and academic scientists, such as conservation biologists and public health researchers, began to corroborate the local knowledge of many grassroots activists in the watershed and environmental justice movements. While there have certainly been varying degrees of contention among actors in these fields, social movement and community actors have often collaborated with administrative and academic professionals to reframe problems and expand the array of action repertoires and usable tools. As a result, the field of environmentalism has continued to become more organizationally diverse and dynamic, with new forms of civic engagement and social capital generated in the process (Sirianni and Sofer 2012).

The EPA and the Watershed Movement

The US EPA has helped to build the watershed field, including the watershed movement, in a variety of ways. Here I focus on three: framing, tools, and networks. The

EPA has become a key partner in helping to develop the watershed frame as a cognitive template for understanding interrelated problems of water, as well as ecosystems more generally. This frame contains a key role for civic associations and local knowledge. The EPA has also produced tools that citizens can use to protect and restore watersheds, in many cases collaborating with civic organizations to coproduce such tools. Finally, it has helped to develop civic capacity in the field by funding associations, conferences, projects, and partnerships, as well as lending expertise, legitimation, resources, and guidance to states to further enable network formation and action at the state and local levels.

Watershed Frame

Watershed associations, councils, and alliances are groups that form to protect and restore particular streams and rivers and often expand their horizon to include much larger watersheds. Such associations often emerge from various groups that refer to themselves as "friends" or "stewards" of a particular creek or lake, or of a species, such as Northwest salmon, and many begin as single-issue advocacy groups in a fight with a local developer or government agency. Many groups see their efforts through a cultural lens that attaches deep meaning to protecting treasured places and symbol-laden species, such as "totem salmon" (House 1999). The structure of local watershed groups varies considerably. Some are stand-alone groups, while others bring together an array of conservation, education, neighborhood, and other civic groups into a separately incorporated nonprofit 501(c)(3). Still others are multistakeholder, including independent watershed and civic groups, plus various farming, ranching, timber, and other business and commodity interests, as well as representatives from local, state, and federal agencies (Lubell et al. 2002, 2003). The multistakeholder model is more typically (though not consistently) called a "watershed council," and is more prevalent in the West, where consensus process is often utilized to move beyond policy stalemate and where state agencies might certify and fund the councils, which are usually not incorporated as separate nonprofits (Lavigne 2004; Moore and Koontz 2003; Woolley, McGinnis, and Kellner 2002).

What distinguishes watershed associations and kindred groups as they develop over time is that they adopt a distinctive watershed frame for their work. Indeed, local movement actors in the early years, as well as some of their partners in agencies, informally referred to themselves as "shedheads," a countercultural reference to "deadheads," or devotees of the famous Grateful Dead rock and roll band, determined to rock the field of water pollution out of its narrow command-and-control silos. By the mid-1990s, after convening in a national workshop and four Watershed Innovators Workshops in specific states leading the field, these innovators were explicitly calling themselves a "watershed movement" with the aim of "watershed democracy" (Lavigne 1995; Born 1999), though the latter term has since been folded into collaborative governance and similar nomenclature. This broad watershed movement included a variety of other movements, such as the volunteer monitoring movement, the estuary movement, and parts of the environmental education, environmental justice, and land trust movements (Sirianni and Sofer 2012). The watershed frame was formulated over the course of the 1980s and 1990s through mutual learning among networks of watershed movement innovators, academic scientists, policy analysts, legal theorists, and public officials (Sirianni 2009, 31, 159–61; Houck 2007). They contested the command-and-control frame favored by powerful environmental advocacy groups and regulators, but in ways significantly different than how sociologists tend to think of contentious movement framing, especially "we versus them" (Benford and Snow 2000; Johnston and Noakes 2005), though there was certainly some contention in getting various actors to move in this direction.

The watershed frame holds that most if not all the key problems pertaining to water—quality, supply, fisheries, habitat preservation, biodiversity, flood control—need to be understood and dealt with at the level of the watershed: hydrologically defined drainage basins that feed particular water bodies. Watersheds, including smaller watersheds nested in much larger ones, such as the Chesapeake Bay or Puget Sound, are systems defined by complex interactions among innumerable natural and social dynamics. Only holistic, problem-solving strategies tailored to specific, place-based contexts and engaging civic associations and institutional actors in active stewardship could hope to maintain and restore them. Even though fragmented federal regulations, command-and-control techniques, and massive investments in wastewater treatment have significantly reduced point-source pollution since the Clean Water Act of 1972, watersheds remain at risk owing to nonpoint-source pollution, primarily from farms, transportation systems, and urban runoff, as well as innumerable everyday activities of ordinary citizens (e.g., use of lawn fertilizers). The familiar regulatory tools are inadequate for nonpoint pollution and ecosystem restoration (Sabatier et al. 2005; Goslant 1988; Adler 1995; Koontz et al. 2004). Climate change brings still further complexity and the need for holistic and collaborative strategies for both mitigation and adaptation (Portney 2013; Kraft and Mazmanian 2009; Bulkeley 2013; Emerson 2011; Poff, Brinson, and Day 2002).

Watershed Tools

The EPA has played a vital role in helping to develop usable watershed tools for public deliberation, participatory planning, citizen monitoring, collaborative management, open and usable information, and hands-on restoration. These tools, as noted, are often coproduced with an array of nongovernmental partners, including civic associations, and are designed to be utilized effectively by ordinary citizens, community groups, watershed associations, service learning programs in schools and youth associations, and conservation partnerships that include public agencies and various other stakeholder groups. The coproduction of tools—sometimes vocally demanded by civic partners, sometimes elicited by the EPA, often both—tends to be the most effective way to tap local knowledge and meld it with professional expertise and quality assurance standards, thus ensuring greater legitimacy among various types of actors, as well as the iterative and interactive refinement of tools in response to continued feedback from practical use. At its best, the coproduction of tools represents a core component of "pragmatist democracy" (Ansell 2011; Briggs 2008; Hess and Ostrom 2003; Wessells 2007). Several examples illustrate how this has worked.

Beginning in the late 1980s, the EPA began sponsoring conferences on volunteer citizen monitoring of water quality, in collaboration with various environmental and conservation groups that had begun their own programs earlier. Such groups either did not trust data being produced by public agencies or did not find such data useful or well-targeted for certain types of watersheds, and especially not for the specific watersheds where citizens themselves were claiming stewardship. Emerging as a form of ecological citizenship that entailed productive action, stewardship went beyond claims making or monitorial roles often associated with advocacy groups (Sirianni and Sofer 2012). In 1987, the Clean Water Act revisions by Congress (supported and framed by the EPA) provided the statutory basis for the National Estuary Program (NEP), a voluntary, multistakeholder, collaborative management program for the nation's most important estuaries—now constituting twenty-eight specific NEPs among the approximately 130 estuaries. While the act did not specify citizen monitoring, estuary groups—and many other watershed associations—began doing this and the EPA sponsored the development of a manual to assist them.

The second iteration of *Volunteer Estuary Monitoring* (Ohrel and Register 2002) provides a good sense of the meticulous combination of technical knowledge and civic practice represented by the EPA's collaborative work with some of these organizations and their local partners. Developed in partnership with the Ocean Conservancy, this 396-page methods manual, available in print and online, covers all manner of project planning, organizing volunteers, managing safety, and testing the broadest spectrum of nutrients, oxygen, toxins, alkalinity, temperature, salinity, turbidity, bacteria, submerged aquatic vegetation, and other living organisms. The process for developing the manual, however, is as significant as the product. With EPA funding, the Ocean Conservancy had been conducting regular training for local networks of volunteer groups since 1998 in all twenty-eight NEPs—some six hundred groups in all as of 2005. As Seba Sheavly, the Ocean Conservancy coordinator at the time, noted, "EPA support has enabled us to operate as a network builder where some activity already exists. We train them [volunteer groups] in data collection, technical methods, but also in fund-raising, organization, and media presentations so that the data can be presented to the public in understandable formats. And the Ocean Conservancy is enriched by their work as well. These are all shared resources" (author interview, 2005). During development of the manual's second edition, the Ocean Conservancy worked with experts in each technical area of monitoring and shared the draft with all its local group trainees over the previous two-year period. As part of an expansive watershed movement network, prominent volunteer monitoring organizations around the country contributed case studies. The final draft was reviewed by a broad array of leading practitioners from these groups, as well as from universities and extension services, local and state agencies, EPA regional and headquarters offices, and the US Fish and Wildlife Service, most of whom had developed long-term relationships and trust through EPA-sponsored activities. From local knowledge and organizing methods on one end to laboratory science and rigorous quality assurance technique on the other, this network has produced and refined a form of democratic knowledge indispensable to the stewardship of estuaries throughout the country.

There are many other tools the EPA has helped develop to assist more robust watershed work among citizens and stakeholder groups (see Table 9.1 for an overview). These include the *Volunteer Monitor*, a journal for the exchange of methods and learning, produced independently through horizontal networks but with EPA funding (until recently). The networks enlisted and constituted through the *Volunteer Monitor* served as a resource for the Ocean Conservancy's work on the estuary manual, and indeed on virtually all other monitoring guides tailored to specific types of water bodies. When New Jersey developed its state program on citizen monitoring and aligned it with its own professional requirements, it tapped into the network resources of the *Volunteer Monitor* and borrowed from relevant state models. Such learning has generated what is arguably the most distributed network form of "street science" (Corburn 2005) existing nationwide today. The EPA also funded the development of a deliberative tool (Firehock, Flanigan, and Devlin 2002) and an eleven-volume series on restoring small watersheds, of which the *Methods to Develop Restoration Plans for Small Urban Watersheds* (Schueler and Kitchell 2005) provides a clear and comprehensive guide for collaborative and participatory work. When developing the Watershed Plan Builder, an online tool, the director of the Office of Wetlands, Oceans, and Watersheds (OWOW), created in 1991 partly to leverage the growing watershed movement, opened the office to vocal input by twenty leaders of the watershed movement. The input was heard first in Washington headquarters and then at the movement's annual 2005 River Rally, a mixture of strategy conference, training, and celebration convened by the River Network and its many partners. The OWOW director, in other words, opened up the bureaucratic box so that her staff could hear how movement leaders thought the planning tool should be designed, as well as how training should be organized and funded, and how regulatory tools, such as TMDLs (total maximum daily load measures for specific pollutants and nutrients), could serve integrated watershed strategies. While movement leaders pressed hard, the OWOW director used this as an opportunity for her staff to learn what kinds of tools would prove most useful to citizens on the ground doing the work (author interviews, 2005, 2006), and thus to promote organizational culture change within the EPA itself.

Table 9.1 EPA Coproduced Tools for Democratic Watershed Collaboration (Sirianni and Schor 2009)

Type of tool	Selected examples (overlapping, integrative uses for many tools)
Organizing	"Watersheds" as cognitive frame for civic organizing and collaboration *Community Culture and the Environment* *Community Watershed Forums: A Planner's Guide*
Network building	EPA cosponsored conferences of watershed movement (see Table 9.2) NEP Citizen Advisory Committees Volunteer Monitor
Management	NEP management conference Watershed Academy trainings, webcasts, partnership with U.S. Office of Personnel Management
Data	Water Quality Exchange, STORET Warehouse
Planning	NEP comprehensive conservation and management plan (CCMP) *Handbook for Developing Watershed Plans to Restore and Protect Our Waters* Watershed Plan Builder
Financing	Matching grants (NEP, Chesapeake Bay; National Fish and Wildlife Foundation) Section 319 nonpoint source grants to states Targeted Watershed Grants OWOW's Watershed Financing Team University-based environmental finance centers Watershed Academy webcasts on financing watershed associations
Restoration	*Methods to Develop Restoration Plans for Small Urban Watersheds* (part of eleven-volume series)
Deliberation	*Community Watershed Forums: A Planner's Guide*
Monitoring	*Volunteer Estuary Monitoring: A Methods Manual* *Volunteer Monitor*
Performance	Region 1: Charles River "measurement that matters" *The Volunteer Monitor's Guide to Quality Assurance Project Plans* *Valuing Ecosystem Services: Toward Better Environmental Decision-Making*

Watershed Networks

As is already evident in the discussion of framing and tools, the EPA has helped to build the capacity of local groups and broader networks that constitute the watershed field, and specifically the watershed movement. The watershed frame has been developed interactively among networks of local watershed groups, social movement and related intermediaries, professional scientists and legal theorists, and public agencies, with a key coordinative role played by the EPA. Usable tools have been produced by the EPA, with input from movement organizations, as well as coproduced with various of these groups, sometimes as part of an extensive network of grassroots organizations, thus democratically anchoring (Sørensen and Torfing 2007) the collaboration of professional movement staff and other kinds of professionals. EPA staffers have exercised the kinds of "social skill" (Fligstein and McAdam 2012) needed to build an institutional field, and many have developed a deeply civic identity as "democratic professionals" (Dzur 2008). Here I wish to focus on three other components of the EPA's role in building networks: funding for local groups and intermediary networks, convening conferences that help constitute networks, and catalyzing state watershed approaches that, in turn, provide similar framing, tools, and network support at the state level.

First, the EPA has been a significant funder of local groups, especially for particular watershed projects (planning and restoration, but also capacity building) and for various movement intermediaries that provide training and technical assistance, as well as pass-through funding. As a NAPA (2007) report noted, meeting pollution reduction and restoration goals on the Chesapeake Bay will require the joint efforts of six states, the District of Columbia, and 3,169 local governments; 23 federal agencies; 678 watershed associations; a large number of citizen-run "riverkeepers"; two interstate river basin commissions, 30 regional councils, 36 state-created tributary strategy teams, and 87,000 farm owners; five to six million homeowners; hundreds of lawn care companies; an uncounted number of land developers, homebuilders, construction companies, agribusinesses, and other companies that pollute the bay; and a large number of other civic and nonprofit organizations. The Chesapeake Bay Program at the EPA has provided small and large grants to local groups, often on a matching basis. The funds were initially administered by the Chesapeake Bay Alliance, a nonadvocacy regional group, and then by the National Fish and Wildlife Foundation, which gathers funding from various public and private sources. The Chesapeake Bay Foundation, the major regional advocacy association, also has been funded by the program, but for its environmental education and restoration work, not typically for its advocacy. Beyond the Chesapeake Bay, the EPA's competitive Targeted Watershed Grants Program, set up in 2002, has also funded national and regional movement groups, such as the River Network, the Southeast Watershed Forum, and Trees, Water, and People, to train and assist local groups, thus drawing them into—or further into—movement networks. Under various statutes passed since the Clean Water Act revisions of 1987, local NEPs have provided matching funds and other grants to local watershed groups, both from the EPA, as well as NOAA's Restoration Center, in many cases helping to leverage significantly more than a one-to-one match. Most watershed grants now require the establishment of a multistakeholder partnership of some form. That is, the policy design is intended to elicit collaboration, not just independent civic action.

Second, the EPA has provided some of the funding, as well as cosponsorship, for convening various networks that have come to constitute the watershed movement.

Table 9.2 EPA Cosponsored/Funded Watershed Network Building Conferences (Sirianni 2009)

Conference(s)	Date(s)	Participants
First National Conference of Estuary Groups	1987	Save The Bay (Providence, RI) convenes emerging coalitions of estuary groups as NEP is established
National Citizen Monitoring Conferences	1988–2000	Bi-annual, 100–300 participants, in conjunction with rotating civic partners (Izaak Walton League, Chesapeake Bay Alliance, etc.); now part of NWQMC network (professional and volunteer monitors)
Watershed '93	1993	1,100 participants from broad range of local, state, and national watershed and conservation groups, tribes, public agencies, University Extension, business and professional associations; hundreds more via satellite broadcast on final day
Restoring Urban Waters: Friends of Trashed Rivers Conference	1993	Coalition to Restore Urban Waters (CRUW), with River Network, Izaak Walton League, National Association of Service and Conservation Corps (now Corps Network), and others; 300 participants (followed by three other trashed rivers conferences)
Watershed '96	1996	2,000 participants, plus several thousand others at 156 teleconference downlinks, from broad range of local, state, and national watershed and conservation groups, public agencies, university extension, K-12 schools, business and professional associations
National River Rally	1995–2012	524 participants in peak year of 2006, convened by River Network, other river advocacy and watershed restoration groups, public agencies (recent falloff in EPA support, but still tools presentations)
Regional Watershed Forums	1999–2001	13 regional, multistakeholder, lay/professional roundtables, 40–85 participants each; some continue as regular roundtables, with state and county offshoots; prepare agenda for National Watershed Forum
National Watershed Forum	2001	480 participants from broad range of local, state, and national watershed and conservation groups, public agencies, university extension, and professional associations
National Conferences on Coastal and Estuarine Habitat Restoration	2003–2012	800–1,500 participants, broad multistakeholder, convened by Restore America's Estuaries, with Save The Bay, TNC, NOAA, USFWS, local and state agencies, business partners

In addition, the EPA has participated actively in these conferences, thus lending legitimacy, important not only to grassroots movement actors and intermediaries, such as the River Network or Restore America's Estuaries, but also to many of the local and state government professionals attending. These conferences have been important in developing strategies for field building. Indeed, it is impossible to think of either the emergence of the social movement field, or the broader institutional field for watershed work, absent these gatherings, where participants share and critically evaluate best cases, tools, and funding strategies, as well as build trust for specific multiorganizational partnerships. The EPA has worked to convene conferences nationally and regionally with leading movement organizations in specific subareas (urban watersheds, volunteer monitoring, estuaries), as well as to develop a more integrative movement that links all kinds of watersheds, as well as related movements, such as land trusts (see Table 9.2).

Third, the EPA has provided guidance and incentives for states to adopt a watershed approach. This tends to happen according to different rhythms and institutional configurations within states, sometimes initiated narrowly as citizen monitoring, sometimes more broadly, and almost always with some agencies or offices leading the way and others resisting. In some cases, the state's watershed movement is considerably ahead of public agencies in seeking innovation; in others, the movement itself coheres in response to innovation within one agency or even one office within one of many agencies. The national and regional watershed forums and other conferences often serve as precursors and trust builders to enable specific state networks to take initiative. Of course, support can also come from a governor or legislature.

Colorado provides a case in point. In the Region 8 office of the EPA—encompassing Colorado, Montana, North Dakota, South Dakota, Utah, Wyoming, and twenty-seven sovereign tribal nations—seven staff members volunteered in the mid-1990s to become coordinators of a national cross-agency initiative known as Community-Based Environmental Protection (CBEP), closely but by no means exclusively aligned with the watershed frame. CBEP coordinators in Region 8 included several relatively senior staff members, who received substantial support from the regional administrator. Because federal land ownership in these western states tends to elicit greater collaboration between the regional EPA office and other environmental agencies than exists in many other regions, Region 8 was more open to the ecosystem management agenda that the Clinton administration was promoting across all agencies. Within the newly organized Ecosystem Protection Program in the region, Karen Hamilton, Ayn Schmit, and Nat Miullo took the lead in team building and culture change internally, as well as developing watershed initiatives and ecosystem partnerships externally. With solid programmatic and technical backgrounds among them, they were insulated from the charges of many regulatory staff that community decision making represented an abdication of agency authority or was "just a lot of fluff." Indeed, with much good humor and gender irony, even as they seriously worked to convince other staff members of the results that could be achieved through voluntary programs and partnerships, Hamilton and Schmit would alternately bestow on one another the honorific title "Queen of Fluff" (author interviews, 2005).

To be sure, CBEP regional staffers were fully aware that the threat of enforcement, for example by the TDML staff in Hamilton's unit, might be needed to elicit a form of collaboration that produced far greater results than the TDMLs alone could do.

The environmental justice and pollution prevention programs in Region 8 have also helped transform the culture, as has the recruitment of younger staff members with interdisciplinary university training. Programs that were at first resistant, such as in the Air Office, then began to dedicate staff members to community-based work and became key to a subsequent cross-media community-based program, Community Action for a Renewed Environment (see below).

To build capacity for community-based collaboration, Region 8's ecosystem program has supported the work of various intermediary organizations, such as the Colorado Watershed Assembly, Colorado River Watch Network, and similar groups in the other states. It worked with the Center for Watershed Protection to produce the eleven-volume Urban Subwatershed Restoration Manual Series, noted previously, to enable communities to develop their own democratic restoration plans and to implement them through technically sophisticated public work (Boyte and Kari 1996; Boyte 2005). Of eight teams in the ecosystem program as of 2005 (since reorganized), the six staff members on the ecosystem stewardship team worked directly with watershed groups and partnerships as "coaches" to develop their leadership skills. Marc Alston, for instance, had worked in drinking water, Superfund, brownfields, and watersheds. As he put it in 2004 before he left the EPA to work directly with the Colorado Watershed Assembly, "My coaching of watershed group leaders has evolved. . . . I came to realize that the sustainability of groups is related to the strength of their leaders. Leadership of a watershed group demands technical, facilitation, organizational, fundraising, and leadership skills." As a generalist who drew upon the technical expertise of his team, Alston provided "information, advice, coordination, advocacy, and networking" (Alston 2004). He helped with financial planning and obtaining resources from a wide variety of sources. He served as liaison between the EPA laboratory and watershed groups who use it for microbiological analyses, and he aligned this work with the Clean Water Act regulatory process. Region 8 has also collaborated with national groups, such as the River Network, American Rivers, and The Nature Conservancy (TNC). *Natural News*, the newsletter of Region 8's ecosystem program, has provided a window onto local, regional, and national innovations, trainings, awards, funding opportunities, information tools, and other resources, as well as movement-building events, such as the national 2005 River Rally in Keystone, Colorado. Articles have been written by EPA field staffers, who have built long-term relationships with local groups, as well as by local citizens. This government publication served, before cuts in 2008, as a civic forum and catalyst for a far-flung learning network.

The synergy among EPA Region 8 staff, watershed groups, and state agency officials is especially evident in Colorado. Responding to EPA framing and funding incentives, the Colorado Water Quality Control Division reorganized around the watershed approach in 1997 and established four regional (within-state) watershed coordinators. As a result, independently organized watershed groups, which numbered only six in 1996, grew quickly to forty by 1998, a more than sixfold increase simply in response to the policy reframing and administrative restructuring. The associations then established the statewide Colorado Watershed Assembly as their coalition, which in turn has spurred growth to more than eighty groups as of 2013. The assembly sponsors training and an annual conference; in October 2007 it collaborated on the Sustaining Colorado Watersheds Conference with a broad range of other civic groups, including AWARE Colorado, the League of Women Voters of Colorado Education Fund, the Colorado Watershed Network, the Colorado Lakes and Reservoir Management Association, and the Colorado Riparian Association. The assembly also publishes an attractive and influential annual report on the state of Colorado's watersheds and the work of its watershed groups. It has lobbied successfully in the statehouse, and collaborated with the state water conservation board and water quality control commission, to create and manage a grant program for watershed groups funded through a voluntary state income tax refund check-off program, which in turn has been used by local groups as a match source for various federal and other grants.

While the assembly is governed by representatives of independent citizen groups, its committees include state and federal staffers working together toward collaborative solutions. "Sometimes we have to push back hard against the good old boys in some of the agencies," says Richard Fox, assembly president from 2002 to 2005. "The head of [a powerful state board], for instance, continually referred to us as 'self-appointed watershed gurus.' And I was always tempted to tell him to kiss my you-know-what. . . . But we just kept showing up and talking the language of collaboration. And they loved it when we said this could minimize lawsuits." Region 8 staff members and state watershed coordinators, in particular, have been "essential" to our work, Fox continues. "I trust them. They became real mensches. . . . They responded *as people* looking for solutions with the watershed groups. And, besides, they helped organize the picnics. . . . And the Colorado Watershed Assembly believes deeply in having fun . . . and celebrating our work in restoring the watersheds. We don't let ourselves be dragged down by just fighting the good fight" (author interview, 2006).

EPA and the Environmental Justice Movement

In October 1991, the National People of Color Environmental Leadership Summit, attended by some six hundred participants from all fifty states, signaled the official birth of the environmental justice (EJ) movement in the United States. Under administrator William Reilly, the EPA began to give a hearing to the movement and to respond to statistical evidence of racial and economic disparities in risk and regulatory behavior. With two strong EJ proponents on president-elect Clinton's environment transition team and the appointment of Carol Browner as the new administrator in 1993, the agency became considerably more systematic in analyzing racial disparities and promoting EJ as an administrative norm and policy goal. In 1994, Clinton issued Executive Order 12898 requiring each federal agency to make EJ part of its mission, and he established the Federal Interagency Working Group on Environmental Justice (EJ IWG), composed of representatives of eleven federal agencies and chaired by the EPA, to develop strategies and model projects. He also created the National Environmental Justice Advisory Council (NEJAC) to provide a formal voice for the movement and other stakeholders across the federal government. Browner renamed the recently established environmental equity office the Office of Environmental Justice (OEJ) (Cole and Foster 2000; Pellow and Brulle 2005; Brown 2007; Szasz 1994).

The EJ movement is considerably different than the watershed movement because it arises much more from poor and working-class communities of color, especially but by no means exclusively in urban areas, and because public health rather than ecosystem health is its central focus. Both movements seek more holistic and integrated strategies to the problems they foreground, and, to be sure, there have been cross-pollination and overlap, especially since issues of sustainable cities, urban watersheds, and climate change have become more prominent. Here I do not attempt a systematic comparison, but I investigate some parallels in terms of the role of the EPA in enabling more robust civic action and collaboration, especially the development of a frame, tools, and networks.

Environmental Justice Frames

Since the EJ movement takes much of its framing from the civil rights movement (Taylor 2000), it is no surprise that it has sought various legal and regulatory remedies and has won important achievements, such as fairer participation of communities of color in state permitting for hazardous waste sites, greater enforcement of existing laws, expanded legal resources for communities, heightened federal administrative scrutiny, and increasing numbers of state EJ statutes and programs (Targ 2005; Gerrard and Foster 2008). Some of these legal resources for the movement have been funded by the EPA (Environmental Law Institute 2001, 2002). But the EPA has also focused on how to engage EJ communities more directly. Community participation has always been a central component of the EJ movement frame, and in recent years some sectors of the movement, along with the EPA and other federal and state agencies, have come to promote collaborative community problem solving as an essential component of the frame. Since the movement is divided on this, framing contests (Benford and Snow 2000) are ongoing. The emergence of the collaborative frame results from several factors.

First, administrative and legal remedies have revealed serious limits to administrators as well as local citizen groups. For the latter, legal action can take many years, consume inordinate organizational resources, and demobilize constituents, often only to lead to disappointment in final outcomes. Courts have systematically refused to apply Title VI of the 1964 Civil Rights Act against polluters without direct evidence of discriminatory intent, which is notoriously difficult to prove, especially in the face of

competing explanations (relative land values, housing market dynamics, agglomera-
tion economies in industry clustering) and scientific uncertainties (differential health
impacts). The EPA has had little more success with such discriminatory intent claims
than have community groups and activist lawyers, and its Title VI guidance has been
met with considerable skepticism by the Conference of Mayors and the Environmental Council of the States. Congress has remained deeply skeptical, if not explicitly
restrictive, and the Supreme Court has ruled in ways that limit invoking disparate
impact (Gordon and Harley 2005; Schweitzer and Stephenson 2007; Foreman 1999;
Ringquist 2006).

Second, key EJ movement networks, working within the multistakeholder policy
forum of NEJAC, have concluded that on key issues such as cumulative risk and pollution prevention, a place-based collaborative approach can deliver substantial payoffs
for communities most vulnerable to multiple and interactive risk factors. Two NEJAC
reports represent this self-described "paradigm shift," though some movement leaders
still remain skeptical both of the specific components and of the frame's endorsement
by government—and, from a different angle, the amount of resources the agency has
been willing and able to put behind it. In *Ensuring Risk Reduction in Communities
with Multiple Stressors: Environmental Justice and Cumulative Risks/Impacts* (NEJAC
2004), the NEJAC work group argues that where there are multiple physical, chemi-
cal, biological, social, and cultural factors, which cumulatively and in the aggregate
contribute to distinct vulnerabilities for low-income and minority communities, a
multimedia, place-based approach can provide the most effective way to generate a
"bias for action" that engages various stakeholders in making quick and tangible improvements. Tackling immediate risks and ones broadly recognized as real problems
can enable local actors and institutions, including polluters, to build trust for addressing more difficult and contentious issues down the line. Residents can directly contribute to local health diagnoses and practical solutions through participatory action
research and community health education campaigns.

In *Advancing Environmental Justice through Pollution Prevention* (NEJAC 2003),
NEJAC made a similar set of arguments. Pollution prevention (P2) strategies have
advanced significantly in recent years through a broad range of initiatives in cleaner
technologies and materials, energy efficiency and green building, transportation and
land use planning, and management and work systems. The Pollution Prevention
Act of 1990 and a host of voluntary programs have encouraged this. To get the full
benefit of P2 approaches at the community level, especially for those most vulnerable,
however, would require far more intentional collaboration among civic organizations,
environmental groups, small and large businesses, health departments, and other local
government agencies. Building the capacity of local groups for multistakeholder collaboration, as well as broad public education to make P2 an everyday habit, would
require serious financial, technical, and programmatic support from public agencies,
as well as private sources.

It is important to reiterate that support for a collaborative EJ community problem-solving frame has been driven by various community and EJ movement leaders, albeit in a context where the EPA and NEJAC have created an institutional framework for genuine policy learning among community groups, regional movement networks, industry representatives, academic scientists, public health experts, and administrators from various local, state, and federal agencies. Charles Lee, author of the formative United Church of Christ report on environmental racism in 1987 and a key organizer of the first EJ leadership summit, chaired the NEJAC subcommittee that conducted public dialogues on brownfields and urban revitalization in five major cities in 1995, where strong support for assets-based community development emerged. In 1999, Lee went from movement leader to OEJ staff, playing a key role in the NEJAC reports on cumulative risk and pollution prevention, as well as chairing the EJ IWG and then becoming OEJ director. The IWG developed the collaborative framework for EJ based upon a wide scan of the community-building field and a series of demonstration projects beginning in 2000, as well as by paying careful attention to the forms of community collaboration that had been emerging from grassroots EJ action over nearly a decade. Given its multiagency composition, the IWG was not only especially attuned to the enormous complexity of EJ problems (housing stock, transportation patterns, industry clusters, waste treatment facility siting, children's health), but also to the limits of addressing such problems though the usual programmatic and regulatory stovepipes of their separate agencies. Communities clearly needed integrative strategies that worked on the ground and involved a broad range of stakeholders, including adversaries, even as those with the least formal power and at greatest risk may still have to mobilize and protest to bring others to the table. They also needed federal, state, and local agencies to provide the institutional supports for local collaboration. As the EPA's strategic plan for EJ has continued to evolve, collaborative community-based models have remained central but have also been further aligned with other tools (rule making, permitting, compliance, enforcement) (Federal Interagency Working Group on Environmental Justice 2002; US EPA 2011; Dixon 2003; author interviews, 2004–2006).

Various prominent EJ community and movement leaders contributed to these NEJAC and IWG activities: Peggy Shepard of West Harlem Environmental Action (WE ACT), Wilma Subra of the Louisiana Environmental Action Network, Mary Nelson of Bethel New Life in Chicago, Connie Tucker of the Southern Organizing Committee for Economic and Social Justice, Tom Goldtooth of the Indigenous Environmental Network, Tirso Moreno of the Farmworkers Association of Florida, Donele Wilkins of Detroiters Working for Environmental Justice, and Bahram Fazeli from Communities for a Better Environment in California (affiliations at the time of the reports). These EJ leaders drew upon their own experiences, as well as those of dozens of other community groups, which had been developing local civic problem-solving and partnership strategies. In some cases, such as Bethel New

Life, an assets-based community development frame and strategy (Kretzmann and McKnight 1993) had preceded EJ work in this congregation-based community development corporation (CDC), as has been the case with other CDCs (Shutkin 2000). Collaborative EJ strategies emerged with the support of OEJ's various small grant programs as early as 1994, as well as funding from other offices at the EPA and several other federal agencies, such as the National Institute of Environmental Health Sciences at the National Institutes of Health. The EPA's Office of Pollution Prevention and Toxics (OPPTS), for instance, provided much relevant experience through its Design for Environment (DfE) program, which utilized civic networking strategies among trade associations in various industries with large numbers of small, often ethnic, businesses (printing, dry cleaning, and auto body repairs), as well as through its intensive research pilot program, Community Partnership for Environmental Protection in South Baltimore and its EJP2 grants program (Sirianni and Friedland 2001). Some on NEJAC also took to heart the poignant criticisms of policy scholars, such as Christopher Foreman Jr. (1998), in *The Promise and Peril of Environmental Justice*, that epidemiologic and community-based approaches to improving health in poor and minority communities were far more promising than regulatory ones, a finding that has received further support in the community and public health fields (Israel et al. 2005; Minkler and Wallerstein 2004; Corburn 2009). Given the strong pull of the original EJ frame and movement ethos toward an all-encompassing radicalism (Foreman 1998; Benford 2005; Bullard 2005), this paradigm shift to a collaborative community problem-solving approach—aligned with regulatory and other tools—has been no small feat. The shift is certainly still selective and incomplete within the larger movement (author interviews, field notes, 2004–2011), and the Center for Health, Environment, and Justice (CHEJ), one long-established movement organization that has served as an important trainer and network builder, rarely uses collaborative language, even if some of its community partners eventually move in this direction.

Environmental Justice Collaborative Tools

Perhaps the best window into the tools the EPA has developed, coproduced, and diffused on issues of environmental justice is provided by the Community Action for a Renewed Environment (CARE) program. Although drawing upon virtually all community-based, watershed, and ecosystem programs and framing documents since the early 1990s, CARE has been deeply influenced by EJ work within the agency and has enlisted EJ staff, as well as EJ movement leadership, in helping to develop training and tools that communities would find most useful. Its establishment as a cross-media program in 2005 was partly prompted by pressure from movement leaders within NEJAC to make media-specific offices, such as the Office of Air and Radiation, more responsive to communities, especially distressed ones. In effect, after being shown by

EPA regulatory staff the positive overall impacts of various media-specific programs, movement leaders asked, "So what have these done to improve *our* communities, as we experience them?" As Robert Brenner, then deputy assistant administrator of the Air office and director of its Office of Policy Analysis and Review, has noted, "to put it politely, I pretty much got beat up at those [NEJAC] meetings. . . . After getting beat up a couple of times too often, I sat down with them and began to focus on some of their specific concerns" (author field notes 2005). With support from the EPA's deputy administrator and the Innovation Action Council, which has a mandate to innovate agency-wide and not just in specific offices, Brenner convened a multidisciplinary team to develop CARE as a competitive grant program, requiring applicants to develop cooperative agreements as multistakeholder partnerships, following a template designed to enable communities to formulate specific priorities of their own, design and implement action plans, and monitor and evaluate performance (Sirianni 2009, 207–13; NAPA 2009).

The tools, many of which serve as EJ tools and are thus not duplicated by EJ offices and programs throughout the agency and in the regional offices, take several forms. One is represented by the compendium of tools one can find in the online CARE Resource Guide (*cfpub.epa.gov/oarweb/care/index.cfm?fuseaction=Guide.showIntro*). Here community activists and partners can find tools specifically designed for CARE but that also have broad application to other collaborative approaches, including EJ, namely, how-to guides on forming partnerships, building consensus, understanding risks in a specific community, developing strategic plans, measuring performance, and tracking progress. The other sets are represented by the very specific tools that have been developed in a wide array of offices and programs over the years: how to protect children from lead exposure, how to reduce pollution (and asthma) from idling school buses, how to reduce exposure to radon and toxic chemicals in homes. Every individual citizen or resident has access to these tools online, but when clustered and combined with other tools for organizing communities, they are especially relevant to strategic campaigns to create healthier communities and to sustain and further build organizational and partnership capacities, thereby motivating more individuals, civic groups, educational and health institutions, trade and professional associations, and public agencies. If, for instance, a partnership sets a specific goal of reducing asthma and chooses several tools to be utilized by various partners (neighborhood associations, health agencies, business partners that may negotiate with a diesel truck fleet or a school bus company), and holds all partners accountable for measurable results, motivation for civic action can increase as targets are met, and leverage for regulatory action can increase as well as various other barriers to improving health become more evident. While professional advocacy, legal and regulatory action, and social protest are indispensable in the EJ field as a whole, the collaborative EJ "bias for action" to engage multiple stakeholders in strategic community-based action, with accountability for results that are valued and visible to ordinary citizens, remains a key component of a form of self-governance amidst enormously complex problems of environmental risk, uncertainty, and inequality.

A second general type of tool is hands-on training of local activists and partners, as well as of agency staff members themselves. In the CARE program, a round of trainings was conducted during the first year among headquarters and regional staff, both in-person and by teleconference. Training partners included movement groups, such as WE ACT, as well as national civic associations with skills in community visioning and collaboration, such as the National Civic League. Other training partners came from university community health programs, as well as trade associations that had significant experience with their corporate members on pollution prevention. In short, the initial trainings were coproduced, with the EPA pulling together training partners from previous work and trusted networks, and all partners open to learning from multiple directions. As CARE's annual grantees came into the program formally (at two levels, one more advanced than the other), many of these same partners, as well as agency staff, were utilized as trainers. The more advanced CARE communities (Level II) played a key role in the trainings, developing cases and reflecting on lessons. The trainings were designed to create an expanding (year-by-year) network of community partnerships that could serve as resources to others, as well as networks with staff across headquarters, regional offices, and labs that could troubleshoot or enlist still other staff most relevant for particular technical and other components of particular community strategies. The CARE team modeled itself as a horizontal learning community, or community of practice (Wenger 1998), which has elicited similar norms and practices across the entire network.

Environmental Justice Networks

The EPA has helped build the networks across the environmental justice movement, and specifically for collaborative problem-solving models, especially through its grant programs. The small grants program of OEJ, as noted above, has proven critical to EPA learning even though overall small grants budgets have remained relatively modest in size—down considerably from the $2 to $3 million annual levels of 1995–1999, which were even then far too low. Even before the grants had an explicitly collaborative focus, community groups were developing innovative ways to utilize local knowledge and mobilize civic networks. Community development corporations engaged neighborhood youth to clean up lots, educate local residents, and conduct participatory planning for long-term remediation. Community health center professionals collaborated with local auto body repair shops to develop alternative work methods and safe disposal practices. On childhood lead poisoning and asthma, Head Start centers and statewide associations led broad community education campaigns. To assist community groups and local government agencies in risk communication and equity planning, students in historically black colleges and universities provided research. Small grants have also been available to watershed associations and volunteer monitoring networks to enable them to incorporate EJ principles and practices into their work, and to intermediary organizations, such as the Center for Neighborhood Technology in Chicago, that work with numerous kinds of community and small business groups. Many other kinds of civic groups have become engaged in EJ work through the small grants: ethnic associations, tribal communities, migrant farm worker groups, YMCAs, 4-H clubs, American Lung Association chapters, and church groups (OEJ 2005).

With the launching of two rounds of EJ IWG demonstration projects beginning in 2000 and then OEJ's Collaborative Problem Solving Cooperative Agreements in 2003, and subsequently with environmental justice "showcase communities," projects have typically come to involve one or more local community or advocacy group, in partnership with several larger institutions, such as health departments, medical centers, universities, environmental agencies, and chambers of commerce. The collaborative grants, in fact, require three signed memoranda of agreement from such partners, as well as more regular consultation and reporting and a greater emphasis on environmental results and sustainability than the small grants program. For example, Bethel New Life, a Lutheran-affiliated CDC that has used assets-based organizing and development strategies in the low-income African American West Garfield Park neighborhood of Chicago for more than two decades, began its EJ journey as a result of two issues, the discovery of a troublesome brownfield site and the announced closing of a main transit line running through the community. After successful coalition organizing (with several suburban communities) to preserve the transit line, Bethel turned to a set of partners to help with transit-oriented development, including a commercial center designed according to green building principles, clean energy, and a walkable community with homes clustered close to the transit stop. Other green businesses complement Bethel's job-development strategy through its successful employment center. Project partners include the Center for Neighborhood Technology and Neighborhood Capital Budget Group, which have provided technical and financial assistance for local projects that empower residents, as well as the Argonne National Laboratory and the City of Chicago's transit, environment, and planning departments. Commonwealth Edison and the Illinois Department of Commerce and Community Development have provided assistance with the photovoltaic cells to power the commercial center (Lee 2005; Fleming and Hanks 2004; King 2012).

EPA funding for local partnerships, as well as trainings and other meetings through the Office of Environmental Justice, Community Action for a Renewed Environment, and related programs, have helped to build important networks within the environmental justice movement field. Some leading EJ movement organizations, such as West Harlem Environmental Action, have served as critical nodes in these networks and have provided training on a regular basis. Wilma Subra, from the Louisiana Environmental Action Network, has played a role as both the vice chair (for seven years) of NACEPT, whose important report on EPA's stewardship and partnership mission was earlier noted, as well as on NEJAC (for six years). Yet the EPA has not generally helped build the capacity of national movement and professional intermediaries, such as the equivalent of the River Network or the Center for Watershed Protection in the watershed field, nor of state-level associations, whose capacity has been aided by grants and trainings through such national groups. Two reasons for this difference suggest themselves, though further comparative analysis is needed. First, environmental justice is not a statutory program, with specific powers and funding streams that devolve to the states, as is the case with water and watersheds under the Clean Water Act and various related congressional statutes. Second, the EJ movement field has generally been more contentious than the watershed field, and the EPA may be wary of devolving funding and training to independent nonprofit intermediaries, at least until it can trust that national intermediaries will consistently operate within a collaborative problem-solving frame. If this is the case, it is certainly justifiable in normative terms; government agencies receive delegated powers to solve problems, ideally in ways that are equitable, but not to systematically enhance group conflict. Contention, of course, exists across a broad spectrum of federal agency programs that seek to work in partnership with civic associations and multistakeholder partnerships, and these dynamics are worthy of more systematic analysis, especially if we are to develop a more refined normative framework for thinking about the federal administrative role in a democratic theory and practice of self-governance for the twenty-first century.

Concluding Thoughts

Before returning to my initial set of questions—*can* a federal administrative agency enable citizens to help solve public problems (analytic), and *should* such an agency be theorized as an essential component of democratic self-governance (normative)—I should indicate some other kinds of questions that require further research and that limit this current analysis. First, of course, is that the US EPA is only one among many other federal agencies, and watersheds and environmental justice are only two relatively small components within it. Thus, at the minimum, we need further comparative analysis within the EPA, across federal environmental and other agencies in the United States, and with similar national agencies in other countries, to further specify and qualify these findings. Examining federal levels comparatively would be an indispensable component of this. Second, specific obstacles within federal agencies to enable robust civic engagement in partnerships and across entire fields need to be examined in depth: how to provide sufficient levels and appropriate kinds of funding for partnerships; how to better align civic and community-based approaches with regulatory and market ones; how to sustain, deepen, and broaden organizational learning and culture change within agencies; how to enable civic action and movement networks that are appropriately anchored in independent civic associations and thus sufficiently resistant to various demobilization and cooptation dynamics. A fuller analysis would reveal democratic deficits at the EPA in all these areas (Sirianni 2009, 217–22), some unfortunately compounded during the Obama administration. Third, how can continued innovation in collaborative self-governance address questions of performance measurement and democratic accountability (Weber 2003; Fung 2004; March and Olsen 1995; Sørensen and Torfing 2007; Behn 2001; Kettl 2002)? The EPA has certainly had to grapple with all these questions, sometimes at the behest of the EPA's Office of Inspector General (OIG 2005) or the Office of Management and Budget (US OMB 2005), and has received both positive reinforcement and critical feedback on shortcomings that require correction. Often movement actors provide critical feedback, on program or tool design, or on funding cuts in critical areas of training and capacity building, especially (but not only) since the 2008 financial crisis and heightened conservative assaults on the very legitimacy of the agency.

There is a growing social science, natural science, and program evaluation literature that addresses these kinds of problems empirically and analytically (Sabatier, Focht, and Lubell 2005; Pellow and Brulle 2005; Layzer 2008; NAPA 2009; Bernhardt et al. 2007; Palmer et al. 2007), and further study needs to build upon these. Here I want to reiterate some core insights provided by this analysis of the EPA and suggest several lines of potential policy design and normative grounding. While this is a bit like trying to sketch the horizon while having assembled one's chalks and pads on the beach, but without all the serious analytic rowing needed to approach the horizon—which, in any case, will keep receding as we row—we nonetheless need to focus our eye on the democratic horizon. Our founding ideals of democratic self-government permit nothing less.

First, a federal agency *can*, at least in some important areas of its work, engage in shared cognitive reframing of public problems with ordinary citizens and civic associations, coproduce usable tools to assist collaborative problem solving, help build networks that can leverage trust and learning on a broad scale, and align collaborative and deliberative tools with other essential tools of the administrative and social welfare state. Agencies are not only capable of doing this, they are capable of refining how they do it, drawing from experience and collaborative learning across a field, which might range from a local water quality monitoring group to a state watershed association to a national movement network to a state university extension service to the Office of Inspector General to the National Academy of Public Administration. All of these kinds of organizations within (or partially drawn into) the watershed field, and still others, have come into productive interplay in refining pragmatic civic action and collaborative problem solving and self-governance. Ideally, other organizations would become part of this policy learning and feedback, thus lending a more robust normative and pragmatic dimension to the study of institutional fields (Fligstein and McAdam 2012). Congress is sometimes engaged, as when it stipulated strong (if vague) norms for public participation in the Clean Water Act in 1972 and when it authorized the National Estuary Program in the 1987 revisions, as well as in several other laws that have provided support for community-based habitat restoration, enabling movement organizations, such as

Restore America's Estuaries, to provide funding and training to local groups. Addressing these issues at the level of Congress—and hence policy design as lawmaking and not simply administrative practice—raises the central question of how to enlist national environmental lobbies to support, or at least to not oppose, such policy designs, since they can and do compete (for legitimacy, budgets) with some favored command-and-control tools and channels of influence. The work of alignment thus needs to occur within agencies and in the broader field where civic associations of various sorts compete as well as collaborate (Sirianni and Sofer 2012). In today's polarized Congress, such policy designs might not be possible, but will eventually have to become one component of moving toward a less polarized and more pragmatic politics generally.

Second, the Executive Office of the President has potential leverage that it has yet to utilize effectively enough. The executive office under President Clinton utilized its authority quite visibly to ensure that environmental justice became a norm across the federal government and that a multistakeholder policy forum (NEJAC) convene EJ movement and other leaders to deliberate over various strategies, including collaborative environmental justice problem solving, a norm of both pragmatist democracy and social equity. In addition, it established an interagency working group to spur strategic learning across the federal government. The Clinton administration also fostered an array of watershed and ecosystem approaches across various federal agencies, which networks of senior and mid-level civil servants and some Bush appointees sustained, partly under the rubric of "cooperative conservation," including a White House conference to share best practice. The Bush administration also provided support for CARE to become institutionalized. President Obama issued an ambitious and promising memorandum on open government (Executive Office of the President 2009) on his first full day in office, which contained strong norms for transparency, participation, and collaboration. While initiative in this and other areas has been hampered by a crowded policy agenda, amidst severe fiscal constraints and party polarization (Skocpol and Jacobs 2011), as well as by inflated faith in the data transparency component of open government (Lukensmeyer, Goldman, and Stern 2011) and a behavioral economics approach to regulatory reform (Mettler 2011; Thaler and Sunstein 2009), there remain various ways of catalyzing change through federal agencies in this or future administrations committed to collaborative governance, indeed to bring the admirable goals articulated by the Obama memorandum and its open government initiative to much greater fruition. Here I would reiterate (but further refine) two components that were among the recommendations of *Investing in Democracy* (Sirianni 2009, 227–35) and that are consistent with richer versions of open government (Noveck 2009).

The first recommendation is to require each federal agency, beginning with those most relevant to community-based work—EPA, Housing and Urban Development, Health and Human Services, Centers for Disease Control, Justice, Transportation, Agriculture, Interior—to develop an explicit and detailed civic mission statement to complement its substantive mission statement. As the EPA has begun to do with its various

Table 9.3 Facilitative Activities of a White House Office of Collaborative Governance

Function	Activity, purpose, capacity (in full collaboration with appropriate agency teams)
Civic mission	Develop civic mission statements for federal agencies Align with substantive agency missions Periodically review
Civic program	Inventory existing community-based and related programs Generate shared understanding of programmatic foundations, opportunities, barriers, limits, past mistakes Inventories are for learning and energizing, not for delaying or renaming
Agency and network capacity	Inventory capacities, including: Agency staff (training, recruitment, performance measures, collaborative culture, professional identity) Usable tools for citizens and communities (data, planning, organizing, collaborative management, performance measurement, social marketing) Processes for developing, coproducing, and field-testing tools (collaboration with user communities, movement network and other intermediaries) Network capacity (appropriate configuration of national, state, local intermediaries and other partners; capacity for training and technical assistance; sufficient democratic anchorage in associations responsive to grassroots membership)
Capacity investments in civic infrastructure, collaborative tools	How much, what measures Determine short-, medium-, and long-term investment needs Develop strategies for leveraging federal investments (among state and local governments, foundations, businesses, universities, other institutions, citizens themselves) Develop appropriate measures and models for resource leveraging; diverse mixes as democratic anchorage Integrate into strategic planning, budget requests
Tool mix	Align civic with other governance tools in a mix appropriate to particular policy challenges, public goods

internal and advisory panel reports on stewardship and collaboration, each agency would be challenged to specify how its programs and tools enable the work of citizens and civic associations, and how it could make such work a more central, indeed normative, ingredient of its mission as a democratic agency in a self-governing republic. The second recommendation would be to institutionalize a White House office of collaborative governance that would facilitate an ongoing civic-mission learning process within each federal agency, and thus with agency teams and perhaps an interagency working group. It would also provide budgetary authority, tools, and staff training to facilitate organizational culture change internally, as well as the robust development of fields, such as watersheds, public

health, community policing, environmental justice, community development, collaborative forest management, city climate planning, and other collaborative approaches. The
best place to locate such an office is debatable, but OMB would provide significant budget and management leverage, and it has recently facilitated place-based approaches that
include an important role for civic engagement. A brief sketch of what such an office of
collaborative governance might do is contained in Table 9.3.

We have enough evidence, especially when we include the experience of other
federal agencies, to suggest that a federal administrative agency *can* enable citizens to
help solve public problems, at least in some important areas of its work. Needless to
say, that evidence is both mixed and incomplete, as it could only be in the relatively
early stages of any systematic effort to transform the administrative state into a vital
component of a self-governing republic—as indeed was the evidence available when
the founders began our noble but risky experiment well more than two centuries
ago. Thus, any strategic effort has to be grounded in policy and administrative design
that promotes learning and is responsive to norms of performance and accountability,
even while it keeps its eyes on the democratic horizon. But that raises the normative
question of whether federal agencies *should* be theorized as an essential component of
democratic self-governance. This is clearly a question that warrants its own extended
analysis, so here I suggest only several lines of argument.

First, if it *can*, then it *should*. Civic engagement has eroded from many directions
in recent decades (Putnam 2000; Skocpol 2003; Macedo et al. 2005), which poses
a threat to democratic institutions. While scholars do not fully agree on causes, it
would be foolish to not utilize the agencies of the administrative state at all levels
of the federal government if they can help reverse this trend, and especially if they
contribute to it. We have many cases of local government as enablers of civic problem
solving (Berry, Portney, and Thomson 1993; Skogan and Hartnett 1997; Fung 2004;
Leighninger 2006; Sirianni 2007; Sirianni and Schor 2009; Nabatchi et al. 2012), and
some at state and federal levels, in some cases providing the legal mandate or funding
for local innovation. Clearly, the argument "if it can, it should" has to be qualified
by other factors, such as relative cost and effectiveness in solving public problems and
risks to relative independence of organizations within civil society. Second, as scholars increasingly stress the policy feedback effects on civic capacities (Campbell 2005,
2012; Mettler 2005)—and hence on further strengthening, weakening, or appropriately revising policy design—we ought to drive policy design for democracy (Ingram
and Smith 1993) and civic feedback strategies further into the workings of federal
administrative agencies of various sorts, especially those that are directly relevant for
communities, and not focus so exclusively on national distributive policies, as important as these are. Third, the administrative state is here to stay and thus should be made
as fully enabling of and complementary to other strategies for strengthening democracy. There are no credibly democratic conservative or neoliberal strategies that could
displace the administrative state in favor of radical market solutions in a complex

democracy. Nor are there credible left strategies that could displace the administrative state in favor of the radical democracy of social movements and fully autonomous civil society. Especially as public problems increase in complexity and publics become more diverse across a broad array of policy arenas, the administrative state will need to deploy regulatory and related tools. But a new New Deal or Progressive era cannot succeed on the back of purely technocratic, behavioral economic, or redistributive tools. The question is whether the administrative state can learn to effectively enable democratic engagement in collaborative public problem solving—as well as public deliberation on related questions of entitlement and distribution—thereby enriching its overall tool mix and knowledge base, as well as enhancing its democratic legitimacy. For this, still further kinds of civic innovation will be required.

References

Adler, Robert W. 1995. "Addressing Barriers to Watershed Protection." *Environmental Law* 25: 973–1106.

Alston, Marc. 2004. "Dispatches." *Grist Magazine*, January 19–23.

Ansell, Christopher K. 2011. *Pragmatist Democracy: Evolutionary Learning as Public Philosophy*. New York: Oxford University Press.

Behn, Robert. 2001. *Rethinking Democratic Accountability*. Washington, DC: Brookings Press.

Benford, Robert D. 2005. "The Half-Life of the Environmental Justice Frame: Innovation, Diffusion, and Stagnation." In *Power, Justice, and the Environment: A Critical Appraisal of the Environmental Justice Movement*, ed. David Naguid Pellow and Robert J. Brulle, 37–53. Cambridge, MA: MIT Press.

Benford, Robert D., and David A. Snow. 2000. "Framing Processes and Social Movements: An Overview and Assessment." *Annual Review of Sociology* 26: 611–39.

Bernhardt, Emily S., Elizabeth B. Sudduth, Margaret A. Palmer, et al. 2007. "Restoring Rivers One Reach at a Time: Results from a Survey of U.S. River Restoration Practitioners," *Restoration Ecology* 15: 482–93.

Berry, Jeffrey, Kent Portney, and Ken Thomson. 1993. *The Rebirth of Urban Democracy*. Washington, DC: Brookings Press.

Booher, David E. 2008. "Civic Engagement as Collaborative Complex Adaptive Networks." In *Civic Engagement in a Network Society*, ed. Kaifeng Yang and Erik Bergrud, 111–48. Charlotte, NC: IAP.

Born, Stephen M., with Kenneth Genskow. 1999. *Exploring the Watershed Approach: Critical Dimensions of State-Local Partnerships*. Four Corners Watershed Innovators Initiative, Final Report. Portland, OR: The River Network.

Boyer, Barry. 1981–1982. "Funding Public Participation in Agency Proceedings: The Federal Trade Commission Experience." *Georgetown Law Journal* 70: 51–172.

Boylan, Anne M. 2002. *The Origins of Women's Activism: New York and Boston, 1797–1840*. Chapel Hill: University of North Carolina Press.

Boyte, Harry C. 2005. "Reframing Democracy: Governance, Civic Agency, and Politics." *Public Administration Review* 65: 536–46.

Boyte, Harry C., and Nancy Kari. 1996. *Building America: The Democratic Promise of Public Work*. Philadelphia: Temple University Press.

Briggs, Xavier de Souza. 2008. *Democracy as Problem Solving: Civic Capacity in Communities Across the Globe*. Cambridge, MA: MIT Press.

Brooke, John L. 1996. "Ancient Lodges and Self-Created Societies: Voluntary Association and the Public Sphere in the Early Republic." In *Launching the Extended Republic: The Federalists Era*, ed. Ronald Hoffman and Peter J. Albert, 273–377. Charlottesville: University of Virginia Press.

Brown, Phil. 2007. *Toxic Exposures: Contested Illnesses and the Environmental Health Movement*. New York: Columbia University Press.

Bulkeley, Harriet. 2013. *Cities and Climate Change*. New York: Routledge.

Bullard, Robert D. 2005. "Environmental Justice in the Twenty-first Century." In *The Quest for Environmental Justice: Human Rights and the Politics of Pollution*, ed. Robert D. Bullard, 19–42. San Francisco: Sierra Club Books.

Campbell, Andrea Louise. 2005. *How Policies Make Citizens: Senior Political Activism and the American Welfare State*. Princeton, NJ: Princeton University Press.

———. 2012. "Policy Makes Mass Publics." *Annual Review of Political Science* 15: 333–51.

Clemens, Elizabeth S., and Debra C. Minkoff. 2004. "Beyond the Iron Law: Rethinking the Place of Organizations in Social Movement Research." In *The Blackwell Companion to Social Movements*, ed. David A. Snow, Sarah A. Soule, and Hanspeter Kriesi, 155–70. Malden, MA: Blackwell.

Cole, Luke W., and Sheila R. Foster 2000. *From the Ground Up: Environmental Racism and the Rise of the Environmental Justice Movement*. New York: New York University Press.

Corburn, Jason. 2005. *Street Science: Community Knowledge and Environmental Health Justice*. Cambridge, MA: MIT Press.

———. 2009. *Toward the Healthy City: People, Places, and the Politics of Urban Planning*. Cambridge, MA: MIT Press.

Davis, Gerald F., Doug McAdam, W. Richard Scott, and Mayer N. Zald, eds. 2005. *Social Movements and Organizational Theory*. New York: Cambridge University Press.

De Tocqueville, Alexis. 2004. *Democracy in America*. Translated by Arthur Goldhammer. New York: Library of America.

Dietz, Thomas, and Paul C. Stern, eds. 2008. *Public Participation in Environmental Assessment and Decision Making*. Washington, DC: National Research Council.

Dixon, K. A. 2003. "Reclaiming Brownfields: From Corporate Liability to Community Asset." In *Natural Assets: Democratizing Environmental Ownership*, ed. James K. Boyce and Barry G. Shelly, 57–76. Washington, DC: Island Press.

Dzur, Albert W. 2008. *Democratic Professionalism: Citizen Participation and the Reconstruction of Professional Ethics, Identity, and Practice*. University Park: Pennsylvania State University Press.

Emerson, Kirk. 2011. "Collaborative Public Management and Climate Change: Managing Climate Change in a Multi-Level Governance System." In *Navigating Climate Change Policy: The Opportunities of Federalism*, ed. Edella Schlager, Kristen H. Engel, and Sally Rider. Tucson: University of Arizona Press.

Environmental Law Institute. 2001. *Opportunities for Advancing Environmental Justice: An Analysis of U.S. EPA Statutory Authorities*. Washington, DC: ELI.

Environmental Law Institute. 2002. *A Citizen's Guide to Using Federal Environmental Laws to Secure Environmental Justice*. Washington, DC: ELI. Companion video, *Communities and Environmental Laws*.

Executive Office of the President. 2009. President's Memorandum on Transparency and Open Government, January 21. *www.whitehouse.gov/the_press_office/TransparencyandOpenGovernment*.

Federal Interagency Working Group on Environmental Justice. 2002. *Environmental Justice Collaborative Model: A Framework to Ensure Local Problem Solving*. Washington, DC: US Environmental Protection Agency.

Fiorino, Daniel J. 2006. *The New Environmental Regulation*. Cambridge, MA: MIT Press.

Firehock, Karen, Fran Flanigan, and Pat Devlin. 2002. *Community Watershed Forums: A Planners Guide*. Baltimore: Alliance for Chesapeake Bay.

Fleming, Cora, and Katrena Hanks. 2004. *Not Business as Usual: Using Collaborative Partnerships to Address Environmental Justice Issues*. Washington, DC: International City/County Management Association.

Fligstein, Neil, and Doug McAdam. 2012. *A Theory of Fields*. Oxford: Oxford University Press.

Foreman, Christopher, Jr. 1998. *The Promise and Peril of Environmental Justice*. Washington, DC: Brookings Press.

Fung, Archon. 2004. *Empowered Participation: Reinventing Urban Democracy*. Princeton, NJ: Princeton University Press.

Gerrard, Michael B., and Sheila R. Foster, eds. 2008. *The Law of Environmental Justice: Theories and Procedures to Address Disproportionate Risk*, 2nd ed. Chicago: American Bar Association.

Gibson, Alan. 2006. *Interpreting the Founding: Guide to the Enduring Debates over the Origins and Foundations of the American Republic*. Lawrence: University Press of Kansas.

Goldsmith, Stephen, and William D. Eggers. 2004. *Governing by Network: The New Shape of the Public Sector*. Washington, DC: Brookings Press.

Gordon, Holly D., and Keith I. Harley. 2005. "Environmental Justice and the Legal System." In *Power, Justice, and the Environment: A Critical Appraisal of the Environmental Justice Movement*, ed. David Naguid Pellow and Robert J. Brulle, 153–70. Cambridge, MA: MIT Press.

Goslant, Kim Herman. 1988. "Citizen Participation and Administrative Discretion in the Cleanup of Narragansett Bay." *Harvard Environmental Law Review* 12: 521–68.

Greenwood, Royston, Christine Oliver, Roy Suddaby, and Kerstin Sahlin-Andersson, eds. 2008. *The Sage Handbook of Organizational Institutionalism*. Thousand Oaks, CA: Sage.

Harris, Richard A., and Sidney M. Milkis. 1996. *The Politics of Regulatory Change: A Tale of Two Agencies*. New York: Oxford University Press.

Hess, Charlotte, and Elinor Ostrom. 2003. "Ideas, Artifacts, and Facilities: Information as a Common-Pool Resource." *Law & Contemporary Problems* 66: 114–18.

Hoffman, Andrew J. 2001. *From Heresy to Dogma: An Institutional History of Corporate Environmentalism*, expanded edition. Stanford, CA: Stanford Business Books.

Houck, Michael. 2007. "Bankside Citizens." In *Rivertown: Rethinking Urban Rivers*, ed. Paul Stanton Kibel, 179–96. Cambridge, MA: MIT Press.

House, Freeman. 1999. *Totem Salmon: Life Lessons from Another Species*. Boston: Beacon.

IAC (Innovation Action Council). 2005. *Everyday Choices: Opportunities for Environmental Stewardship*. Technical Report prepared by the EPA Environmental Stewardship Staff Committee. Washington, DC: US EPA.

Ingram, Helen, and Steven Rathgeb Smith, eds. 1993. *Public Policy for Democracy*. Washington, DC: Brookings Press.

Innes, Judith E., and David E. Booher. 2010. *Planning with Complexity: An Introduction to Collaborative Rationality for Public Policy*. New York: Routledge.

Israel, Barbara A., Eugenia Eng, Amy J. Schulz, and Edith A. Parker, eds. 2005. *Methods in Community-Based Participatory Research for Health*. San Francisco: Jossey-Bass.

John, DeWitt. 1994. *Civic Environmentalism: Alternatives to Regulation in States and Communities*. Washington, DC: Congressional Quarterly Press.

John, Richard R. 1997. "Governmental Institution as Agents of Change: Rethinking American Political Development in the Early Republic, 1787–1835." *Studies in American Political Development* 11: 347–80.

Johnston, Hank, and John A. Noakes, eds. 2005. *Frames of Protest: Social Movements and the Framing Perspective*. Lanham, MD: Rowman & Littlefield.

Kemmis, Daniel. 2001. *This Sovereign Land: A New Vision for Governing the West*. Washington, DC: Island Press.

Kettl, Donald F. 2002. *The Transformation of Governance: Public Administration for the Twenty-First Century*. Baltimore: Johns Hopkins University Press.

King, Marva E. 2012. "Collaboration Program Effectiveness: Comparing Two Community Partnership Programs." PhD dissertation, George Mason University.

Klandermans, Bert. 1992. "The Social Construction of Protest in Multiorganizational Fields." In *Frontiers in Social Movement Theory*, ed. Aldon D. Morris and Carol McClurg Mueller, 77–103. New Haven, CT: Yale University Press.

Kloppenberg, James. 1987. "The Virtues of Liberalism: Christianity, Republicanism, and Ethics in Early American Political Discourse." *The Journal of American History* 74 (June).

Koontz, Tomas, et al. 2004. *Collaborative Environmental Management: What Roles for Government?* Washington, DC: Resources for the Future.

Kraft, Michael E., and Daniel A. Mazmanian, eds. 2009. *Toward Sustainable Communities: Transition and Transformations in Environmental Policy*. Cambridge, MA: MIT Press.

Kretzmann, John P., and John L. McKnight. 1993. *Building Communities from the Inside Out*. Chicago: ACTA Publications.

Landy, Marc. 1993. "Public Policy and Citizenship." In *Public Policy for Democracy*, ed. Helen Ingram and Steven Rathgeb Smith, 19–44. Washington, DC: Brookings Press.

Landy, Marc, Marc Roberts, and Stephen Thomas. 1990. *The Environmental Protection Agency: Asking the Wrong Questions*. New York: Oxford University Press.

Lavigne, Peter M. 1995. *The Watershed Innovators Workshop: Proceedings*. Cummington, MA, June 4–5. Portland, OR: River Network.

———. 2004. "Watershed Councils East and West: Advocacy, Consensus, and Environmental Progress." *UCLA Journal of Environmental Law and Policy* 22 (2).

Layzer, Judith A. 2008. *Natural Experiments: Ecosystem-Based Management and the Environment*. Cambridge, MA: MIT Press.

Lee, Charles. 2005. "Collaborative Models to Achieve Environmental Justice and Healthy Communities." In *Power, Justice, and the Environment: A Critical Appraisal of the Environmental Justice Movement*, ed. David Naguid Pellow and Robert J. Brulle, 219–49. Cambridge, MA: MIT Press.

Leighninger, Matt. 2006. *The Next Form of Democracy*. Nashville, TN: Vanderbilt University Press.

Lubell, Mark, Mark Schneider, John T. Scholz, and Mihriye Mete. 2002. "Watershed Partnerships and the Emergence of Collective Action Institutions." *American Journal of Political Science* 46: 148–63.

———. 2003. "Building Consensual Institutions: Networks and the National Estuary Program," *American Journal of Political Science* 47 (1): 143–58.

Lukensmeyer, Carolyn J., Joe Goldman, and David Stern. 2011. *Assessing Participation in an Open Government Era: A Review of Federal Agency Plans*. Washington, DC: IBM Center for the Business of Government.

Macedo, Stephen, et al. 2005. *Democracy at Risk*. Washington, DC: Brookings Press.

Maier, Pauline. 2010. *Ratification: The People Debate the Constitution, 1787–1788*. New York: Simon & Schuster.

Mansbridge, Jane. 1980. *Beyond Adversary Democracy*. New York: Basic Books.

March, James G., and Johan P. Olsen. 1995. *Democratic Governance*. New York: Free Press.

Mettler, Suzanne. 2005. *Soldiers to Citizens: The G.I. Bill and the Making of the Greatest Generation*. New York: Oxford University Press.

———. 2011. *The Submerged State: How Invisible Government Policies Undermine American Democracy*. Chicago: University of Chicago Press.

Minkler, Meredith, and Nina Wallerstein, eds. 2004. *Community Organizing and Community Building for Health*, 2nd ed. New Brunswick, NJ: Rutgers University Press.

Moore, Elizabeth A., and Tomas M. Koontz. 2003. "A Typology of Collaborative Watershed Groups: Citizen-Based, Agency-Based, and Mixed Partnerships." *Society and Natural Resources* 16: 451–60.

Nabatchi, Tina, John Gastil, G. Michael Welksner, and Matt Leighninger, eds. 2012. *Democracy in Motion: Evaluating the Practice and Impact of Deliberative Civic Engagement*. New York: Oxford University Press.

NACEPT (National Advisory Council for Environmental Policy and Technology). 2008. *Everyone's Business: Working Towards Sustainability Through Environmental Stewardship and Collaboration*. Washington, DC: US EPA.

NAPA (National Academy of Public Administration). 1995. *Setting Priorities, Getting Results: A New Direction for the Environmental Protection Agency. A National Academy of Public Administration Report to Congress*. Washington, DC: NAPA.

———. 1997. *Resolving the Paradox of Environmental Protection: An Agenda for Congress, EPA, and the States*. Washington, DC: NAPA.

———. 2000. *Environment.gov: Transforming Environmental Protection for the 21st Century*. Washington, DC: NAPA.

———. 2007. *Taking Environmental Protection to the Next Level: An Assessment of the U.S.*

Environmental Services Delivery System: A Report to the U.S. EPA. Washington, DC: NAPA.

———. 2009. *Putting Community First: A Promising Approach to Federal Collaboration for Environmental Improvement. An Evaluation of the Community Action for a Renewed Environment (CARE) Demonstration Program.* Washington, DC: NAPA.

NEJAC (National Environmental Justice Advisory Council). 2003. *Advancing Environmental Justice through Pollution Prevention.* Washington, DC: US EPA.

———. 2004. *Ensuring Risk Reduction in Communities with Multiple Stressors: Environmental Justice and Cumulative Risks/Impacts.* Washington, DC: US EPA.

Novak, William J. 2001. "The American Law of Association: The Legal-Political Construction of Civil Society." *Studies in American Political Development* 15: 163–88.

Noveck, Beth S. 2009. *Wiki Government: How Technology Can Make Government Better, Democracy Stronger, and Citizens More Powerful.* Washington, DC: Brookings Press.

OEJ (Office of Environmental Justice). 2005. *Environmental Justice Small Grants Program: Emerging Tools for Local Problem Solving,* 2nd ed. Washington, DC: US EPA.

Ohrel, Ronald L., Jr., and Kathleen M. Register. 2002. *Volunteer Estuary Monitoring: A Methods Manual,* 2nd ed. Washington, DC: Ocean Conservancy and US EPA.

OIG (Office of Inspector General, US Environmental Protection Agency). 2005. *Sustained Commitment Needed to Further Advance Watershed Approach: Evaluation Report.* Washington: US EPA, Office of Inspector General.

O'Leary, Rosemary, and Lisa Blomgren Bingham, eds. 2009. *The Collaborative Public Manager: New Ideas for the Twenty-first Century.* Washington, DC: Georgetown University Press.

Ostrom, Elinor. 1990. *Governing the Commons: The Evolution of Institutions for Collective Action.* New York: Cambridge University Press.

———. 2005. *Understanding Institutional Diversity.* Princeton, NJ: Princeton University Press.

Palmer, Margaret, J. David Allan, Judy Meyer, and Emily S. Bernhardt. 2007. "River Restoration in the Twenty-First Century: Data and Experiential Knowledge to Inform Future Efforts." *Restoration Ecology* 15: 472–81.

Partnering with Communities. 2009. *Partnering with Communities: Federal Models of Community-Based Programs: Final Summary Report.* April 8, 2009. Washington, DC: Brookings Institution. *community-plan.net/nationalworkshop/docs/partnering_with_communities_federal_models_of_community_based_programs_final_report.pdf.*

Pellow, David Naguid, and Robert J. Brulle, eds. 2005. *Power, Justice, and the Environment: A Critical Appraisal of the Environmental Justice Movement.* Cambridge, MA: MIT Press.

Poff, N. LeRoy, Mark M. Brinson, and John W. Day Jr. 2002. *Aquatic Ecosystems and Global Climate Change: Potential Impacts on Inland Freshwater and Coastal Wetland Ecosystems in the United States.* Arlington, VA: Pew Center on Global Climate Change.

Portney, Kent E. 2013. *Taking Sustainable Cities Seriously: Economic Development, the Environment, and Quality of Life in American Cities.* 2nd ed. Cambridge, MA: MIT Press.

Putnam, Robert. 2000. *Bowling Alone.* New York: Simon & Schuster.

Richardson, Henry. 2002. *Democratic Autonomy: Public Reasoning about the Ends of Policy.* New York: Oxford University Press.

Ringquist, Evan J. 2006. "Environmental Justice: Normative Concerns, Empirical Evidence, and Government Action." In *Environmental Policy: New Direction for the Twenty-First Century*, 6th ed., ed. Norman J. Vig and Michael E Kraft, 239–63. Washington, DC: Congressional Quarterly Press.

Robertson, Stacey M. 2010. *Hearts Beating for Liberty: Women Abolitionists in the Old Northwest*. Chapel Hill: University of North Carolina Press.

Sabatier, Paul A., W. Focht, M. Lubell, et al. 2005. *Swimming Upstream: Collaborative Approaches to Watershed Management*. Cambridge, MA: MIT Press.

Scheberle, Denise. 2004. *Federalism and Environmental Policy: Trust and the Politics of Implementation*, 2nd ed. Washington, DC: Georgetown University Press.

Schueler, Tom, and Anne Kitchell. 2005. *Methods to Develop Restoration Plans for Small Urban Watersheds*. Ellicott City, MD: Center for Watershed Protection.

Schweitzer, Lisa, and Max Stephenson Jr. 2007. "Right Answers, Wrong Questions: Environmental Justice as Urban Research." *Urban Studies* 44: 319–37.

Shutkin, William. 2000. *The Land That Could Be: Environmentalism and Democracy in the Twenty-First Century*. Cambridge, MA: MIT Press.

Sirianni, Carmen. 2007. "Neighborhood Planning as Collaborative Democratic Design: The Case of Seattle." *Journal of the American Planning Association* 73 (4): 373–87.

———. 2009. *Investing in Democracy: Engaging Citizens in Collaborative Governance*. Washington, DC: Brookings Press.

Sirianni, Carmen, and Lewis Friedland. 2001. *Civic Innovation in America: Community Empowerment, Public Policy, and the Movement for Civic Renewal*. Berkeley: University of California Press.

Sirianni, Carmen, and Jennifer Girouard. 2012. "The Civics of Urban Planning." In *The Oxford Handbook of Urban Planning*, ed. Rachel Weber and Randall Crane, 669–90. New York: Oxford University Press.

Sirianni, Carmen, and Diana Marginean Schor. 2009. "City Government as Enabler of Youth Civic Engagement: Policy Designs and Implications." In *Engaging Young People in Civic Life*, ed. James Youniss and Peter Levine, 121–63. Nashville, TN: Vanderbilt University Press.

Sirianni, Carmen, and Stephanie Sofer. 2012. "Environmental Organizations." In *The State of Nonprofit America*, 2nd ed., ed. Lester M. Salamon, 294–328. Washington, DC: Brookings Press.

Skocpol, Theda. 2002. *Diminished Democracy: From Membership to Management in American Civic Life*. Norman: University of Oklahoma Press.

Skocpol, Theda, and Lawrence Jacobs, eds. 2011. *Reaching for a New Deal: Ambitious Governance, Economic Meltdown, and Polarized Politics in Obama's First Two Years*. New York: Russell Sage.

Skogan, Wesley G., and Susan Hartnett. 1997. *Community Policing, Chicago Style*. New York: Oxford University Press.

Smith, Steven Rathgeb. 2010. "Nonprofits and Public Administration: Reconciling Performance Management and Citizen Engagement." *The American Review of Public Administration* 40 (2): 129–52.

Smith, Steven Rathgeb, and Helen Ingram. 2002. "Policy Tools and Democracy." In *The Tools of Government*, ed. Lester Salamon, 565–84. New York: Oxford University Press.

Sørensen, E., and Jacob Torfing, J. 2007. *Theories of Democratic Network Governance*. Basingstoke: Palgrave Macmillan.

Stivers, Camilla. 1990. "The Public Agency as Polis: Active Citizenship in the Administrative State." *Administration and Society* 22: 86–105.

Szasz, Andrew. 1994. *Ecopopulism: Toxic Waste and the Movement for Environmental Populism*. Minneapolis: University of Minnesota Press.

Targ, Nicholas. 2005. "The States' Comprehensive Approach to Environmental Justice." In *Power, Justice, and the Environment: A Critical Appraisal of the Environmental Justice Movement*, ed. David Naguid Pellow and Robert J. Brulle, 171–84. Cambridge, MA: MIT Press.

Taylor, Dorcetta. 2000. "The Rise of the Environmental Justice Paradigm: Injustice Framing and the Social Construction of Environmental Discourses." *American Behavioral Scientist* 43: 508–80.

Thaler, Richard, and Cass R. Sunstein. 2009. *Nudge: Improving Decisions About Health, Wealth, and Happiness*. New York: Penguin.

US EPA. 1999. *EPA's Framework for Community-Based Environmental Protection*. Washington, DC: EPA Office of Policy, Office of Reinvention.

———. 2000. *Engaging the American People: A Review of EPA's Public Participation Policy and Regulations with Recommendations for Action*. Washington, DC: OPEI.

———. 2003. *Public Involvement Policy of the U.S. Environmental Protection Agency*. 2003. Washington, DC: Office of Policy, Economics, and Innovation.

———. 2011. *Plan EJ 2014*. Washington, DC: US EPA.

US OMB (US Office of Management and Budget). 2005. *Ocean, Coastal, and Estuary Protection: Program Assessment*. Washington, DC: OMB.

Vasi, Ion Bogdan. 2011. *Winds of Change: The Environmental Movement and the Global Development of the Wind Energy Industry*. New York: Oxford University Press.

Weber, Edward P. 2003. *Bringing Society Back In: Grassroots Ecosystem Management, Accountability, and Sustainable Communities*. Cambridge, MA: MIT Press.

Weber, Edward P., and Ann M. Khademian. 2008. "Wicked Problems, Knowledge Challenges, and Collaborative Capacity Builders in Network Settings." *Public Administration Review* 68: 334–49.

Wenger, Etienne. 1998. *Communities of Practice: Learning, Meaning, and Identity*. New York: Cambridge University Press.

Wessells, Anne Taufen. 2007. "Constructing Watershed Parks: Actor-Networks and Collaborative Governance in Four U.S. Metropolitan Areas." PhD dissertation, University of California.

Wondolleck, Julia M., and Steven L. Yaffee. 2000. *Making Collaboration Work: Lessons from Innovation in Natural Resource Management*. Washington, DC: Island Press.

Woolley, John T., and Michael Vincent McGinnis, with Julie Kellner. 2002. "The California Watershed Movement: Science and the Politics of Place." *Natural Resources Journal* 42 (1): 133–83.

Young, Oran R., Heike Schroeder, and Leslie A. King, eds. 2008. *Institutions and Environmental Change: Principal Findings, Applications, and Research Frontiers*. Cambridge, MA: MIT Press.

10

A Systemic Approach to Civic Action

JANE MANSBRIDGE

■ The many forms of civic action are all embedded in larger systems of deliberation, representation, and political pressure. As part of a system, one feature does not have to fill all the functions that a good system should fill. That feature can be incomplete in itself but provide a part of the necessary whole. In a deliberative system, for example, one case of civic action may be of low deliberative quality—biased, disrespectful, and exclusive—but still fill an important function if it adds information or the voices of systemically disrespected and marginalized individuals or groups to the system as a whole. On the other hand, even when a new form of civic action is itself of excellent deliberative quality—productive of useful knowledge, respectful, and inclusive—adding that new form to a deliberative system can detract from the best functioning of the whole whenever the new form displaces or reduces the effect of an existing form that makes the whole system work well.

In addition to these complementary and displacement effects, a systemic approach also alerts us to the subtle system-wide effects of any one civic action or collection of civic actions through the dynamics of emergence. In emergence, the micro-influences between proximate parts create a whole that is more than the sum of the parts, as when each fish in a school communicates only with the adjacent fish, but the entire school turns in one direction or another as if it were one organism. Thus the full effects of any one case of civic action cannot be known without a systemic analysis.

The cases in this book all form parts of larger systems of political deliberation, representation, and pressure within their neighborhoods, cities, states, nations, and the planet. We all implicitly judge each case for its practical use, its emancipatory power, and its conformity to criteria that we implicitly or explicitly harbor for such cases. In this concluding reflection, I will focus on the deliberative system and suggest explicit criteria for judging such cases within the framework of such a system as a whole. My larger point is that any judgment of a particular case should take place within an understanding of the larger system of which each case is a part, so that each succeeds, fails, or partially succeeds according to our different criteria, not only in its own setting but in the system more broadly.

Deliberative systems, I and colleagues have argued, should be judged according to how well they serve the epistemic, ethical, and democratic functions of deliberation. Epistemically, they should produce preferences, opinions, and decisions that are appropriately informed by facts and logic and that derive from the meaningful consideration of relevant reasons. Ethically, deliberative systems should produce mutual respect among citizens. Democratically, deliberative systems should give voice to multiple and plural perspectives, interests, concerns, and claims on the basis of feasible equality and equal opportunity. From all three perspectives, a healthy deliberative system is one in which relevant considerations are brought forth from all corners, aired, discussed, and appropriately weighed.[1]

When we make these systemic judgments, I urge that we examine each case not only in its legal place within a system but also in its effects more broadly, in complementing or displacing other forms of civic action, in changing the ongoing behavior of those who act within it, and in modeling behavior to others outside its immediate environs. From this perspective we may see this book itself as having a place in the deliberative system. It extends the lessons and modeling effects of every case to each of its readers and, beyond those readers, through the acts they may take that are influenced by the cases and the words they use to convey this influence to others.

Thus, Carmen Sirianni's analysis of the coproduction of beneficial environmental outcomes by government groups and various forms of citizen groups has the potential to inspire more of these efforts and give them some guidelines for success. He describes the effects of a long process that combined funding from the federal Environmental Protection Agency (EPA), work by an ongoing and committed EPA staff, and the mobilizing and information-producing efforts of hundreds of local groups to make the "watershed" a meaningful area of investigation, concern, and eventual policy reform. Although the process he describes has some participatory deficits, it should be judged overall on the basis of the degree to which it contributed to the system-wide understanding of the environment, to mutual respect among citizens, and to the inclusion and equality of voices in the system. On these measures, it seems to bear up well. So too the environmental justice movement on which Sirianni reports seems to have contributed across the deliberative system to understanding, respect, and inclusion. Certain moments in this process were actively exclusionary, but their overall effect was to add to the system voices that had not previously been heard. The analysis does not tell us how the representation of different perspectives and interests in these two cases played out in the representative system as a whole. In the pressure system, however, the watershed groups undoubtedly strengthened environmental as opposed to industry forces, even though the groups worked cooperatively with local and national industry and building interests at times. In addition, from all three perspectives of deliberation, representation, and pressure, without any intention necessarily to do so, the very reporting and analysis of these cases in this book itself promotes the amplification of muted voices, the representation of underrepresented interests, and the organization of pressure for environmental causes.

Elena Fagotto and Archon Fung make a convincing case in this volume for embedding civic deliberation in the ongoing political institutions and social practices of a community. They thus implicitly portray the community as a system. To be embedded, they argue, public deliberation must be iterative, or regularly repeated, anchored in its links to ongoing organizations, and encompassing in treating a variety of problems. Recognizing the role of deliberative entrepreneurs, they suggest that organizational leaders are more likely than individual activists to promote embedded deliberation precisely because their organizations are ongoing and connected in multiple ways to other parts of the deliberative, representative, and pressure systems. Their analysis points out effectively the systemic strengths of embedded organizations, but it does not argue that embedded deliberation necessarily affects the larger deliberative system more than sporadic deliberation. Occupy Wall Street is perhaps the quintessential nonembedded deliberation. Emerging seemingly out of nowhere, propelled by individual more than organizational activists, it reveled in its lack of connection to ongoing organizations or frameworks of goals. Yet it had a profound effect in drawing public deliberative attention to the phenomenon of massive, growing inequality in the United States, previously relatively unnoticed except by scholars. The effects of Occupy Wall Street on the deliberative system of the United States, and even to some extent globally, were profound. The authors might reply that some of the most lasting effects of the Occupy movement may come about through more embedded civic deliberation, as a number of unions picked up the theme in their ongoing revitalization efforts and students used the themes and techniques of the movement to inspire their organization in universities. But even though it was not embedded, the increases in knowledge, the cultivation of mutual respect, and the inclusion of less frequently heard voices in the Occupy Wall Street movement had modeling effects throughout the system. Here, as in the nine cases on which Fagotto and Fung report, the implication of formal public authorities (as mayors had to decide what stance to take to the Occupy encampments), the promotion of lasting deliberative capacity, and the mobilization of demands for democracy had effects on cities, states, and the entire nation.

Jason Corburn uses the case of how an organization originally formed to block the displacement of local residents seized on a fortuitous opportunity to use health concerns to further their ends. The process required delicately negotiating the material and recognition interests of the different constituent groups, including relatively poor African Americans and relatively affluent white young people. The organization's efforts included convening small and large subgroups, surveys of residents, studies, and many meetings, toward the end of which attendance flagged as the group failed to reach consensus. Yet the next stage, a "visioning process," produced transformations, at least among some participants, in understanding the interconnections among issues in their community. Perhaps most important from a systems perspective, the process also resulted in new networks and finally in a regional "Healthy Places Coalition" that coalesced a set of previous concerns around the concept of "healthy places," just as the work on which Sirianni reported coalesced around the concepts of "watershed" and "environmental justice." The major effects of this work were, in short, system-wide.

Lewis Friedland takes an explicitly systemic approach to his discussion of local sources of civic communication. Given a dramatic change in the ecology of local communication, with newspapers losing subscribers and advertising revenue to the Internet, he suggests that many locales can learn from the example of Seattle, which combined neighborhood governance, grants to promote Internet technology skills at the neighborhood level, the development of neighborhood blogs and social networking tools, transparent and accessible city data, and an active city and university promotion of television, radio, print, and Internet forms of "new regional neighborhood media." He suggests conditions that will help make civic communication successful, including a "robust micro-ecology, among individuals, niches, groups, and neighborhoods, that generates information from below." Each of the elements in his ecology supports and is supported by the others, so much so that he considers each "necessary" for sustaining the system. At the same time, he recognizes that the system is dynamic and that some of the new elements with the most promise have the potential to drive out the first requirement, "a robust, healthy local newspaper" that can continue to serve as a "hub" for the other forms. He leaves us in the midst of a systemic transformation that, if successful, can serve as a model nationwide and perhaps globally.

Anne Taufen Wessells also makes a systemic point as she analyzes the "interrelated, reinforcing elements within a local ecology of governance." Any complex policy issue, she points out, is inherently a set of issues, requiring "multiple, concurrent" designs and initiatives. Whenever any overall goal requires interlocking goals and initiatives, the required integration can arise spontaneously, as each part reflexively adapts to the changes in the others, or it can require conscious planning. Wessells presents two cases. In one, the Cal-FED Bay Delta program brought together twenty-five state and federal agencies to negotiate existing conflicts among these agencies and force or entice them to coordinate with one another. An evaluation matrix based on the state's existing measures for such projects "depersonalized" contention. A consultant helped the group come to "collective understandings of their project priorities" by insisting that "the door is still open" for change until the moment that everyone realized the matrix was "not going to change." A democratic theory focused on action would probably approve of this process (Mansbridge 2012). But a skeptical outsider might note that depersonalization in this case included depoliticization, and stress on the possibility of change served as a cover for the increasing incapacity to change. In Wessells' second and unrelated case, two initiatives—a book of walks along the Los Angeles River and an artistic installation inspired by the river—sprang from the efforts of two "individual activists." Both individuals were, she notes, deeply embedded in a larger system of civic activism, organization, and "informal constituency building" combined with government management and government-organized citizen participation. These cases suggest, perhaps, that the more complex the processes of conceiving, formulating, implementing, and mobilizing around a policy issue, the more each part of the system will produce reverberations in the other parts.

Thamy Pogrebinschi's chapter examines how a set of innovative participatory initiatives in Brazil, sponsored by both city governments and the national government, have made it possible for minority group members to participate in policy making and get results that meet their needs to a degree unprecedented in Western democracy. As in the other chapters in this volume, these initiatives can be seen as parts of a larger system. Some initiatives, such as the regional conferences, are explicitly designed to work as parts of a formal system, while others, such as certain civil society groups, have emerged or adapted informally as the deliberative, representative, and pressure systems in which they are enmeshed dynamically evolved. As Pogrebinschi points out, the new venues for participation stimulate civil society in large part because they heavily reward inputs from civil society. They also encourage the participants to think of their demands as "rights" and so change the larger discourse. They have had, she plausibly suggests, significant effects on policy statements and legislative bills. At the end of her chapter, Pogrebinschi suggests the effects that these innovations might have on the larger representative and deliberative systems. She points out that these deliberations are "imbued with a strong legitimacy claim," although they are shaped "in a nonelectoral setting" relatively "free from party influences" and "media appeal." Their unorthodox legitimacy claims can hardly avoid affecting the legitimacy of the existing parties and media. They are thus not merely additions, "parallel to elections and party politics," but may to some extent, and for better or worse, be displacing elections and parties.

Robert Fishman examines two pairs of cases in which factors "located *outside* the specialized terrain of elections and official institutions" facilitated the success of disadvantaged groups' efforts to improve their lot. In his first pair of cases, in Portugal, a national narrative grounded in the 1974 "Carnation Revolution" stressed political inclusion and resistance to domination. This national-level discourse contributed to the success of an immigrant march to protest eviction from their homes. In Spain, protests against a similar eviction failed in part for the lack of these elements at the national level. In his second pair of cases, a village with "boundary-crossing" and "intrinsically meaningful" social ties between intellectuals and workers succeeded in grounding its protest against the closing of the local coal mines in a rhetorical "globalizing discursive" frame. A nearby village, where such ties were primarily instrumental, had access only to a frame of "narrow localism," in which it "could hardly be thought to contribute to any public goal lying outside the immediate context of the town." Fishman concludes that "culturally rooted understandings, meanings, and practices . . . shape the emergence and significance of social network ties" while "these networks, in turn, strongly influence the extent to which cultural innovations and assumptions can spread." Social networks and culture are thus "mutually constitutive" (Pachuki and Breiger 2010, 209) across local and national levels in a self-reinforcing system. The systemic reinforcing effects or backlash effects of any local action or rhetorical frame probably depend in part on the context. Although in good times we could expect using the inclusivity of the Carnation Revolution to enhance success, in bad times attempts to draw upon that frame might only weaken the effectiveness of the frame.

In a chapter that highlights one of the strong themes of this volume, Caroline Lee points out that "the contemporary social context of political life in the United States is one of hybrid, multilayered forms of activism, organization, and politics," blending public and private, and "nested in institutional domains of different scales and sectors." This hybridity and multilayered quality may multiply opportunities (Briggs 2008), but it also makes each move heavily system-dependent. Two of Lee's three cases of multistakeholder collaborative partnerships for resource conservation illustrate perfectly how a part of a system that does not meet or even approach many of the normative standards for deliberation in its internal organization nevertheless plays a useful role in the larger deliberative system. In San Diego, the deliberative process met many of the classic standards. It was public, with consultants and facilitators, transparent procedures, and a variety of public workshops and hearings that actively included stakeholders and interested citizens. In Charleston, the process was authoritarian and private, open only to a self-selected few, and actively excluded developers and local jurisdictions. As an individual case, the San Diego process approached far more closely the classic norms for good deliberation. Yet in practice its length and complexity "ended up wearing down stakeholders with less resources and capacity and generating substantial skepticism and bad will" and it never produced the hoped-for better cooperation. Its effect on the larger deliberative system may have been minimal or negative. By contrast, the exclusive, nontransparent Charleston group was able to informally initiate dialogue with and solicit participation from even strongly opposed stakeholders. Lee concludes, "Paradoxically, fluidity of roles and responsibilities, the informalization of government involvement, and the avoidance of legal rules and obligations can make participants' commitments to collective enterprise stronger, not weaker." It can also produce better results. Deliberative theorists have come to realize only recently that transparency and publicity, although traditionally considered hallmarks of high-quality deliberation, are often the enemy of good information, respect, and even inclusion—although closed-door negotiations must be embedded in larger systems that produce accountability by other means (Chambers 2004; Mansbridge 2005; Mansbridge et al. 2010). Lee ends with a plea for understanding specific instances of collaborative governance "within complex multi-institutional contexts," that is, within the larger system in which they are embedded. Only with a systemic analysis can she explain how, in the context of other institutions, the Charleston group might accomplish deliberative goals better than the San Diego group, which consciously tried much harder to achieve those goals.

Does the concept of a system add anything to the concepts of "connection," "network," and "context"? A "system" has a set of distinguishable, differentiated, but to some degree interdependent parts, often with distributed implicit functions and a division of labor, connected in such a way as to form a complex whole. It requires both differentiation and integration among the parts, so that some parts do work that others cannot do. It also requires some relational interdependence, so that a change in one component will bring about changes in some others. In this analysis the term "system" is not intended to be mechanistic. It does not require that every component have a specific function in the system or that every component be interdependent on every other so that a change in one automatically brings about a change in all the others. If a component does contribute to a function, that function need not be fulfilled optimally in a single location because within the larger system the same function may be distributed across various subsystems. A system may be highly redundant, with overlapping functions. It may be inefficient. It may lack components that would make it work better. In this analysis the term is intended only to draw attention to the complex interdependence of a set of institutions and relationships (including networks and discourses) that human beings can use to achieve their goals (Mansbridge et al. 2012).

A systemic analysis should alert us to possible relationships of displacement as well as complementarity. In the cases in this book, the analytic emphasis has been almost entirely on the positive synergies in the system, and rarely if ever on the way that one initiative, admirable in itself, might drive out or disadvantage other initiatives. In the 2004 nationwide deliberation in Britain over the national health service, for example, the introduction into the debate of government-sponsored randomized deliberative "citizen juries" partially displaced existing advocacy groups in legitimacy and influence (Parkinson 2006). In Caroline Lee's case in this volume, the existence in San Diego of a government-sponsored, inclusive, highly deliberative process on the issue of resource conservation made it far less likely that an informal, exclusive, but successful private process such as the one in Charleston would emerge.

A systemic analysis should also alert us to the dynamics of emergence, which a single case or even multiple case studies can rarely capture. Robert Fishman in this volume shows how networks of individuals and the narratives that sometimes travel along these networks can make the difference between organizational success and failure. The deliberative force of both the "Carnation" and the globalization frame came in part from the way each of these ideas had been diffused, adapted, and applied in a larger deliberative system. To understand these processes even better, we would need the close analysis of individual talk in everyday life in conjunction with overall data on the ebb and flow of different concepts on the national or even global level. So too, to understand the provenance and also the full impact of any particular civic action, we need to place it within a web of interactions, networks, and discourses that facilitate or prevent other actions.

In these concluding reflections I have suggested only briefly how the cases in this book might use and contribute to a systemic analysis of civic action. For those concerned with the quality of deliberation in civic life, these cases provide important insights into the conditions of successful cooperation. If citizens in democracies globally become increasingly more affluent, they will probably begin to demand more "postmaterial" goods, such as "giving people more say in important political decisions" (Inglehart 1971). But we do not know much yet about how best to give people such a say. The cases in this book provide many lessons in civic "say." A next step will be to set such cases in the context of larger deliberative and democratic settings, to try to judge the degree to which each form of civic action adds to our resources overall—or perhaps detracts from them.

Note

1. Mansbridge et al. 2012, 18–19. These standards are contestable; indeed contest is built into the concepts of "appropriately" and "feasibly." For the evolution of standards of good deliberation, see Mansbridge et al. 2010. The reflections in this chapter do not include a discussion of the representative or pressure systems. I argue that representative systems should be judged by the criteria of whether they provide equal opportunities for the expression of diverse perspectives on the common good and equal power when interests conflict. Pressure systems, which are systems of coercive power—that is, systems involving threats of sanction and the use of force—should, in a democracy, reflect the equal power of every individual.

References

Briggs, Xavier de Souza. 2008. *Democracy as Problem Solving: Civic Capacity in Communities Across the Globe.* Cambridge, MA: MIT Press.

Chambers, Simone. 2004. "Behind Closed Doors: Publicity, Secrecy, and the Quality of Deliberation." *The Journal of Political Philosophy* 12 (4): 389–410

Inglehart, Ronald. 1971. "The Silent Revolution in Europe: Intergenerational Change in Post-Industrial Societies." *American Political Science Review* 65 (4): 991–1017.

Mansbridge, Jane. 2005. "The Fallacy of Tightening the Reins." *Österreichische Zeitschrift für Politikwissenschaft* 34 (3): 233–47.

———. 2012. "On the Importance of Getting Things Done." The 2011 James Madison Lecture. *P.S.: Political Science and Politics* 45 (1): 1–8.

Mansbridge, Jane, James Bohman, Simone Chambers, Thomas Christiano, Archon Fung, John Parkinson, Dennis F. Thompson, and Mark E. Warren. 2012. "A Systemic Approach to Deliberative Democracy." In *Deliberative Systems*, ed. John Parkinson and Jane Mansbridge. Cambridge: Cambridge University Press.

Mansbridge, Jane, with James Bohman, Simone Chambers, David Estlund, Andreas Follesdal, Archon Fung, Cristina Lafont, Bernard Manin, and José Luis Martí. 2010. "The Place of Self-Interest and the Role of Power in Deliberative Democracy." *Journal of Political Philosophy* 18 (1): 64–100.

Pachuki, Mark A., and Ronald L. Breiger. 2010. "Cultural Holes: Beyond Relationality in Social Networks and Culture." *Annual Review of Sociology* 36: 205–24.

Parkinson, John. 2006. *Deliberating in the Real World: Problems of Legitimacy in Deliberative Democracy.* New York: Oxford University Press.

Contributors

Jason Corburn is associate professor in city and regional planning, as well as public health, at the University of California-Berkeley. He is author of *Street Science: Community Knowledge and Environmental Health Justice* (MIT Press, 2005), *Toward the Healthy City: People, Places and the Politics of Urban Planning* (MIT Press, 2009), and most recently *Healthy City Planning: From Neighborhood to National Health Equity* (Routledge, 2013).

Elena Fagotto is a Democracy Fellow at the Ash Center for Democratic Governance and Innovation, Kennedy School of Government, Harvard University. She is also a faculty affiliate at LUISS School of Government in Rome and PhD candidate at Erasmus University Rotterdam. She has published widely on government transparency, public deliberation, and collaborative governance.

Robert M. Fishman is professor of sociology at the University of Notre Dame. He is author of *Democracy's Voices: Social Ties and the Quality of Public Life in Spain* (Cornell University Press, 2004), *Working Class Organization and the Return to Democracy in Spain* (Cornell University Press, 1990), and has edited *The Year of the Euro: The Cultural, Social and Political Import of Europe's Common Currency*, with Anthony Messina (University of Notre Dame Press, 2006). His current book project is *Constituting Democratic Practice: The Iberian Divide in Political Equality*.

Lewis A. Friedland is Vilas Distinguished Professor, School of Journalism and Mass Communication, University of Wisconsin-Madison. He is author of *Public Journalism: Past and Future* (Kettering Foundation Press, 2003), and *Civic Innovation in America* with Carmen Sirianni (University of California Press, 2001), among other works. He is also an innovator of various online civic journalism projects and won the Public Broadcasting Gold Award for PBS documentary.

Archon Fung is the Ford Foundation Professor of Democracy and Citizenship at the Ash Center for Democratic Governance and Innovation, Kennedy School of Government, Harvard University. He is the author of *Empowered Participation: Reinventing Urban Democracy* (Princeton University Press, 2004), *Full Disclosure: The Perils and Promise of Transparency* (Cambridge University Press, 2007), with Mary Graham and David Weil, among other books. His most recent edited collection is *Open Budgets: The Political Economy of Transparency, Participation, and Accountability* (Brookings Institution Press, 2013) with Sanjeev Khagram and Paolo de Renzio.

Jennifer Girouard is a PhD candidate in sociology at Brandeis University. Her dissertation research is on the spatial, legal, and deliberative dynamics of statewide affordable housing in Massachusetts. She is coauthor (with Carmen Sirianni) of "The Civics of Urban Planning," in *The Oxford Handbook of Urban Planning*, ed. Rachel Weber and Randall Crane (Oxford University Press, 2012).

Daniel Kreiss is an assistant professor in the School of Journalism and Mass Communication at the University of North Carolina at Chapel Hill. He is author of many articles on online politics, as well as *Taking Our Country Back: The Crafting of Networked Politics from Howard Dean to Barack Obama* (Oxford University Press, 2012). He is currently working on a book on networked politics and campaigning at the ward level.

Caroline W. Lee is associate professor of sociology, Lafayette College. She is the author of articles in the *American Journal of Sociology, Sociological Forum,* and *Society and Natural Resources* and is currently writing *Disciplining Democracy: Public Engagement Experts and the New Participation Economy.* Her edited collection, *Democratizing Inequalities,* with Michael McQuarrie and Edward T. Walker, will be published by New York University Press in 2014.

Jane Mansbridge is Adams Professor of Political Leadership and Democratic Values, Kennedy School of Government, Harvard University. She is the author of *Beyond Adversary Democracy* (Basic Books, 1980), *Why We Lost the ERA* (University of Chicago Press, 1986), and various edited volumes (*Beyond Self-Interest, Oppositional Consciousness*), and most recently of *Deliberative Systems: Deliberative Democracy at the Large Scale* (Cambridge University Press, 2012). She is past president of the American Political Science Association.

Laura Meadows is a PhD candidate in the School of Journalism and Mass Communication at the University of North Carolina at Chapel Hill. Her dissertation research examines the LGBT movement in the South through a case of study of the movement in North Carolina.

Thamy Pogrebinschi is a professor of political science at the Institute of Social and Political Studies, State University of Rio de Janeiro, where she coordinates the Laboratory on Studies in Democracy. She has recently been Alexander von Humboldt Fellow at the Wissenschaftszentrum für Sozialforschung in Berlin. She is the author of various books in Portuguese on pragmatism, law, political theory, and democracy. Her most recent publication in English is "Participation as Representation: Democratic Policymaking in Brazil," in *New Institutions for Participatory Democracy in Latin America: Voice and Consequence* (Palgrave Macmillan, 2012), edited by Cameron A. Maxwell, Eric Hershberg, and Kenneth E. Sharpe.

Carmen Sirianni is the Morris Hillquit Professor of Labor and Social Thought, and professor of sociology and public policy at Brandeis University. He is also Faculty Fellow at the Center for Democratic Governance and Innovation, Kennedy School of Government, Harvard University. Among his books are *Investing in Democracy: Engaging Citizens in Collaborative Governance* (Brookings Press, 2009) and *Civic Innovation in America* (University of California Press, 2001), with Lewis Friedland. He is currently writing a two-volume work, *Self-Governance in American Political Development.* His work on civic renewal has recently been translated and published by the Chinese Academy of Social Sciences.

Anne Taufen Wessells is an assistant professor in urban studies at the University of Washington, Tacoma. Her work on watershed planning, governance networks, and urban sustainability has appeared in *Urban Studies, Planning Theory and Practice, Policy Studies Journal, Natural Resources Journal,* and elsewhere.

Index

Numbers in **bold** refer to tables;
numbers in *italic* refer to figures.

ACE Basin Task Force (Charleston, SC)
    formation and administration of partnerships in,
        136–38
    inclusion and, 137, 138, 140, 141–43
    instrumental ties in, 146–50
    overview, 133–35, **134**
    systemic approach to civic action and, 244, 245
*Advancing Environmental Justice through Pollution
    Prevention* (NEJAC), 220
Allen, George, 80
Alston, Marc, 217
Amadora (Portugal), 159–60, 166
American Rivers, 217
AmericaSpeaks, 11
Anderson, C. W., 80
Armour, Mark, 81, 83
AWARE Colorado, 218

Babbitt, Bruce, 135
Baeza, Javier, 159
Ballard News-Tribune (Seattle newspaper), 110
Baltimore Sun (newspaper), 99
Baristanet (local news website), 121
Barnett, Erica, 113
Bennett, Lance, 106–7
Bergman, Corey, 115
Bergman, Kate, 115
Berk, Gerald, 130
Best, Kathy, 112–13
Bethel New Life, 221–22, 225
Bhatia, Rajiv, 46–47, **47**, 69
Black, Dustin Lance, 81
blogs
    intramovement agenda setting and, 81–89
    role in civic communication ecology in Seattle,
        108–9, 111, 114–15, 116, 117, 120
    social movements and, 78–80
Boardman, David, 109
Brazil. *See* national public policy conferences (Brazil)
Breiger, Ronald L., 162
Brenner, Robert, 223
Brewster, David, 110
Briggs, Xavier de Souza, 132, 138, 144, 147
British Columbia Citizen Assembly, 21n2
Brokerage and Closure (Burt), 173–74

Brookings Institution, 207
Browner, Carol, 218–19
Burt, Ronald, 173–74
Bush administration, 228

Caetano, Marcelo, 165
CalFED Bay Delta program, 27–28
California. *See* Eastern Neighborhoods Community
    Health Impact Assessment (ENCHIA); Multiple
    Species Conservation Program (San Diego, CA)
California Endowment (TCE), 68, 71–72
California Environmental Quality Act (CEQA), 47, **52**
campaigns, 77–78. *See also* Coalition to Protect ALL
    NC Families
Campbell, Amber, 115
Campbell, Stuart, 75
Capitol Hill Blog/Central District News (blog),
    115–16
Captains of April (film), 164
Carder, Justin, 115–16
Carnation Revolution (Portugal, 1974), 163–69
Carter administration, 208
Center for Health, Environment, and Justice
    (CHEJ), 222
Center for Neighborhood Technology, 225
Center for Watershed Protection, 217, 226
Central Seattle Grassroots Radio, 110
Chambers, Simone, 9
Charleston (SC). *See* ACE Basin Task Force
    (Charleston, SC)
Chesapeake Bay Alliance, 214
Chesapeake Bay Foundation, 214
Chesapeake Bay Program, 214
Chion, Miriam, 46
civic communication ecology
    future of, 119–21
    new media and, 99–101
    overview, 92–93
    role of newspapers in, 93, 94–99, 119
    role of television in, 96
    in Seattle: governance policy and, 103–8; layers of,
        117–19; media ecology and, 108–11; overview,
        102; role of new media in, 111–17
    systemic approach to, 242
civic practice
    role of narratives in, 160–69, 176–77
    role of networks in, 160–63, 169–77
    systemic approach to, 239–46

Civil Rights Act (1964), 219–20
Clean Water Act (1972)
    MSCP and, 135, 136
    NEPs and, 211, 214, 227–28
    watersheds and, 226
Clinton administration, 218–19, 228
Coalition to Protect ALL NC Families
    ethnographic study of, 80–81
    intramovement agenda setting and, 82–89
    overview, 75–77
Coglianese, Cary, 129
Cohen, Joshua, 129
collaborative environmental problem solving
    comparison of case studies, 150–51
    formation and administration of partnerships in,
        135–38
    ideals and realities in, 128–32
    inclusion and, **137**, 138–43
    instrumental ties in, 144–50
    introduction to case studies, 132–35, **134**
    systemic approach to, 244, 245
collaborative policy design
    challenges in, 24
    EPA and, 204, 226–31, **229**
Colorado, 216–18
Colorado Lakes and Reservoir Management
    Association, 218
Colorado Riparian Association, 218
Colorado River Watch Network, 217
Colorado Water Quality Control Division, 217
Colorado Watershed Assembly, 217, 218
Colorado Watershed Network, 218
Commonwealth Edison, 225
communication. *See* civic communication ecology
Communities for a Better Environment (CBE), 71,
    221
Community Action for a Renewed Environment
    (CARE) program, 217, 222–24
Community Conversations on Public Education, 18
community organizing, 10
Community Partnership for Environmental
    Protection, 222
Community Technology Program (CTP, Seattle),
    104–7, 111, 116, 121
Community-Based Environmental Protection
    (CBEP), 216–18
Corburn, Jason, 241–42
Cronon, William, 127, 152
Crosscut (Seattle news website), 113

Dahl, Robert, 166
Deerfield (NH), 119
deliberation, 24–25
deliberative democracy
    assessment of, 151–53
    definition of, 9
    functions of deliberation and, 240
    See also public deliberations

deliberative entrepreneurs, 12, 14–15, 17, 241
Deliberative Polls, 11
Delli Carpini, Michael X., 9
Democracy in America (Toqueville), 203–4
Democratic Party, 79–80
Design for Environment (DfE) program, 222
Detroiters Working for Environmental Justice, 221
Dewey, John, 206
Diers, Jim, 104
Down by the Los Angeles River (Linton), 34–37, *39*
Downie, Len, 98
Drezner, Daniel W., 80
Durkin, Jessica, 122n4

Earl, Jennifer, 78–79
Eastern Neighborhoods Community Health Impact
    Assessment (ENCHIA)
    community experts and, 58–59
    evidence base for, 57
    guiding principles of, 47–48, *49*
    HDMT and, 46, 63–64, *63*, 69, 70
    inequalities and, 55–56
    measurements and, 57–58
    objectives of, **48**, 49–55, **52–54**, 56–57, **56**
    outcomes of, 64–65, 69–70
    overview, 45–47
    participants, 48–49, **50**, 61–62, 65–66, 68–69
    policy briefs by, 59–61, **60**
    role of networks in, 66–68
    systemic approach to civic action and, 241–42
Ecker, Jeffrey, 138–39, 144, 146
Ecosystem Protection Program, 216
Edwards, John, 87
embedded deliberation
    conditions for, 18–21
    definition of, 7
    dimensions of, 13–18, *15*
    methodology and, 8–9
    vs. occasional deliberation, 10–11
    process of, 11–13
    success of, 131
    systemic approach to, 241
*Ensuring Risk Reduction in Communities with
    Multiple Stressors* (NEJAC), 220
environmental justice movement
    EPA and: framing and, 219–22; networks and,
        224–26; overview, 218–19; systemic approach
        to civic action and, 240; tools and, 222–24
    origins of, 218
Environmental Protection Agency (US EPA)
    command-and-control regulatory regime and,
        205, 207–8
    environmental justice movement and: framing
        and, 219–22; networks and, 224–26; overview,
        218–19; systemic approach to civic action and,
        240; tools and, 222–24
    need for collaborative governance in, 204, 226–
        31, **229**

watershed movement and: framing and, 209–10; networks and, 213–18, **215**; overview, 208–9; systemic approach to civic action and, 240; tools and, 210–12, **213**

Equality NC, 75, 76, 80

Fagotto, Elena, 131, 241
Fancher, Mike, 108, 110
Farmworkers Association of Florida, 221
Farrell, Henry, 80
Fazeli, Bahram, 221
Feit, Josh, 113
Feldman, M. S., 24, 41n2
Ferrao, Joao, 159
Fishman, Robert, 131, 243–44, 245
Five Models Afloat (gallery installation), 34, 37–39, *39*
Ford administration, 208
Foreman, Christopher, Jr., 222
Fox, Richard, 218
Freedom to Marry, 85
Friedland, Lewis A., 108, 113, 242
Friends and Neighbors of North Admiral (FANNA), 114–15
Friends of the Los Angeles River (FoLAR), 28, 34, 41
Fung, Archon, 131, 241

Gates Foundation, 112
Goldman, Joe, 21n5
Goldtooth, Tom, 221
Goode, Bobby, 139–40, 144–45
Gothenburg Statement (WHO), 47
Gran Limpieza, La, (Great Los Angeles River Clean Up), 37
Great Bay Resource Protection Partnership (Portsmouth, NH)
  formation and administration of partnerships in, 136–38
  funding and, 153–54n3
  inclusion and, **137**, 138, 140–41, 142–44
  instrumental ties in, 146–50
  overview, 133–35, **134**
Great Communities Collaborative (GCC), 70–71
Greene, Iris, 138
Griffin, Chad, 81, 83, 87–88
Guertin, Joshua, 145

Haas, Tanni, 108
Hahn, Nation, 75, 80–81, 82–85, 87, 88
Hamilton, Alexander, 203
Hamilton, James T., 94
Hamilton, Karen, 216
Hartig, Dennis, 114
Harvard University, 207
Hawley, Amos H., 94
health impact assessments. *See* Eastern Neighborhoods Community Health Impact Assessment (ENCHIA)

Healthy Development Measurement Tool (HDMT), 46, 63–64, *63*, 69, 70
Healthy Places Coalition, 71
Highline Times (Seattle newspaper), 110
Hindman, Matthew S., 100
Hirotaka, Amy, 106
How to Create and Implement Healthy General Plans (TCE), 72
Hughes, Chris, 76
Human Impact Partners (HIP), 71
Human Rights Campaign, 76, 85
HUNOSA (Spanish state-owned coal company), 160

Ikegami, Eiko, 175
immigrants and immigration, 159–60
inclusion, 24–25, **137**, 138–43
Indigenous Environmental Network, 221
Indigenous Issues Forums, 10, 17
inequalities, 55–56
Ingram, Helen, 42n5
Innovation Action Council (IAC), 204, 207, 223
institutions, 24–25
Integrated Regional Watershed Management (IRWM), 23, 25–26, 27–34, *29*, 39–41
Interagency Working Group on Environmental Justice (EJ IWG), 218–19, 221, 225
Internet
  blogs and: intramovement agenda setting and, 81–89; role in civic communication ecology in Seattle, 108–9, 111, 114–15, 116, 117, 120; social movements and, 78–80
  decline of newspapers and, 97–98
intramovement agenda setting
  actors in, 86–88
  narratives and, 83–86
  networks and, 82–83, 89
  overview, 75–77
InvestigateWest (Seattle news website), 113

Janowitz, Morris, 120
Jefferson, Thomas, 203
J-Lab, 99, 112, 117

Karpf, David, 80
Katz, Mitch, 61–62
Kauffman Foundation, 18
KCTS-TV (Seattle television station), 109
KDNA (Seattle radio station), 110
Keiki Caucus (Children Caucus), 10, 18, 19
Kennedy, Jeremy, 75, 80–81, 82, 83–85, 86–88
Keyes, David, 105
Kimport, Katrina, 78–79
KING (Seattle television station), 109, 111
Kitchell, Anne, 212
Knight Foundation, 121
Knighton, Betty, 21n3
KOMO (Seattle television station), 109, 113, 116

Konieczna, Magda, 113
Korfmacher, Katrina S., 138
KRAB (Seattle radio station), 110
Kreiss, Daniel, 76
KSER (Seattle radio station), 110
Kuna ACT, 17, 19
KUOW (Seattle radio station), 109–10

Lake, Celinda, 81, 83, 85–86
Lansman, Jeremy, 110
Lasch, Christopher, 169
Lasswell, Harold D., 122n1
Latour, Bruno, 41n3
Layzer, Judith, 129, 132
League of Women Voters, 18
League of Women Voters of Colorado Education
 Fund, 218
Lecomte, Josee, 77
Lee, Caroline, 244, 245
Lehrer, Jim, 144
LGTB movement
 history of, 78
 intramovement agenda setting and, 75–77, 82–89
 marriage equality and, 82
Lichterman, Paul, 175
Linton, Joe, 34–37, 39
Lippmann, Walter, 94
Los Angeles and San Gabriel Rivers Watershed
 Council, 28
Los Angeles City Council, 34
Los Angeles County Bicycle Coalition, 34
Los Angeles River Watershed
 constituency building and, 23, 26, 34–39, 39,
  40–41
 IRWM planning and, 23, 25–26, 27–34, 29,
  39–41
 overview, 23–27
 systemic approach to civic action and, 242–43
Louisiana Environmental Action Network, 221,
 225–26
Lula da Silva, Luiz Inácio, 181, 185–87, 191, 195,
 199–200

MacAdams, Lewis, 35
Macedo, Timoteo, 167
MacNeil, Chris, 81
Macris, Dean, 61
Madison, James, 203
Madrid (Spain), 159–60
Maeda, Sharon, 110
Maltzer, Paul, 46–47
Margerum, Richard D., 136
marriage equality. See Coalition to Protect ALL NC
 Families
Masket, Seth E., 79
McChesney, Robert, 98–99
Medeiros, Maria de, 164
Mernit, Susan, 121

Methods to Develop Restoration Plans for Small Urban
 Watersheds (Schueler and Kitchell), 212
Milam, Lorenzo, 110
Minnesota United, 85
Mission Anti-displacement Coalition (MAC). See
 Eastern Neighborhoods Community Health
 Impact Assessment (ENCHIA)
Mission Economic Development Association
 (MEDA), 67–68
Miullo, Nat, 216
money bombs, 76
Moreno, Tirso, 221
Morrison, Patt, 35
MoveOn, 79
Multiple Species Conservation Program (San Diego,
 CA)
 formation and administration of partnerships in,
  135–36, 138
 inclusion and, 137, 138–40, 143
 instrumental ties in, 144–47, 149
 overview, 133–35, 134
 systemic approach to civic action and, 244, 245
Murteira, Mario, 167
My Ballard (blog), 115, 116

NAACP, 76, 89
narratives
 intramovement agenda setting and, 83–86
 role in civic practice, 160–69, 176–77, 243, 245
National Academy of Public Administration
 (NAPA), 205, 214
National Advisory Council for Environmental Policy
 and Technology (NACEPT), 204
National Civic League, 224
National Environmental Justice Advisory Council
 (NEJAC), 204–5, 219, 220–21, 228
National Estuarine Research Reserves, 133, 134
National Estuary Programs (NEPs), 211, 214,
 227–28
National Federation of Community Broadcasters,
 110
National Fish and Wildlife Foundation, 214
National Issues Forums, 10, 11, 16
National People of Color Environmental Leadership
 Summit, 218
national public policy conferences (Brazil)
 characteristics of, 181–83
 minority groups and: governmental responses
  to, 194–200, 195, 197–99; overview, 184–89,
  185–86; policy guidelines by, 189–94, 193
 policy areas deliberated in, 184, 184
 process of, 183–84
 representation and, 200–202
 systemic approach to civic action and, 243
National Wildlife Refuges, 133, 134
Natural News (newsletter), 217
Nature Conservancy, The, (TNC), 217
Neighborhood Capital Budget Group, 225

Nelson, Mary, 221
networks
  ENCHIA and, 66–68
  environmental justice movement and, 224–26
  EPA and, 213–18, **215**, 224–26
  intramovement agenda setting and, 82–83, 89
  role in civic practice, 160–63, 169–77, 243–44, 245
  watershed movement and, 213–18, **215**
New Hampshire. *See* Great Bay Resource Protection Partnership (Portsmouth, NH)
New Kind (consulting firm), 80
newspapers
  role in civic communication ecology, 93, 94–99, 119
  in Seattle, 108–9, 110–13
Next Door Media (regional news website), 115
Nichols, John, 98–99
Nixon administration, 207, 208
North American Wetlands Conservation Act (NAWCA), 153n3
North Carolina. *See* Coalition to Protect ALL NC Families
Northeast Trees, 28

Oakland Local (local news website), 121
Obama administration, 228
Obama campaign (2008), 79
Occupy Wall Street, 241
Ocean Conservancy, 211–12
Office of Air and Radiation, 222
Office of Environmental Justice (OEJ), 219, 221, 224–25
Office of Inspector General (OIG), 227
Office of Management and Budget (US OMB), 227
Office of Pollution Prevention and Toxics (OPPTS), 222
Office of Wetlands, Oceans, and Watersheds (OWOW), 212
Ohrel, Ronald L., Jr., 211–12
One Economy, 106–7
Open Government Initiative, 129, 228

Pachucki, Mark A., 162
participation, 24–25
participatory budget, 181
Payne, Bob, 111–12
Pew Center for Civic Journalism, 110
Pew Center for Excellence in Journalism, 99
Philadelphia Inquirer (newspaper), 99–100
Pogrebinschi, Thamy, 243
PolicyLink, 71–72
pollution prevention (P2) strategies, 220
Porto Alegre (Brazil), 181
Portsmouth (NH). *See* Great Bay Resource Protection Partnership (Portsmouth, NH)
Portsmouth Listens, 17, 19
Portugal

immigration and civic action in, 159, 166
  role of narratives in civic action in, 163–69, 243, 245
Promise and Peril of Environmental Justice, The, (Foreman), 222
public deliberations, 7, 8, 9–10. *See also* embedded deliberation
Public Health Law and Policy, 72
PubliCola (Seattle news website), 113
Puget Sound Off, 106–7
Putnam, Robert, 92, 120, 162

Qualitative Comparative Analysis (QCA), 122n3
Quick, K. S., 24

racism, 55–56
radio, 109–10
Ragin, Charles, 122n3
Raimi Associates, 72
Rainier Valley Post (regional news website), 115
Reade, Virginia, 139
Record, Tracy, 108–9, 114
Register, Kathleen M., 211–12
Reidel, Will, 142
Reilly, William, 218
representative democracy, 9
republican self-government, 7, 203–4
Resource Protection Partnership (RPP). *See* Great Bay Resource Protection Partnership (Portsmouth, NH)
Restore America's Estuaries, 215, 227–28
Results from a Community Assessment of Health and Land Use (SFDPH), 58
Reyes, Ed, 35
Rhodes, Philip, 137, 141–42, 143, 148
Rice, Norman, 109
Richmond (CA), 70
Richmond Equitable Development Initiative (REDI), 70
River Network, 214, 215, 217, 226
River Project, 27–28
Roberts, Nancy, 24
Rogers, Jim, 84
Rogers, Joel, 129
Rojas, James, 34, 37–39, *39*
Rosen, Jay, 108
Rosenberg, Matt, 107–8
Roussef, Dilma, 181
Rowe, Ryan, 75, 81, 84, 85

San Diego (CA). *See* Multiple Species Conservation Program (San Diego, CA)
San Francisco (CA). *See* Eastern Neighborhoods Community Health Impact Assessment (ENCHIA)
San Francisco Recreation and Parks Department (SFRPD), 57
Sand, Patrick, 114

Santa Monica Mountains Conservancy, 28
Santos, Boaventura de Sousa, 164–65
Schaffer, Jan, 112
Schell, Paul, 104
Schmit, Ayn, 216
Schneiberg, Marc, 130
Schneider, Anne, 42n5
Schrier, Bill, 103, 107
Schudson, Michael, 94, 98
Schueler, Tom, 212
Seattle (WA)
    civic communication ecology in: governance
        policy and, 103–8; layers of, 117–19; media
        ecology and, 108–11; overview, 102; role of
        new media in, 111–17
    economy and population of, 102–3
Seattle Communities Online Project (SCOP), 106, 116
Seattle Post-Intelligencer (newspaper), 108, 113
Seattle Times (newspaper), 108–9, 110–13, 116, 117
Seattle University, 112
Serrano, Estrela, 167
Shepard, Peggy, 221
Sigler, Christopher, 145
Sirianni, Carmen, 41n1, 240
Skocpol, Theda, 169
social capital, 131
Soeiro, Jose, 166–67
SOMCAN, 67–68
South Carolina. *See* ACE Basin Task Force
    (Charleston, SC)
Southeast Watershed Forum, 214
Southern Organizing Committee for Economic and
    Social Justice, 221
Spain, 159–60, 169–76, 243–44, 245
Stadler, Anne, 109
Staggenborg, Suzanne, 77
Stiefel, Todd, 81, 83
Stone, Amy, 78, 82
Stranger, The, (Seattle newsweekly), 110, 113
study circles, 10, 11, 16, 18, 19
Subra, Wilma, 221, 225–26

Tales of the City's Workers (SFDPH), 58
Tanner, Veronica, 145
Targeted Watershed Grants Program, 214
television
    role in civic communication ecology, 96
    in Seattle, 109, 111, 113, 116
theories of change, 12–13

Thomas, Craig, 144
timber wars, 128–29
Toqueville, Alexis de, 203–4
transparency, 130
Transportation and Land Use Coalition (TALC),
    70–71
Tree People, 28
Trees, Water, and People, 214
Truitt, Kay, 136–37, 140–41, 147–48
Tucker, Connie, 221
Twin Cities Daily Planet (local news website), 119

Ulibarri, Joshua, 81
United Way, 18, 19
University of Washington, 106–7
Urban Habitat, 70, 73n13

Virginian-Pilot (Norfolk newspaper), 114
Volunteer Estuary Monitoring (Ohrel and Register),
    211–12
Volunteer Monitor (journal), 212

Warhover, Tom, 114
Watershed Innovators Workshops, 209–10
watershed movement
    EPA and: framing and, 209–10; networks and,
        213–18, 215; overview, 208–9; systemic
        approach to civic action and, 240; tools and,
        210–12, 213
    Linton and, 35
    See also Los Angeles River Watershed
Webb, Jim, 80
Wessells, Anne Taufen, 242–43
West Harlem Environmental Action (WE ACT),
    221, 224, 225
West Seattle Blog, 108–9, 111, 114–15, 116, 117,
    120
West Seattle Herald (Seattle newspaper), 110
West Virginia Center for Civic Life, 17
wilderness, 127
Wilkins, Donele, 221
Workers Party (Partido dos Trabalhadores, Brazil),
    181
World Health Organization, 47

YMCA, 106–7
YWCA, 12, 18

Zaverukha, Lydia, 68

www.ingramcontent.com/pod-product-compliance
Lightning Source LLC
Chambersburg PA
CBHW080416270326

41929CB00018B/3047